Law and Criminal Justice

Law and Criminal Justice

An Introductory Survey

David R. Lynch
David C. Brody
Michelle Heward
Steven Burge

Carolina Academic Press
Durham, North Carolina

Library of Congress Cataloging in Publication Data

Law and criminal justice : an introductory survey / by David R. Lynch ...
[et al.].
p. cm.
Includes bibliographical references and index.
ISBN 10: 1-59460-437-1
ISBN 13: 978-1-59460-437-9 (alk. paper)
1. Criminal justice, Administration of--United States. 2. Criminal
procedure--United States. I. Lynch, David R. (David Richard) II. Title.

KF9223.L39 2008
345.73'05--dc22

2008005283

Carolina Academic Press
700 Kent Street
Durham, NC 27701
Telephone (919) 489-7486
Fax (919) 493-5668
www.cap-press.com

Printed in the United States of America

Table of Contents

Table of Principal Cases xiii

Chapter One Fundamentals of Criminal Law, Part I: What is a Crime?; Constitutional Limitations on Criminalizing "Bad" Conduct; Basic Elements of a Crime 3

What Is a Crime? 3

Constitutional Limits on Criminalizing "Bad" Conduct 5

Cruel and Unusual Punishment (Status Offenses) 6

Robinson v. California 6

Offensive Speech 7

People v. Rokicki 8

Religion 9

Reynolds v. United States 9

Wisconsin v. Yoder 10

The Right to Privacy 11

Lawrence v. Texas 12

The Void for Vagueness Doctrine 13

Minnesota v. Reha 14

Equal Protection 15

Allam v. State 15

Basic Elements of a Crime 16

State v. Dalton 17

Morissette v. United States 18

Chapter Two Fundamentals of Criminal Law, Part II: Justifications and Excuses for Crimes 21

Justification Defenses 22

Self-Defense 22

Defense of Others 22

Defense of Property 23

Bishop v. State 23

Execution of Public Duties 23

Tennessee v. Garner 24

Necessity 25

Lightner v. State 25

Resisting Unlawful Arrest 26
Excuse Defenses 27
Insanity 27
State v. Johnson 29
Mistake 30
Duress 31
Entrapment 32
Jacobson v. United States 33
Youthful Age 34
Involuntary Intoxication 35
United States v. Sewell 35

Chapter Three Basic Search and Seizure Law 37
How to Obtain a Warrant 38
Do All Searches and Seizures Require Warrants? 39
The Exclusionary Rule 39
Mapp v. Ohio 39
United States v. Leon 41
What Is a Search? 43
Katz v. United States 43
California v. Greenwood 44
Warrantless Searches 45
Consent Searches 46
Florida v. Bostick 46
Automobile Searches 48
California v. Carney 48
Plain View 49
Exigent Circumstances 50
Frisk for Weapons 50
Terry v. Ohio 50
Searches Incident to a Lawful Arrest/Regulatory Searches 52
Seizures 53
Investigative Stops 53
Delaware v. Prouse 54
Arrests 55
Arrest Warrants 56

Chapter Four Self-Incrimination, Right to Counsel, Speedy Jury Trials 57
Self-Incrimination 57
Miranda v. Arizona 58
New York v. Quarles 60
Right to Counsel 61
Gideon v. Wainwright 62
Right to a Speedy Jury Trial 64
Speedy: A Promise Unfulfilled? 64
Barker v. Wingo 65

The Right to an Impartial Jury 69
Lockhart v. McCree 70
The Correct Size of Juries 71
Williams v. Florida 71

Chapter Five Law and the Proper Roles of Prosecutors, Defense Attorneys, and Judges 73
The Prosecutor 74
Duty to Seek Justice 74
Miller v. Pate 76
Kyles v. Whitley 77
Prosecutorial Discretion and the Charging Decision 78
Wayte v. United States 79
Bordenkircher v. Hayes 81
Defense Attorneys 81
Right to Counsel 82
Argersinger v. Hamlin 82
Effective Assistance of Counsel 83
Strickland v. Washington 83
Right to Counsel of One's Choice 85
U.S. v. Gonzalez-Lopez 85
Counsel's Duty to the Client 87
Nix v. Whiteside 87
Judges 88
Duty to Promote a Just Trial 88
Sheppard v. Maxwell 89
Duty to Remain Neutral and Detached 90
Conclusion 92

Chapter Six The Law of Bail, Plea Bargaining, and Guilty Pleas 93
Bail 93
History and the Legal Right to Bail 94
Legitimate and Extra-legal Uses of Bail 94
Stack v. Boyle 94
United States v. Salerno 96
Types of Bail 98
Legal Rights of Bounty Hunters 98
Plea Bargaining 99
The Constitutionality of Plea Bargaining 100
Santobello v. New York 100
Types of Plea Bargains 101
Judicial Participation in Deal-making 102
State v. Davis 102
Guilty Pleas 103
"Voluntarily and Knowingly Entered" Requirement 104

Boykin v. Alabama 104
Libretti v. United States 105
Types of Guilty Pleas 106
North Carolina v. Alford 107
Withdrawing One's Guilty Plea 108

Chapter Seven Law of Evidence, Part I: Categories of Evidence, Relevancy, and Prejudicial Impact 111
A Forward to Your Study of the Law of Evidence 111
Categories of Evidence 112
Direct Evidence 113
State v. Long 113
Circumstantial Evidence 115
People v. Basciano 116
Real Evidence 116
Byerly v. Ashley 117
Documentary Evidence 118
United States v. Maxwell 119
Relevancy 120
United States v. Brown 121
Prejudicial Impact 122
United States v. Layton 123
Prior Records 124
Offers to Plea Bargain 125
United States v. Mezzanatto 125
Rape Shield Laws 127
United States v. Withorn 127
Leg Irons and Jail Clothes 128
United States v. Stewart 128
Victim Impact Evidence 130
Commonwealth v. Means 130

Chapter Eight Law of Evidence, Part II: Competency of Witnesses, Privileged Communications, Opinion Evidence, Hearsay and Its Exceptions 133
Competency of Witnesses 133
Personal Knowledge 134
Oath/Affirmations & Religion 135
Judges and Jurors 135
Mental Incapacity and Children 136
United States of America v. Allen J. (a Juvenile) 136
Other Categories of Disqualification 137
Privileged Communications 137
Attorney/Client 139
In re Grand Jury Subpoena 140

Priest/Penitent Privilege 142
In re Grand Jury Investigation 143
Husband/Wife 144
Trammel v. United States 144
Other Privileges 146
Testimonial Evidence 146
Lay Opinions 147
Expert Opinion 148
Kumho Tire Company, Ltd., et al., v. Patrick Carmichael, et al. 149
Basis for an Expert Opinion 150
Opinion of the Ultimate Issue 151
Hearsay 152
Definition of Hearsay 153
Exceptions to Hearsay and Non-Hearsay 155
1. Prior Statements and Admissions 155
Michael Nowell v. City of Cincinnati, et al. 156
2. Excited Utterances 157
United States of America v. Jean Brito 158
3. Dying Declarations 160
United States of America v. Melvin Troy Two Shields 161
4. Other Exceptions 162

Chapter Nine Proof beyond a Reasonable Doubt 163
Guilty or Not Guilty: You Make the Call 165
Introductory, Non-Technical Definition of Reasonable Doubt 167
Proof beyond a Reasonable Doubt: A Constitutional Requirement 168
In re Winship 169
Attempting to Further Define and Understand
Proof beyond a Reasonable Doubt 170
A. What Proof beyond Reasonable Doubt Is Not! 170
B. Defining Proof beyond a Reasonable Doubt through Case Law 172
Victor v. Nebraska 173
C. Numerical Quantification 174
Constitutional Ideals Related to the Burden of Proof 176
Guilty Pleas Affected by the Reasonable Doubt Standard 177
Ordeals: Proof of Guilt from a Historical Perspective 178
Cage v. Louisiana 180
The Constitutionality of Non-Unanimous Jury Verdicts 181
Johnson v. Louisiana 181
Sufficient or Insufficient Evidence? 182
A. Guilt or Mere Presence at a Crime Scene? 182
B. Is Mere Flight Enough to Prove Guilt? 183
C. Mere Confession 184
Michigan v. McMahan 184
Conclusion 185

Chapter Ten Criminal Juries and the Law 187
Limitations on the Right to Trial by Jury 188
Blanton v. City of North Las Vegas 188
A Jury of One's Peers 190
United States v. Shinault 190
Juries in Death Penalty Cases: The Death Qualified Jury 192
Wainwright v. Witt 193
Anonymous Juries 195
United States v. Ross 196
Jury Nullification and the Sanctity of Jury Deliberations 197
United States v. Thomas 198
Breaking Deadlocked Juries: The Use of Dynamite Charges 200
United States v. Arney 200
Conclusion 202

Chapter Eleven Law of Sentencing; Cruel and Unusual Punishments 203
Four Classical Goals of Punishment 203
Harmelin v. Michigan 204
Sentencing Guidelines 206
How Guidelines Work 206
Mandatory vs. Non-mandatory Guidelines 207
Constitutionality of Guidelines 207
Blakely v. Washington and *United States v. Booker* 207
Cruel and Unusual Sentences 209
Torture 210
Dawson v. State 210
Shaming 212
United States v. Gementera 212
Banishment 213
Doe v. Miller 214
Crafting a Sentence 215
Legal Factors in Crafting a Sentence 215
United States v. Grayson 216
Extra-legal Factors in Crafting a Sentence 218
Sentencing Factors vs. Elements of a Crime 218
Apprendi v. New Jersey 218

Chapter Twelve Inmate Rights 221
Eighth Amendment Rights 221
Safe Environment 222
Farmer v. Brennan 222
Use of Force 224
Hudson v. McMillian 224
Medical Care 226
Estelle v. Gamble 226

Conditions of Confinement 227
Wilson v. Seiter 228
Fourth Amendment Rights 229
Hudson v. Palmer 229
First Amendment Right to Religious Exercise 230
Spratt v. Rhode Island Department of Corrections 231
Conclusion 233

Chapter Thirteen Death Penalty Law 235
The Spotlight and Infamy through Execution 235
General Overview and Data on the Death Penalty 237
Pros and Cons 239
Why the Death Penalty Is Right (Hypothetical Argument for Study) 240
Why the Death Penalty Is Wrong (Sample Argument for Study) 241
Historical Background for the Death Penalty 242
The Eighth Amendment 243
Wilkerson v. Utah 244
Proportionality and Cruel and Unusual Punishment 245
Abolishment and Re-Birth of the Death Penalty 245
Furman v. Georgia 245
Gregg v. Georgia 246
Race and the Death Penalty 247
Mentally Disabled Subjects and the Death Penalty 248
Atkins v. Virginia 249
The Execution of Juvenile Murderers 249
Stanford v. Kentucky 250
Roper v. Simmons 250
Death Penalty for Rape as
Cruel and Unusual Punishment 252
Coker v. Georgia 252
Errors and the Death Penalty 253
Conclusion 253

Chapter Fourteen Juvenile Law 255
Part I: Development and Evolution 255
Common Law through 19th Century 255
Houses of Reform 256
State Establishment of Juvenile Courts 256
Due Process Era 257
A. Treatment of Juveniles as Adults 258
Kent v. United States 258
B. Due Process Rights during Adjudication 259
In re Gault 259
Deinstitutionalization Era 261
"Get Tough" Era—Waiver, Certification and Automatic Transfer 262

Age 262
Characteristics of Waiver Statutes 264
Part II: Current Juvenile Justice System 265
Jurisdiction 265
Terminology 268
Processing through the Juvenile Justice System 269
Specialty Courts 271
Adjudication Rights of Juveniles 272
A. Preventative Pretrial Detention 272
Schall v. Martin 272
B. Burden of Proof 273
In re Winship 273
C. Right to a Jury Trial 274
McKeiver v. Pennsylvania 274
D. Double Jeopardy 274
Breed v. Jones 274
E. Death Penalty 275
Conclusion 276

Chapter Fifteen Appellate Law 277
Purposes of an Appeal 277
Error Correction 278
A. Error Correction: Double Jeopardy 279
Ashe v. Swenson 280
B. Error Correction: Lawyer's Duty to Object and the Plain Error Doctrine 281
United States v. Young 282
Commonwealth v. Clair 283
C. Error Correction: The Harmless Error Doctrine 285
State v. Campbell 285
Arizona v. Fulminante 286
Policy Review 288
A. Policy Review: The Historic Case of *Marbury v. Madison* 289
Marbury v. Madison 289
B. Policy Review: Strict Construction vs. "Living Constitution" 290
C. Policy Review: The *Stare Decisis* Doctrine 292
Planned Parenthood of Southeastern Pennsylvania v. Casey 293
Mechanics of an Appeal 294
Appeals of Right vs. Discretionary Appeals 295
Right to Counsel in Appeals of Right 296
Douglas v. California 296
Anders Briefs and the Frivolous Appeal 297

Index 299

Table of Principal Cases

Allam v. State, 15
Apprendi v. New Jersey, 218
Argersinger v. Hamlin, 82
Arizona v. Fulminante, 286
Ashe v. Swenson, 280
Atkins v. Virginia, 249
Barker v. Wingo, 65
Bishop v. State, 23
Blakely v. Washington, 207
Blanton v. City of North Las Vegas, 188
Bordenkircher v. Hayes, 81
Boykin v. Alabama, 104
Breed v. Jones, 274
Byerly v. Ashley, 117
Cage v. Louisiana, 180
California v. Carney, 48
California v. Greenwood, 44
Coker v. Georgia, 252
Commonwealth v. Clair, 283
Commonwealth v. Means, 130
Dawson v. State, 210
Delaware v. Prouse, 54
Doe v. Miller, 214
Douglas v. California, 296
Estelle v. Gamble, 226
Farmer v. Brennan, 222
Florida v. Bostick, 46
Furman v. Georgia, 245
Gideon v. Wainwright, 62
Gregg v. Georgia, 246
Harmelin v. Michigan, 204
Hudson v. McMillian, 224
Hudson v. Palmer, 229
In re Gault, 259
In re Grand Jury Investigation, 143
In re Grand Jury Subpoena, 140
In re Winship, 169
In re Winship, 273
Jacobson v. United States, 33
Johnson v. Louisiana, 181
Katz v. United States, 43
Kent v. United States, 258
Kumho Tire Company, Ltd., et al., v. Patrick Carmichael, et al., 149
Kyles v. Whitley, 77
Lawrence v. Texas, 12
Libretti v. United States, 105
Lightner v. State, 25
Lockhart v. McCree, 70
Mapp v. Ohio, 39
Marbury v. Madison, 289
McKeiver v. Pennsylvania, 274
Michael Nowell v. City of Cincinnati, et al., 156
Michigan v. McMahan, 184
Miller v. Pate, 76
Minnesota v. Reha, 14
Miranda v. Arizona, 58
Morissette v. United States, 18
New York v. Quarles, 60
Nix v. Whiteside, 87
North Carolina v. Alford, 107
People v. Basciano, 116
People v. Rokicki, 8
Planned Parenthood of Southeastern Pennsylvania v. Casey, 293
Reynolds v. United States, 9
Robinson v. California, 6
Roper v. Simmons, 250
Santobello v. New York, 100

Schall v. Martin, 272
Sheppard v. Maxwell, 89
Spratt v. Rhode Island Department of Corrections, 231
Stack v. Boyle, 94
Stanford v. Kentucky, 250
State v. Campbell, 285
State v. Dalton, 17
State v. Davis, 102
State v. Johnson, 29
State v. Long, 113
Strickland v. Washington, 83
Tennessee v. Garner, 24
Terry v. Ohio, 50
Trammel v. United States, 144
U.S. v. Gonzalez-Lopez, 85
United States of America v. Allen J. (a Juvenile), 136
United States of America v. Jean Brito, 158
United States of America v. Melvin Troy Two Shields, 161
United States v. Arney, 200
United States v. Booker, 207
United States v. Brown, 121
United States v. Gementera, 212
United States v. Grayson, 216
United States v. Layton, 123
United States v. Leon, 41
United States v. Maxwell, 119
United States v. Mezzanatto, 125
United States v. Ross, 196
United States v. Salerno, 96
United States v. Sewell, 37
United States v. Shinault, 190
United States v. Stewart, 128
United States v. Thomas, 198
United States v. Withorn, 127
United States v. Young, 282
Victor v. Nebraska, 173
Wainwright v. Witt, 193
Wayte v. United States, 79
Wilkerson v. Utah, 244
Williams v. Florida, 71
Wilson v. Seiter, 228
Wisconsin v. Yoder, 10

Law and Criminal Justice

Chapter One

Fundamentals of Criminal Law, Part I: What is a Crime?; Constitutional Limitations on Criminalizing "Bad" Conduct; Basic Elements of a Crime

We begin our journey into the legal world of the criminal justice system by first looking at the fundamentals of criminal law. It is good place to start since without criminal law there would be no criminals and no criminal justice system. Every robber, rapist, thief, murderer, burglar, and drug dealer owes his or her official status to the criminal law. Every police officer, prosecutor, defense attorney, judge, probation officer, jailer, and prison official owes his or her job to the fact that the state has chosen to make certain acts crimes.

At the outset, the reader should be warned that since this book is not meant to be solely a criminal law text, it will not be practical to go into great detail about the definitions of specific crimes like burglary, rape or drunk driving. Rather, it will highlight concepts that are common to these and all crimes.

Thus, we will begin (in this chapter) by considering "what is a crime." Then we will examine what restraints the Constitution has placed on overly enthusiastic legislators who might want to criminalize just about anything that they consider offensive. Next, we will look at the essential elements of all crimes.

In the next chapter, we will look at defenses to crimes. These defenses are important for understanding the basic nature of all crimes since they all tend to eliminate the same critical element of any crime, that being the bad mind.

What Is a Crime?

This sounds like a simple enough question but could you easily give a definition without simply resorting to examples? People have been struggling with this definition for hundreds of years.

Some try to suggest that crimes are "public wrongs" rather than "private wrongs." **Public wrongs** are believed to hurt the general public and thus should be punished by the state, whereas **private wrongs** only hurt individuals and should be the subject of civil law suits between private parties. Hence, if I beat a small, defenseless child I have committed a crime because I have not only harmed an individual but wounded the rest of us. This makes some sense. One could easily come up with a list of ways the general public is harmed by child abuse. But, what if I choose to go to Las Vegas and play rather than to pay my rent and thereby stiff my landlord? This is not considered to be a crime as it is somehow deemed to be merely a "private wrong." I supposedly have not hurt anyone but the individual landlord. Do you see the silliness in all of this? In what ways does intentionally harming my landlord hurt the general renting public?

Perhaps a better starting point is to suggest that all crimes share this one characteristic: *immorality*. Can you think of any crime currently enforced that society as a whole does not consider to be immoral? (Please note that traffic violations and ordinance transgressions do not count: they are characterized as "violations" rather than crimes.) Let us see how this "immorality" characteristic is present in all crimes by considering the three broad categories of crimes.

First, there are **crimes against the person** (e.g., homicide, rape, assaults, kidnaping, robbery, threats of violence). Certainly, most people would consider these to be immoral actions. Next, there are **crimes against property** (e.g, theft, forgery, burglary, arson, vandalism). Again, when people commit any of these they are generally considered to have done something immoral. Finally, there are **crimes against public order and morals** (e.g., drunk driving, public nudity, sale of illegal drugs, publishing child pornography). Though, there is perhaps less of a societal consensus about the virtue or vice of some of these, most people would still consider these to be in the category of moral wrongs.

What all this is attempting to demonstrate is that "immorality" (as subjectively decided through community consensus) is a common denominator of any crime. This is necessarily so since we **punish** criminals (we do not merely require them to pay restitution as in civil court but in addition we fine them and/or take away their liberty). It would be senseless to punish someone who has acted morally. We only punish people who have acted immorally. If I accidentally cave-in your car's trunk during a routine collision, I will only be expected to pay for the damages to your car. After all, I have not acted immorally. But if I intentionally plow into your car in a fit of road rage, I may be punished in addition to paying for your loss. Why not just restitution? Would not restitution restore the equilibrium? No, because I acted immorally and deserve to be punished. Mere **restitution** (making the individual victim whole) is not punishment and hence not satisfactory.

Of course, immorality is not synonymous with crime. "Immorality" is a necessary but insufficient criteria to labeling something a crime. Can you think of anything that someone has ever done to you that was hurtful and immoral but not a crime? The fact that you probably can suggests that crimes are merely a small subset of a greater world of moral wrongdoings.

It would seem that society has developed a hierarchy of sorts when it comes to cracking down on improper conduct. William Graham Sumner (1840–1910) developed a classic and still famous way to conceptualize this long, long ago.[1]

1. Sumner, William Graham. (1992). *On Liberty, Society, and Politics: The Essential Essays of William Graham Sumner*, edited by Robert C. Bannister. Indianapolis: Liberty Fund.

He suggested that some offensive acts are petty enough to require merely a weak societal response because, though offensive, the acts simply are not immoral. An example of this might be picking one's nose in public or failing to shower on a regular basis. Few would consider these to be immoral acts, but we still feel that there should be consequences to such misdeeds. Otherwise, everyone might start doing them. The weapons society uses to fight against such **folkway violations** are ridicule and/or ostracism. Would you be tempted to gossip about or avoid socializing with someone who picks his nose in class?

A greater misdeed would be what Sumner labeled a **mores violation**. Unlike violating folkways, when one violates mores, he or she is deemed to have acted not just inappropriately but immorally. But, not so immorally as to yet warrant a governmental response. Thus, if I were to constantly belittle my spouse in public many people would not only ridicule and ostracize me (as with a folkway violation) but in addition would feel moral outrage. But, the government would not be summoned.

Finally, the most serious norm violation is a **law violation**. In committing a criminal act that is against the law, I have not only acted immorally but so offensively that the government now seeks to punish me. Private ridicule, ostracism, and moral condemnation are not enough. The state will seek to intervene and punish me by taking away my property, liberty or life.

Of course, an immoral act, even a grievous one, is only a crime if the legislature gets around to saying so. An immoral act may deserve a governmental response but unless the legislature chooses to criminalize it, it simply is not a crime. Politics, practicality, enlightenment, legislative will, and even tradition all are part of the mix in determining what a legislature will or will not make a crime. Some mores violations arguably should be made crimes but simply have not yet been properly dealt with by our lawmakers. Can you think of any examples?

So, it appears that a workable definition of a crime would be: A **Crime** belongs to that subset of immoral acts which some offended legislature has determined to punish above and beyond any restitution that might be owed individual victims.

Constitutional Limits on Criminalizing "Bad" Conduct

Though it is true that the legislature sometimes fails to criminalize that which ought to be criminalized, it is also true that legislatures sometimes attempt to criminalize that which should be tolerated. Just because something is offensive or even immoral, does not mean that it should be a crime. Imagine a society in which every immoral act were made a crime and punished by governmental officials. Would this be the utopia some seek or a hellish police state?

Of course, in a democracy legislatures are not free to go overboard in generating over-the-top crime codes. Politics and voter-backlash see to that. But, politics aside, could a state legislature theoretically make any offensive act a crime that it wanted to? As long as most of the voting public agreed, would there be nothing to restrain it?

For example, in some future world, if the voting public of your state became utterly hostile to cigarette smokers, could your future state legislature make smoking cigarettes a crime? Could it make it a crime to be hideously and offensively ugly? Could it make it a crime to have a highly contagious disease? Could it make it a crime to worship at the local Church of Satan? Could it make it a crime to use hurtful racial slurs? Could it make it a crime to be a "hooligan?"

Here is the key to resolving these and all similar questions: assuming that fear of voter backlash does not get in the way, the legislature can make anything it wants to a crime with the exception of that conduct which is protected by a constitution. In other words, the only thing ultimately stopping a legislature (be it your state legislature or Congress) in its quest to limit offensive conduct is the federal and/or state constitution. If a reviewing court cannot find something in a constitution that prohibits the legislation, then the legislation will stand.

So, could cigarette smoking be made a crime? Absolutely. There is no constitutional right to smoke. Could drinking alcohol be made a crime? Yes, it has been made illegal before and could be made so again (in fact, some counties even today are "dry"). But, could the government make it a crime to be ugly or to be a "hooligan?" Read on.

Cruel and Unusual Punishment (Status Offenses)

Almost every American is aware of that fact that a sentencing judge could not sentence someone to "**cruel and unusual punishment**." Such a prohibition is found in the Eighth Amendment. That is why one can not be sentenced to being buried alive, burned at the stake, drawn and quartered, castrated against one's will or having one's eyes poked out. But what is perhaps less well-known is the fact that it is not only sentencing judges who have to worry about the Eighth Amendment. Legislatures also are subject to the prohibition against cruel and unusual punishment during the very act of defining what can be made a crime in the first place. Certain statutes will be deemed to violate the Eighth Amendment merely by criminalizing certain things at all.

Specifically, courts have ruled that legislation which creates a "status offense" violates the guarantee against cruel and unusual punishment. A **status offense** is the criminalizing of a mere state of being or state of existence. This is why it is unconstitutional to punish someone for the status of being ugly or for being mentally ill or for being old or for being handicapped. People do not "act" in such situations. They simply "are." It would be cruel and unusual to punish people for something over which they have no control.

Most people agree that it would be wrong to punish someone for a mere illness. But, what about drug addiction? Is that a mere illness and hence a "status?" The case below explores that question.

Robinson v. California

370 U.S. 660 (1962)

Robinson was convicted under a California statute that made it a crime not just to possess narcotics in violation of law but also to "be addicted to the use of narcotics." The expert and other evidence against Robinson tended to prove that he was indeed addicted to heroin. Robinson appealed. The U.S. Supreme Court eventually had to decide whether or not a statute making it a crime to be addicted to narcotics was in effect criminalizing a status and hence constituted cruel and unusual punishment.

The Court found that such a statute did indeed punish a mere status. It reasoned that drug addiction was an illness like having a cold or the flu and courts have always maintained that an illness is nothing more than a status. When one is addicted to something, one is not doing anything. It would be cruel and unusual to punish someone for being sick. True, a person could in theory be involuntarily quarantined for having a highly contagious disease or involuntarily hospitalized for being dangerously mentally ill. But, that is not the same as criminally punishing someone. What the state of California is attempting to do to Robinson is criminal punishment and as such would be cruel and unusual.

The dissent thought that the majority was making a mistake. In his dissenting opinion, Justice White said that he did "not consider appellant's conviction to be punishment for having an illness ... but rather a conviction for the regular, repeated or habitual use of narcotics immediately prior to his arrest and in violation of California law."

Do you think that drug addiction is an illness like cancer or tuberculosis or do you agree with the dissent? If you think it is an illness, would you mind living next door to someone addicted to narcotics? If it is not an illness, would you favor locking up all the country's addicts (including perhaps the millions of potentially dangerous alcoholics)?

Offensive Speech

One of the more obvious constitutional protections we enjoy is freedom of speech. This is guaranteed not just in the first ten amendments to the Constitution (collectively known as our "**Bill of Rights**") but in the very first of these ten amendments. The fact that speech was included in the first of the amendments was probably intentional. It is arguably the single most important right a free people possesses.

Yet, speech can wound deeply. Some speech may be so offensive that a legislature may be tempted to criminalize it. This is where the First Amendment steps in. Remember, the First Amendment only is necessary to protect offensive speech. Nobody is going to want to criminalize warm and fuzzy speech. Such agreeable speech needs no protection.

Not all speech is protected by the First Amendment even though a literal reading of the amendment seems to suggest otherwise. The First Amendment speaks in absolute terms when it comes to speech: "Congress shall make no law ... abridging freedom of speech." Despite the words "no law" courts have been forced to use common sense and allow "some laws." This is alright since it is doubtful the drafters meant for ridiculous results. Hence, speech which puts people in **"clear and present danger"** can be made a crime. That is why it is illegal to jokingly yell "fire" in a crowded theater or to incite a riot. Threatening violence against another can also be made a crime. You have the right to free speech but courts sometimes must balance this right against the rights of others to not be terrorized. The freedom I enjoy to offend you with my speech does not include my right to threaten you with physical violence. When your right to speech conflicts with my right to not be put in danger or terrorized, courts will balance the two competing rights and rule on the side of those whose rights are obviously greater. However, if your speech merely is offensive rather than posing a "clear and present danger" or so threatening as to likely terrorize, courts will generally protect it no matter how offensive it is.

What about "hate speech?" Some democracies, not subject to the American Constitution, have chosen to make certain forms of "hate speech" a crime. Would you fault Germany for example for making anti-Jewish diatribes a crime? Could this or other "hate speech" be made a crime here despite our First Amendment? The case that follows explores this question.

People v. Rokicki

718 N.E.2d 333 (Ill.App. 1999)

Ronald Rokicki was convicted in Illinois for disorderly conduct for making a "scene" in a Pizza Hut where he went to order a pizza. What enraged Rokicki was his assessment that the person taking his order and touching his food was gay. Rokicki claimed the victim had touched his food after putting his fingers in his mouth. Rokicki was deeply offended and demanded his money back. He yelled for ten minutes, disrupting the restaurant with words like "faggot," and "Molly Homemaker," while pounding his fist on the counter and pointing his finger at the victim. The victim was understandably terrified by the defendant's aggressive words and behavior. Finally, the manager gave Rokicki his money back and Rokicki left. After being arrested (the store manager managed to get his license plate number), the defendant was not only charged with "disorderly conduct" but also under an Illinois statue providing for enhanced penalties for various crimes (including assault, vandalism, theft and disorderly conduct) when the motive for the crime was based on hatred of someone's actual or perceived race, religion, gender or sexual orientation.

Because of the enhanced penalty due to the anti-gay motive, Rokicki got two full years of probation plus 100 hours of community service. Rokicki argued on appeal that he was being punished extra for his beliefs and for his expressions regarding homosexuality and that such beliefs and expressions are protected by freedom of speech.

The issue therefore was this: Even if the state can punish someone for disorderly conduct for making a verbal scene at a restaurant, can it punish that person extra without violating freedom of speech on the grounds that the motive behind the disorderly conduct was hatred of someone based on his or her perceived sexual orientation?

In its decision, the court ruled that a state can indeed punish someone extra in such circumstances without violating the First Amendment's guarantee of free speech. The defendant is correct when he suggests that he cannot be punished for hating anybody or for peacefully expressing or calmly vocalizing his ideas about homosexuals. But, he is not being punished for the crime of hating homosexuals or peacefully expressing opinions but rather for the crime of disorderly conduct. He clearly was disorderly when he was disrupting the restaurant and should be punished. That said, the question becomes what criteria can a court use in deciding an appropriate sentence for disorderly conduct? Can a court legitimately consider the defendant's motive when deciding the proper sentence? Of course it can. Courts routinely consider motives in deciding proper sentences. Should not a court punish someone less for the crime of punching someone in the nose when the motive was revenge for the sexual abuse of that person's child than when the motive for the punch was revenge for insulting someone's favorite sports team? Motive properly matters when it comes to sentencing people and legislatures (through enhanced penalty statutes) have the right to care about motives just as judges do.

Religion

The First Amendment not only guarantees free speech but also freedom of religion: "Congress shall make no law respecting an establishment of religion, or prohibiting the free exercise thereof ..."

Just about everyone would agree that we do not want a preferred state-religion (as exists in Saudi Arabia, for example). But what is more "tricky" is the "prohibiting the free exercise" guarantee.

Just as with free speech, the First Amendment sounds like the government cannot prohibit any religious practices, period (the language is absolutist). But, as with free speech, courts feel compelled to use common sense. Beginning with the case below, courts have always differentiated between religious *belief* (which can never be prohibited) and religious *practices* (which sometimes can be prohibited). Let us examine the case that first made this distinction. It involved the question of polygamy.

Reynolds v. United States

98 U.S. 145 (1879)

George Reynolds, a 19th Century Mormon and personal secretary to Brigham Young, was convicted of polygamy in violation of a federal statute that made it a crime to marry or sexually cohabit with more than one woman at the same time. He appealed the conviction to the U.S. Supreme Court claiming that the law violated his First Amendment right to freely exercise his religion. He argued that polygamy was an important part of his sincerely held religious beliefs and that it was unconstitutional for the government to punish him for its practice.

So, can the government make it a crime to practice polygamy even if it is a very important aspect of someone's religion? Yes, the Supreme Court reasoned. The Court noted that while it is true that one cannot be punished for a religious belief or opinion, it is sometimes constitutionally permissible to punish someone for a harmful religious practice. For example, if someone sincerely believed that God wanted that person to offer human sacrifices would anyone argue that the First Amendment would prohibit laws against that? The Court asserted that "polygamy has always been odious among the northern and western nations of Europe, and until the establishment of [this early form of the Mormon Church], was almost exclusively a feature of life of Asiatic and of African people." It went on to note that no American colony or state before, during or since the passage of the First Amendment recognized polygamy as a right. It was not the intent of those who wrote the First Amendment to guarantee polygamy or to prohibit future legislation with respect to something so fundamental to society as marriage.

Given the drastic changes in values that seem to have occurred and continue to occur in American society with regard to sex, living together, and marriage, do you believe that consenting, unrelated adults today should be prevented from sexual cohabitation if they wish to do so for religious reasons? What if they wish to do so for non-religious reasons?

Though the *Reynolds* decision is still helpful in helping us to see that there is a distinction between religious belief and religious actions, it did not give much guidance as to how future courts should actually balance the rights of religious minorities against the rights of the rest of society alleging harm caused by the minority religion.

Cases in the Twentieth Century attempted to give more guidance. Specifically, courts began to require that a state prove a **"compelling interest"** before it interfered with some religious practice. This "compelling interest" was deemed to be much more than a legitimate reason or a good reason. The key word is "compelling." The case that follows shows how this often played out.

Wisconsin v. Yoder

406 U.S. 205 (1972)

Wisconsin made it a crime for a parent to refuse to send his or her child under the age of 16 to school. Yoder, an Amish man, was tried and convicted of this offense. On appeal, he argued that the law was an unconstitutional interference with the free exercise of his religion.

For religious reasons, Amish people traditionally only educate their young up through the eighth grade (until about 13 years of age). Though the Amish believe in learning the "three R's," education beyond that point is believed to be excessive and even harmful to the Amish way of life. It is felt that "excessive" levels of education can lead to worldly values such as competition, individualism and nationalism. Such values, Amish believe, tend to lure children away from the Amish religion which emphasizes farming and working with one's hands. At about age 13, Amish children are expected to leave school and start working in the community.

The state of Wisconsin, on the other hand, argued that it had good reasons to require parents to send their children to school beyond the eighth grade. Society benefits greatly from an educated citizenry and children are shielded from having to work at too young an age in many potentially dangerous adult occupations.

In deciding this case, the U.S. Supreme Court noted that when both sides have a good point, a balancing test must be used to decide whose rights are heavier. However, it is not a simple balancing test because before a state can interfere with a fundamental right like the free exercise of religion, it must not only show that it has a good reason to do so but a "compelling" one.

Ultimately the Court decided that the Amish right to pull their children out of school outweighed the state's legitimate right to see that all children are educated up until the age of sixteen. The Court did not believe that the state's interests were compelling enough to outweigh the interest of the Amish to practice core religious beliefs that ultimately did not harm anybody. The Amish alternative to schooling, which at the time was essentially farming, was seen as a viable alternative to schooling and posed no danger to Amish children or the greater non-Amish society.

From the above, we see that the "compelling interest" standard held sway throughout much of the 20th Century. But, what about today? To the horror of many religious-rights advocates, courts recently began ruling that the "compelling interest" standard (also known as "strict scrutiny") is no longer sacrosanct. Following the example of the U.S. Supreme Court, courts have begun ruling that a law hurting minority religious practices is ok whether or not there is a compelling state interest as long as it is "**facially neutral and uniformly applied.**" (See, e.g. *Employment Division of Oregon vs. Smith*, 494 U.S. 872 (1990)). What this means is that a law is ok even if it harms a particular religion as long as that religion was not targeted for harm. If the law just happens to hurt the religion as "collateral damage" of sorts, then it is constitutional. Hence, a law against the use of narcotics that happens to make it a crime for certain Indians to make religious use of peyote is ok (according to the *Smith* case just cited) since the legislature was not specifically going after their religion. This is so even though the aims of the law (stopping drug abuse) probably would not have been found compelling enough (under the old standard) to outweigh the Indians' rights to their religious use of peyote.

This abandonment of the "compelling interest" standard and its replacement with the "facially neutral test" has so outraged Congress (both liberal and conservative members) that it legislatively resurrected the "compelling interest" standard by statute. So, we are back to the religion-friendly strict scrutiny used throughout much of the 20th Century. But this is thanks only to a statute passed by Congress (known as the **Religious Freedom Restoration Act**) rather than to the First Amendment as interpreted by the Supreme Court.

The Right to Privacy

We learned earlier that a legislature can make anything it wants to a crime as long as a constitution is not violated. Certainly, free speech and free exercise of religion are clearly constitutional rights that potentially trump legislation. But, what about the so-called "right to privacy?" Perhaps you have heard of this right.

The "**right to privacy**" is not expressly found anywhere in the black letter text of the Constitution. Rather, it has been found "between the lines" so to speak. If one reads the Constitution as a whole, advocates of a general right to privacy argue that its existence becomes necessary and obvious.

Some legal scholars and even some current Supreme Court justices do not believe in any of this. They do believe in specific rights of privacy (like freedom against unreasonable searches, freedom against self-incrimination, etc.). These are mentioned in the Bill of Rights. But they do not believe that there is some general right of privacy—at least not in the Constitution. They would argue that to hold otherwise leads inevitably to judicial imposition of personal values on American society.

The "right to privacy" came about in a 1965 case known as *Griswold v. Connecticut*, 381 U.S. 479 (1965). At the time, Connecticut still made it a crime for a doctor to help women obtain artificial birth control. The majority of the Supreme Court found that such a statute violated a general right to privacy. Though the dissent said no such right can be found in the wording of the Constitution and hence simply does not exist, the majority believed that such a right can be found through implication. The majority pointed out that many mini-rights to privacy exist in the Constitution (e.g, First Amendment right to associate, the Third Amendment right to not be forced to house troops in one's home, the Fourth Amendment right against unreasonable searches, the Fifth Amendment right against compulsory self-incrimination). They believed that the cumulative effect of these mini-rights to privacy was to create a larger, general right to privacy. They went on to reason that the extremely personal decision of whether or not to use birth control was one aspect of this newly discovered general privacy right.

Whether or not a general right to privacy should be found to exist in the Constitution, few people today would lobby their state legislature to criminalize birth control. But the next big privacy case still causes intense debate. It was *Roe v. Wade*, 410 U.S. 113 (1973), and despite some close calls it still remains the law of the land. In this, the most famous "privacy" case of all time, the U.S. Supreme Court reaffirmed a general right to privacy in the Constitution. That said, it went on to hold that such a right covers elective abortion up until the point that a fetus could survive on its own (albeit with medical help) outside the mother's womb. This point, known as "**viability**," occurs at the end of the second trimester, or about six months into a pregnancy.

Roe remains controversial for several reasons. First, some people still do not agree that there is any such thing as a general right to privacy in the Constitution. It may sound laudable, but that does not give courts the right to pencil-in rights that do not exist. Second, some say that even if a general right to privacy exists, it may cover such things as birth control but should not cover elective abortions. Finally, some argue that even if the right covers elective abortions, it certainly should not cover abortions as deep into a pregnancy as the six months *Roe* allows. By then, the fetus is clearly so human that its right to live outweighs any privacy rights of the mother.

Defenders of *Roe* say that women should have the right to control their own bodies and reproductive choices. They say that *Roe* was a great leap forward in women's rights and vigorously oppose any interference with what they consider to be one of life's most private matters. They further argue that it would be harmful to upset a precedent that has been in place and relied upon for so long and that a repeal of *Roe* would lead to disrespect for the Supreme Court and unduly aggravate societal tensions.

Roe continues to divide Americans like no other case currently the law of the land. It will remain to be seen if it stands the test of time or eventually is overturned.

The "right to privacy" continues to expand. The next case considers whether or not it should be deemed to cover consensual gay sex.

Lawrence v. Texas

123 S.Ct. 2472 (2003)

In Houston, Texas, police officers legally entered a private residence pursuant to the report of a weapons offense. While inside, they observed John Lawrence engaging in sex with another man. Both men were arrested and convicted of "deviate sexual intercourse," basically for engaging in anal sex with someone of their own gender.

On appeal, Lawrence argued that the right to privacy should be deemed to cover gay sex and therefore the Texas state legislature should not be allowed to make it a crime. But, lower appellate courts upheld the convictions citing a 1986 U.S. Supreme Court decision (*Bowers v. Hardwick*, 478 U.S. 186 (1986)) which held that the right to privacy did not cover gay sex, even in the privacy of one's home. The Court in *Bowers* did not believe a fundamental right to gay sex existed given the history and traditions of our country. It opined that upholding morality was a legitimate function of government, otherwise many criminal laws would have to be turned on their heads.

The vote in *Bowers* was as close as it can get: five to four. Now, less than a decade and a few personnel changes later, the Supreme Court once again considered whether the general right to privacy, originally found in the *Griswold* birth control case and later extended to the *Roe* abortion case, should now be considered to include consensual gay sex as well.

Over the outraged dissent of three of the Justices, the majority of the Supreme Court found that the general right to privacy does indeed cover consensual gay sex. The majority ruled that *Bowers*, decided just seven years earlier, was poor law and should be overturned. In reaching its decision, the Court reasoned that the reliance in *Bowers* on history and tradition was misguided because of the "emerging awareness" in the past fifty years that private sex between consenting adults is purely a private matter. It noted that The European Court of Human Rights has recognized the right to such activities and held laws to the contrary there invalid. It noted that even here in America, those states that criminalized sodomy rarely enforced the law (including the state of Texas). Given all of this, it was the opinion of the Court that privacy is part of liberty and gay sex is part of privacy.

The stinging opinions of the dissenters is best illustrated by the ideas penned by Justice Scalia. He wrote that the Court clearly took sides in the culture wars and allied itself with the liberal agenda of the academic legal community, of which Scalia said the High Court was apparently a kindred soul. He said it was not the role of the court to "invent" constitutional rights that do not exist simply because some states are believed to be slow in changing what may or may not be backward laws. Scalia wrote that he had nothing personally against homosexuals, but that he did not see that he had any right to create new constitutional rights regardless of how he might personally feel. He ended by warning that this decision, despite the majority's assurances to the contrary, must inevitably lead to an eventual recognition of a constitutional right to gay marriage.

The Void for Vagueness Doctrine

Earlier, you were asked to consider whether a state could make it a crime to be a "hooligan." Do you see any problems with such a law? In fact, "hooliganism" was a crime in the former Soviet Union. Towards the end of the Soviet era, a German youth out to have some fun, flew a small airplane into Russia, somehow evaded air defenses, and landed smack dab on Red Square in Moscow. Several Soviet generals lost their jobs over the incident and the German lad was charged with being a "hooligan." No doubt he did misbehave and probably should have been punished. But hooligan? What is a hooligan?

In America, it would be unconstitutional to charge someone with the crime of being a hooligan. Why? Because the Fourteenth Amendment to the Constitution says you cannot punish someone criminally without first giving that person "due process of law." "Due process" basically means fair procedures. Fair procedures traditionally include such things as a trial, legal advice, and the right to confront and question one's accusers. Fair procedures would also include being charged with a statute that is not too vague. **Vague statutes** are unfair and hence violate the guarantee of due process for two reasons: 1) they fail to give fair notice of what conduct is prohibited; and 2) they allow police and prosecutors to target people they do not like.

Suppose the state you live in made it a crime to be a "hooligan." Do you see how making this a crime would fail to give people fair notice of what is expected of them? Do you also see how such a law would empower police and prosecutors to go after people they simply do not like for whatever reason. No doubt the Soviet authorities loved the fact that they could pass vague statutes. But here in America, such statutes would be "void for vagueness," by violating the "due process" guarantee of the Fourteenth Amendment. The case that follows illustrates this "void for vagueness" doctrine and the points just covered.

Minnesota v. Reha

474 N.W.2d 360 (Minn. App. 1991)

The city of Minneapolis made it a crime for occupants of dwellings to fail to keep them in a "clean and satisfactory condition." A Minnesota Health Department official decided to visit and inspect Reha's home after having received a complaint. Arriving at the house, the inspector found "severe clutter" in the yard, five plastic garbage bags on the back porch, ground-in dirt on the interior walls, clutter on the stairs, boxes stacked against an interior wall, and clothing and food lying about the house. Some of the clothing apparently contained roach and mice droppings.

Reha denied having an unclean house but instead maintained that it was merely disorganized. Nevertheless, a jury found her guilty and the judge sentenced her to 35 days or a $700 fine. Reha appealed to the Minnesota Court of Appeals claiming that the ordinance was so vague as to deny her due process of law under the 14th Amendment.

On appeal, the Court agreed with Reha. It found the words "clean and satisfactory" to be so vague as to violate due process. The phrase failed to define the criminal offense "with sufficient definiteness that ordinary people can understand what conduct is prohibited and in a manner that does not encourage arbitrary and discriminatory enforcement."

The court noted that "clean and sanitary" is not a "term of art" with well-understood meanings. These words could mean many things to different people. In fact, even employees of the Health Department apparently differ greatly as to their meaning. Given this, how could ordinary people know what is expected? Because Reha was not put on reasonable notice and because enforcement officials were given so little guidance in determining whom to prosecute, Reha was punished without first having been given minimal standards of due process.

Laws like the one in the case discussed above which are held to be too vague can often be fixed. Lawmakers simply need to be more precise in the way they word the statute. Ridiculous amounts of precision will not be required, however. Courts are composed of reasonable human beings who will cut lawmakers some slack if it is obvious they have done as good a job with their wording as can be reasonably expected. But, if courts feel that legislatures have simply been stupid or lazy, they will often strike the law down.

Equal Protection

The last constitutional limit on the criminal law that we will cover is that of "equal protection." Like "due process," the words "equal protection" are found in the 14th Amendment. According to the 14th Amendment, no state may "deny to any person within its jurisdiction the equal protection of the laws." What **equal protection** means is that states should treat all similarly situated people the same (there should be no improper discrimination on the part of government). Not all discrimination is bad though. The government can treat people differently if there are valid reasons to do so, but it should not play favorites merely for the sake of playing favorites.

Think of the state as a parent of sorts. If you were a parent with three children wouldn't you be denying your children "equal protection" if you left your two sons everything in your will but left your daughter nothing merely because of her gender? You would be playing favorites and that is morally wrong. On the other hand, there may be valid reasons to treat your three children differently in your will. Suppose for example, that you left half of your estate to a retarded child who was unable to support himself and the other half to be shared by the two remaining children. Even though you treated your children differently, you did not deny them your "equal protection." You had a valid reason for treating them differently and were not merely playing favorites.

The same holds true with the way the equal protection clause of the 14th Amendment is interpreted. Race or gender discrimination aside (scary categories that cause suspicious courts to engage in a form of heightened scrutiny), courts will not have a problem with laws treating people unequally as long as the state can come up with a legitimate or **rational basis** for the unequal treatment. Normally, this is a very, very easy standard to meet. The case that follows illustrates this point.

Allam v. State

830 P.2d 435 (Alaska App. 1992)

Allam was an 18-year-old senior at an Anchorage high school. During a school-sponsored event at a local park known as "senior fun day," Allam was caught rolling marijuana cigarettes with three other boys, two of whom had not yet turned 18 years of age. Allam and the other 18-year-old were arrested under an Alaska statute which (at the time) allowed people 19 and older to possess small amounts of marijuana (up to four ounces) but not 18-year-olds. In other words, just as many states today do not allow people to use alcohol until they are 21, Alaska did not allow people to use small amounts of marijuana until they turned 19 years of age. The other two youths caught with the marijuana were not arrested because they were still juveniles.

On appeal to the Alaska Court of Appeals, Allam claims that Alaska was denying him equal protection of the laws. He asserts that a ridiculous situation is created by the law in that the only people in Alaska that could be prosecuted for possessing small amounts of marijuana were 18-year-olds and nobody else. People aged 19 to 119 could not be prosecuted because the legal marijuana smoking age was set at nineteen. People 0 to 17 could not be criminally prosecuted because they are still juveniles, and if anything would be processed through the juvenile justice system rather than charged with an adult crime. He claims that Alaska could have no possible rational basis for making 18-year-olds criminals with this law and nobody else.

In its decision, the appellate court sided with the State of Alaska. It said since neither race nor gender were involved here, the statute would be constitutional so long as the state merely had a rational basis for the different treatment based on age. The court found a rational basis in that 18-year-old "adults"—unlike those 19 and older—are often still in high school and thus in a position to corrupt minors who attend school with them. It also noted that even though a strange, ultimate result is produced, there is nothing irrational about treating people under the age of 18 as juveniles and there is nothing irrational about setting the legal age for marijuana smoking at 19 years of age. Since the state does have a rational basis for the law, it did not deny Allam its equal protection.

Basic Elements of a Crime

Let us turn our attention now away from constitutional limits on the criminal law and consider something else. Are there any basic elements which virtually all crimes have in common? The answer is "yes." There are two such basic elements to crimes. These two elements are known as "actus reus" and "mens rea." Think of this as an equation. This equation would look like this: Actus Reus + Mens Rea = Crime. If either actus reus or mens rea is missing, there is no crime.

Generally speaking, the **actus reus** (or "bad act") is the physical part of the crime and the **mens rea** (or "bad mind") is the mental part of the crime. Both are necessary for a crime to occur.

For example, suppose I admit to a group of friends to having the most foul and evil thoughts imaginable and they go and tell the police exactly what I have been thinking. Even though I may be considered disgusting and even dangerous, I could not be charged with a crime? Why not? Because there is no actus reus.

On the other hand, suppose I kill somebody whom I very reasonably but mistakenly believe is about to kill me. I cannot be charged with their murder. Why not? Because I have no mens rea.

Students often make the mistake of equating mens rea with "intent." For example, if I intend to kill you I had mens rea but if I did not intend to kill you there is no crime. Actually, intent is merely one type of mens rea. One acts with **intent** when the result obtained was the conscious objective that one was seeking (in other words the harmful result was the goal all along). If intent were the only type of mens rea, I could kill you while drunk driving and claim that I committed no crime since, after all, it was not my goal that you die.

Obviously there are other types of mens rea in addition to "intent." For example, recklessness is a type of "bad mind" and so qualifies as mens rea. **Recklessness** is defined as being aware of a substantial risk of causing harm yet taking that risk anyway (e.g., killing a small child while zooming by a stopped, flashing school bus—can you see how such a person has a bad mind even without intent to kill?). Negligence is another type of mens rea. **Negligence** is defined as not being aware of a substantial risk of harm even though a reasonable person would be aware.

The level of mens rea can matter a lot. If I kill you intentionally, that would typically be murder and I would get life in prison. If I kill you recklessly, that would only be manslaughter and I might only have to serve a few years in prison. If I kill you negligently (e.g., running a red light without even realizing it), that would only be negligent homicide and I could conceivably get probation. As you can see, "intent" is one type of mens rea but there are other types as well.

Let us now look at a couple of cases that illustrate the concepts of actus reus and mens rea. We will begin with a case in which there is no actus reus then look at a case in which there is no mens rea.

State v. Dalton

793 N.E.2d 509 (Ohio App. 10th Dist. 2003)

Brian Dalton was on probation after serving time in prison for various possession of child pornography charges. While on this probation, Dalton's mother found his diary in his apartment and read distressing fantasies regarding children written by him. She contacted Dalton's probation officer and asked him to take the diary away. The probation officer subsequently read the diary and became aware of Dalton's written fantasies about the violent torture and rape of a number of fictitious children.

The probation officer contacted a police detective who took the journal and charged Dalton with two counts of creating obscene material involving the portrayal of a minor. Both charges were based not on images but solely on Dalton's writings located in the diary found in his apartment.

Under the advice of his court-appointed lawyer, Dalton pled guilty to one of the counts in exchange for the other being dropped. The trial court judge then sentenced Dalton to seven years in prison for the one count. In addition to this, Dalton received additional time as a consequence of his probation being revoked for his having pled guilty to the new offense.

Later, Dalton tried to withdraw his guilty plea on the grounds that he had been denied effective assistance of counsel. He argued that his lawyer allowed him to plea guilty to conduct that could not constitutionally be made a crime since the state could not punish mere thoughts. In other words, Dalton is arguing that since there is no actus reus there can be no crime.

The trial court judge refused to allow Dalton to withdraw his guilty plea. It ruled that Dalton's lawyer had advised Dalton of all possible defenses but he nevertheless chose to plead guilty. Dalton appealed this decision to the Ohio Court of Appeals.

The appellate court ruled in favor of Dalton. It said that the trial court abused its discretion in not allowing Dalton to withdraw his guilty plea. It reasoned that Dalton's lawyer let him plea guilty to something that, even if proved, would have failed to show an essential element of the offense (an actus reus). The court determined that Ohio could not constitutionally punish the private possession of thoughts written down in a diary. Otherwise, the state would in effect be punishing an individual for his or her thoughts. Because Dalton's lawyer did not understand this, she was clearly ineffective and Dalton must be allowed to withdraw his guilty plea. Also, the sentence for the probation violation would have to be eliminated since the probation revocation was based on defendant's conviction of a new crime based on the wrongful guilty plea.

Do you agree with this decision? How would you feel if Dalton moved next door to you and your young children? Do you agree with the court that writings in a diary are mere thoughts or would you consider them to be an actus reus of sorts?

Morissette v. United States

342 U.S. 246 (1952)

Morissette went hunting on a large tract of uninhabited and untilled land that the government used as a bombing range. The range was marked, "Danger—Keep Out—Bombing Range." Nevertheless, the range was well-known as a good place to hunt and was extensively used by civilians for that purpose. While hunting there, Morissette came across some spent bomb casings which he apparently thought had been abandoned. They were not stacked in any way but rather dumped into heaps. Many of the casings had begun to rust by having been sitting there for as many as four years. Morissette decided to gather these casings and sell them as salvage to help him recoup some of the expenses of his hunting trip. The loading and transporting of these casings were in full view of people passing by and Morissette made no efforts to act secretly.

When the government found out what Morissette had done it launched an investigation. When confronted, Morissette very candidly explained what he had done and what he had believed. Nevertheless, he was charged with "stealing and converting property of the United States" in violation of a federal theft statute.

Morissette tried to explain during his trial that he honestly did not intend to cheat the government out of its property but rather sincerely believed that the casings were abandoned property. The trial judge said that it did not matter whether or not Morissette intended to steal: "He took it because he thought it was abandoned.... That is no defense." The trial judge felt this way because the statute itself was completely silent as to a requirement for intent or any other type of mens rea. Literally read, the statute seemed to suggest that Morissette was guilty of theft regardless of his state of mind. The physical act of taking was all that was needed. Morissette was convicted of theft of the casings.

On appeal, the U.S. Supreme Court overturned Morissette's conviction for theft. It ruled that "intent" has been a required element of theft for centuries in Anglo-American law. The court reasoned that it would be hard to believe that Congress really meant to do away with mens rea in this type of crime. Though there are minor infractions known as **strict liability offenses** that do not require any type of mens rea (e.g., minor traffic offenses or minor regulatory offenses), true crimes with significant potential penalties or which actually stigmatize people—like theft for instance—have always carried with them a requirement for some type of mens rea.

Since Congress was silent in its statute with regards to what mens rea, if any, it would require, the Court will assume it meant to require "intent" as an element of this offense. To assume by its silence on the matter that it meant to do away with the "intent" element for theft would fly in the face of hundreds of years of tradition. That is just too hard to believe. Since Morissette was not proven to have intended to steal, he could not rightfully have been convicted of theft of these rusting and seemingly abandoned casings.

This completes this chapter. The next chapter will cover "defenses" to crimes. Now that you have learned what mens rea is, you will be in a better position to see that nearly all of the defenses to crime have this in common: they recognize that people who are more or less lacking a bad mind should not be punished for a crime.

Chapter Two

Fundamentals of Criminal Law, Part II: Justifications and Excuses for Crimes

It is likely that the most common defense raised by those accused of committing a crime would be, “I did not do it.” In such cases a defendant may be asserting mistaken identity, an alibi defense, or fabrication on the part of the alleged victim.

But suppose harm was done and the defendant was the one who committed it. What then? Is there no further defense? There are in fact many remaining defenses.

What these remaining defenses all tend to have in common is that though the defendant may have perpetrated a harm of sorts, he or she lacks the mind set of a criminal. In other words, these defenses tend to negate the “evil mind” element rather than the “harmful act” element of a crime.

Neatly put, there are two broad categories of such “I did it but should be let off anyway” defenses: justifications and excuses. A **justification defense** asserts that even though a perpetrator’s action was harmful, it was the morally correct thing to do. The perpetrator has nothing to apologize for. The jury has nothing to forgive. A good example of justification is self-defense. If I shoot some burglar who is coming at me with a large knife, did I do anything morally wrong? Do I need forgiveness on the part of the jury? Of course not. If anything a jury would probably applaud what I have done and would hope that others in similar circumstances will act the same way.

On the other hand, an **excuse defense** asserts that even though what I did was wrong (not justified), I should be forgiven (excused) because there is something wrong with me. The jury does not like what I have done and hopes that others in similar circumstances will act differently. But because I have a mental defect or handicap of sorts, they will not hold me responsible for my actions. Insanity is the clearest example of an excuse defense. If I am found not guilty by reason of insanity, the jury is not justifying what I have done (saying it was good) but rather excusing what I have done (saying it was bad but nevertheless forgiven).

Can you see how both justification defenses and excuse defenses go to the heart of the mental element of a crime? If I am justified in what I have done, I have no guilty mind. Similarly, if there is something so wrong with my thinking processes that a jury wishes to excuse me, then once again I apparently lack the mental element of a true crime. An understanding of justifications and excuses is fundamental to the understanding of criminal law. By studying them, one is studying the lack of moral culpability.

Justification Defenses

Let us now look at the justification defenses. Justifications include self-defense, defense of others, defense of property, execution of public duties, necessity, and resisting unlawful arrest. Keep in mind that what they all have in common is the perpetrator's having done "justice."

Self-Defense

One is justified when one has acted in self-defense. However, before asserting self-defense there is a "technical detail" that one has to worry about: A **reasonable and proportional** level of force is allowed but not an excessive level (more than is reasonable and proportional). If you punch me in the face I am probably justified in punching you back, perhaps even several times. But would you still consider me justified if, after my attacker went down, I were to repeatedly kick him in the face, stomp on his head, and kick him in the gut all while he begged me to stop? The point is, that the concept of self-defense permits me to use that level of force required to defend myself, but does not give me permission to go overboard.[1]

What about killing someone in self-defense? Certainly, most people would say that if I kill to avoid being killed then the homicide is usually justified. But what if I shoot someone who is merely going to punch me? Should I be allowed to use deadly force to defend myself against non-deadly force? Or should I just suffer the blow if necessary?

The rule is that deadly force can only be used to repel deadly force. If non-deadly force is being used against me, I can respond only with non-deadly force. However, **deadly force** is usually defined in such a way as to include danger of serious bodily injury in addition to the danger of death.[2] Hence, if someone is about to poke my eye out with a screwdriver, I may be justified in shooting him in order to prevent this very serious bodily injury.

Defense of Others

In addition to protecting one's self, one may also protect others who are in genuine need of assistance from attack. For example, if I see a vagrant beating up an old man for refusing to make a donation, I may come to the assistance of the old man. The rule here is that the helper steps into the shoes of the person whom he or she is attempting to help. What this means is that the helper can use the same amount of force as the person being aided but no more. So, if the person being aided could use deadly force, so can the helper. But if the person being aided could only use non-deadly force, then that is the only level of force the good Samaritan can use.

---

1. Model Penal Code, Section 3.04(1).
2. Model Penal Code, Section 3.04(2)(b)

Defense of Property

Growing up, I liked to watch reruns of old movies on television. I liked it when John Wayne would shoot the thief who was stealing his horse as the thief was about to disappear out of range. Was John Wayne justified in protecting his property in this manner? Today the "Duke" would be considered to have committed criminal homicide. Why? The next case will explain.

Bishop v. State

356 S.E.2d 503 (Ga. 1987)

Robert Bishop lived in a Georgia trailer court and was sick and tired of burglars breaking into his trailer while he was away. So, one day before going to work, Bishop rigged a booby trap. He placed a rifle on two chairs near the front door with a string attached to both the doorknob of the trailer and the trigger of the rifle. If anyone entered his trailer while he was away, the gun would discharge a bullet into the intruder.

While Bishop was at work, an acquaintance of Bishop tried to gain entrance to Bishop's trailer (perhaps to steal or perhaps to just visit Bishop—the facts are not clear). Sure enough, the gun discharged and a bullet fractured the arm of the uninvited visitor. The intruder went to the hospital but later died from a blood clot that developed as a result of his wound.

Bishop was convicted of murder. On appeal he argued that a man's home is his castle and that he should be allowed to defend it with a deadly booby trap.

The appellate court rejected Bishop's defense. It reasoned that though one may use reasonable, non-deadly force to protect property that is being taken in one's presence, one can never use deadly force merely to protect property. True, the law in some states does allow people to defend an attack upon their homes with deadly force, but only when the homeowner is present. Here, Bishop was at work. When the homeowner is present, there is always the chance that he or she will determine that deadly force is not necessary. But traps involving loaded guns can show no such mercy. Also, to allow such devices would put firefighters, police officers, and children at risk should they enter. This cannot be tolerated.

Do you agree that Bishop should go to prison for what he did? Would it make a difference if the intruder was actually planning to steal rather than merely visit? Does even a burglar's right to live outweigh the right of someone to protect his or her things?

Execution of Public Duties

We have learned that private citizens ordinarily may not use deadly force unless they are being put in danger of death or serious bodily injury. But, would you make an exception for police officers who are trying to carry out their duties? Suppose a tired and out of shape police officer is chasing someone and yells "freeze" but the suspect refuses to stop. Should the police officer be required to just let that person get away? Does it depend upon what that defiant person is suspected of having done? The case that follows gives us guidance on this point.

Tennessee v. Garner

471 U.S. 1 (1984)

Garner was the father of a teenaged boy who was shot in the back of the head while running from the police. The father is suing the government civilly for wrongful death. He claims that his son was unreasonably "seized" in violation of the Fourth Amendment prohibition against unreasonable searches and seizures.

A Memphis police officer shot the teen, who appeared to the officer to be 17 or 18 years old and who looked to be unarmed. The officer had responded to a residence pursuant to the report of a prowler called in by a neighbor. Upon arriving at the neighborhood, the police officer saw the neighbor gesture towards the adjacent house while exclaiming that she had heard glass breaking.

The officer went around to the back of the house in question, whereupon the officer heard a door slam shut and saw the teen running toward the fence at the end of the back yard. The officer yelled, "police, halt," but the boy did not halt. Instead, he started climbing the fence. Convinced that the burglar would escape unless he were shot, the officer shot the youth, killing him.

At the time, Tennessee law made the police officer's actions perfectly legal. The Tennessee statute provided that "if, after notice of the intention to arrest the defendant, he either flee or forcibly resist, the officer may use all the necessary means to effect the arrest."

Because of this statute authorizing the officer to use deadly force, the officer could not be charged with any crime. But, was the father of the teen correct when he argued that the Tennessee statute was a violation of the Fourth Amendment and therefore he should at least receive monetary compensation from the government for the wrongful death of his son? Was the shooting of his fleeing son an unreasonable seizure?

Yes, the U.S. Supreme Court decided. It ruled that the use of deadly force to prevent the escape of all fleeing suspects, regardless of their crimes, is constitutionally unreasonable. It said that even a rule allowing for the shooting of all fleeing felons (the teen apparently had committed burglary, a felony) would be constitutionally unreasonable. The only suspects that could be reasonably shot to prevent their escape are those felons whose escape would pose a real risk of serious harm to others. Some escaping felons would qualify under this rule, but not burglars.

The court justified its decision by saying that "it is not better that all felony suspects die than that they escape ... It is no doubt unfortunate when a suspect who is in sight escapes, but the fact the police arrive a little late or are a little slower afoot does not always justify killing the suspect. A police officer may not seize an unarmed, non-dangerous suspect by shooting him dead."

The three dissenters felt very differently. They seemed to agree that police should not be allowed to shoot just any fleeing criminal, but argued that burglars of homes "pose a real risk of serious harm to others." They pointed out that, at the time, "three-fifths of all rapes in the home, three-fifths of all home robberies, and about a third of home aggravated and simple assaults are committed by burglars." In short, the dissenters believed that burglary was just too serious a crime to just let the suspect get away.

So, where does this leave us? Can a police officer shoot a fleeing shoplifter? Absolutely not. Could an officer shoot a fleeing felon? That would depend upon the nature of the felony: how violent and dangerous it was. What felonies do you think people should be shot for if trying to escape. Income tax evasion? Drug trafficking? Rape? Armed robbery?

Necessity

The next justification defense is that of **necessity** or choosing the lesser of two evils. Suppose that you were freezing to death in the wilderness and you finally came across a cabin that said, "No Trespassing—Keep Out." Instead of obeying the law, you break into the cabin, build a fire in the fireplace, and eat some cans of food found in the pantry. Were you justified in committing this burglary? Consider your alternative: freezing and starving to death.

The above illustrates the principle of necessity. When a person is confronted with the evil of breaking the law vs. suffering an even greater evil if he or she were to obey the law, he or she is generally justified in breaking the law.

Who would say that someone acted wrongfully by throwing cargo overboard from a sinking boat, or by stealing medicine for a dying child during a natural disaster, or by speeding to a hospital when a passenger is having a heart attack? Sometimes we are forced to break the law in order to choose the lesser harm.

One of the scary things about necessity is that if we are not careful, it could lead to anarchy. For this reason, courts are sometimes reluctant to recognize the defense in cases involving poor people resorting to "self-help." It is one thing to steal during a natural disaster. But what if one steals just because one is poor? The case that follows pursues this issue.

Lightner v. State

843 S.W.2d 161 (Tex.App. 1992)

An off-duty police officer working as a guard in an office building noticed a vagrant out in the parking lot entering the car of a woman who worked in the building. The officer walked over to the car and saw Lightner inside the vehicle going through the glove box. He was in the process of removing music tapes he found in this glove box. The officer arrested Lightner and he was subsequently tried for burglary of an automobile.

At the end of his trial, Lightner asked the trial judge to instruct the jury on the defense of necessity. Lightner explained to the court that at the time of the crime he had been a street person for about a year and that he had not eaten for a day. He was hungry and broke into the car in order to look for food or something of value he could use to get food. The judge refused to instruct the jury on the necessity defense. As a result, the jury never considered the defense in its deliberations. The jury convicted Lightner.

On appeal, Lightner claims that the refusal of the trial judge to charge the jury on the necessity defense denied him a fair trial. Lightner argued that whether his necessity defense was weak or strong is irrelevant. The jury should have decided the issue.

The appellate court disagreed with Lightner and upheld his conviction. It ruled that the trial judge had made no error, since the evidence submitted at trial did not raise any reasonable possibility of a successful necessity defense. It is true that necessity involves the weighing of a choice of evils and one can be justified in breaking the law when that is the lesser of two bad outcomes. But, Lightner was not actually forced to choose between two evils. Necessity is only a defense when "the actor reasonably believes the conduct is immediately necessary to avoid imminent harm." Lightner was not in danger of "imminent harm" and his burglary was not "immediately necessary." Consequently, his necessity defense as a matter of law was doomed to failure and the trial judge acted properly in not confusing a jury by presenting it as a viable option.

Do you agree with the decision above? If you were homeless and hungry would you steal if you could? How hungry would Lightner have to become before you would consider him to be in danger of "imminent harm?" Would this ever develop? Do hungry, homeless people like Lightner always have options available that do not involve breaking the law? Do people in poor countries always have such options? Do you think any government on the planet would ever allow necessity to be used as a defense to thefts committed by poor, hungry people?

Resisting Unlawful Arrest

The last justification defense that we shall consider is that of Resisting an Unlawful Arrest. Suppose that a young, attractive female in her early 20s is approached by a bored, lonely police officer walking his beat. Suppose that at some point while conversing with her, the officer makes unwanted romantic contact with the woman and as a consequence the woman slaps him on the face. If the officer were to attempt to arrest this woman for "assaulting" a police officer, would she be justified in resisting the bogus arrest?

Or, suppose that a religious person is proselyting door to door in a wealthy area when an irritated homeowner of influence calls the police. The police officer shows up and attempts to unconstitutionally "escort" the religious person out of the officer's jurisdiction by way of the back of a police car. Would the religious person be justified in resisting this unlawful arrest?

Traditionally, citizens were allowed to use reasonable, non-deadly force in resisting an unlawful arrest. To expect a citizen to passively acquiesce to a police officer abusing his arrest power would have been considered to be "un-American."

Times have changed. Today, the defense of "Resisting an Unlawful Arrest" has been rejected by the courts. The modern reasoning is that allowing citizens to resist arrest (even unlawful arrests) could lead to an escalation in tensions, potentially leading to lethal violence. Remember, police have guns. And, citizens may think an arrest is unlawful when in fact it is the opposite. Citizens should just submit to the arrest and fight it out later in a court of law.

Do you agree with the traditional view of your great-grandparents or with the view of your modern contemporaries? Do you think that the anti-government radicals who founded our republic would be proud of our abandonment of the defense? Would they be morally outraged or would they see us as practical and enlightened? Does it matter to you what they would think?

Excuse Defenses

We shall now leave justification defenses and turn our attention towards excuses. Excuse defenses include insanity, mistake, duress, entrapment, youthful age, and involuntary intoxication. Remember, when a jury excuses a defendant, the jury is not saying that he or she was justified (morally correct in his or her actions). Rather, it is saying that even though the defendant acted badly, the defendant will be forgiven due to a mental handicap of some kind. Essentially, the jury is saying that the defendant is not responsible for his or her bad conduct.

Insanity

Insanity is perhaps the most famous of the excuse defenses. But legally, it is tricky. We casually use the words, "insane," and "insanity" in our every day conversation. When we say that a person is "insane," we generally mean (to be rather vulgar about it) that he or she is "crazy." Basically, we equate insanity with severe mental illness.

Medical professionals obviously would not use a word like "crazy." It is not a proper medical term. But, neither are the words "insane" and "insanity" medical terms.

"Insanity" is strictly a legal term, not a medical term. It was invented by lawyers and legal scholars. A medical doctor would never diagnose someone as being "insane." Only a criminal court would use that term. When a court finds that someone is insane, it is not merely saying that the defendant is severely mentally ill. It is saying that the defendant is mentally ill *and* should be let off the criminal justice system hook.

Not every severely mentally ill person is let off the hook by juries. In fact, very few are. Prisons are full of delusional psychotics, extreme paranoids, and hallucinating schizophrenics whom juries refused to find "insane." Remember, if a jury says someone is insane, the jury is excusing that person for whatever harm he or she has caused. Juries are not very inclined to forgive and forget, even when the perpetrator is obviously intensely disturbed. Very, very people in this country are found not guilty by reason of insanity.

This is so for several reasons. First of all, many mentally ill people think they are better off pleading guilty than being found insane. So they accept plea bargains. Most plea bargains result in probation or a little jail time. If you are found not guilty by reason of insanity, you may feel more stigmatized by that label than you might feel for being convicted of a crime. In addition, people found insane may be civilly committed to a mental hospital for a minimum of one year without any further hearings. What would you prefer? A little jail time as a noble criminal or the mental hospital for a year?

Second, only two percent of cases that wind up at trial even involve an insanity defense to begin with.[3] It is very rarely raised in trials (probably much less frequently than it could be).

Third, even in that two percent of cases in which it is raised, defendants are found not guilty by reason of insanity in only two to five percent of those few cases.[4] In other words, insanity results in an acquittal in only about two to five percent of two percent of trials (not even counting all of the convictions gained from the plea bargains).

At this point you might be asking what exactly is the test for insanity that juries use in their deliberations. What is the precise definition of the legal term, "insanity?"

There are several tests out there. States choose which one to use. One test is known as the **product test**. Simply put, the jury merely asks itself whether or not the crime was a "product" of mental illness. If it was the product, then the defendant should be found not guilty by reason of insanity.

When you think of it, this "product test" is very defendant-friendly. That is perhaps why almost no states use it. Suppose as a juror you were presented with a very disturbed person who kidnaps people in order to chop off their heads so that he could supplement his boiled head collection. Would you say that his actions were somehow a product of mental illness? Perhaps. It is because of this "perhaps" that so few states use this test. Most states instead look for a test that is much more conviction-friendly. The most famous of these conviction-friendly tests is the M'Naghten Rule.

M'Naghten was a mentally ill man who lived in England in the early 1800s. He believed that the British Prime Minister, Sir Robert Peel, was out to destroy him. So, he went over to Peel's house and attempted to shoot Peel in a preemptive strike. He missed and killed Peel's personal secretary instead. When he was tried for murder, the English jury acquitted him by finding him not guilty by reason of insanity. This verdict so upset British society that the House of Lords (the British version of a supreme court) decided to come up with a new test of insanity that would make it very difficult for future bad actors like the hated M'Naghten to avoid responsibility for their harms. The test they devised is now known as the M'Naghten Rule and it is still used by nearly half of the United States.

The **M'Naghten Rule** requires one of two things before a jury may find someone to be insane. "Owing to a disease of the mind," the person must be unable to either (1) understand the nature or quality of his or her act; or (2) appreciate the wrongfulness of what he or she has done. Confused? Juries often are too.

Basically, I only fail to understand the "nature or quality" of my act when I am so utterly delusional that I am unable to perceive what is taking place. For example, if I "see" that I am shooting a deer while hunting while I am actually shooting my work colleague in his office, then I probably am failing to understand the nature or quality of my act. Very few mentally ill criminals could claim this (the person who boiled heads knew he was dealing with human heads and not cabbage).

---

3. Morris, Norval. *Madness and the Criminal Law.* (Chicago: University of Chicago Press, 1982).
4. Walker, Samuel. *Sense and Nonsense about Crime,* 5th ed. (Monterey, CA: Brooks/Cole, 2001).

I am unable to appreciate the "wrongfulness" of what I am doing if I am able to understand that what I am doing is considered by society to be morally wrong. Again, very few mentally ill criminals could claim this (the person who boiled human heads —Jeffrey Dahmer—hid the heads in his basement because he knew murder was wrong).

Can you see how the M'Naghten Rule is much harder than the Product Test in gaining an acquittal? Many scholars think that it is too hard. They argue that the M'Naghten Rule is unfair because it focuses solely on the intellect. In other words, people may intellectually know the quality of their act and may intellectually know that it is wrong but despite this awareness they are powerless to stop themselves. Perhaps there is a non-intellectual aspect to insanity: some people simply cannot control themselves despite what their brain knows. For this reason, many states have modified M'Naghten to make room for this impulsive form of mental illness. They have adopted an expanded test that is not so defendant-friendly as the Product Test but still more defendant-friendly than a straight M'Naghten Rule. The new test (used by nearly half the states) is now known as the **substantial capacity test** (also known as the **model penal code test**). The case that follows defines the test.

State v. Johnson

399 A.2d 469 (R.I. 1979)

Johnson was convicted of a crime (the published opinion does not specify which crime) despite asserting an insanity defense. The trial court that found him guilty did so by applying the old M'Naghten Rule to his case. On appeal, Johnson asked that his conviction be overturned on the grounds that the M'Naghten Rule was too harsh on defendants who suffer from severe mental illness and that it should be replaced with a test that is more understanding of the realities of mental disease.

The sole issue in this case then was whether or not Rhode Island should abandon the M'Naghten Rule and adopt a different test instead. In its decision, the Rhode Island Supreme Court agreed with Johnson and adopted a new formulation for legal insanity.

The Rhode Island Supreme Court noted the history of the M'Naghten Rule. It suggested that the rule came about due to the pressure of an angry British public and a frightened Queen. The queen herself had been threatened by the same disturbed M'-Naghten who had attempted to kill her prime minister and who did kill her prime minister's secretary. Under heavy pressure, the House of Lords rejected further use of a rather enlightened test that M'Naghten's jury was permitted to use. This pre-M'Naghten test had recognized that insanity could be more than just the cognitive inability to distinguish right from wrong. The House of Lords made it clear that henceforth British juries would only find a defendant to be insane if, the "accused was laboring under such a defect of reason, from disease of the mind, as not to know the nature and quality of the act he was doing, or if he did know it, that he did not know that what he was doing was wrong."

This new M'Naghten test quickly became the predominant test in the United States. However, it is now subject to intense criticism because it "refuses to recognize volitional or emotional impairments, viewing the cognitive element as the singular cause of conduct." It does not give any sympathy to someone who is "unable to resist sustained psychic compulsion or to make any attempt to control his conduct." In other words, some ill people may intellectually understand what they are doing and intellectually understand that what they are doing is wrong, yet lack the free will to control themselves. A better test would be one that acknowledges lack of free will and not just cognitive impairment.

The test that Rhode Island chose to adopt is the Model Penal Code Test adopted by about half the states as well as by the federal courts. This test, also known as the "substantial capacity test," provides that a person will not be held responsible for his criminal conduct if, due to mental illness or defect, "his capacity either to appreciate the wrongfulness of his conduct or to conform his conduct to the requirements of the law is so substantially impaired that he cannot justly be held responsible."

We see in this test a sort of M'Naghten "plus." Like M'Naghten there is the cognitive or intellectual element: "not appreciating right from wrong." But in addition to this there is the lack of free will or volitional element: unable to "conform his conduct to the requirements of the law."

Because Rhode Island adopted this new, more expansive test that it believed better reflected a modern understanding of mental illness, Johnson's case was sent back to the trial court for a new trial regarding the sole issue of criminal responsibility.

Unlike the court above that is very sympathetic to the mentally ill charged with crimes, some people argue that insanity should simply be abolished entirely as a defense. Would you agree with that? Apparently there is no constitutional right to an insanity defense. States are free to abolish it or keep it as they deem fit.

Mistake

Not every excuse defense involves mental illness. Suppose for example that I simple make a mistake. We all make mistakes. Can you see how making a mistake can negate the mental element of a crime?

For example, suppose that as a joke my best friend wears a stocking mask over his face and jumps out of an alley with a toy gun in order to frighten me. Out of mistaken belief that my life is in jeopardy, I take out my concealed firearm (which I have a permit for) and fatally shoot my friend. Obviously I am not mentally ill but neither do I correctly perceive what is going on. My friend meant no harm, yet my friend is now dead. Should I be excused? Most people would agree that I am not responsible for the death of my friend. Though my actions killing him were regrettable, my mind-set was not a bad one.

Such mistakes certainly can constitute a legal excuse to a crime. But, we have to be careful when we look for a mistake to excuse us. There are two kinds of mistake and only one of them constitutes a defense. A **mistake of law** occurs when a person is not aware that some act has been made a crime. A mistake of law is no excuse to a crime. You already knew that this type of mistake was no legal excuse. Have you ever heard the expression, "ignorance of the law is no excuse?" What this of course means is that just because someone is unaware that what he or she has done is illegal, that does not entitle that person to avoid responsibility for his or her bad acts.

Mistake of law is not a legal defense for a couple of reasons. First, if it were a defense, criminals could too easily take advantage of the defense by pretending ignorance. Hence, frauds would constantly be perpetrated on the courts. But, there is a second and arguably more profound reason not to recognize mistake of law as a valid excuse. Remember, by definition, crimes are immoral acts (that is why we punish criminals rather than just requiring restitution as in civil court). If a person who commits an immoral act does not realize it was against the law, the fact still remains that the person acted immorally. In a sense the wrongdoer still has a guilty mind (the bad actor knew or should reasonably have known that the harmful act was morally wrong even if he or she did not realize it was illegal). After all, if a strong enough societal consensus existed to make it a crime, it must have constituted a fairly serious deviation from societal norms. So, whether the perpetrator of a harmful act actually knew it was against the law, only knew it was morally wrong, or only should have known it was morally wrong, he or she still possesses a bad mind-set of sorts and should not be excused for the harm he or she has caused.

The other kind of mistake is a mistake of fact. A mistake of fact (unlike a mistake of law) can be a defense to a crime. A **mistake of fact** occurs when a person understands the circumstances surrounding a particular situation to be different than what they truly are. That is why I should be excused for shooting my friend who dressed up like a thug and pointed a toy gun at me. My mistake was a mistake of fact and not a mistake of law. Mistakes of facts (unlike mistakes of law) negates the evil mind.

But, should we forgive all mistakes of facts or just reasonable ones? What if (as I was asked once on a law exam) I were to go over to my married friend's house and he tells me that his wife (whom I have never met) is asleep in the bedroom. My friend (unknown to me) is angry with his wife and wants revenge. So, he tells me that his wife enjoys having sex with complete strangers and being a "player" himself he lets her have her fun. He suggests that I should just go on in to her room and have my ways with her. He also tells me that she will probably vigorously protest, but I should just ignore her screams because she has rape fantasies and just resists as part of the fun. Assuming that I make a mistake of fact regarding the poor woman's consent to sex, should I be forgiven for raping her? Does my unreasonable mistake still warrant my being excused? Did my unreasonable mistake negate my bad mind? Most of you probably do not think that this kind of a mistake should be a defense. You would be right. It is only a **reasonable mistake of fact** that constitutes a defense.[5]

Duress

Another type of lawful excuse to a crime is that of duress. Someone acts under **duress** when he or she feels compelled to commit a crime due to another person's threatening immediate serious bodily harm to that person or someone he or she cares about. Under such circumstances, one becomes mentally handicapped because his or her will is over-

5. See, *People v. Williams*, 52 CrL 1350 (Calif 1993). This rape case involved a reasonable but mistaken belief that consent to sex was given.

come and he or she can no longer think straight. Because such a person lacks willfulness, he or she should be excused.

For example, if a drug dealer with a violent reputation ordered me to deliver drugs or else I would have my legs broken, a jury might excuse my crime because I was acting under incapacitating fear. True, a rational person might have gone to the police or have found some other alternative to breaking the law, but who can think rationally under such circumstances?

Often, the excuse defense of duress can seem very similar to the justification defense of necessity (lesser of two evils). It is true that there can be some overlap. Maybe I deliver drugs because my will was overcome but at the same time it constituted the lesser of two evils. But, there also can be situations where duress fits the facts while necessity does not. This occurs when someone chooses the greater (rather than the lesser) of two evils yet should be forgiven anyway because he or she could not think straight. In the Hollywood movie, *Air Force One*, the U.S. president (played by Harrison Ford) is ordered to telephone the leader of Russia and demand that he release from incarceration a general that would no doubt attempt to undo Russia's progress towards democracy. Harrison Ford refuses even when the terrorists put a gun to his head. But, when they put a gun to the head of his young daughter, he agrees to their demands and makes the phone call. Back in Washington, members of the president's cabinet realize that he has acted under duress and decide to counter-measure the president's actions by lawfully unseating him from power. They justify this by noting that the president is no longer able to think rationally. He is thinking like a father and not like a president. In other words, the movie is demonstrating the concept of duress (and not necessity). We feel sympathy for the president's choice to call Russia not because making the telephone call was the lesser of two evils (the lesser evil would have been to let his own daughter die rather than plunge Russia into a civil war). Rather, we feel sympathy for the president because he clearly was acting under duress and should not be held responsible for his bad choice. His will was overcome. His actions should be forgiven, not justified.

Entrapment

Just about everyone is aware of the defense of entrapment. But how exactly does this defense work? Consider the following two scenarios.

In the first scenario, a lost motorist trying to get back to the interstate requests directions from a person standing outside of the motorist's car on a street corner. Instead of giving the motorist directions, the person on the corner asks the motorist if he would like to buy some marijuana, quoting the lost person a very good price. The person refuses and again asks for directions. The individual on the corner gives the motorist the directions but again also offers to sell him some marijuana, this time for a very, very good price. The motorist hesitates but after repeated solicitations agrees and hands over the money. When the motorist reaches out of the window to receive the bag of marijuana, the drug dealer (who is actually an undercover vice cop) slaps handcuffs on his wrist and tells him he is under arrest. In your opinion, should this motorist be forgiven for having bought the illegal drug?

Now, consider the second scenario. The same undercover police officer is standing on the corner in a neighborhood notorious for high levels of drug trafficking. While standing there, the officer notices the defendant circle the block four or five times before finally stopping his car right next to the officer. The driver then asks the officer "what's up?" The officer asks the driver if he would like to buy a souvenir of the neighborhood. The driver asks the officer what he has in mind and the officer says he is selling marijuana for a good price. The driver agrees and the deal is made. The officer then places the driver under arrest. In your opinion, should this driver be forgiven for having bought the illegal drug?

The first scenario (involving the lost motorist) demonstrates entrapment. The second scenario (involving the driver circling the drug block) demonstrates legitimate undercover police work. **Entrapment** is usually defined as government inducement (seduction) of a person who is not already *predisposed* to commit a crime to engage in conduct that is against the law. The key word in this definition is "predisposed." That is the word a judge or jury will properly focus on. In other words, if the police tempt an otherwise law-abiding, innocent-minded person to break the law, then entrapment has taken place and that person should be excused. On the other hand, if the police merely afford opportunity to someone who is already **predisposed** (e.g., desiring or seeking) to break the law, then that it is simply an appropriate police sting operation and not entrapment.

Sometimes what at first glance appears to be good police work targeting a predisposed bad guy turns out on closer look to be unfair entrapment. The famous U.S. Supreme Court entrapment case that follows demonstrates this.

Jacobson v. United States

112 S.Ct. 1535 (1992)

Keith Jacobson was a farmer who earlier in his life had purchased two magazines in a bookstore, entitled, "Bare Boys I" and "Bare Boys II." These magazines depicted nude teenage and preteen boys. At the time of purchase, possession of such magazines was not against the law. However, that soon changed with the passage in 1984 of the federal Child Protection Act. Agents of the Postal Service and of the Customs Service who were charged with enforcing the new act became aware of Jacobson's earlier purchases from the bookstore's mailing lists and decided to target him with special attention.

Over the course of the next two years, the agents would send Jacobson literature supposedly from organizations that were fighting governmental censorship and "hysteria" surrounding child pornography. For example, the bogus "American Hedonist Society" sent him a letter claiming that "we have the right to seek pleasure without restrictions being placed on us by outdated puritan morality." The fictional "Heartland Institute for a New Tomorrow (HINT)" sent him material which stated that it was an "organization founded to protect and promote sexual freedom and freedom of choice," and further stated that "we must be ever vigilant to counter attack right wing fundamentalists who are determined to curtail our freedom." What these and other repeated mailings had in common was an offer to sell pornographic images of underage boys to be sent discretely through the mail, the profits from which the organizations could use to fight the right wing censors. After two years of being bombarded with such solicitations, Jacobson finally attempted to purchase some child pornography in violation of the federal act.

Jacobson argued for an entrapment defense at his trial but the jury refused to excuse his conduct. On appeal, Jacobson argued that no reasonable jury could have failed to see that he had been entrapped.

The U.S. Supreme Court agreed with Jacobson. Noting that the jurisdiction that tried Jacobson used the traditional "predisposition test," the Court opined that there was simply no evidence that Jacobson was predisposed to break the law. True, Jacobson had earlier ordered child pornography, but that was before it was a crime to do so in his area. The Court said that "evidence of predisposition to do what once was lawful is not, by itself, sufficient to show predisposition to do what is now illegal, for there is a common understanding that most people obey the law even when they disapprove of it." The Court ruled that "in their zeal to enforce the law ... government agents may not originate a criminal design, implant in an innocent person's mind the disposition to commit a criminal act, and then induce commission of the crime." The Court concluded that "the evidence that petitioner was ready and willing to commit the offense came only after the Government had devoted 2½ years to convincing him that he had or should have the right to engage in the very behavior proscribed by law. Rational jurors could not say beyond a reasonable doubt that petitioner possessed the requisite predisposition prior to the Government's investigation ..."

Do you agree with the reasoning of the Supreme Court? If you were on the original jury that tried Jacobson, would you too have probably convicted him?

Youthful Age

There are certain concepts of criminal responsibility that could be categorized as ancient. The fact that children under a certain age are incapable of truly judging right from wrong is one of them. Though societies may disagree as to what that certain age is, all societies would probably agree that there necessarily comes a point where a child is so young that he or she in incapable of forming mens rea. For example, who could hold a three-year-old criminally liable for theft?

Here in America, we have varying ideas about when adulthood begins. For purposes of drinking alcohol, it is set at twenty one. For purposes of voting, it is set at eighteen. For purposes of serving as president, it is constitutionally set at thirty-five. For purposes of driving a car, it is generally set at about age sixteen. What about for purposes of criminal liability? Most states set the age presumptively at 18, though a few choose 17 and a very few choose 16.[6]

People under the "presumptive" age for criminal liability are usually processed as juveniles through the juvenile justice system rather than as adults through the criminal

6. Puzzanchera, Charles M. 2001. "Delinquency cases waived to criminal court, 1989–1998." Washington, D.C.: Office of Juvenile Justice and Delinquency Prevention.

justice system (though there are exceptions made on a case by case basis at the discretion of the judge). In other words, for purposes of a crime, children are technically excused for what they have done and the adult courts with their focus on punishment will step back and allow the juvenile courts (with their focus on helping the child) to take jurisdiction.

What about old age? Should that ever be an excuse for a crime? No. Unlike youthful age, there is no plausible old age point past which someone could safely be presumed to have problems distinguishing right from wrong. What if an elderly person acquires dementia and hits a caretaker in imagined self-defense? Even then, the proper defense would not be age. What excuse defense would apply in such a situation?

Involuntary Intoxication

The final excuse defense that we will cover is that of involuntary intoxication. Think of involuntary intoxication as a form of temporary insanity. **Involuntary intoxication** occurs when a person unwillingly or unwittingly takes in a mind-altering substance that substantially interferes with his or her ability to judge right from wrong. It can occur from being forced to drink alcohol or to take drugs against one's will; from being tricked into consuming something disguised as something else; or from a bizarre reaction to a prescription. It is up to a jury to decide if the involuntary intoxication should excuse the particular criminal conduct in question.

Voluntary intoxication, unlike involuntary intoxication, is not usually recognized as an excuse to a crime. Since the person chose to become intoxicated, he or she has chosen to assume the risk of any potential bad behavior. Some people try to argue that voluntary intoxication should excuse their misdeeds if they were so far "out of it" that they did not know what they were doing. Such an argument is not looked upon favorably by most courts, as the following case illustrates.

United States v. Sewell

252 F.3d 647 (2001)

On an early December afternoon, Keith Sewell walked into a bank in suburban Rochester, New York. He was wearing sun glasses and a hat and carried a brief case. He approached a teller and presented a hold up note demanding money. The teller gave Sewell $4,399 in cash and Sewell left with the money. The teller hit the silent alarm and the police soon responded. Sewell's get away car developed engine problems during the subsequent police chase. With the engine smoking, Sewell abandoned the car before it had come to a complete stop and the car continued on until it hit a light pole. Sewell then tried to escape on foot but was soon apprehended by the police. The police noticed that Sewell was acting very strangely. He seemed to be irrational and incoherent. The defendant later claimed that at the time of the robbery he was high on crack cocaine and had been consuming it almost continuously since the day before in the company of witnesses.

At the trial, Sewell wanted to present evidence that he was high on crack cocaine at the time of the crime. The judge refused to allow him to do so, ruling that it was irrelevant to the case. Sewell also wanted the judge to instruct the jury at the end of the trial on the defense of intoxication. Again the judge refused to comply with Sewell's desires. Subsequently, the jury convicted Sewell of robbery and related crimes and he was sentenced to 156 months in prison.

On appeal Sewell argued that he was denied a fair trial because he was not allowed to present his defense. He argued that he was so high on cocaine that he was unable to form the intent to rob and therefore had a valid excuse defense. He said that even voluntary intoxication can blot out the intent or knowledge that robbery requires.

The appellate court rejected Sewell's arguments. It said that voluntary intoxication "does not negate the intent element of a crime ... such as robbery." All that was required in such a situation involving voluntary intoxication was the "intention to make the bodily movement which constitutes the act which the crime requires." Because Sewell chose to get high, and because he intended to make the bodily movements of walking into a bank and of handing the teller a note, the trial court did not err when it refused to allow Sewell to present irrelevant evidence regarding an intoxication defense that just does not apply.

This completes our discussion of defenses to crimes. Remember, when one claims justification, one accepts responsibility for what one has done but claims that one's actions were virtuous. When one seeks an excuse, one denies responsibility for one's actions. In effect, the person claiming an excuse is asking the jury to shift responsibility for the act from the actor onto the disability. It is the disability that did the crime, not the person.

Chapter Three

Basic Search and Seizure Law

How would you like it if the police searched your house while you were out simply because they thought that you looked like the "type" who might use drugs? Or, how would you like it if the police stopped your car and questioned you because you looked too "rough" to be driving such a nice vehicle? Have you ever known anyone to be wrongfully stopped or searched by the police?

Americans have long had an intense dislike for unreasonable searches and seizures. In the 1700s, colonists were enraged by the fact that Parliament chose to give residents of Britain more protection from unreasonable searches and seizures than it chose to give British citizens living in America. Americans particularly despised the infamous **Writs of Assistance.** These were watered-down versions of what we would now call search warrants, but with a sinister twist. Unlike proper search warrants, they required neither a description of the particular place to be searched nor of the particular items to be seized. Furthermore, these general warrants lasted as long as the monarch who issued them was alive.

Armed with these writs, British custom officials obsessed with enforcing the hated stamp tax laws (remember the Boston Tea Party?) could search any home or place of business at will without having to justify their actions in advance with a judge or magistrate.[1] Their actions became so abusive that the colonists knew all too well the "relationship between security of property and political liberty."[2]

After a successful revolution (largely motivated by a hatred not just of taxation without representation but of British taxation, period), the victorious Americans wanted a guarantee that future abuses of searches and seizures would not take place. Hence, the Fourth Amendment to the Constitution states that

> The right of the people to be secure in their persons, houses, papers, and effects against unreasonable searches and seizures shall not be violated, and no warrants shall issue but upon probable cause, supported by oath or affirmation and particularly describing the place to be searched and the persons or things to be seized.

---

1. Peak, K.J. (1993). *Policing America: Methods, Issues, Challenges.* Englewood Cliffs, NJ: Regents/Prentice Hall.
2. Zalman, M. & Siegel, L.J. (1997). *Criminal Procedure: Constitution and Society* (2nd ed.). Belmont, CA: West/Wadsworth.

How to Obtain a Warrant

From the words of the Fourth Amendment we see that search warrants, unlike the old and despised Writs of Assistance, do not last for decades at a time (each individually must be "supported by oath and affirmation"). We further see that many searches and seizures apparently require something referred to as "probable cause." We also see that the searching or arresting official must be able to describe with specificity just what or whom he or she is after.

Suppose that the police wish to search someone's house. With rare exception, they could not just barge into the house without judicial permission first. They would have to go to a neutral judge or magistrate and get pre-approval of their actions. Before signing the warrant (a standard form police fill out and bring to a judge), the judge will want to see that the police officers have particularly described on the form the items they expect to find. The police cannot simply state, "criminal evidence." What criminal evidence? They have to be specific. They also have to specifically identify the place they will search. For example, they cannot say "all houses and apartments on the south side of town." They have to specify an exact address or give some other precise identifier. The judge will also look on the form to see what facts they have written down in support of their "probable cause."

Probable cause to search and probable cause to arrest are two slightly different concepts. **Probable cause to search** means that there are enough circumstances to lead a reasonable person to believe that "there is a fair probability that contraband or evidence of a crime will be found" in the particular place to be searched.[3] **Probable cause to arrest** means that there are enough circumstances to lead a reasonable and prudent person to believe that a crime has probably been committed and that the person to be seized is the one who likely committed it.[4] The key word is "probable," rather than the words "beyond a reasonable doubt." In deciding whether or not police have enough probable cause to deserve a warrant, courts will not look at just one or two points in isolation but rather will consider the **totality of the circumstances.**[5] This means that even though the police might come up with a set of weak points, no one of which by itself creates probable cause, the sum of all the weak points considered together might constitute probable cause.

If a judicial officer is satisfied that the police have particularly described what it is they are after and have demonstrated probable cause, he or she will sign the warrant (after first requiring the officer verbally or in writing on the form to swear that what the officer has put down is truthful). The police are now clearly authorized to do the search or the arrest. The warrant will be good for a reasonable period of time (often set by local statute as being ten days or so). If too much time passes (more than what is "reasonable"), then the warrant will become a **stale warrant** and no longer any good (otherwise we are back to the decades-lasting Writs of Assistance). Warrants clearly become

3. *Illinois v. Gates*, 462 U.S. 213 (1983).
4. *Draper v. United States*, 358 U.S. 307 (1959).
5. *Gates*, supra note 3.

stale when the information that was used to demonstrate the probable cause is now too old to reasonably rely on anymore.[6]

Do All Searches and Seizures Require Warrants?

The short answer is, "NO." Though the Fourth Amendment specifically talks of "warrants," courts have not interpreted the Amendment to mean that warrants are always required. Courts have come up with what they consider to be common-sense exceptions to the search warrant requirement. They have also identified traditional exceptions to the arrest warrant requirement. Though virtually all searches and all arrests require probable cause, courts do not always make the police run the probable cause by a judicial officer in advance. Maybe there simply is not time or it would be ridiculous to do so. The exceptions to the search warrant and to the arrest warrant requirement will be discussed later in the chapter. But first, let us examine why any of this even matters. What will be the consequences if police violate somebody's Fourth Amendment rights?

The Exclusionary Rule

For a long time the Fourth Amendment was just a bunch of words on paper without any real teeth. Suppose the police did violate somebody's rights? What then? Should the police officer who violated the Constitution be arrested? Police departments rarely if ever could be expected to arrest a fellow officer for doing an illegal search or a bogus arrest. Furthermore, victims of police abuse are unlikely to sue (or even know that they can). And, even if somebody did sue the police, would a jury sympathize more with the "victim" or more with the cop just trying to do his or her job?

The famous case of *Mapp v. Ohio* fixed this problem. *Mapp v. Ohio* came up with what is now referred to as the **exclusionary rule**. To understand what this rule means, let us look at the *Mapp* decision itself.

Mapp v. Ohio

367 U.S. 643 (1961)

Cleveland, Ohio police officers suspected Mapp of being involved with a recent bombing. They went over to her house in order to search for policy paraphernalia that they believed might be there that could help link her to the crime. Upon arriving at the home, the officers knocked on the door and demanded to be let in to search. Mapp refused to let them in. The officers came back a few hours later and would not take "no" for an answer. Over the protests of Mapp and her attorney (who was now at the scene), the officers entered the house and began the search. In the hallway, Mapp demanded that they

6. See, *United States v. Nepstead*, 424 F.2d 269 (9th Cir. 1970).

show her a search warrant. One of the officers produced a piece of paper which he claimed was a search warrant and waived it in the air. Mapp grabbed it and stuck it down her bosom. Officers then wrestled with Mapp and retrieved the apparently bogus warrant from her.

The officers never did find any evidence linking her to the bombing. However, during the search they did find obscene materials which Mapp possessed in violation of the law. She was therefore arrested and tried for the offense of possessing obscene materials. Following her conviction, she appealed claiming that the police had no search warrant and therefore searched her house illegally. She argued that any evidence found should have been suppressed and kept secret from the jury.

So, should evidence obtained pursuant to an illegal search be suppressed? Remember, the evidence we are talking about is truthful evidence. It may have been obtained illegally, but it would help a court determine the truth. As Justice Cardozo famously once asked long ago, "Should a criminal go free because the constable has blundered?" In other words, why punish society for the mistakes of the police?

The majority in *Mapp* held that despite Justice Cardozo's concerns, evidence obtained in violation of the Fourth Amendment prohibition against unreasonable searches or seizures must henceforth be excluded from evidence during trial. The jury will never know that the evidence exists. If the police can prove their case without the illegally obtained evidence, then the state may proceed on that basis. If not, the state will just have to lose its case.

This "exclusionary rule" was justified by the court on several grounds. First, it said that no other remedy will work to deter the police from violating people's search and seizure rights. Other remedies (like internal discipline by one's police chief or allowing people to sue for money) just have not worked. Second, it said because no other remedies seem to work, that unless police know that their illegally obtained evidence will be thrown out of court, the Fourth Amendment will be reduced to a "mere form of words," a "valueless" right without any real bite. Next, it noted that there was a real concern regarding "judicial integrity." The Court noted that "nothing can destroy a government more quickly than failure to observe its own laws, or worse, its disregard of the charter of its own existence ... If the government becomes a lawbreaker, it breeds contempt for the law ..." Finally, the court noted that the federal government and many states have already voluntarily adopted the exclusionary rule in their courts without any apparent catastrophic consequences. There has been no evidence that the FBI or other police agencies living under such a rule have been rendered ineffective in their fight against crime.

Do you agree with the Exclusionary Rule? Most democracies do not. They still believe that the public should not be punished for the illegal blunders of the police. Can you think of any way to coerce the police into respecting the Fourth Amendment without resorting to the Exclusionary Rule?

American courts are not satisfied simply with suppressing evidence directly associated with the illegality but also with any other evidence to which the tainted evidence may lead. For example, if the police illegally search your house and find a map of where you buried a dead body, not only will the map be suppressed but so will the dead body to which the map led them. This doctrine is known as the **fruit of the poisonous tree** and is believed to be a natural consequence of the courts' desire to deter illegal police searches and seizures.

Suppose though that the police think that they might have probable cause to do a search and ask a judge for a warrant. When the judge asks them to explain their probable cause, they honestly and straightforwardly explain their reasons. Suppose that the judge then issues a warrant based on the supposed probable cause but a reviewing court later determines that the judge made a mistake: that probable cause actually was lacking. What then? Should the evidence be suppressed? The Fourth Amendment requires probable cause to search. But in this situation there objectively was none. The next case deals with this dilemma.

United States v. Leon

468 U.S. 897 (1984)

Leon apparently possessed large quantities of illegal drugs. Though he was arrested and charged, all of the drug evidence was suppressed in a pre-trial hearing by the trial judge because of the exclusionary rule. The prosecutor consequently was unable to proceed with his case and appealed the pre-trial ruling of the court suppressing the drug evidence.

What made the prosecution so upset was that the police had obtained a search warrant from a judicial officer prior to conducting the search. The magistrate the police had gone to for the search warrant had found probable cause to grant the warrant, but the probable cause was later found lacking by the trial court judge who disagreed with the magistrate's assessment. Specifically, the trial judge found that probable cause should not have been found based merely on the "allegations of an untested informant" backed up only by police surveillance evidence that was "as consistent with innocence as with guilt."

So, this case (as the Supreme Court so aptly put it) presented "the question of whether the Fourth Amendment exclusionary rule should be modified so as not to bar the use in the prosecution's case-in-chief of evidence obtained by officers acting in reasonable reliance on a search warrant issued by a detached and neutral magistrate but ultimately found to be unsupported by probable cause." In other words, should there be a **good faith exception to the exclusionary rule** for police officers who try to do the right thing by getting a search warrant but who unfortunately go to a magistrate who erroneously finds probable cause and issues the warrant?

The U.S. Supreme Court decided it was time to allow a good faith exception to the exclusionary rule (something courts never allowed before). The Court reasoned that the question of whether or not a good faith exception should exist is one of costs v. benefits.

First, it asked itself what were the costs of suppressing evidence under such circumstances as those in this drug case or any criminal case. It found a couple of very significant costs. One cost would be that suppressing the evidence would "impede unacceptably the truth-finding functions of judge and jury." This would result in a criminal going free or enjoying the benefits of an overly generous plea bargain. Another cost would be the generation of disrespect for courts among the general public who become outraged upon hearing that juries were kept in the dark about what was really true. These costs of the exclusionary rule are very high indeed.

Because the costs of the rule are so high, the rule should only be reserved for those situations in which the benefit is even higher. When is the benefit higher than the costs? This occurs when deterrence of police illegality can actually take place. But, when the police act in good faith and it is the magistrate (not the police) who makes a mistake, the deterrence benefit does not apply. Deterrence will not come into play if the police, believing that there might be probable cause, act on a good faith reliance on the competency of the magistrate. The reason the exclusionary rule exists is to deter police, not to let criminals go free. When deterrence is not at play there is no reason to reward the criminal. The costs are high and the benefit non-existent.

The Court noted that in order for the prosecution to take advantage of this newly articulated good faith exception to the exclusionary rule, the police must indeed have been acting in good faith. There are several possible examples of "bad faith" on the part of police. For example, this would occur when police intentionally mislead a magistrate in order to get a search warrant. It would also occur when police act with reckless disregard for the truth of the facts they present to the magistrate. It also would occur when the police know that they are dealing with a magistrate who has "wholly abandoned his judicial role" of neutrality. It also clearly would occur when the police affidavit of probable cause is so ridiculous as to render any official belief in its sufficiency to be utterly unreasonable. Finally, the police application for the warrant may be so facially defective that it would be obvious to anyone—including the police officers—that it is undeniably deficient (e.g., it utterly fails to particularly describe the place to be searched or the items expected to be seized).

The Court's point is that good faith means good faith. But, if the police act with such, they will be protected even if the magistrate drops the ball.

What do you think of the above decision? Some argue that magistrates are part of the same government as the police and it should not matter who makes the mistake: a mistake is a mistake. Others suggest that the U.S. Supreme Court is naive when it comes to putting faith in local magistrates. These critics suggest that magistrates in real life rarely are neutral and detached but instead are typically pals of the local cops. These cynics argue that there should be no good faith exception to the exclusionary rule since cops and magistrates are so often in cahoots and that many magistrates are nothing more than rubber stamps. Is this too dark a view?

The good faith exception is one way for prosecutors to try to get around the harshness of the exclusionary rule. But, there is a second way as well. This second way is known as the inevitable discovery exception. The **inevitable discovery exception to the exclusionary rule** holds that evidence that was obtained without a search warrant (or otherwise illegally) can still be admitted at trial if the prosecutor can convince the judge that the evidence would have unavoidably been discovered eventually by the police anyway. In other words, if there is a virtually 100 % chance that the evidence would have been uncovered whether or not the police had acted unlawfully, courts will still allow the jury to hear it. For example, suppose the police are dragging a pond systematically for a missing person they think might be in there. While they are doing this, other police conduct an illegal search of a suspect's home and find a diary saying that he dumped the body in the north side of the same pond the police are already searching. If the police who found the diary show up at the pond right before the body is about to be found anyway and announce the location of the body, the trial court may refuse to suppress the evidence under the inevitable discovery exception. What rationale would you expect there to be for such an exception to the exclusionary rule?

The exclusionary rule, and its exceptions, apply to the fruits of both illegal searches and illegal arrests (an example of the latter would be a confession obtained after an illegal arrest). But, we still need to ask ourselves a couple of very basic questions: what legally constitutes a search and what legally constitutes an arrest? Let us now turn our attention to these matters.

What Is a Search?

Before asking whether or not a search was unreasonable (e.g., was there a valid search warrant when required), it is always wise to first ask whether or not a search has even occurred. If a search has not taken place, then who cares what the Fourth Amendment requires?

Can you recognize a "search" when you see one? Obviously, if the police were to rifle through your bedroom underwear drawer, a search has taken place and you can expect Fourth Amendment protections. But, what if the police intentionally sit behind you in a movie theater in order to eaves drop on a conversation you and your criminal buddy are having? Have they committed a search? Or, what if the police linger outside a confessional box in order to eaves drop on a confession you are attempting to discretely make to your priest? Would that be a search? What if binocular-equipped police watch you snorting drugs at your kitchen table from their secret perch in an apartment across the street? Would that be a search?

The key to all of these scenarios is whether or not a reasonable expectation of privacy exists. If there is a reasonable expectation of privacy then there is a search and Fourth Amendment protections apply. But, if there is no reasonable expectation of privacy, there is no search (at least not in a Fourth Amendment sense). This concept was articulated well in the classic case of *Katz v. United States* that follows.

Katz v. United States

389 U.S. 347 (1967)

Katz was convicted of using a telephone line to conduct illegal gambling activities in violation of a federal statute. The evidence against Katz was obtained by the FBI who listened in on a telephone call Katz made from a closed, public telephone booth. The FBI was able to listen to and record Katz's telephone conversation thanks to an electronic listening device they had placed on the outside of the booth.

The issue that Katz raised on appeal to the U.S. Supreme Court was whether this evidence should be suppressed. Katz argued that the FBI conduct constituted a search done without a warrant and that the exclusionary rule should shield him from the fruits of this flagrant Fourth Amendment violation. It does appear that if this were indeed a search, then a search warrant would have been required. But was this even a search?

The FBI argued that no search took place because there was no physical penetration of the booth. It further pointed out that the booth was made of glass and anybody could easily look into the booth to see what was going on inside. The Court did not accept either of these arguments.

As to the "booth made of glass" argument, the Court noted that what Katz sought to shield himself from by entering the booth was "not the intruding eye—it was the uninvited ear." As to the "no physical penetration of the booth" argument the Court pointed out that "the Fourth Amendment protects people—and not simply 'areas'—against unreasonable searches and seizures [and so] it becomes clear that the reach of that Amendment cannot turn upon the presence or absence of a physical intrusion into any given enclosure."

Then the Supreme Court summed up its analysis by articulating its now famous doctrine: a search occurs whenever the state violates a *reasonable expectation of privacy.* "The government's activities in electronically listening to and recording the petitioner's words violated the privacy upon which he justifiably relied while using the telephone booth and thus constituted a 'search and seizure' within the meaning of the Fourth Amendment. The fact that the electronic listening device employed to achieve that end did not happen to penetrate the wall of the booth can have no constitutional significance."

Certainly the Framers who drafted the Fourth Amendment could not have envisioned all future technologies that could be eventually used to invade people's privacy. But the Supreme Court in *Katz* apparently believed that the core value of the Amendment, protecting citizens from governmental invasion of their privacy, transcends time. The Supreme Court apparently believes that if they were alive today, the drafters would be appalled at the idea of warrantless use of governmental electronic listening devices.

Now that you know that a "search" occurs when the police violate a **reasonable expectation of privacy**, what would you make of a situation in which the police search through someone's garbage left at the curb without first getting a search warrant? That is the precise issue facing the High Court in the next case. This is a famous case that students delving into what constitutes a "reasonable expectation of privacy" seem to love to debate.

California v. Greenwood

486 U.S. 35 (1988)

Officers of the Laguna Beach, California police department received information leading them to believe that Greenwood might be trafficking in illegal drugs. So, on garbage pick-up day the police went over to Greenwood's street and asked the garbage collector they found there to not mix his curb-side trash with those of the other houses. Rather, they asked the trash collector to segregate it and to hand it over to them at the end of the block. The trash collector did as asked. The police then looked through Greenwood's trash and found evidence which eventually led to his arrest and conviction on drug charges.

The question on appeal was whether the police violated a reasonable expectation of privacy when they went through Greenwood's curb-side trash. Did this warrantless examination of abandoned property constitute a "search" within the context of the Fourth Amendment? If so, the evidence would need to be suppressed.

Would you feel violated if a police officer or a neighbor went through your trash? The U.S. Supreme Court did not think it was that big a deal. It found that Greenwood could have no reasonable expectation of privacy regarding his curb-side trash. It said that what Greenwood may have subjectively considered to be an invasion of his privacy does not matter. Rather, the standard is what "society accepts as objectively reasonable." The court pointed out that "plastic garbage bags left on or at the side of a public street are readily accessible to animals, children, scavengers, snoops, and other members of the public." Since anybody can lawfully go through someone's trash, the police can as well.

Two of the justices disagreed vigorously with the majority's conclusions. Justice Brennan (with Justice Marshall joining him) wrote in a dissenting opinion that Greenwood most certainly had a reasonable expectation of privacy to his garbage, even if it were left at the curb for pick-up. The opinion noted that "most of us ... would be incensed to discover a meddler—whether a neighbor, a reporter, or a detective—scrutinizing our sealed trash containers to discover some detail of our personal lives." It noted the many personal facts that could be exposed by looking through a person's trash. "A single bag of trash testifies eloquently to the eating, reading, and recreational habits of the person who produced it ... [It] can relate intimate details about sexual practices, health and personal hygiene ... [It] can divulge the target's financial and professional status, political affiliations and inclinations, private thoughts, personal relationships, and romantic interests." In effect, the dissenters saw little difference between going through someone's sealed trash and rifling through someone's desk drawers. They rejected the majority's reasoning that since any neighbor or animal could go through the trash, that the police may as well. "The mere *possibility* that unwelcome meddlers *might* open and rummage through the containers does not negate the expectation of privacy ..." [Italics in original.]

Despite the dissent's point that mere possibilities should not negate privacy expectations, courts have consistently held that activities that are easily observable by the public at large hold no reasonable expectation of privacy. Hence, police eaves dropping on conversations made in public places do not typically require warrants (after all, if a nosy citizen can snoop this way, why should the police not be permitted?). Police can even use binoculars and other devices to "snoop" as long as they are readily accessible to the general public. Would you feel that your privacy were violated if the police or a neighbor used binoculars to watch you through your window?

Warrantless Searches

Up to this point, we have basically equated a warrantless search with an unreasonable search. One might get the impression that police must get a warrant before doing any snooping that violates a reasonable expectation of privacy—that searches without warrants automatically violate the Fourth Amendment. This is not the case.

Though the Fourth Amendment hints that warrants will often be required, modern courts have carved out some common-sense exceptions to the search warrant requirement. There are enough of these exceptions that the general rule requiring search warrants can almost seemed swallowed up by them. But, you still have to find an exception to avoid the exclusionary rule. The easiest way to keep it all straight is to follow these three simple steps:

1. Was there a reasonable expectation of privacy? If not, the discussion is over and the police win (no "search" even occurred). But, if a "search" did occur we must then ask,
2. Did the police obtain a search warrant? If so, discussion is over—the police have covered themselves (in most states) as long as they acted in good faith with the magistrate. If no search warrant, then ask,
3. Did the search fall under one of the exceptions to the search warrant requirement? If so, the police are covered. If not, then the evidence will have to be suppressed.

So, what are the exceptions that fall under step #3 above? Courts have come up with the following **exceptions to the search warrant requirement**: consent, automobiles, plain-view, exigent circumstances, frisk for weapons, search incident to a lawful arrest, and regulatory searches. Let us consider each of these in turn.

Consent Searches

Consent is a beautiful thing. If police can get you to consent to one of their searches, not only do they not need a search warrant, they do not even need probable cause. All they need is your consent and they are completely covered.

For example, if police knock on your door tonight and say, "Hi, we're the cops. We just happen to be in the neighborhood with nothing to do. Can we search your house for drugs?" If you say, "yes," the police can search at will (however, you do have the right to limit the scope of your consent to certain areas of the house).

Of course, true consent is **voluntary consent,** meaning the police cannot coerce you in order to get your consent (e.g., "if you do not let us search, we'll arrest you"). It also should be noted that your refusal to give consent cannot be used against you later as part of the probable cause to get a search warrant from a magistrate.

Courts often seem to give the benefit of doubt to the police with regards to the issue of voluntariness of consent. See what you think of the next case.

Florida v. Bostick

501 U.S. 429 (1991)

Terrance Bostick was a passenger on a bus heading from Miami to Atlanta. During a stopover in Fort Lauderdale, two police officers in full-uniform boarded the bus in order to do a "drug sweep." They had no reason to suspect anybody on the bus. One of the officers held a recognizable zipper pouch containing a pistol.

After eyeing the passengers, the officers zoned in on Bostick. They approached him and asked to see his ticket. After returning his ticket to him, they then asked him if they could search the luggage he was carrying with him on board. They told him he had the right to refuse. Bostick gave his permission and the police found cocaine in one of his two bags. Bostick was convicted of trafficking drugs.

On appeal, Bostick convinced a lower appellate court that the cocaine evidence found in his bag should have been suppressed. He had argued to this lower court that a police encounter in this setting is inherently coercive making true consent impossible. Unlike an encounter with the police on a sidewalk, the police on the bus towered over him while he was in a confined space. He was not free to just walk away since to do so would mean that the bus would leave without him. The lower appellate court agreed with him but the government appealed this decision to the U.S. Supreme Court.

The U.S. Supreme Court reversed the decision of the lower appellate court. It said it disagreed with the idea that the encounter was automatically so coercive that consent was not possible. It said the facts must be re-examined by a trial court regarding this issue, but it made absolutely clear that drug sweeps of buses, even ones involving no reasonable suspicion, are not automatically so coercive as to make voluntary consent for a search impossible. It said that even though Bostick was not free to leave the bus, this was not due to the police investigation but rather because he chose to be a passenger. As a passenger wanting to get to Atlanta, he would not have been free to leave the bus whether or not the police had boarded it. The Court said the test should not be whether the bus passenger was free to leave but whether a reasonable person would have felt free to decline the officers' request for a search. "The crucial test is whether, taking into account all of the circumstances surrounding the encounter, the police conduct would have communicated to a reasonable person that he was not at liberty to ignore the police presence and go about his business."

The dissent thought that, as a matter of law, the encounter was inherently so coercive as to make voluntary consent impossible. It did not think there was any need to send the case back down for further fact-finding. It wrote that Bostick only had two choices open to him, neither of which were real options. First, he could just say "No," to the police request to search. But, "in light of the intimidating show of authority that the officers made upon boarding the bus, respondent reasonably could have believed that such behavior would only arouse the officers' suspicions and intensify their interrogation." The dissenters pointed out that non-legally trained people like Bostick have no way of knowing that a refusal cannot be used in any way against them. Second, instead of saying, "No," Bostick could attempt to leave. "But because doing so would have required respondent to squeeze past the gun-wielding inquisitor who was blocking the aisle of the bus, this hardly seems like a course that respondent reasonably would have viewed as available to him." The dissent concluded by saying that because police know that these choices are not real choices, the police shamefully and regularly take advantage of vulnerable bus passengers in their fishing expeditions for evidence.

Given that you have the right to refuse consent to a search without your refusal being used against you by the police, would you nevertheless be reluctant to refuse? Would you have had the courage to refuse before reading these materials? Under what circumstances, if any, might you refuse to give consent for a search even though you have nothing at all to hide? If you were to enter law enforcement, would you routinely use consent as a way to get around Fourth Amendment repercussions?

Automobile Searches

Automobiles are not like buildings. They are very mobile. Because of this fact (and the fact that they have less privacy associated with them than buildings), courts do not require warrants in order for the police to search them. Probable cause, yes. But, not warrants. Police are permitted to explain to a judge after-the-fact (if the issue is raised by a defense attorney) the basis for their probable cause. In other words, though they still need probable cause to search, they do not have to run this probable cause by a judge ahead of time.

This is a very old exception to the general requirement for a search warrant. As the Supreme Court said in *Carroll v. United States*, 267 U.S. 132 (1925), back in the early days of the automobile,

> ... The Fourth Amendment has been construed practically since the beginning ... as recognizing a necessary difference between a search of a store, dwelling house, or other structure in respect of which a proper official warrant readily may be obtained and a search of [a moving vehicle like a cart] where it is not practicable to secure a warrant, because the vehicle can be quickly moved ...

So, we see that due primarily to this mobility concern, courts allow searches of automobiles without warrants (as long as the police still have probable cause). An interesting issue then becomes, "what is an automobile?" The next case struggles with this.

California v. Carney

471 U.S. 386 (1985)

Drug Enforcement Agents were keeping a watch on a Dodge Mini Motor Home that was parked in a lot in downtown San Diego. The motor home could be driven away at will. The agents had received a report that someone staying in the motor home had been trading drugs for sex. On the day in question, the agents saw a youth enter the motor home with Carney. The shades were pulled down by both the youth and by Carney. Over an hour later, the youth came out and was stopped and questioned by the agents. He told the agents that while he was inside, Carney had given him marijuana in exchange for sexual contacts. Based on this information, but without first securing a search warrant, the agents entered the motor home and observed marijuana, plastic bags, and a scale. Carney was subsequently convicted of possessing marijuana for sale.

In appealing the conviction, Carney argues that the evidence must be suppressed because the police did not have a search warrant. He argues that his motor home was a residence. Though automobiles are excepted from the search warrant requirement, homes are not.

So, is a motor home an automobile or is it more in the nature of a residence? The former never requires search warrants whereas the latter traditionally does.

To answer this question, the court considered the purposes behind the automobile exception to the search warrant requirement. It said that ever since the days of the *Carroll* decision in 1925, courts have carved out an exception for automobiles based on their inherent mobility. "The capacity to be 'quickly moved' was clearly the basis of the holding in *Carroll*, and our cases have consistently recognized mobility as one of the principle bases of the automobile exception." The Dodge Mini Motor Home that Carney, the drug dealer, was living in clearly had the capacity to be quickly moved. It was not elevated on blocks or connected to any utilities. It was in a parking lot with easy access to a public road.

In addition to mobility, the court noted that decisions after the *Carroll* case added a second justification for the automobile exception to the search warrant requirement. "Besides the element of mobility, less rigorous warrant requirements govern because the expectation of privacy with respect to one's automobile is significantly less than that relating to one's home or office." Automobiles are highly regulated by the government and are made largely of glass. Homes and businesses are less regulated and made largely of walls. The court went on to reason that even though Carney's Mini Motor Home was capable of functioning as a home, it was more like an automobile than like a structure. True, it had some aspects of a home but so do ordinary cars when people live out of them, and courts do not require warrants for ordinary cars being lived in. "To distinguish between respondent's motor home and an ordinary sedan for purposes of the vehicle exception would require that we apply the exception depending upon the size of the vehicle and the quality of its appointments." That would be asking too much.

The dissent argued that the DEA should have been required to get a warrant. True, the motor home may have been mobile but there is still the privacy problem which cannot be overcome. "Although it may not be a castle, a motor home is usually the functional equivalent of a hotel room, a vacation and retirement home, or a hunting and fishing cabin." Since a motor home constitutes a "living quarters," it should not be searched without first getting a warrant, the dissent unsuccessfully argued.

Plain View

Police may seize contraband or evidence of a crime that is in plain view without bothering to get a search warrant first. It would be silly to expect a police officer who is lawfully in a home (e.g., investigating a domestic dispute) and who sees a pile of drugs on someone's kitchen table to go to a judge to get a search warrant before he or she can seize the evidence. Contraband or evidence in plain view can be seized instantly by the police. In a sense, if the material is in plain view, no search is needed. It has already been discovered. Nobody can expect any privacy with regards to it.

The key to understanding the doctrine is this: things are in **plain view** as long as the officer's eyes are allowed to be where they are. Hence, if an officer has a search warrant to look for drugs in your house but instead stumbles across a counterfeiting machine in the closet, the machine is in plain view (the officer's eyes were allowed to be in that closet looking for the drugs). If an officer knocks on a residential door as part of an "officer friendly" program and sees a marijuana cigarette in the mouth of the person who opens the door, that marijuana cigarette is in plain view (police do not need a search warrant to knock on someone's door).

On the other hand, suppose the police have a search warrant to look for a stolen car in your garage and instead find an unregistered handgun in a cigar box on the garage shelf. Would you consider these drugs to be in plain view? (They would not be in plain view since the officers have no business looking for a car in a cigar box.)

Exigent Circumstances

Another common-sense exception to the search warrant requirement is that of exigent circumstances. **Exigent circumstances** simply mean urgent circumstances or circumstances requiring immediate action.

For example, suppose a police officer is walking a beat and hears blood-chilling screams coming from a window of a town home she is passing. She knocks on the door several times but the screams go silent and nobody answers the door. What would you have the officer do? Go get a search warrant and come back later? Or, suppose a transit officer hears something ticking in a brief case being carried by a trembling passenger on a subway car. Would you expect the officer to "freeze the situation" while a search warrant was obtained? Or, suppose DEA agents knock on someone's door as part of an investigation and hear someone yell, "it's the narc cops, flush everything!" Should the officers refrain from rushing inside to stop the obvious destruction of evidence because they do not have a search warrant?

Simply put, the exigent circumstances exception exists whenever taking the time to obtain a search warrant would put criminal evidence in jeopardy of being destroyed or a person in jeopardy of being seriously harmed.

Frisk for Weapons

Police who are doing their job often come in close contact with rough and/or deranged people who very well may be armed and dangerous. Certainly, there is nothing wrong with an officer stopping a suspicious character for a quick question or two but what about "searching" such a person for weapons? Here we have the privacy of the citizen in conflict with the safety of the officer. The famous case that follows addressed this dilemma some time ago.

Terry v. Ohio

392 U.S. 1 (1968)

A plainclothes, city detective noticed two men standing on a Cleveland, Ohio street corner who were acting very suspiciously. One of the men would walk down the street, peer into a store window, walk on, and then return to his friend on the corner. The friend would then do the same thing while the first man waited. The two continued this behavior, taking turns about a dozen times in all. The detective felt that the two might be "casing" the store for a stickup.

The officer approached the men and asked them their names. The men simply mumbled something so the officer, fearing that they may be armed, spun Terry around and patted him down. During the pat down, the officer felt a gun in Terry's breast pocket and removed a pistol. The officer then patted down Terry's friend and found a pistol on him as well. Terry was charged and convicted of possessing a concealed firearm without a license. He appealed this conviction, claiming that he was subjected to a seizure and a search without a warrant.

The U.S. Supreme Court agreed with Terry that he had been both seized and searched and that the Fourth Amendment would therefore apply. People who are stopped and spun around, though not arrested, are still seized. People who are patted down suffer from an invasion of privacy so they are searched. This is not Nazi Germany. The police cannot just walk down the sidewalk stopping anybody they want for no reason in order to frisk for weapons. As the Court put it, "It must be recognized that whenever a police officer accosts an individual and restrains his freedom to walk away, he has 'seized' that person. And it is nothing less than sheer torture of the English language to suggest that a careful exploration of the outer surface of a person's clothing all over his or her body in an attempt to find weapons is not a 'search.'"

But, the Court went on to say that even though the Fourth Amendment protects people from being stopped, harassed and patted down for no legitimate reason, it does not always require police to obtain an arrest warrant before stopping suspicious people for brief questioning or a search warrant before conducting a sensible pat down for weapons of scary people. Not all seizures and searches are of equal magnitude. Some are much less intrusive than others and so will require less in order to be held reasonable.

Specifically, where a police officer "reasonably concludes in light of his experience that criminal activity may be afoot and that the person with whom he is dealing may be armed and dangerous, he may stop such persons; and if after identifying himself and making reasonable inquiries, his fears are not dispelled, he can frisk outer clothing for weapons."

Courts do not expect police officers to get either an arrest warrant or a search warrant under such circumstances. This is because the Court felt a need to balance the rights of citizens vs. the needs of the police to do their job. There is a difference between a "stop" and an "arrest" and between a "pat down" of outer clothing for weapons and a "full-blown search." The seizure and search to which Terry was subjected were relatively minor compared to the legitimate needs of the detective to prevent a possible armed robbery and to protect himself. The court pointed out that the Fourth Amendment does not prevent seizures and searches, only unreasonable ones. What the detective did here was very reasonable. In fact, most people would be outraged if the officer had just let these two men go without stopping them. And nobody is going to fault this detective for patting these potential stickup men down to protect himself. The Fourth Amendment cannot be reasonably construed to require even probable cause let alone a warrant in such a situation. Suspicion alone is adequate justification.

The above case generated new terms used by police and courts to this present day. A brief stop for questioning of someone who may be engaged in criminal activity is now known as a **Terry stop**. It is a seizure but something less than an arrest. A brief pat down of the outer clothing for weapons of someone who may be armed and dangerous is now known as a **Terry search**. It violates privacy but not overly so. Police doing such a mini-seizure and mini-search need only **reasonable suspicion** of criminal activity or reasonable suspicion of a weapon rather than probable cause. And if during the pat down for weapons they happen to feel contraband instead (e.g., a lump of powdery cocaine), they may reach in and take this contraband as criminal evidence. Such contraband would be considered **in plain feel** (similar to the doctrine of "in plain view" discussed earlier).[7]

Searches Incident to a Lawful Arrest/Regulatory Searches

Two more common exceptions to the search warrant requirement are worth discussing. One of these is the venerable, old **search incident to a lawful arrest**. Under this exception, police may do a thorough search of a person they have lawfully placed under arrest. They do not need a warrant. They do not need probable cause. They do not even need reasonable suspicion. As the U.S. Supreme Court pointed out in the case of *Chimel v. California*, 395 U.S. 752 (1969), police may search people they have arrested because of the need "to remove any weapons that the [person] might seek to use in order to resist arrest or effect his escape" and to "seize any evidence on the arrestee's person in order to prevent its concealment or destruction." This exception to the search warrant requirement is the oldest of all the exceptions. It long predates the *Chimel* case just noted above, and in fact has been recognized by American courts as far back as colonial days and even ultimately to England itself.[8]

The last important exception to the search warrant requirement is the regulatory search. **Regulatory searches** are usually done by government officials other than police officers and include such things as health inspections of restaurants, searches of vehicles crossing borders, airport screening of passengers, and building fire inspections. These searches, like "Terry" pat downs, require neither probable cause nor warrants. In fact they go beyond Terry in that they (like searches incident to an arrest) do not even require reasonable suspicion. They are justified by courts' balancing the need of people to have privacy v. the even greater need of the government to protect its citizens.[9] Protecting citizens is perhaps the most basic function of government. Imagine how difficult air travel would be if the government was required to have probable cause or even reasonable suspicion before asking a passenger to empty his or her pockets. Or, imagine how crazy it would be to require border agents to have probable cause or reasonable suspicion before looking into someone's car trunk. Sure, some people feel a little bit violated when subjected to such searches. But, most are sensible enough not to take such minor invasions personally, especially given the obvious need of the government to engage in such routine activities.

---

7. *Minnesota v. Dickerson*, 508 U.S. 366 (1993).
8. See, *Weeks v. United States*, 232 U.S. 383 (1914).
9. See, *Camara v. Municipal Court*, 387 U.S. 523 (1967) for an early reliance of the Supreme Court on such a balancing test in the area of regulatory searches.

Seizures

We already began discussing seizures while covering the so-called "Terry stops." But, mostly we have been examining the law as it specifically relates to searches. Let us now turn our attention more fully to the law surrounding seizures.

Generally, when lawyers discuss seizures they are contemplating the seizures of people rather than property. The taking of property is generally covered quite well under the principles of search law.

When it comes to the seizures of human beings, there are basically two types of seizures that concern the legal community: investigative stops and arrests. An **investigative stop** is a minimal type of seizure, but a seizure nonetheless, and therefore subject to Fourth Amendment safeguards. An **arrest** is a major seizure and therefore subject to even more Fourth Amendment protection than a mere stop. Let us look at both of these types of seizures in more detail.

Investigative Stops

Not all stops by the police are "seizures." Hence the placement of the word, "investigative" before the word "stop." Consider the following two scenarios. You are walking in a city park with your spouse on a leisurely stroll when a police officer stops you in order to engage you in pleasant conversation about the beauty of the park. Or, an officer trying to build ties with the community she serves, stops you on a sidewalk near your home to ask you if there is anything she could do to help make your neighborhood a better place. Would you feel "seized" under either of these situations? Probably not. In fact, since these stops were not done for investigative purposes, they are not considered seizures by the courts.

On the other hand, suppose you were stopped on the sidewalk by an officer wanting to know if you had anything to do with a recent burglary in the neighborhood. The officer questions you for a couple of minutes until he is satisfied with your answers. You do not feel free to leave during this encounter until the officer has finished. Would you feel seized? Probably. Courts would agree—they would consider an investigative stop like this to be a seizure.

Investigative stops, being true seizures, fall under constitutional protections. The question then becomes what requirements the Fourth Amendment should be deemed to impose on the police before stopping someone for questioning. Think back to the *Terry v. Ohio* case discussed a little earlier in this chapter. As you recall, Terry was seized when the police detective stopped him and spun him around. Did the Court require the detective to have probable cause? No. In order to stop (but not arrest) Terry, the Court only required what is commonly referred to now as **reasonable suspicion**. Reasonable suspicion is obviously something much less than probable cause. Investigative stops (unlike arrests) merely require reasonable suspicion rather than probable cause.

Courts would never attempt to define such concepts as reasonable suspicion or probable cause in numerical terms, preferring to use words rather than numbers in crafting definitions. However, one unofficial survey of federal judges found that this group of jurists on average would ascribe a 31% degree of certainty to the concept of "reasonable suspicion," while attributing a much higher degree of certainty—46%—to the concept of "probable cause".[10] Though we may quibble with such numbers (I personally would put reasonable suspicion at a much lower numerical level and probable cause at a slighter higher one), it is clear that all courts hold that even the relatively lower standard of reasonable suspicion has to be based on something more than just a gut feeling or a mere hunch. The next case illustrates this point well.

Delaware v. Prouse

440 U.S. 648 (1979)

At about 7:00 pm on a November evening, a New Castle County, Delaware patrol officer stopped an automobile driven by Prouse. Prouse was not violating any traffic laws nor was any equipment associated with his car out of order. The patrolman just decided to check Prouse out. As he put it, "I saw the car in the area and wasn't answering any complaints, so I decided to pull them off."

After pulling Prouse's car over, the officer saw marijuana in plain view on the floor of the automobile. Prouse was arrested for illegal possession of a controlled substance.

Prior to trial, Prouse moved to suppress the marijuana evidence. He argued that the police officer's stop was an illegal seizure. The so-called "in plain view" marijuana was fruit of the poisonous tree (the illegal stop) and therefore ought to be subject to the exclusionary rule. The trial court agreed that the marijuana would have to be suppressed. The state appealed this pre-trial ruling and the issue eventually worked its way to the U.S. Supreme Court.

The U.S. Supreme Court affirmed the decisions of the courts below and ruled that the evidence must be suppressed. The Court said that the stopping of a car for investigative purposes clearly constitutes a seizure within the meaning of the Fourth Amendment. As such, it could only be justified by reasonable suspicion that a traffic violation or some other crime was taking place. In order to prove reasonable suspicion, a police officer asserting such would have to be able to convey "specific and articulable facts" in court. He could not simply explain that he was going on a hunch or declare that he had a vague intuition of some kind. He had to give clear, sound, and credible reasons justifying his suspicions.

The Court took pains to emphasize that a police stop of an automobile is indeed a seizure. People who are pulled over in their cars are inconvenienced and often experience substantial anxiety. Their freedom of movement is interfered with and their time is taken up. As the Court noted, "Automobile travel is a basic, pervasive, and often necessary mode of transportation.... Were the individual subject to unfettered governmental intrusion every time he entered an automobile, the security guaranteed by the Fourth Amendment would be seriously circumscribed."

---

10. McCauliff, C. *Burdens of Proof: Degrees of Belief, Quanta of Evidence, or Constitutional Guarantee?"* 35 Vand.L.Rev. 1293, 1325 (1982).

The state had tried to argue that since police do roadblocks all the time in trying to catch escaping criminals or detect drunk drivers, they should also be allowed to randomly "check out" motorists as part of their patrol function. But, the Supreme Court refused to accept this analogy. It opined that Prouse's situation was different than that of a roadblock where all cars are stopped. "At traffic checkpoints the motorist can see other vehicles being stopped ... and he is much less likely to be frightened or annoyed by the intrusion."

The need to insist on reasonable suspicion that police can back up with **articulable facts** (facts that, unlike hunches, can be pointed out and explained by the officer in court) is dramatized by allegations from ethnic minorities that they are often being subjected to racial profiling. This phenomenon, sometimes referred to as "Driving While Black" or "Driving While Hispanic" has appropriately been the subject of many appeals.[11] Gender and age profiling no doubt also occurs, though being harassed for"Driving While Young and Male" would probably be even harder to prove.

Arrests

Though being stopped on foot or in your automobile for questioning may be inconvenient, imagine how inconvenient it would be to be placed under arrest. Since arrests are much more vexing and frightening than investigative stops, the Fourth Amendment has been construed to require something more than mere reasonable suspicion to justify them. This "something more" is **probable cause.**

But, at what point does a mere stop turn into an arrest? What if the "mere stop" goes on for fifteen minutes? What if it goes on for forty minutes? Would the stop then turn into an arrest requiring probable cause?

Courts refuse to set an artificial "time limit" on investigative stops. However, such stops must meet the **requirement of brevity** or else they will turn into an arrest. As the court in *United States v. Sharpe*, 470 U.S. 675 (1985) puts it, "Obviously if an investigative stop continues indefinitely, at some point it can no longer be justified as an investigative stop. But our cases impose no rigid time limit ... Much as a 'bright line' rule would be desirable, in evaluating whether an investigative detention is unreasonable, common sense and ordinary human experience must govern over rigid criteria." In deciding whether or not the "brevity" requirement has been met the court suggested that one important factor to consider would be "whether the police diligently pursued a means of investigation that was likely to confirm or dispel their suspicions quickly."

In addition to time considerations, people may feel arrested rather than merely stopped if they are transported somewhere. For example, what if the police simply wish to take you downtown for questioning? Is that necessarily an arrest requiring probable cause? It apparently is if you have no choice in the matter. In the case of *Kaupp v. Texas*, 538 U.S. 626 (2003), a young man suspected of the abduction and murder of a 14-year-old girl was woken up by police officers in his bedroom after his father had given the police permission to come inside. The police did not have probable cause or a warrant to take him into

---

11. See, e.g., *Whren v. United States*, 517 U.S. 806 (1996).

custody but nevertheless told him that "We need to go and talk," to which Kaupp replied, "Okay." The police then put handcuffs on him and led him in his bare feet, boxer shorts, and T-shirt to the police car outside. The police took him to the police station where he confessed to the murder.

On appeal the Supreme Court ruled that what happened to Kaupp was a full-blown arrest. It said that since Kaupp essentially had no choice but to go with the police this episode was "sufficiently like arrest to invoke the traditional rule that arrests may constitutionally be made only on probable cause." The fact that Kaupp had said "Okay" to going with the police could hardly be construed under the circumstances to constitute voluntary consent. Since Kaupp's transportation was involuntary, an unconstitutional arrest had taken place, and the confession that was the fruit of this illegality would have to be suppressed.

Arrest Warrants

Before leaving the topic of arrests, we need to address the topic of arrest warrants. When are police required to get an arrest warrant before taking someone into custody? The answer is: very rarely. Stemming from old English traditions apparently accepted by those who drafted the Fourth Amendment, police do not need an arrest warrant to effectuate the arrest of anyone they have probable cause to believe committed a felony (unless they wish to arrest the person in the home). Neither do they need a warrant to arrest someone for a misdemeanor committed in their presence. Police do need a warrant to arrest someone for a misdemeanor not done in their presence (e.g., a simple assault reported by a neighbor). The bottom line is that well over 90% of arrests do not require warrants (just probable cause).

This completes this chapter on the basics of search and seizure law. If you were to take an entire course devoted to this topic, you would be able to learn many more important details concerning the subject. But, if you understand everything that was covered in this chapter, you know more about search and seizure law than the vast majority of the American public and even more than many lawyers engaged in non-criminal practice.

Chapter Four

Self-Incrimination, Right to Counsel, Speedy Jury Trials

In Chapter Three we looked at the Fourth Amendment and search and seizure law. In this Chapter we shall look at rights generated by the next two Amendments: the Fifth Amendment and its prohibition against self-incrimination, and the Sixth Amendment and its guarantees of legal counsel and a speedy jury trial.

Self-Incrimination

The Fifth Amendment to the Constitution says that "No person ... shall be compelled in any criminal case to be a witness against himself ..." But, why should we not expect a person to give an account of what he or she knows? What would be so wrong, if during a trial, the state called the defendant to the stand and asked her to explain her side of things. After all, after the victim, the defendant is probably the person from whom juries most want to hear.

The simple answer is that most people would consider compelling people to "rat themselves out" to be cruel. It would put people in the terrible position of having to choose between breaking a sworn oath (and thus perjuring themselves) and being the instrument of their own downfall. This would be an affront to human dignity and to privacy.[1]

Of course, in order to really protect the right against self-incrimination, we would have to extend the right to events that occur long before any court was convened. For example, what good would the right be at trial if we already spilled the beans, pre-trial, to the police? The police would then be in a position to testify in our place.

All of this is common sense, at least if one agrees with the spirit of the Fifth Amendment. But, what was not considered obvious for a very long time was the current requirement that police have to explicitly inform us of our rights before questioning us after arrest. All of this changed with the blockbuster case of *Miranda v. Arizona*, covered just below.

Today, thanks to Hollywood police dramas, nearly every U.S. resident (and probably most of the world) knows of the American "right to remain silent" and that anything

1. These stated purposes behind the privilege against self-incrimination were expressed by Chief Justice Warren in *Miranda v. Arizona*, 384 U.S. 436 (1966).

"you say can and will be used against you in a court of law." In fact, thanks to the cinema, foreigners sometimes erroneously believe they too have the right to be **Mirandized** by the police before being asked any questions (to their dismay when their lawyer tells them otherwise).[2]

Miranda v. Arizona

384 U.S. 436 (1966)

Miranda confessed to a rape after being questioned by the police for two hours without ever having been apprised of his right to remain silent nor of his right to counsel. He, along with three other defendants in separate cases who also were never fully apprised of their rights, collectively appeal their convictions on the basis that their confessions should not have been used against them. None of the four defendants alleged threats or violence on the part of the police, although one of the four (a man named Stewart) only confessed after having been interrogated nine different times while in custody.

The main issue in this case was whether the police should be required, prior to any questioning, to inform people they have taken into custody of their basic Fifth Amendment rights to remain silent and to legal counsel. There are good arguments on both sides of this issue. On the one hand, you could argue that a right is of little value if one does not know it exists. On the other hand, you could argue that though the police must respect constitutional rights by not coercing confessions, it is not their responsibility to encourage non-compliance by giving out legal advice. After all, police are not required to tell people of their legal right to refuse consent to a search when the police simply ask permission to search a house or automobile. People have the right to refuse but the police do not have to explain this right to them.

The U.S. Supreme Court decided that the time had come to deny the prosecution from using any incriminating statements "stemming from custodial interrogation of the defendant unless it demonstrates the use of procedural safeguards effective to secure the privilege against self-incrimination." These "procedural safeguards" include mandatory warnings (now called **Miranda rights**) given prior to any questioning of the defendant of the "right to remain silent, that any statement he does make may be used as evidence against him, and that he has a right to the presence of an attorney either retained [privately hired] or appointed [provided free of charge]" during the interrogation.

It should be emphasized (as the Court itself well did) that these warnings only need be given before **custodial questioning.** If a person has not been taken into custody (i.e., arrested), then there is no need to **Mirandize** him or her before asking any questions.

---

2. The author had a conversation with a Canadian attorney at a conference who told of a client who admitted that he had confessed to the police but that it would be no problem since the police "never read me my rights." The lawyer had to explain that this was an American right, not a Canadian one, and that he shouldn't rely on American TV shows for his legal education.

This is why the police can knock on your door or stop you on the street and ask you questions without first reading you your rights. You are not yet in custody.

The reasoning of the Court in requiring that these rights be explained to you in advance of custodial questioning has to do with its concerns about the inherent coercive atmosphere of post-arrest questioning. It described such a situation as being a "police dominated atmosphere" which carries its "own badge of intimidation ... Unless adequate protective devices are employed to dispel the compulsion in custodial surroundings, no statement obtained from the defendant can truly be the product of his free choice."

So, what can dispel this compulsion to surrender one's rights? The Court believed that requiring the police interrogators to inform the defendant of his constitutional options would go a long way in equalizing the balance of forces. This would be so for two reasons. First, people would know their rights under the Constitution. People are not lawyers. We cannot assume that they know of their right to remain silent or their right to have counsel with them before answering. Without being informed of their rights, they might assume (as many people around the world do) that they have no right to refuse to answer questions put to them by the police. Second, just hearing the police enunciate these rights will help decrease the intimidating atmosphere associated with police questioning. This is so because the suspect will know that the police know of these rights and "the warning will show the individual that his interrogators are prepared to recognize his privilege should he choose to exercise it."

What will be the result if police henceforth question people taken into custody without telling them of these *Miranda* rights? According to the Court, the incriminating statements (and any fruits thereof) must be suppressed. This will be the case even if the state can prove that the defendant already knew of these rights without the police having to articulate them (e.g., a sophisticated criminal or someone legally trained). Anyone arrested and questioned (including the legally knowledgeable) still need to have the rights told to them so that they will know that the police will honor these rights. After all, there has been a long history of abusive questioning in the annals of policing.

After the warnings are given, the police are required to respect them. For example, once a suspect in custody invokes her right to remain silent, all questioning must immediately cease. If the suspect states her desire to have an attorney present, all questioning must cease until the attorney arrives. The police may not attempt to persuade the suspect to change her mind.

The case above has accomplished what it set out to do. Thanks to the ritualistic reading of these rights (both in real life and on television shows), Americans have come to know these rights now as well as any police officer does. There are no precise words that need to be recited when giving somebody the rights. Courts will be satisfied as long as the essential meanings are conveyed. Nevertheless, just to be careful, many police departments require police officers to read or recite from memory the verbatim wording found on cards provided by the local prosecutor's office. It may sound mechanical but it gets the job done.

We already learned that *Miranda* rights only must be given when the suspect has been taken into custody. It is also important to remember that the *Miranda* decision will only apply when a person is actually being interrogated (questioned). A person can be arrested, tried and convicted without ever having been read *Miranda* rights as long as the police never question the person. Of course, it is likely that the police will almost always wish to question a suspect to at least try to get a lawful confession. But, sometimes the police get lucky and obtain incriminating statements without having advised someone in custody yet of his or her rights. How can this occur? If a person is arrested and simply volunteers information (e.g. while riding in the back of a squad car) without ever actually being asked anything, then no suppression of the statements is required. The person may be in "custody" but he or she has not been "interrogated." *Miranda* applies to custodial *interrogations.*

Assuming that a suspect is both in custody and interrogated, are there no exceptions whatsoever to the rule that incriminating statements made without being first "Mirandized" must be suppressed? In fact, there are two very important exceptions: the inevitable discovery rule and the public safety exception.

The **inevitable discovery rule** holds that even though statements were obtained in violation of *Miranda*, additional evidence that these statements lead to will not have to be suppressed as long as this additional evidence would have been unavoidably discovered anyway. This rule was first created in the case of *Nix v. Williams*, 467 U.S. 431 (1984). In this case, officers with the Des Moines, Iowa police department took a suspect into custody on suspicion of kidnaping and murder. While transporting him from one Iowa town to another, they tricked him into confessing to the murder and into telling them where he dumped the body. They did this by playing on his deeply held religious beliefs, telling him it would be a shame if the victim were not given a proper Christian burial. All of this was done in violation of *Miranda*. At trial, the prosecution presented evidence of the body (which was found exactly where the defendant had directed the police to look) on the theory that the police would have inevitably found it anyway since they were already doing a careful grid search of the same area. The U.S. Supreme Court agreed that such inevitable discovery would henceforth be an exception to the exclusionary rule.

The **public safety exception** (the second exception to *Miranda*) recognizes that sometimes the reading of *Miranda* rights has to take back seat to more important issues of public safety. Would you want the police to read a terrorist his *Miranda* rights before asking him how to disable a ticking bomb? This doctrine was first articulated in the case that follows.

New York v. Quarles

467 U.S. 649 (1984)

A woman reported having been raped to the police by someone fitting the description of Quarles. The woman told the police that the rapist had just entered a nearby supermarket and that he was carrying a gun. When the police entered the supermarket, Quarles spotted them and took off running to the back of the store. Officer Kraft ran after him and caught up with him in the back of the store. Officer Kraft put handcuffs on Quarles and, after frisking him, did not find a gun but did find an empty shoulder holster. The officer asked Quarles where he had disposed of the gun.

Quarles nodded in the direction of some empty boxes and told the officer that "the gun is over there." Officer Kraft swiftly located the gun in the boxes and then read Quarles his *Miranda* rights. Prior to his trial on gun charges, the judge suppressed both the gun itself as well as the statement, "the gun is over there." Both were ruled to be in violation of the *Miranda* decision.

On appeal to the U.S. Supreme Court, the state asked for an exception to the *Miranda* decision in a case such as this. The Court agreed to create a "public safety exception" to *Miranda*. It said that "we do not believe that the doctrinal underpinnings of *Miranda* require that it be applied in all its rigor to a situation in which police officers ask questions reasonably prompted by a concern for public safety." In this particular case, the gun, if not promptly located, could have been found by a potential accomplice or by an employee or customer of the store. If Quarles had been read his rights, he might very well have decided not to answer when asked where this dangerous gun was.

The Court went on to reason that as long as the "cost" of the *Miranda* decision was limited to suppression of incriminating evidence at trial, the *Miranda* decision made sense. But the *Miranda* decision became too costly when its existence put the public safety at grave risk. The Court concluded that "the need for answers to questions in a situation posing a threat to the public safety outweighs the need for the prophylactic rule protecting the Fifth Amendment's privilege against self-incrimination."

In her dissent, Justice O'Connor agreed that the police acted correctly in asking where the gun was without first reading Quarles his rights. But, she went on to say that the gun nevertheless should be suppressed. In her view, the police should bear the cost of ensuring public safety by violating *Miranda*, not defendants. In other words, they should violate *Miranda* under such circumstances and just take their lumps. By way of example, she gives a hypothetical of a bomb about to explode. She says the police can and should ask a suspect in custody where the bomb is, even use trickery to find out, all in violation of *Miranda*. The *Miranda* decision would not stop them from doing these appropriate things. All *Miranda* says is that if they do so, any statements made cannot be used at trial.

The public safety exception is potentially a large loophole for the police to get around the *Miranda* decision. Can you see how many judges might be reluctant to play "Monday morning quarterback" in second-guessing a police officer's assessment that a public safety situation existed?

Right to Counsel

The Sixth Amendment says, in part, that "the accused shall enjoy the right ... to have the Assistance of Counsel for his defense." This right to a lawyer exists because of the adversary nature of our criminal court system. The idea is that a neutral body of fact finders (i.e., juries or judges) will be exposed to a clash of two opposing sides, each striving zealously to skillfully advance their positions, and that out of this clash the truth will emerge. But to guarantee a fair contest, the two sides must be somewhat equally represented. The state has the prosecutor. So, the defendant too must be allowed to have his or her articulate spokesperson.

However, the right to legal counsel originally meant that an accused had the right to hire a lawyer if he or she could afford one. There was no right to a public defender or some other kind of free lawyer. If an accused could not afford to hire a lawyer, then he or she simply had to stumble along through the process as best as he or she could manage. The idea of requiring states to provide poor people accused of crimes with free lawyers seemed silly. After all, there is no constitutional right to free food even if one is starving to death. There is no constitutional right to free medicine if one is sick; free dental care if one's tooth aches; free shelter if one is freezing; or a free education if one is illiterate. True, government eventually chose to start providing these services voluntarily, but not because the Constitution required it: it was done for political and cultural reasons. If the government wanted to, it could abolish all public schools, food stamps, housing assistance, medicaid, etc. to the poor without violating the Constitution. There simply is no constitutional right to governmental charity.

How then did there get to be a constitutional right to state-supplied, free lawyers in criminal cases? This came about largely due to the efforts of an elderly, small-time, career criminal named Clarence Gideon.

Gideon v. Wainwright

372 U.S. 335 (1963)

Clarence Gideon allegedly burglarized a poolroom in Florida and requested the Florida trial judge to provide him with a free lawyer at his trial. The trial judge refused, informing Gideon that he had no right to free counsel. Gideon told the trial judge that the U.S. Supreme Court said he had the right to a government furnished defense attorney. The Florida judge told Gideon that such was not the case and that he would just have to defend himself as best he could.

Gideon did as good a job as could reasonably be expected of a lay person in defending himself. He gave an opening statement, cross-examined witnesses, wisely declined to testify himself, and gave a short closing argument. But, he lost anyway. He was sentenced to five years in prison. But, Gideon was not finished. He eventually appealed the trial judge's refusal to give him free legal counsel all the way up to the U.S. Supreme Court.

In one of the most dramatic decisions of the Twentieth Century, the Supreme Court ruled that henceforth anyone charged with a serious crime (later expanded to include even most petty crimes[3]) had the right to a state-provided defense attorney if the person was too poor hire one privately. The Court reasoned that all states are constitutionally required to give criminal defendants a fair trial under the Sixth and Fourteenth Amendments to the Constitution. It further ruled that a fair trial requires the services of a defense attorney. It pointed out that, "Lawyers to prosecute are everywhere deemed essential to protect the public's interest in an orderly society. Similarly, there are few defendants charged with crime, few indeed, who fail to hire the best lawyers they can get to prepare and present their defenses. That government hires lawyers to prosecute and defendants

3. *Argersinger v. Hamlin*, 407 U.S. 25 (1972) ruled that even a petty crime requires free legal counsel if the conviction results in any jail time.

who have the money hire lawyers to defend are the strongest indications of the widespread belief that lawyers in criminal courts are necessities, not luxuries."

The Court noted that providing criminal defendants with government-furnished lawyers is not the same thing as charity. A free lawyer, unlike free food, shelter or medical care, is not the granting of charity because in a criminal prosecution, the government (not nature or happenstance) is the aggressor. Since the government initiates the ordeal, it has a responsibility to ensure that the process is fair.

Defense lawyers can help the process be fair in many critical ways. They can file important pre-trial motions, provide skillful opening statements, deliver impassioned closing arguments, engage in vigorous cross-examination of state witnesses, counsel defendants on whether or not to take the stand in their own defense, and maximize the chances of an acquittal by remaining objective.

After winning his appeal, Gideon was appointed a free lawyer by the Florida courts and tried again. This time he was acquitted of the charges. His new lawyer was able to establish that the government's main witness, who claimed to have seen Gideon emerge from the business, had likely committed the crime himself.[4]

The *Gideon* decision ushered in a new era of government-provided defense attorneys. What the *Gideon* case did not resolve however was how states had to go about providing such lawyers. States are free to provide free lawyers any way they want to.

States follow three main methods for providing **indigent defense** (defense for people without any means).[5] The first system is that of the **public defender**. Public defenders are salaried government officials just like prosecutors. They may work full-time or part-time but are not paid per case but rather by way of a full-time or part-time salary. If full-time, they usually receive paid vacation days, medical insurance, and a government pension plan. Public defender systems only exist in slightly more than a third of counties nationwide, yet more than 70 percent of the American population lives in these counties.[6]

The second method of providing indigent defense is that of **assigned counsel** programs. It is the second most popular method (in terms of number of clients served), used in about half of all American counties (many of which though have small populations).[7] In jurisdictions using assigned counsel programs, privately practicing attorneys wishing to make some extra money may have their names placed on a list kept at the courthouse by a clerk or some other official. When it is their turn to receive a case, the courthouse official contacts them and offers them the case. Typically they are paid an hourly fee (e.g., fifty dollars per hour). But these attorneys are not salaried government employees like public defenders with an ongoing caseload. They work for themselves and merely are appointed cases from time to time with a fee paid for each individual case (they submit a bill to the court when the case is finally over).

---

4. Lewis, Anthony. 1963. *Gideon's Trumpet*. New York: Random House, at 237–238.

5. The following discussion is found in my book, Lynch, David R. *Inside the Criminal Courts*. 2004. Durham, N.C.: Carolina Academic Press, at 71.

6. U.S. Department of Justice. 1988. "Criminal Defense of the Poor." *Bureau of Justice Bulletin*, September.

7. Id.

The last method for providing the indigent with a defense is that of **contract systems**. This is the least common method used in the United States. Under this system, private law firms act as sub-contractors for the government and provide all of the indigent defense for a county for a specified period of time (e.g., a one year contract). Often, the law firm willing to put in the lowest bid will be awarded the contract. If the law firm of *Smith and Jones* were to win this year's contract, then all poor criminal defendants would be referred to the law firm of *Smith and Jones* for legal representation.

Which system a particular area uses depends upon the county in which one lives. Though counties within the same state tend to copy one another, a particular county may or may not use the system that most sister counties use.

The question arises regarding which system—assigned counsel, public defender, or contracts with firms—provides the best quality of representation. It appears that public defenders provide the best representation of the three and contracts with law firms the worst.[8]

Right to a Speedy Jury Trial

In addition to guaranteeing the right to a defense attorney, the Sixth Amendment provides that "the accused shall enjoy the right to a speedy and public trial, by an impartial jury ..." Let us now consider what is legally meant by the word "speedy." Later, we shall turn our attention to the meaning of the words, "impartial jury."

Speedy: A Promise Unfulfilled?

Justice delayed is indeed justice denied. Victims want closure. Slow justice not only denies victims timely closure, they may also see their case evaporate when key prosecution witnesses move out of the area, simply disappear, or forget critical details of the matter.

Defendants also are harmed when cases take too long to process. Those unable to make bail have to languish in jail not knowing their ultimate fates. If by cruel irony they are ultimately acquitted, they are simply told that they are free to go: no compensation and no apology. Defendants able to make bail suffer as well. Though "free," they too have their futures put on hold. Will they be acquitted, given probation, or incarcerated? Should they bother continuing with their schooling, get married, avoid pregnancy, look for a better job? Like victims, defendants need closure. Waiting around can be much more stressful than the eventual sentence.

If victims and defendants are both harmed by delay, then why does it exist? The conventional wisdom about case delay is that it is caused by too much volume and too few

8. See Worden, Alissa Pollitz. 1993. "Counsel for the Poor: An Evaluation of Contracting for Indigent Criminal Defense." *Justice Quarterly* 10:613–637.

resources. But, there may be an even more powerful explanation: a human desire for delay on the part of self-interested prosecutors, defense attorneys, and judges.[9]

Prosecutors might like delay in order to postpone weak cases they do not want to face. They also like delay when a defendant sits in jail unable to make bail since the delay might soften the accused up for an eventual "time served" plea agreement. Defense attorneys might like delay in the hope that prosecution witnesses might forget or move away, that victims might become less angry over time and not oppose generous plea bargains, or that they will have more time to collect fees owed them. Judges might like delay in the hope that a yet unresolved case might in the interim be resolved by a plea bargain instead of via a time-consuming trial. Still, these court house professionals cannot drag their feet forever. There is a constitution they have to worry about.

So, what then constitutes a "speedy" trial? Lay people might think of "speedy" in terms of weeks or perhaps a couple of months or so. But, modern courts refuse to put a number on it. They believe that would be too simplistic and a little dangerous. Simplistic because every case is different. Dangerous because, after beating around the bush for decades, the U.S. Supreme Court finally ruled that the remedy for excessive tardiness in the processing of a criminal case is complete and final dismissal of that case. No watered-down remedy (e.g., reduction in sentence) would be allowed to substitute for dismissal.[10]

If courts do not like to use numbers in defining "speedy," what then do they use? The case below will tell us.

Barker v. Wingo

407 U.S. 514 (1972)

An elderly couple, living in Christian County, Kentucky, were beaten to death by two intruders wielding a tire iron. Two people were arrested in connection with these murders: Manning and Barker. The state decided to try each of these two men separately.

The state elected to try Manning first because its case against Barker was weaker. In fact, the state was not confident that it could convict Barker without Manning's testimony. The state had a problem. Manning was not about to voluntarily testify against Barker, and because of his Fifth Amendment privilege against self-incrimination, the state could not compel Manning to take the stand against Barker. However, this privilege against self-incrimination would disappear if and when Manning were convicted prior to Barker's trial. Manning could then be forced to take the stand at Barker's trial and tell what he knew of these crimes.

For the next four years, the state tried to convict Manning in multiple trials. The first Manning trial ended in a hung jury. A second trial resulted in a conviction but was overturned on appeal due to illegally obtained evidence not being properly suppressed. A third trial also resulted in a conviction but was overturned on appeal due to the trial court's failure to change the venue of this locally highly-publicized case. A fourth trial

---

9. This idea and the brief discussion that follows is found in my book, *Inside the Criminal Courts*, supra note 5, at 45.

10. *Strunk v. United States*, 412 U.S. 434 (1973).

resulted in another hung jury. Finally, a fifth trial resulted in Manning being convicted of one of the murders, with a sixth trial resulting in him being convicted of the other murder.

Now, after four long years, the state was finally ready to try Barker. It could now use Manning as a witness against Barker since Manning (convicted himself) no longer had to worry about self-incrimination.

During the four year wait, Barker had spent the first ten months in jail but was then able to post bail. The state had asked for a dozen or so continuances (postponements) in Barker's case during the four years it took to process Manning, but Barker never bothered to object to any of them. Apparently, he was gambling that Manning would be acquitted. But, Barker's gamble did not pay off.

Now that the state was finally ready to call Barker's case to trial, it had to ask for yet another postponement because the sheriff who had investigated the case fell seriously ill. Barker objected to this continuance on the grounds that his right to a speedy trial was being denied him (he pointed out that he had been arrested four long years ago at this point). The trial court overruled Barker's objection and granted the state's request for the continuance. Eventually the sheriff got well and Barker went to trial. Barker was convicted of the murders and sentenced to life in prison.

Barker appealed his convictions on the grounds that his right to a speedy trial had been denied. He asked that he be set free as a remedy. The U.S. Supreme Court eventually was asked to decide this matter.

The Supreme Court acknowledged that high stakes were involved. Should it rule that Barker's right to a speedy trial was violated, it would have no choice but to let a murderer go free. Letting a criminal go free is an even more serious remedy than that given defendants who benefit from the exclusionary rule due to illegally executed searches or improperly obtained confessions. When the exclusionary rule is invoked, it is still possible that the state might be able to prove its case without the suppressed evidence. But, in the case of the denial of a speedy trial only one outcome—freedom for the criminal—is possible.

The Supreme Court reviewed the harms done both to society and to the criminal defendant when trials are not speedily brought to court. Society is hurt because large backlogs of cases often result in prosecutors' offering overly generous plea bargains to move things along. Society also suffers from having to put up with defendants who make bail who now have the opportunity to commit new crimes while awaiting their day in court (in fact, Barker who was charged with murders was free for all but the first ten months of his four year wait). Also, if a defendant does not make bail (such as Barker for his first ten months), not only does society have to bear the costs associated with jail overcrowding, but families of defendants often loose the wages of their breadwinner.

But, as serious as these societal harms are, even more grave are the harms to the individual defendant. Those unable to make bail often experience job loss, anxiety, boredom, separation from loved ones, and increased difficulty in locating witnesses and preparing their defense. Those able to make bail suffer less, but still face anxiety and often live under a cloud of suspicion.

The problem facing the Court then was how should "speedy" be defined. The Court expressed its frustration that this concept was necessarily much more "vague" than other procedural rights. True, some state legislatures have eliminated this vagueness by voluntarily passing statues that define the right in terms of a set period of days or months. The Supreme Court, however, felt that it could not require state legislatures to do this. It has no right to force states to adopt particular procedures unless the Constitution mandates it. Given the fact that every case is different, the Supreme Court could find "no constitutional basis for holding that the speedy trial right can be quantified into a specified number of days or months. The states, of course, are free to prescribe a reasonable period consistent with constitutional standards, but our approach must be less precise."

The Court ruled that there is just no way around the fact that each case must be analyzed using a balancing test to be administered on a case by case, *ad hoc* basis. The Court went on to identify **four key speedy trial factors** that are to be used in this balancing test: "length of delay, the reason for the delay, the defendant's assertion of his right, and prejudice to the defendant." It then went on to illustrate each of these four factors.

The "length of delay" was described as the "triggering mechanism." Until there is some delay, there is nothing to complain about. One has to be careful in looking at length of delay. "The delay that can be tolerated for an ordinary street crime is considerably less than for a serious, complex conspiracy charge."

"Reason for delay" means the reasons the government gives for not bringing its case to trial sooner. Here too, good judgement must be used in assessing this factor. "A deliberate attempt to delay the trial in order to hamper the defense should be weighed heavily against the government. A more neutral reason such as ... overcrowded courts should be weighed less heavily but nevertheless should be considered ..." since it is not the defendant's fault that courts are overcrowded.

"The defendant's responsibility to assert his right" is a factor because some defendants like the delay and for this reason fail to object to government requests for trial postponements. "The more serious the deprivation, the more likely a defendant is to complain ... Failure to assert the right will make it difficult [though not impossible] for a defendant to prove that he was denied a speedy trial."

The last factor, "prejudice to the defendant" simply means the harm the delay has caused the defendant. Speedy trials are meant to minimize "oppressive pretrial detention," "anxiety and concern of the accused," and "the inability of the defendant to adequately prepare his case."

The Court made it very clear that even though it articulated four factors, "these factors have no talismanic qualities." There is no need to have all four of these factors in order to find that the right to a speedy trial was denied. "Courts still must engage in a difficult and sensitive balancing process."

Now that the Court had articulated its four-factor balancing test, it was prepared to specifically rule on the Barker case. If found it to be a "close" call.

It began with the first factor—length of delay. It found the nearly five years from arrest to trial (including the four years to first process Manning plus the sheriff's illness) to be "extraordinary."

It next considered the "reasons for the delay" and again felt that this factor favored Barker's position. "Only seven months of that period can be attributed to a strong excuse, the illness of the ex-sheriff who was in charge of the investigation."

The next two factors, however, tended to favor the state's position. First, the Supreme Court found the "prejudice to the defendant" to be "minimal." Though Barker no doubt suffered from anxiety, he did spend most of the time out of jail and "there is no claim that any of Barker's witnesses died or otherwise became unavailable ..."

The final factor—"defendant's assertion of the right"—hugely favored the government's side of this controversy because Barker allowed eleven continuances to be advanced over a four year period without ever objecting to any of them. "The probable reason for Barker's attitude was that he was gambling on Manning's acquittal. The evidence was not very strong against Manning, as the reversals and hung juries suggest, and Barker undoubtedly thought that if Manning were acquitted, he would never be tried ... Barring extraordinary circumstances, we would be reluctant indeed to rule that a defendant was denied [his right to a speedy trial] on a record that strongly indicates ... that the defendant did not want a speedy trial. We hold, therefore, that Barker was not deprived of his due process right to a speedy trial."

As the opinion above indicates, some state legislatures have voluntarily adopted specific time frames for defining what is "speedy" in terms of bringing cases to trial. Apparently, they do not feel comfortable leaving it to trial judges to do the difficult and sensitive four-factor balancing act that the Supreme Court came up with. They consider these four factors to be too "squishy" to be of reliable use.

Under so-called **speedy trial statutes**, cases are mandated to be processed within so many months despite the traditional willingness of appellate courts to be less time-sensitive. Congress helped to get the ball rolling by passing the **Federal Speedy Trial Act** which requires that defendants charged with federal crimes be indicted within thirty days of arrest and brought to trial within another seventy days thereafter. (Cases can sometimes exceed these deadlines if a judge determines the case to be unusually complex or if the "ends of justice" otherwise demands the extension. Also, the clock stops running whenever the defense—rather than the prosecution—causes the delay.)[11]

Since the first passage of the Federal Speedy Trial Act in 1974, many states have followed suit by passing similar speedy trial statutes for crimes tried in their state courts. Many of these states, however, have much longer time-frames than the federal courts (e.g., a case must be brought to trial within six months for those who cannot make bail and twelve months for those out on bail).[12]

The scary thought is that despite cases requiring four-factor balancing tests (a very dubious and subjective process) and despite speedy trial statutes (with time frames that can be very long indeed), we may very well live in an era in which the right to a speedy trial in many areas of the country is simply an unfulfilled promise. If true, this would not be the first time that a constitutional promise remains unenforced. For most of American history, the Fourth Amendment's prohibition of unreasonable searches and seizures

---

11. *Speedy Trial Act*, 18 U.S.C. sections 3161–3174 (2000).
12. This was the time frame in Pennsylvania where I practiced criminal law.

was simply not effectively enforced by the courts. The Amendment was indeed a "mere form of words." It was not until the *Mapp decision*[13], deep into the Twentieth Century, that the Supreme Court finally made the exclusionary rule applicable to state courts, thus finally giving the Fourth Amendment some real teeth. Could it be that the same atmosphere of judicial neglect exists today with regards to the Sixth Amendment right to a speedy trial that existed pre-*Mapp* with regards to Fourth Amendment unreasonable searches and seizures?

The Right to an Impartial Jury

The Sixth Amendment not only mandates a "speedy trial" but a trial conducted by an "impartial jury of the State and district wherein the crime shall have been committed." Obviously, if a defendant is convicted by a jury that includes members who are biased and unwilling to hold the state to its heavy burden of proof, then due process has not been provided. Defendants are entitled not just to a jury but to an impartial jury who has not pre-judged the case.

Voir Dire is the mechanism that American courts use to ensure that jurors who serve are impartial. During the voir dire process, lawyers and judges question prospective jurors in an attempt to ferret out any who are too biased to serve in a fair and just manner. Any potential juror in the group asked to assemble in the courtroom who answers a question in such a way as to expose bias will be **challenged for cause** by the lawyer wishing to eliminate that prejudiced juror. If the judge agrees that the prospective juror is biased, that juror will be excused from service in that trial. For example, a juror who admits knowing one of the parties or who admits that they are too upset with the charges to think straight would be successfully challenged for cause. There is no limit to the number of challenges for cause in a voir dire. If so many members of the jury panel turn out to be biased that twelve are no longer remaining, additional prospective jurors will be summoned to the courtroom.

In addition to challenges for cause, lawyers are also given a limited number of (usually about a half dozen or so) **peremptory challenges.** Using a peremptory challenge, a lawyer (either the prosecutor or defense attorney) may ask to have a potential juror excluded for any reason or no reason whatsoever. The idea behind the peremptory challenge is that a lawyer might have a strong intuition that a juror is biased yet be unable to prove it.

Once jurors have been successfully challenged, either for cause or peremptorily, they leave the courtroom. The first twelve of those remaining (going down a pre-drawn list of names) will serve as the jury.

Perhaps the most important case in terms of selecting truly impartial jurors would be a trial in which a jury may ultimately be asked to consider the death penalty. Americans are split on whether or not they believe in the death penalty. Would you expect Americans who philosophically support the death penalty to also be more prosecution-prone than defense-prone in terms of returning guilty verdicts in capital murder trials?

---

13. *Mapp v. Ohio*, 367 U.S. 643 (1961).

See what you think of the next case which struggles with the prosecution's right to a jury that will carry out the law when it comes to imposing death vs. a defendant's right to have a jury that is not stacked with prosecution-prone jurors.

Lockhart v. McCree

476 U.S. 162 (1986)

McCree was charged with capital murder in federal court. Since he faced the death penalty, McCree felt that it was wrong that he should be given a group of trial jurors who collectively stacked up to be more prosecution-prone than would randomly be the case. McCree's lawyer argued in a hearing before the trial judge that it would be wrong for a trial court to allow the prosecutor to successfully "challenge for cause" every prospective juror who admitted during a jury selection process that he or she, for moral or philosophical reasons, could not impose the death penalty. McCree's argument was based on numerous social science studies which his attorneys presented that provided support for his contention that people who support the death penalty tended to be more likely to convict people generally than those who were philosophically opposed to the death penalty. The prosecution on the other hand argued that it had the right to exclude from jury service in a death penalty case those jurors who absolutely would refuse to carry out the law of the land, including imposing the death penalty if the facts warranted it.

The trial court found in favor of the defendant, McCree, and granted him the habeas relief he sought. The federal prosecutors appealed to the Eighth Circuit, but this intermediate-level appellate court also sided with McCree, finding "substantial evidentiary support for the District Court's conclusion that the removal for cause of [those who cannot ever impose the death penalty] resulted in 'conviction-prone' juries and ... such removal for cause violated McCree's constitutional right to a jury selected from a fair cross-section of the community." Not liking this decision, the prosecution appealed the matter to the U.S. Supreme Court who agreed to hear the case.

The U.S. Supreme Court overruled the courts below, and sided with the prosecution. It said that even assuming that the social science studies cited were correct in their conclusions that "death qualified" juries were more prosecution-prone than "non-death qualified juries," the Constitution still does not prohibit the use of "death qualified" juries in capital cases.

The Court pointed out that the right to have a "fair cross-section of the community" cannot be taken too literally. The Court has never interpreted that phrase to mean that trial juries are required to exactly "reflect the composition of the community at large." To interpret it that way would be impractical. It would require that every trial jury be balanced with the "proper number of Democrats and Republicans, young persons and old persons, white-collar executives and blue-collar laborers, and so on." What "fair cross-section" really means is that the jurors selected will "conscientiously and properly carry out their sworn duty to apply the law to the facts of the particular case." A jury composed entirely of "death penalty qualified" jurors is capable of doing this.

The Court went on to say that any group whose attitudes make it impossible for its members to apply the facts of a case to the laws of the land can be excluded from jury service. Excluding people who are unable to do their sworn duty has never been held to violate the "fair cross-section" guarantee. Both the prosecution and the defense have the right to a jury who will carry out the law.

Three justices dissented. Justice Marshall (writing for all three) referred to the majority as exhibiting "glib nonchalance ill-suited to the gravity of the issue presented and the power of [McCree's] claims." He said that "the Court upholds a practice that allows the State a special advantage in those prosecutions where the charges are the most serious and the possible punishments, the most severe." He went on to complain that the decision of the Court gives the "prosecution license to empanel a jury especially likely to return" the guilty verdict it is after. He praised the social-science studies cited by McCree as displaying strength lying in the "essential unanimity of the results obtained by researchers using diverse subjects and varied methodologies." He concluded that McCree, like all defendants, had "the right to a fair trial and an impartial jury whose composition is not biased toward the prosecution."

The Correct Size of Juries

Most Americans think of juries as being composed of twelve members. But, where does this number twelve come from? Could a jury composed of fewer than twelve people be constitutionally acceptable? Would you feel cheated if you were brought to trial before just eight jurors? What about four? Two? The case that follows explores this area.

Williams v. Florida

399 U.S. 78 (1970)

Prior to his trial for robbery, Williams filed a motion demanding a 12-person jury instead of the 6-person jury the Florida court was planning to give him. Florida statute allowed 6-person juries, despite the American tradition of juries of twelve. Williams claimed that anything less than a 12-person jury would violate his Sixth Amendment constitutional right to a real jury trial. His motion was denied. He appealed this denial until it reached the U.S. Supreme Court.

The U.S. Supreme Court sided with the Florida legislature and courts and against Williams. In its opinion, it admitted that 12-person juries went back centuries in Anglo-American jurisprudence. But, just because a practice was old did not mean that the U.S. Constitution required it. The Court noted that nobody knows where this number "12" came from. It cited Lord Coke in suggesting that perhaps it rested "on little more than mystical or superstitious insights ..." in that the "the number of twelve is respected in holy writ, as 12 apostles, 12 stones, 12 tribes, etc." The Court went on to say that, "In short, while sometime in the 14th Century the size of the jury at common law came to be fixed generally at 12, that particular feature of the jury system appears to have been a historical accident, unrelated to the great purposes which gave rise to the jury in the first place. The question before us is whether this accidental feature of the jury has been immutably codified into our Constitution."

Ruling that the accidental number "12" was indeed not unalterably welded into the Sixth Amendment right to a jury trial, the Court went on to knock down earlier Court pronouncements that seemed to indicate the opposite. In particular, it criticized its own late 19th Century utterances in *Thompson v. Utah*, 170 U.S. 343 (1898), in which the Court reversed the conviction of someone who had been given an 8-person jury under (then) Utah law. In that decision, the Court cited the Magna Carta and subsequent unbroken tradition as authority for the proposition that legitimate juries required "twelve persons, neither more nor less." But, suggesting that this decision was ill-reasoned, the modern Court pointed out that "noticeably absent [from the decision] was any discussion of the essential step in the argument: namely, that every feature of the jury as it existed at common law—whether incidental or essential to that institution—was necessarily included in the Constitution wherever that document referred to a 'jury.'"

The modern Court said that it doubted the Framers of our Constitution even gave much thought to this whole issue when they wrote the Sixth Amendment. This being the case, the real inquiry should not be centered on murky history and blind tradition but rather on the real purpose behind requiring trials to be decided by lay juries. The Court said that the real function of the jury is "to prevent oppression by the Government." Citing words it had penned in an earlier case, it went on to say that "providing an accused with the right to be tried by a jury of his peers gave him an inestimable safeguard against the corrupt or overzealous prosecutor and against the compliant, biased, or eccentric judge." The High Court went on to add that the size of the jury is really not all that relevant in accomplishing the protective purpose: six lay citizens could do just as good a job of checking government as twelve.

The Court also discussed the often-mentioned secondary purpose of a jury: having a cross-section of the community decide a case. Regarding this, it brought up the point that there is no reason to believe that 12-person juries did a much better job at achieving a fair cross-section of the community than 6-person juries. Whether six or twelve members were employed, it was not likely that all voices in the community would be adequately represented anyway. The Court did say that "to be sure, the number should be large enough to promote group deliberation ... and to provide a fair possibility for obtaining a representative cross-section of the community." But six was nearly as good as twelve in achieving a fair possibility of diversity [though statisticians might strongly disagree with the Court's math on this]. In conclusion, the Court refused to "ascribe a blind formalism to the Framers" not supported by reason or logic.

Well, if six is acceptable to the Supreme Court, what about fewer than six? Eight years after the *Williams* decision above, the Court was asked to give its approval to a five-person jury. In *Ballew v. Georgia*, 435 U.S. 23 (1978), it said that any jury smaller than six members was pushing things too far. Juries have to be large enough to constitute a body that can engage in deliberations and large enough to counterbalance biases that might exist among the jurors. Anything smaller than six members would just not be up to these tasks.

This completes our chapter on rights found in the Fifth and Sixth Amendments to the Constitution. The next chapter will look at the proper legal roles of those who perpetually inhabit our criminal courthouses: our prosecutors, defense lawyers, and judges.

Chapter Five

Law and the Proper Roles of Prosecutors, Defense Attorneys, and Judges

Following the arrest of a suspect, the focus of the criminal justice process centers on the criminal court system. There exist two tracks in the study of criminal trial courts: the individuals, or actors who work in the courts, and the processes and procedures that occur as part of a criminal prosecution. These processes, including pre-trial release and bail decisions, plea bargaining, trials, and sentencing will be discussed in later chapters. This chapter will focus on the actors—prosecutors, defense attorneys, and judges—that work daily in the criminal courts.

Trial courts are much like a bureaucracy. They often appear to operate with a systematic smoothness as the individuals who work in them process case after case. What makes the functioning of trial courts fascinating is the fact that the key personnel that make them function work for different institutions, with different missions, goals, and rules. Given the adversarial design of the criminal court system, the fact that cases get processed in a systematic manner is truly amazing.

The reason for the sustained operation of the criminal courts is that the key actors in the system, while having theoretically different goals, each have one goal in common: completing their work and processing cases as quickly and painlessly as possible. The reality of this goal, and the way it shapes the operation of trial courts and relationships between prosecutors, defense attorneys, and judges, was brought to the forefront of trial court analysis by James Eisenstein and Herbert Jacob in their 1977 book *Felony Justice*.[1] Eisenstein and Jacob labeled the individuals who regularly work in the same court as the **courtroom workgroup**. While at times prosecutors and defense attorneys duke it out in very adversarial proceedings (with the judge sitting as referee), much of their work is done in a cooperative manner. This happens largely out of necessity. Without unwritten guidelines and standard practices within a courtroom workgroup, the time and effort needed to complete the court's business would increase exponentially. By working together to dispose of the court's caseload, all members of the workgroup are better able to perform their duties expeditiously, and have more time to focus on the issues and cases that require full, adversarial proceedings. In this chapter we will study how the law shapes the duties and responsibilities of prosecutors, defense attorneys, and judges in this workgroup setting.

1. Eisenstein, J. and H. Jacob (1977). *Felony Justice*. Boston: Little, Brown, and Company.

The Prosecutor

The prosecuting attorney, sometimes referred to as district attorney or county attorney, represents the government in criminal prosecutions. That simple definitional statement does not begin to convey the critical functions performed, and the power and the control the prosecutor exhibits in the criminal court system.

Prosecutors' offices are very decentralized and independent. Federal prosecutions are handled by the United States Attorney's Office in each of the 93 federal judicial districts. State prosecutions are normally pursued by county—or district-level prosecuting attorneys' offices. Violations of city ordinances are often prosecuted by city attorneys.

In most states county and city prosecutor's offices are independent of each other. Additionally, over 90% of chief prosecutors (district attorneys) are locally elected, answerable only to the jurisdiction's voters. This autonomy provides them with tremendous discretion to operate and make decisions as they deem fit.

This independence is compounded by the fact that a vast majority of the work done by prosecutors and the decisions they make occur behind closed doors. While the prosecutor in the courtroom is the image most people have when they think about prosecuting attorneys at work, most of the actual work done by a prosecuting attorney's office is done by attorneys, paralegals, investigators, and other staff outside the courtroom walls and beyond the view of the public.

Depending on their size, prosecuting attorney offices are usually made up of an elected chief, a number of assistant or deputy prosecuting attorneys, investigators, and support staff. The elected chief prosecutor sets department policy and makes major decisions on staffing and supervisory positions. Rarely do chief prosecutors appear in court let alone conduct trials. It is the job of deputy prosecutors to appear in court on a daily basis, present cases to grand juries, and make decisions on a myriad of issues to put the chief prosecutor's policies into action.

Prosecuting attorneys perform a number of duties that are critical to the functioning of the criminal court system. These include working with law enforcement agencies on obtaining search and arrest warrants, running grand juries, and representing the government at trial and in plea negotiations. While these functions are critical to the operation of the criminal justice system, the overarching duty of a prosecutor is to seek justice. As we will see in the next section, it is not always clear how far a prosecutor may go in quest of a conviction before he/she loses sight of the duty to seek justice.

Duty to Seek Justice

The prosecutor represents the government in criminal prosecutions. While the criminal court process is centered largely around an adversarial system, with attorneys doing all they can to persuade a judge or jury to make decisions favorable to their client, the roles of the prosecution and defense are quite different. As we will discuss later in this chapter, defense attorneys are obligated to do all they can do (within the ethical rules) to obtain a favorable outcome for their clients. This is true even for clients who they know are guilty of the crimes with which they have been charged.

The prosecutor, on the other hand, has a much different duty. The prosecutor represents not only the government, but all of the citizens within the jurisdiction. "The duty of the prosecutor is to seek justice, not merely to convict."[2] The scope of this duty was famously explained by Supreme Court Justice Sutherland in *Berger v. United States*:

> The [prosecutor] is the representative not of an ordinary party to a controversy, but of a sovereignty whose obligation to govern impartially is as compelling as its obligation to govern at all; and whose interest, therefore, in a criminal prosecution is not that it shall win a case, but that justice shall be done. As such, he is in a peculiar and very definite sense the servant of the law, the twofold aim of which is that guilt shall not escape nor innocence suffer. He may prosecute with earnestness and vigor—indeed, he should do so. But, while he may strike hard blows, he is not at liberty to strike foul ones. It is as much his duty to refrain from improper methods calculated to produce a wrongful conviction as it is to use every legitimate means to bring about a just one.[3]

The basis for this duty is twofold. First, as stated in *Berger*, it is simply wrong to convict an innocent person of a crime. Along with the presumption of innocence which is the cornerstone of the American prosecutorial system, a prosecutor must operate with ethical safeguards to limit the chance of a wrongful conviction. The second basis revolves around the place the prosecutor holds in representing the government in criminal prosecutions. If prosecutors are perceived as operating unjustly, outside the rule of law, respect for the government and court system's authority and legitimacy will undoubtedly be diminished. "Recognizing a [prosecutor's] role as a shepherd of justice, we must not forget that the authority of the Government lawyer does not arise from any *right* of the Government, but from *power* entrusted to the Government. When a Government lawyer, with enormous resources at his or her disposal, abuses this power and ignores ethical standards, he or she not only undermines the public trust, but inflicts damage beyond calculation to our system of justice."[4]

During the past decade there has been a great deal of publicity surrounding the use of DNA evidence to exonerate and free from prison wrongly convicted individuals years after their trial.[5] While in most of these cases the wrongful conviction was not due to inappropriate conduct by the prosecutor, overzealous actions by prosecutors and the abandonment of their duty to seek justice has been a factor in a number of such cases.[6] The classic example of this is the pre-DNA era case of *Miller v. Pate*.

---

2. American Bar Association's Standards for Criminal Justice, Standard 3-1.2(c).
3. *Berger v. United States*, 295 U.S. 78, 88 (1935).
4. *In re Doe*, 801 F. Supp. 478, 480 (D.N.M. 1992) emphasis in original.
5. An updated list of cases involving exoneration by DNA evidence is maintained by the Innocence Project, a non-profit legal clinic affiliated with the Benjamin N. Cardozo School of Law at Yeshiva University, at http://www.innocenceproject.org/.
6. *Id.*

Miller v. Pate

386 U.S. 1 (1967)

Lloyd Miller was charged with sexually assaulting and murdering an eight-year-old girl in late 1955. The key piece of evidence at trial was a pair of men's undershorts covered with "large, reddish brown stains" that were found close to the crime scene. Prior to trial Miller filed a motion to have his own experts scientifically examine the shorts. The prosecution objected to the motion and it was denied.

At trial the state's expert witness, a chemist from the Illinois Bureau of Crime Identification testified regarding the shorts. He stated unequivocally that the stain found on the shorts was "type A" human blood. It was further established that Miller had Type O blood and the victim's blood was Type A. During closing argument the prosecutor repeatedly referred to the shorts and testimony regarding them being stained with the same blood type as the victim. Miller was found guilty and sentenced to death.

Nearly a decade after he was convicted and sentenced to death, the Northern Illinois District Court, as part of a habeas corpus proceeding, granted Miller's request to have the shorts examined by his own experts. These new tests found that the stain on the shorts was in fact not blood, but rather paint. Further investigation showed that the prosecutor knew the stain on the shorts was paint and that he intentionally misled the court and jury to believe that it was human blood. The District Court granted Miller's habeas petition and ordered he be released from prison or granted a prompt retrial. The 7th Circuit Court of Appeals reversed, ruling that the discovery that the shorts were not stained with blood, or the prosecutor's intentional use of perjured testimony, were insufficient to overcome the jury's verdict of guilt.

The United States Supreme Court reversed the Court of Appeals decision. In a very short, terse, and unanimous opinion Justice Stewart stated that the Constitution cannot tolerate a "criminal conviction obtained by the knowing use of false testimony." With that simple statement the Court made clear that if the prosecutor abdicates his or her role to seek the truth and obtains a conviction based on known falsehoods, in spite of other evidence that might indicate guilt, such a conviction will be vacated. After spending 11 years on death row, and coming within eight hours of being put to death, Lloyd Miller was released from prison in 1967.[7]

The knowing use of perjured testimony is obviously contrary to the prosecutor's duty to seek justice. A much more difficult question involves what evidence in his or her possession a prosecutor must turn over to a defendant. In *Brady v. Maryland*[8] the Supreme Court held that the prosecution has an obligation to disclose to the defense evidence requested that is "favorable to [the] accused" (**exculpatory evidence**) and "material to either guilt or punishment." Subsequent cases established that the prosecution must turn over material exculpatory evidence regardless of a specific request from the defense. This requirement is founded on the prosecution's duty to seek justice rather than obtain a conviction at any cost.

---

7. For an excellent account of Lloyd Miller's saga see Radelet, M., H. Bedau, and C. Putnam (1992) *In Spite of Innocence*. Boston: Northeastern University Press.

8. 373 U.S. 83 (1963).

Despite the apparent clarity of the requirements under *Brady*, issues involving the obligation to disclose exculpatory evidence are not uncommon. Questions such as who should determine the exculpatory nature or materiality of evidence, must evidence in the possession of the police and not the prosecutor be disclosed, and does evidence not intended to be used by the prosecution at trial need to be disclosed have caused sharp divisions among the Supreme Court Justices. In *Kyles v. Whitley*, the Supreme Court considered these and related issues.

Kyles v. Whitley

514 U.S. 419 (1995)

On September 20, 1984, a sixty-year-old woman was murdered as she was putting her groceries in the trunk of her car in a grocery store parking lot. After shooting the victim in the head, the assailant took her keys and drove off in her red LTD. The police investigating the murder obtained statements from six eyewitnesses, which were inconsistent with each other as to the gunman's hair, height, and body type. The police also traced the license plates of the cars in the parking lot at the time of the murder to find suspects, although none of the plates were registered to Kyles.

The investigation was stalled until two days after the killing when police were contacted by man known as "Beanie." Over the next several days Beanie provided the police with several statements implicating Curtis Kyles. While each statement implicated Kyles, each statement also contradicted others on a number of factual elements. Additionally, following his first statements to the police, but before Kyles was arrested, Beanie visited Kyles' apartment several times. Two days after Beanie's initial statement to the police Kyles was arrested in his apartment. A search of the apartment uncovered the murder weapon and other items taken from the victim. None of the items found in Kyles' home had his fingerprints. After his arrest three of the eyewitnesses identified Kyles as the killer. Kyles was subsequently indicted and put on trial for capital murder.

Prior to trial, Kyles' lawyer filed a discovery motion asking for all exculpatory and impeachment evidence as required under *Brady*. Despite the fact that the police had taken numerous written and recorded statements from Beanie which contradicted one another, evidence that Beanie was a suspect in other robberies, and the reports containing the varied descriptions of the murderer provided by the six eyewitnesses, the prosecution responded that there was no exculpatory evidence.

At trial Kyles argued that he was framed by Beanie. Beanie was not called to testify, the prosecution instead relying on the eyewitnesses and evidence found in Kyles' apartment. The trial ended with a deadlocked jury. After the trial Beanie again met with prosecutors and provided additional and contradictory information against Kyles. At a second trial this new information was used by the prosecution. Once again Beanie, who was accused of framing Kyles, did not testify. Kyles was found guilty and sentenced to death.

During collateral proceedings several years after the trial, Kyles became aware of exculpatory evidence in the possession of the government which had never been disclosed to the defense. This evidence consisted of the eyewitness statements taken by the police, Beanie's recorded and written statements, and a computer print-out of the license plate numbers of the cars parked in the parking lot where the murder occurred in which Kyles' car was not listed. Kyles argued that the failure of the prosecution to disclose these items denied him due process. This argument was rejected by the District Court and Circuit Court of Appeals.

In a five to four decision, the Supreme Court reversed Kyles' conviction and ordered a new trial. The key question was whether or not the undisclosed exculpatory evidence was **material**. Justice Souter, writing for the majority, wrote that exculpatory evidence is material if "there is a reasonable probability that, had the evidence been disclosed to the defense, the result of the proceeding would have been different." The Court set forth several key aspects regarding the consideration of materiality that bear special emphasis.

1) There does not need to be proof by a preponderance of the evidence that the undisclosed evidence would have resulted in an acquittal, only that there is a "reasonable probability" that the defendant might have been acquitted.
2) The test for materiality does not call for weighing the sufficiency of the evidence. Instead, a court should consider whether the "favorable evidence, taken as a whole, could reasonably be taken to put the whole case in such a different light as to undermine confidence in the verdict."
3) The undisclosed evidence should be considered collectively and not item by item.

Using these precepts, the Court held that the undisclosed evidence was material and the nondisclosure was unconstitutional. Beanie provided the key information that led to Kyles' arrest. The fact that the defense was based on a claim that Beanie framed Kyles, evidence that points to that possibility, combined with the discrepancies in the eyewitness descriptions of the killer, were found by the Court to be sufficient to cause distrust in the jury's verdict.

Importantly, the Court also held that the prosecutor is responsible for disclosing material, exculpatory evidence that is in the possession of the police, even if the prosecution is not aware of its existence. It is the prosecutor's duty to be aware of such evidence. To rule otherwise would encourage police to keep evidence hidden from the prosecution and therefore a defendant.

In dissent Justice Scalia argued that the materiality of each piece of exculpatory evidence that was not disclosed should be considered independently of one another. In doing this, it is clear that no piece of undisclosed evidence rises to the level of materiality, and the conviction and sentence should remain in place.

Note that the key to the decisions on *Kyles* is how evidence is determined to be material. The Court concluded that the prosecution is given the responsibility and authority to make an initial determination of materiality. If there is any doubt in the prosecutor's mind, it would be prudent to present the evidence to the judge *in camera* (without disclosure to the defense) and let the court make the determination.

Prosecutorial Discretion and the Charging Decision

The most important function performed by prosecutors is deciding which cases brought to them by police should be prosecuted and which should not. As part of the executive branch of government, whose duty is to enforce the laws of a jurisdiction, the prosecutor is as much a law enforcement officer as a judicial officer. Once a person is arrested by the police, it is the prosecutor's duty to determine whether to formally prosecute that individual's case. In making these decisions, the prosecutor has broad, nearly limitless discretion. This led Supreme Court Justice Robert Jackson to remark that the prosecutor has "more control over life, liberty, and reputation than any other person in America.[9]

Research has consistently found that in the United States between one-third and one-half of arrests are not formally prosecuted. The Supreme Court has repeatedly held that it is generally not for the judiciary to evaluate how and why these decisions are made. How laws are enforced is a matter for the executive branch of government; not the judiciary. While the prosecutor's discretion over which cases to prosecute is immense, it is not limitless. Three motives which are not permitted to be a basis of the decision to prosecute an individual are vindictiveness against a person, or targeting based on personal characteristics such as race, gender, religion, or the exercise of a constitutional right, such as free speech. The next two cases look at how the court examines whether a prosecutor has conducted an unconstitutional selective and vindictive prosecution.

Wayte v. United States

470 U.S. 598 (1985)

In 1980, President Jimmy Carter signed a Presidential Proclamation requiring all males born in 1960 to register with the Selective Service System. Rather than registering as required, David Wayte sent letters to numerous government officials informing them that he refused to register. At the time the Selective Service operated primarily under a policy of "passive enforcement" under which they investigated and prosecuted only individuals who disclosed their intent not to register and actually failed to register. If after being warned of potential criminal prosecution for failing to register, steps to enforce the law would be taken. Wayte and other individuals who disclosed their intent not to register were referred to the FBI and local US Attorneys offices. Pursuant to this procedure, Wayte was indicted for intentionally failing to register with the selective service. Wayte moved to dismiss the indictment on the grounds that he was being selectively prosecuted for exercising his First Amendment right to free speech by voicing his intent not to register.

The United States Supreme Court rejected Wayte's selective prosecution argument. The Court noted that so long as there is probable cause to believe a person committed a crime, the decision of whether or not to prosecute "generally rests entirely in the [prosecutor's] discretion." As the representative of the executive branch charged with enforcing the criminal laws, the prosecutor is in the best position to consider factors such as resource allocation, deterrence value, and the strength of the case against an individual

9. Robert Jackson, "The Federal Prosecutor," 24 *Journal of the American Judicature Society* 18 (1940).

when determining whether or not to pursue a prosecution against an individual. The judiciary is in no position to undertake such an analysis.

That being said, prosecutorial discretion in charging decisions is not limitless and is subject to constitutional constraints. Specifically, the decision to prosecute may not be "based upon an unjustifiable standard such as race, religion or other arbitrary classification, including the exercise of protected statutory and constitutional rights." Claims of selective prosecution are judged using equal protection standards. To prevail, Wayte was required to show that the government's passive enforcement policy (1) had a discriminatory effect, and (2) was motivated by a discriminatory purpose.

The Court found that he failed to prove either. While some people who informed the government that they would not register with the selective service were prosecuted, a number of them did not face prosecution. Moreover, the prosecution was not based on the exercise of free speech given the fact that individuals who disclosed that they would not register but later decided to do so were not criminally charged. It is the act of not registering, regardless of the exercise of one's freedom of speech that leads to a prosecution. This is further evidenced by the many prosecutions of non-registrants who did not explicitly protest the registration requirement.

The Court also held that there was no evidence that charging decisions were made with discriminatory intent. To establish such intent, Wayte would have to show the decision was made because it would adversely affect vocal protesters, not merely in spite of such an effect.

Claims of **selective prosecution** are very difficult to prove. Under the standard stated by the Court it is not enough that a person can show that he or she merely appears to have been singled out for prosecution based on race, religion, or the exercise of a right. The person must show that the impermissible criterion was the actual reason for the prosecution. In other words, a defendant must prove the subjective intent of the prosecutor. Such evidence is nearly impossible to obtain, making the standard nearly impossible to meet.

Vindictive prosecution is a prosecution to deter or punish the exercise of a protected statutory or constitutional right. [10] Claims of vindictive prosecution most often center around plea bargaining. During plea negotiations the prosecution, in an effort to induce a defendant to accept a reduced sentence in return for a plea of guilty, will frequently threaten to pursue the greatest number of charges possible and seek the longest sentence permissible if the defendant refuses to enter into a plea agreement. As we'll see in *Bordenkircher v. Hayes*, where the defendant, charged with writing a bad check with two prior convictions, was offered a sentence of five years in prison if he plead guilty, or a life sentence if convicted at trial, prosecutors have enormous bargaining power and leverage in pursuing favorable plea bargains. In *Hayes* the Court examined whether this use of prosecutorial discretion violated the defendant's right to due process.

---

10. *United States v. Goodwin*, 457 U.S. 368 (1982).

Bordenkircher v. Hayes

434 U.S. 357 (1978)

Paul Hayes was charged with passing a bad check in the amount of $88.30 which was punishable by a term of 2 to 10 years in prison. Mr. Hayes, however, had two prior felony convictions. Under Kentucky's Habitual Criminal Act, a person convicted of a third felony faced a mandatory life sentence. During plea discussions, the prosecutor told Hayes that if he pleaded guilty as charged, the prosecutor would recommend a five-year sentence, but that if the case went to trial, Hayes would be reindicted under that Habitual Criminal Act and face a sentence of life imprisonment if convicted at trial. Hayes refused to plead guilty, was reindicted, convicted at trial, and sentenced to life.

The Supreme Court stated that while the actions of prosecutors as part of the plea negotiation process may appear vindictive to a defendant, as long as the defendant is made aware of the terms of the negotiations throughout the process, due process has not been violated. The Court acknowledged that such an outcome is necessitated in part by pervasiveness of plea bargaining in the criminal justice system. Rather than acting in a vindictive manner in reindicting Hayes and obtaining a life sentence, the Court found that the prosecutor was merely doing what the law permitted him to. In fact, the offer of 5 years in prison instead of insisting on full prosecution under the recidivist statute could be viewed as an act of mercy by the prosecution which Hayes had no right to expect. Hayes knowingly and intelligently rejected receipt of the plea bargain with full understanding of the risk he faced. As long as the reindictment was part of open plea negotiations and not based on a discriminatory intent, it was not impermissibly vindictive.

Threats of and actual reindictment are commonly used by prosecutors as inducements to convince defendants to enter into plea agreements. Do you think it is fair for prosecutors to be able use such extreme leverage to obtain guilty pleas? What are the pros and cons of the practice?

This power and control over charging decisions and plea bargaining practices have been built into the criminal court system. Items such as mandatory sentencing, three strikes and you're out laws, and determinate sentencing schemes, often place individuals charged with serious crimes in the position of choosing between giving up the right to a jury trial in exchange for a non-draconian sentence, or demanding a jury trial at the risk of a very long prison term. As we will see in the following section, this has important ramifications for the job performed by criminal defense attorneys.

Defense Attorneys

The Sixth Amendment to the Constitution provides, "In all criminal prosecutions, the accused shall enjoy the right ... to have the Assistance of Counsel for his defense." While this simple statement seems to be self-defining, when put into practice it has given rise to a number of complex issues. In this section we will examine when does a person actually have a right to counsel, what level of expertise and effectiveness is included in the right to counsel, and what is counsel's duty to his/her client as opposed to his/her duty to the criminal justice and legal systems.

Right to Counsel

In 1963, the Supreme Court held that the right to counsel under the Sixth Amendment is a fundamental right, and therefore applicable to the states under the Fourteenth Amendment.[11] As famously stated by Justice Black in the case of *Gideon v. Wainwright*, "... in our adversary system of criminal justice, any person haled into court, who is too poor to hire a lawyer, cannot be assured a fair trial unless counsel is provided for him. This seems to us to be an obvious truth."[12] Read literally, this right could apply equally to a person charged with murder and a person charged with jaywalking. On the other hand, since Gideon was charged with a felony, one could argue that the right to counsel applied only in cases involving felonies. Not surprisingly, states did not take the Court and Sixth Amendment literally, and instances when counsel was provided for non-felony prosecutions varied greatly. It wasn't until 1972, nine years after *Gideon* was decided, that the Court clarified under what circumstances indigent defendants charged with misdemeanors had a right to counsel.

Argersinger v. Hamlin

407 U.S. 25 (1972)

Jon Argersinger, an **indigent** (person without any financial means), was charged with carrying a concealed weapon, a misdemeanor punishable by imprisonment up to six months, a $1,000 fine, or both. Despite his request for an attorney, he was not provided with counsel. Argersinger was found guilty by a judge at a non-jury trial. He was sentenced to serve 90 days in jail. Argersinger brought a *habeas corpus* action in the Florida Supreme Court, alleging that, being deprived of his right to counsel, he was unable as an indigent layman to properly raise and present to the trial court adequate defenses to the charge he faced. The Florida Supreme Court refused to provide relief, holding that a defendant has a right to counsel only if he is facing a potential period of incarceration longer than six months.

The Supreme Court reversed in an opinion written by Justice Douglas. The Court noted the critical role counsel plays in providing a defendant with a fair trial regardless of the seriousness of the charges being faced. Given the large number of misdemeanants prosecuted in local courts, the potential that indigent defendants in those courts face assembly line justice is real. This same large number of cases would make a requirement that all misdemeanants be provided with counsel daunting if not unfeasible.

Facing these realities the Court struck a balance, holding that absent a knowing and intelligent waiver, no person may be imprisoned for any offense unless he was represented by counsel at his trial. This requirement will only affect cases where imprisonment is sought, a fraction of all misdemeanor prosecutions. "But in those [cases] that

11. *Gideon v. Wainwright*, 372 U.S. 335 (1963).
12. *Id.* at 344.

end up in the actual deprivation of a person's liberty, the accused will receive the benefit of 'the guiding hand of counsel' so necessary when one's liberty is in jeopardy."[13]

As Argersinger was convicted and sentenced to jail without being appointed counsel, his conviction and sentence were vacated.

While the Supreme Court was unanimous in the finding that Argersinger's rights had been violated, several justices disagreed with the standard set forth in the majority opinion. The primary concern was that the criminal justice system would be overwhelmed with the new requirement for the appointment of counsel in thousands of new cases. These concerns have not come to fruition. As it tends to do, the criminal justice system adapted to this new requirement with minimal problems. A more difficult and persistent problem has been the ability of the system to provide and evaluate effective assistance of counsel.

Effective Assistance of Counsel

In the 1932 case of *Powell v. Alabama*,[14] the United States Supreme Court held that a person who has a right to counsel has a right to **effective assistance** of counsel. What actually constituted effective (or ineffective) assistance of counsel was not clarified by the Court until 1984. Prior to that time most federal and state courts adopted the *mockery of justice* standard. Under this standard, only representation that was so shockingly poor as to render the trial a farce would be considered ineffective. The problem with this standard was that it was completely subjective and difficult to evaluate.

The Supreme Court took up the issue of what standard should be used in evaluating ineffectiveness of counsel claims in *Strickland v. Washington*. As you read this case, consider if the new standard is an improvement over the mockery of justice standard.

Strickland v. Washington

466 U.S. 668 (1984)

Over a 10-day period in 1976, David Washington went on a crime spree in which he committed three murders, and several acts of kidnaping, torture, attempted murder, and theft. Following his arrest Washington gave a detailed confession to the police. Washington was appointed an experienced criminal defense attorney to represent him. Against his attorney's advice, Washington plead guilty to all of the charges, including three counts of capital murder. During the plea hearing, Washington told the judge he committed the crimes because he was under stress and accepted responsibility for his actions. Again acting against counsel's advice, he waived his right to an advisory jury for his sentencing hearing, leaving the decision to the judge.

In preparation for the sentencing hearing, defense counsel did not seek out character witnesses, request a presentence report, or request Washington be examined by a psychiatrist. The decision not to present evidence about Washington's character and

13. *Argersinger v. Hamlin*, 407 U.S. 25, 40 (1972)
14. 287 U.S. 45 (1932)

emotional state reflected his attorney's opinion that it would be better to rely on the prior statements made at the plea hearing as evidence regarding Washington's background and mental state, thus preventing the State from cross-examining Washington and from presenting psychiatric evidence of its own. At the sentencing hearing, Washington's attorney chose not to present any evidence regarding Washington's character and emotional state. At the hearing the trial judge found numerous aggravating circumstances related to the crime spree and no mitigating circumstance. Washington was sentenced to death.

After his direct appeals were unsuccessful, Washington sought collateral relief on the grounds that he was provided with ineffective assistance of counsel during the sentencing proceeding. After an evidentiary hearing the federal district court denied his petition for *habeas corpus*, however the Circuit Court of Appeals reversed and granted relief. The U.S. Supreme Court reversed, ruling that he was not denied effective assistance of counsel.

Writing for a seven-member majority, Justice O'Connor noted that the benchmark for judging a claim of ineffectiveness is whether counsel's conduct so undermined the proper functioning of the adversarial process that the trial cannot be relied on as having produced a just result. In examining if this standard was met, the Court set forth a two-pronged test. Under this test counsel will be found to have been ineffective if it can be shown that (a) the attorney's performance was deficient and (b) the deficient performance prejudiced the defendant.

In considering the deficient performance prong, the Court held that a court must consider whether counsel's performance was reasonable. Specifically the court should consider "whether, in light of all the circumstances, the identified acts or omissions were outside the wide range of professionally competent assistance." The majority went on to hold that "counsel is strongly presumed to have rendered adequate assistance and made all significant decisions in the exercise of reasonable professional judgment." Importantly, decisions made by the attorney concerning strategy will not be second guessed in hindsight.

If it is determined that counsel's performance was below acceptable standards, a claim of ineffective assistance of counsel will not succeed unless it is also shown that counsel's ineffectiveness prejudiced the defendant. This requires proof that there is a reasonable probability that, except for counsel's unprofessional errors, the result of the proceeding would have been different.

In applying this standard to the facts before it, the Court held that counsel's performance was not deficient. Faced with a difficult situation, David Washington's attorney made a reasonable strategic choice on how to handle the sentencing hearing. Moreover, given the nature of the crimes, the confession, and the large number of aggravating factors found by the trial judge, any error that may have been made by counsel would not have been prejudicial. There simply was no "reasonable probability" that had counsel presented mitigating evidence at the sentencing hearing the outcome would have been different.

The two-pronged standard laid out by the Court in *Strickland* has proven very difficult to meet. In particular, the prejudice prong of the test is difficult to pass. In most criminal trials, there is extensive evidence against the accused. In reviewing potential prejudice to a defendant caused by an attorney's ineffectiveness, a court will consider if a competent attorney would have made a difference in the outcome. In most cases, courts have found the result would have been the same and have denied relief. There is a class of cases, however, for which prejudice need not be shown.

On the same day the Court issued its opinion in *Strickland*, it laid out an exception to the requirement that prejudice be proven. In *United States v. Cronic* the Court ruled that when a defendant is "denied counsel at a critical stage of his trial" or where "counsel entirely fails to subject the prosecution's case to a meaningful adversarial testing," prejudice to the defendant will be presumed.[15] In reality, such cases are very rare.

Right to Counsel of One's Choice

The vast majority of defendants in the criminal justice system are indigent. As they cannot afford to hire an attorney, the government is required to provide one. As such, regardless of whether the defendant and the attorney like or trust each other, the experience level of the attorney, or the lawyer's reputation for effectiveness in prior cases, a defendant has no right to choose who he/she wants as counsel. The Constitution guarantees that an indigent defendant must be provided with effective counsel, not great or preferred counsel.

What if a defendant has the money to hire an attorney? What limits can the government or court place on an attorney which a defendant wants to hire with his or her own funds? If a defendant is prevented from being represented by counsel of his or her choice, has the right to counsel been violated? Those questions were answered in *United States v. Gonzalez-Lopez.*

U.S. v. Gonzalez-Lopez

126 S. Ct. 2557 (2006)

Cuauhtemoc Gonzalez-Lopez (respondent) was arrested in Missouri and charged with conspiracy to distribute more than 100 kilograms of marijuana. The respondent's family hired attorney John Fahle to be Gonzalez-Lopez's lawyer. Gonzalez-Lopez himself hired Joseph Low, an attorney from California who had recently prevailed in a well-publicized drug sale case not dissimilar to the case against Gonzalez-Lopez. At an evidentiary hearing shortly after arraignment, respondent was represented by both attorneys. At the hearing attorney Low broke the court's rules by passing notes to attorney Fahle. Shortly thereafter, respondent fired Fahle and stated he wanted Low to be his only attorney. Due to Low's rule violations and alleged unethical conduct in unrelated cases, the trial court rejected this hot shot California attorney's petition to practice law in Missouri (limited to this case). This had the practical effect of preventing Low from appearing in court to represent Gonzalez-Lopez. The trial judge went so far as to deny respondent's new counsel's request to have Low sit at counsel table during the trial, requiring him to sit in the gallery and have no contact with respondent or his attorney during the trial. The trial proceeded without Low, and Gonzalez-Lopez was convicted.

15. *United States v. Cronic*, 466 U.S. 648, 659 (1984)

After several post-conviction hearings and appeals, the case was heard by the Supreme Court regarding the issue of whether Gonzalez-Lopez's Sixth Amendment right to counsel was violated by the trial judge's refusal to allow him to hire an attorney of his own choosing. Two critical issues were stipulated to by the parties by the time the appeal had reached the Supreme Court. First, it was agreed to that the district court judge had committed error in denying Low's application to appear for the defendant. Secondly, it was agreed that Gonzalez-Lopez received a fair trial. Everyone agreed that the lawyer who represented Gonzalez-Lopez did not commit significant errors nor did he provide ineffective assistance of counsel.

With these stipulations in place, the Court was faced with the issue of whether denying a defendant the counsel of his choice (this does not involve indigent defendants) constitutes a reversible error absent a showing of ineffectiveness or harm to the defendant. Justice Scalia, writing for a five-member majority, held that denying a non-indigent defendant counsel of his choice violates the Sixth Amendment right to counsel, a fundamental right regardless of whether or not a fair trial took place. The Court held that depriving a person the counsel of his or her choice affects the entire context in which the trial is held making it a structural error rather than simply a procedural error. Justice Scalia stated that the Sixth Amendment right to counsel of choice requires "not that a trial be fair, but that a particular guarantee of fairness be provided —to wit, that the accused be defended by the counsel he believes to be best." Furthermore, the Court noted that the right at stake was the right to counsel of choice, ***not*** the right to a fair trial, and that right was violated because deprivation of counsel was erroneous. As such, no additional showing of prejudice was required to make the violation "complete."

The majority opinion repeatedly emphasized that it is important to remember that indigent defendants with court-appointed counsel are not affected by the Court's holding: it only applies to cases where a defendant can afford to hire private counsel. The Court made a point to emphasize there is no right to counsel of choice for defendants who require appointed counsel.

Four justices dissented. Justice Alito, writing for the dissenters, did not believe that a criminal conviction must automatically be reversed whenever a trial court errs in not permitting a defendant from being represented at trial by the his first-choice attorney. "Instead, a defendant should be required to make at least *some* showing that the trial court's erroneous ruling adversely affected the quality of assistance that the defendant received." The dissent argued that it made no sense to ignore the quality of the representation actually provided the defendant before deciding that his or her rights were violated.

Note that no one argued that Gonzalez-Lopez was denied effective assistance of counsel or that he did not receive a fair trial. Rather, once Low was not permitted to represent Gonzalez-Lopez, the constitutional violation was complete and reversal was mandated under the view of the majority. This would be the case even if the defendant were represented by the best attorney in the country but was denied the right to be represented by his nephew just out of law school. Justice Scalia would respond that there are intangible qualities possessed by individuals and the attorney-client relationship that can't and shouldn't be quantified.

Counsel's Duty to the Client

An attorney has a duty to provide zealous representation for his or her client. This includes adequately investigating matters relevant to the case, pursuing a favorable disposition (plea bargain) prior to trial, zealously presenting the defendant's case and cross-examining prosecution witnesses at trial, and most of all, ensuring that the defendant's rights are protected. Additionally, an attorney has an obligation to maintain confidentiality of communications with a client.

While a defense attorney owes these (and other duties) to his or her client, a lawyer also has an obligation to be honest and candid with the court. An attorney cannot lie or misrepresent facts to the court or knowingly allow the admission of perjured testimony in a trial. These limitations apply even when requested or demanded by a client.

In *Nix v. Whiteside*, the Supreme Court was called on to consider what an attorney should do if a he or she knows the client intends to commit perjury at his murder trial.

Nix v. Whiteside

475 U.S. 157 (1986)

On February 8, 1977, in Cedar Rapids, Iowa, Emmanuel Whiteside and two companions were at the apartment of Calvin Love. An argument over a drug deal took place. At one point Love said to his girlfriend, "Honey get my piece." Whiteside, believing Love was going to kill him, stabbed Love to death. Whiteside was arrested and charged with first degree murder.

Gary Robinson was appointed to represent Whiteside at trial. During several meetings prior to trial, Whiteside consistently told attorney Robinson, that, although he had not actually seen a gun, he was convinced that Love had a gun in his hand because of the circumstances of the fight and Love's reputation for carrying weapons. In fact, no gun was found in the apartment and none of the other witnesses to the stabbing saw a gun.

A week before his trial, Whiteside changed his story, telling his attorneys that he had seen something metallic in Love's hand. When Robinson questioned him about this new story, Whitehead explained, "If I don't say I saw a gun, I'm dead." Robinson warned Whiteside that if he so testified about seeing a metallic object he would advise the court of his proposed perjury, withdraw from the case, and testify against him. At trial Whiteside testified truthfully, stating that he "knew" Love had a gun but that he had not actually seen a gun in his hand. Whiteside was convicted of second degree murder and sentenced to forty years in prison.

After his conviction was affirmed on appeal, Whiteside filed a writ of *habeas corpus* in the United States District Court for the Southern District of Iowa, alleging denial of due process and ineffective assistance of counsel. The district court denied the writ. On appeal, however, the Eighth Circuit Court of Appeals reversed. The court ruled that while a criminal defendant's right to testify does not include a right to commit perjury, Robinson's warning that he would inform the court of the planned perjury constituted a threat to violate an attorney's duty to preserve confidentiality and therefore violated the standards of effective representation as stated in *Strickland* v. *Washington*.

The Supreme Court thought otherwise and reversed. The Court unanimously held that Robinson's actions fell "well within accepted standards of professional conduct ... under *Strickland*." The Court went on to state that whatever right a defendant may have to testify in his own defense, this does not include the right to commit perjury.

While all nine justices agreed that Whiteside's rights were not violated, and also agreed that defense counsel should do all that he/she can to dissuade a client from committing perjury, only five justices joined in the majority's suggestions for dealing with potential client perjury. Chief Justice Burger wrote that an attorney faced with such a situation must reveal his client's conduct to the court, and if necessary, withdraw his representation. Under no circumstances should the lawyer permit or assist his client in giving false testimony. According to the majority, "No system of justice worthy of the name can tolerate a lesser standard."

Defense attorneys are often faced with differences of opinion with their clients. While the client has the right to make major, fundamental decisions regarding how to proceed with a case (plead guilty, testify), matters of strategy are left to the attorney. Moreover, an attorney has an overriding obligation to protect the integrity of the justice system. Though criminal defense lawyers must do all within their power to obtain favorable outcomes for their clients, lawyers must do so within the rules of the court and ethical standards laid out by state bar associations.

Judges

Duty to Promote a Just Trial

While the prosecutor is the catalyst of the criminal court system, and the criminal defense attorney is the most publicized in the popular press, the judge is the symbolic focal point. The overarching responsibility of a trial court judge is to ensure justice. This responsibility goes beyond presiding over the proceedings and ruling on matters of law. As summed up in the American Bar Association's Standards for Criminal Justice:

> The trial judge has the responsibility for safeguarding both the rights of the accused and the interests of the public in the administration of criminal justice. The adversary nature of the proceedings does not relieve the trial judge of the obligation of raising on his or her initiative, at all appropriate times and in an appropriate manner, matters which may significantly promote a just determination of the trial.[16]

The judge has the responsibility to take the initiative to ensure that all parties appearing in court are treated fairly and equally. The importance of this duty goes far beyond the interests of the prosecution and defendant. Maintaining the dignity of the proceedings

16. American Bar Association Standards for Criminal Justice, Standard 6-1.1.

and the appearance of fairness, the judge conveys to the general public the trustworthiness and legitimacy of the court. This responsibility and the failure of a judge to take the necessary steps needed to ensure a fair trial were at the heart of the Supreme Court's decision in *Sheppard v. Maxwell.*

Sheppard v. Maxwell

384 U.S. 333 (1966)

On July 4, 1954, Dr. Sam Sheppard, a prominent member of Cleveland society, called the police to report that his pregnant wife had been beaten to death in their home. Sheppard told police that he fought off and chased the assailant but was knocked unconscious and could not identify the attacker. From the outset the police and media suspected Sheppard of killing his wife. In the days following the murder, newspapers editorialized about Sheppard's guilt, reported that he was not cooperating with the police investigation including his refusal to take a lie detector test, and published evidence provided them by the police that was never used at trial. The coroner's inquest into the cause of death lasted three days, was held in a gymnasium, was conducted in front of hundreds of spectators, and was broadcast live on television and radio. After repeated calls for his arrest, Sheppard was taken into custody by local police on July 30 and charged with the murder of his wife.

The trial itself was a media circus. Prior to the trial the media published the names and addresses of all the prospective jurors. During the trial the media dominated the courtroom. In addition to assigning nearly all of the available seats in the courtroom to the media, the trial judge had an extra table placed behind the defendant for an additional twenty members of the media to sit. Photographers were permitted to take pictures of jurors during the trial; the jury even posed for newspaper photographers while on a lunch break during deliberations. Special telephone and telegraph equipment was installed in all of the rooms on the floor where the trial was held and made available to the media. Radio station WSRS was allowed to broadcast from a room adjacent to the jury room while the jury took recesses and deliberated. Despite the potential problems with disruption to the courtroom, the repeated inflammatory headlines and articles in the media regarding Sheppard's guilt, and the effect the atmosphere and media coverage was having on the jury, the trial judge took no steps to limit press access to the trial and jurors' access to media reports on the trial. After several months of testimony, Sheppard was found guilty of murder and sentenced to life in prison.

Sheppard's direct appeals were unsuccessful. Several years after his conviction, the Supreme Court, acting on habeas corpus review, vacated the conviction on the grounds that the massive pretrial publicity and carnival atmosphere denied him his right to a fair trial. The Court repeatedly chided the trial court judge for losing control of his courtroom. The Court stated that the trial judge should have taken whatever steps were necessary to isolate the jury from prejudicial material and outside influences, and prevent the court from taking on a "carnival atmosphere." The Court further criticized the trial judge for failing to "control the release of leads, information and gossip to the press by police officers, witnesses, and the counsel for both sides."

The Court noted that there were a number of remedial actions the judge could have taken to prevent the situation from getting out of control. These measures included placing gag orders on the trial participants, limiting media access to the courtroom to normal spectator confines, prohibiting media broadcasts from within the courthouse, protecting the privacy and identity of jurors, investigating whether jurors were exposed to and influenced by the media coverage, moving the trial to another county, sequestering the jury, and postponing the trial until the furor died down. As the trial court took none of these steps, and the defendant was prejudiced as a result, the Court ruled it had no choice but to vacate the conviction.

In November of 1966 Sam Sheppard was retried for the murder of his wife. Following sixteen days of testimony, a jury found him not guilty. The case against Sam Sheppard has grown in notoriety since the 1954 trial. The saga of the Sheppards inspired the television show and movie *The Fugitive*, which involved a respected doctor, his murdered wife, and an alleged intruder in their suburban home. For an excellent depiction of the Sheppard case see the book *Mockery of Justice: The True Story of the Sheppard Murder Case* ,[17] which was coauthored by Sam Sheppard's son.

Duty to Remain Neutral and Detached

A key component of maintaining public trust in the criminal court system is the ability of judges not only to serve as neutral and detached arbiters of the law but also to avoid the appearance of bias and impropriety. The American Bar Association's Standards for Criminal Justice describe this duty thusly:

> (a) The trial judge should avoid impropriety and the appearance of impropriety in all activities, and should conduct himself or herself at all times in a manner that promotes public confidence in the integrity and impartiality of the judiciary. The judge should not allow family, social, political or other relationships to influence judicial conduct or judgment.
>
> ...
>
> (e) A judge should not be influenced by actual or anticipated public criticism in his or her actions, rulings, or decisions.[18]

A judge who believes that he or she is biased for or against a party in a case has a duty to consider whether hearing further matters in the case would be appropriate. The act of a judge voluntarily removing himself or herself from hearing a particular case because of bias; conflict of interest; relation to a party, attorney, or witness; or for any other reason is known **recusal**. Standard 6-1.9(a) of the American Bar Association's Standards for Criminal Justice states that, "The trial judge should recuse himself or herself whenever the judge has any doubt as to his or her ability to preside impartially or whenever his or her impartiality reasonably might be questioned." Instances where a judge is related to, a business associate of, or a close friend with a party or attorney in

17. Cooper, C.L. and S.R. Sheppard (1995). *Mockery of Justice: The True Story of the Sheppard Murder Case*, Boston: Northeastern University Press.

18. American Bar Association's Standards for Criminal Justice, Standard 6-1.6.

the case are readily identifiable and cause little controversy. An area that has become very controversial is whether a judge should sit on a case where a party or attorney has helped the judge get elected to the bench.

Trial court judges in a majority of states are selected by popular election. These elections frequently require extensive campaigning as well the need to raise thousands of dollars in campaign contributions. In most states the vast majority of contributions to trial court judges are from attorneys, often attorneys who routinely appear before the judge. This fact is not only acknowledged but also encouraged by practically every appellate court that has considered the matter. The basis for this encouragement is that attorneys who appear before a judge are in an excellent position to evaluate the judge's performance on the bench. If the judge is doing a good job, it is only appropriate for a civic-minded attorney to help the judge be reelected. While this may well be true, it can create the appearance of impropriety when an attorney who contributed to a judge's reelection campaign, or even worked on the campaign, appears before the judge in court. This may even be exacerbated if the opposing attorney or party contributed to the unsuccessful candidate who opposed the judge now hearing his or her case.

The actual effect campaign contributions have on individual judges is difficult, if not impossible, to measure with any certainty. The perceived effect, however, has been measured and is somewhat troubling.

In 2001, *Justice at Stake*, a non-partisan partnership whose stated mission is to educate the public and work for reforms to insulate the judiciary from politics and special interests, commissioned a national survey to measure the perceived effect campaign contributions have on judicial behavior.[19] One thousand registered voters and 2,428 state court judges were asked "How much influence do you think campaign contributions made to judges have on their decisions?" The results, presented in Table 5-1, were startling.

Table 5-1

How Much Influence Do You Think Campaign Contributions Made to Judges Have on Their Decisions?

	Public	Judges
A Great Deal of Influence	36%	4%
Some Influence	40%	22%
Just a Little Influence	14%	20%
No Influence	5%	36%
Don't Know/Refused	5%	18%

Nine out of ten of the registered voters who answered the question felt campaign contributions had at least a little influence on judges. What is truly shocking is that nearly half of the judges also believed campaign contributions influenced judicial decisions. Moreover, only 36% responded that contributions had no influence. While

19. 2001 Greenberg Quinlan Rosner Research Inc. for Justice at Stake.

these results are based on the perception of judges as a group rather than admissions, the fact that judges view campaign contributions as affecting the decision-making of their colleagues is amazing.

Despite what may appear to be an inherent bias in favor of one side over another when a case involves an attorney or party who contributed to the trial judge's campaign, appellate courts have repeatedly held that the fact that a party or attorney contributed money to the judge's election campaign is not grounds requiring the recusal of the judge. Generally, recusal is only required if there are other factors that would make a reasonable person believe a judge cannot be impartial. Almost all courts have ruled that it is mere speculation to assume that a judge will be influenced by a contribution. As attorneys routinely contribute to the reelection campaigns of many judges, and as police officer unions, prosecuting and defense attorney organizations, and many other groups routinely endorse and support judicial candidates, to require recusal of all judges who received contributions or support from individuals or groups associated with a case would likely bring the criminal court system to a standstill. In the end, it is up to an individual to fairly consider if he or she can judge a case impartially.

Conclusion

The operation of the criminal trial court is dependent on the work of well-trained professionals. Though they enter the courtroom with different backgrounds, duties, and goals, they are also able to function as a working unit. In the next chapter we will examine how many of the specific tasks they are called upon to perform actually get done.

Chapter Six

The Law of Bail, Plea Bargaining, and Guilty Pleas

The legal topics to be covered in this chapter—bail, plea bargaining, and guilty pleas—are of intense importance to anyone who has just been arrested. The first thing that most people want more than anything else upon their arrest is to make bail. After making bail, people then move swiftly on to worrying about the ultimate outcome of their case. At that point, plea bargaining inevitably becomes of intense concern to most of them. Once a bargain has been made, professional court actors (lawyers and judges) start worrying about how to properly finalize the deal in court via a defendant's guilty plea. This chapter will cover the law as it relates to the three important topics of bail, plea bargaining, and guilty pleas.

Bail

When a person is arrested he or she is promptly taken before a judge or magistrate (low-level judicial officer) for a brief encounter known as the **first appearance** (sometimes called an initial appearance, preliminary arraignment or magistrate's review). Local rules vary as to how soon such an appearance must occur but the U.S. Supreme Court has ruled that in order to be "prompt" the judicial encounter must occur at least within 48 hours of the arrest.[1] At this first appearance, the judicial officer advises the defendant as to why he or she was arrested, how the defendant may apply for a free lawyer if the defendant so desires, and how much bail must be posted in order to be released pending further court proceedings.

From the point of view of frightened people just arrested, the setting of the bail amount is of extreme importance. Getting released is of utmost concern and occupies all of their thoughts. This human obsession with securing immediate freedom when first arrested is not new. It dates far back in time and was consequently on the minds of those who wrote the American Constitution.

1. *McNabb v. United States*, 318 U.S. 332 (1943).

History and the Legal Right to Bail

Bail has been around for a long time. It dates back at least as far as the ancient Greeks.[2] At one time bail was not just the posting of hostage money but involved an actual hostage.[3] For example, if I wanted to post bail for my cousin, I would have to post myself as the surety. In the event my cousin did not show up for court, the court would seize me and do to me whatever punishment would have befallen my cousin (including execution)!

Bail today has exchanged hostage money for human hostages. Nevertheless, it arguably remains a primitive way of providing for pre-trial release. Yet, what is a better alternative? Our court systems are notoriously slow and clogged up. One of the most serious consequences of the resultant delayed justice is the chance that potentially innocent people might lose their freedom while waiting for a chance to exonerate themselves in court. A person experiencing delayed justice can lose a job or even a career. A college student can miss all of his or her classes. Incarceration can cause one to become socially stigmatized once word gets out of where "so and so is." Jail to some presents a frightening, violence-prone atmosphere. Being incarcerated prior to trial severely handicaps one in preparing a defense. A defendant's family can also suffer while a person sits in jail waiting for his or her day in court, and families have been known to even break up over the stress.

The drafters of the Constitution worried enough about this to not only require that trials be speedily offered but to back up this safeguard by providing for a right to bail prior to trial. The Eighth Amendment to the Constitution, reflecting old English law dating back many centuries,[4] states that "excessive bail shall not be required." The wording of the Eighth Amendment is completely ambiguous regarding a couple of critical points: (1) what is meant by "excessive" bail and (2) is ensuring appearance for trial the only legitimate reason for requiring bail (i.e., do dangerous criminals have to be offered bail just because they are likely to appear for trial)?

Legitimate and Extra-legal Uses of Bail

As noted, in order for bail to be legitimate it cannot be set at an excessive amount. What constitutes an "excessive" amount? The case below grapples with that.

Stack v. Boyle

342 U.S. 1 (1951)

The defendant, along with eleven others, was charged with violating the Smith Act (which prohibited membership or affiliation with organized crime societies). The maximum penalty for this was five years and/or a fine of $10,000. Bail was set at $50,000

---

2. Samaha, Joel. (1994). *Criminal Justice* (3rd ed.). St. Paul: West Publishing Company, at 335.
3. See, *Stack v. Boyle*, 342 U.S. 1 (1951) which briefly discusses the history of bail.
4. Goldfarb, Ronald L. (1965). *Ransom: A Critique of the American Bail System*. New York: Harper & Row.

for each and every defendant. The defendants filed motions asking the court to reduce their bail amounts but the court refused to do so. In support of their motions, the defendants had offered proof of their various family relationships, prior criminal records, financial resources and other information. The government did not offer anything other than to demonstrate that four people previously charged under the Smith Act in otherwise completely unrelated cases had failed to appear for court.

The defendants appealed their denials for bail reduction relief all the way up to the U.S. Supreme Court which agreed to hear their complaints. The U.S. Supreme Court agreed that their bail was excessive and remanded the cases to the lower courts with instructions to reconsider the proper amount of bail.

In deciding as it did, the Supreme Court expressed deep concern that bail in this case far exceeded that which federal courts normally require for crimes involving maximum five year sentences. It was further upset by the fact that the lower courts gave no rationale whatsoever for departing from its norms. It said that the purpose of bail was twofold: to enable people to help prepare their defense and to prevent punishment before a finding of guilt. The requirement of posting money or property exists merely to ensure that the accused will show up for court. The Court emphasized that, "Bail set at a figure higher than an amount reasonably calculated to fulfill this purpose [showing up for court] is 'excessive' under the Eighth Amendment."

The Court said that it is conceivable that bail higher than normal for a certain grading of crime could legitimately be required. But, there has to be a basis for such higher bail. The government had asked the lower courts to assume that anyone violating the Smith Act was a pawn of organized crime and would inevitably flee the jurisdiction if released. But, the Court said that to merely "infer from the fact of indictment alone a need for bail in an unusually high amount is an arbitrary act" and would "inject into our own system of government the very principles of totalitarianism which Congress was seeking to guard against in passing the [Smith Act]."

So, what can we learn from the Supreme Court's opinion in *Stack*? First, bail usually is excessive when it exceeds the amount reasonably calculated to ensure appearance for court. Second, when courts require an amount of bail that far exceeds what they normally require in cases of similar gravity, they better have specific reasons for doing so.

Stack seems to suggest that there is only one possible legitimate purpose for requiring defendants to post bail: ensuring their appearance for subsequent court proceedings. But, though that may be the sole purpose in most cases, is that really the only possible legitimate purpose?

In looking for other potential legitimate purposes we need to proceed with extreme caution. This is so because mischievous judges do sometimes use **extralegal factors in setting bail** (criteria that they should not properly use but do anyway). For example, an outraged magistrate may set bail higher than it should be in order to start punishing the defendant in advance of a determination of guilt. A magistrate may raise or lower bail in an arbitrary manner according to the amount of space available in the local jail: the more space the higher the bails. A magistrate might improperly set high bail to help "soften up" a defendant for an eventual time-served guilty plea. Finally, a magistrate might allow himself or herself to be influenced by such irrelevant criteria as race (magistrates tend to give lower bail to whites than to minorities—all other things equal) or gender (magistrates tend to give lower bail to women than to men—all other things equal).[5]

But, despite these clearly inappropriate criteria there stands one potentially valid concern that we still must consider: future dangerousness. What should a bail-setting magistrate do if he or she believes a particular defendant is a "safe bet" in terms of returning for court but also believes the defendant is likely to hurt others in the meantime if set temporarily free? Can the magistrate use future dangerousness as a valid factor in the bail decision? Let us read the case that follows to find out whether so-called **preventive detention** (denying bail based on supposed future dangerousness) is constitutionally permissible or not.

United States v. Salerno

481 U.S. 739 (1987)

Anthony Salerno was the alleged "boss" of the Genovese Crime Family of La Cosa Nostra. He and an associate (a "captain" in this Mafia organization) were both arrested on various federal charges including mail fraud and conspiracy to commit murders. At a bail hearing, the court refused to offer these two defendants any bail in any amount whatsoever, citing a new federal statute that said a federal judicial officer could refuse bail entirely if the government could prove by clear and convincing evidence that a defendant's pre-trial release would pose a substantial danger to the safety of others. The government's evidence at the bail hearing consisted of statements revealing murderous intentions these defendants made during telephone calls recorded by government agents pursuant to court-ordered wiretaps. The defendants tried to counter this evidence of future dangerousness by putting on character witnesses and by claiming that their statements were merely "tough talk."

So, the issue that eventually was considered by the U.S. Supreme Court was whether a Congressional statute that provides that bail can be denied if a person is proven by clear and convincing evidence to pose a substantial danger to the safety of others is constitutional. The U.S. Supreme Court ruled that reasonable belief in the future dangerousness of someone was a valid basis for refusing to set bail. In ruling the way it did, the Court knocked down two arguments advanced by Salerno and his criminal associate.

First, the Court rejected the defendants' argument that denying bail based on future dangerousness constituted impermissible, pre-conviction punishment (hence a violation of due process). The Court said that after examining the legislative history behind the new, federal preventive detention statute, it became convinced that Congress never intended to punish anybody but rather only sought to protect the public. Whereas an intent on the part of Congress to engage in punishment before a conviction would violate 14th Amendment due process, an intent merely to protect the public from a rea-

5. Patterson, E. Britt and Michael J. Lynch. (1991). "Biases in Formalized Bail Procedures," in Michael J. Lynch and E. Britt Patterson (eds.), *Race and Criminal Justice*. New York: Harrow and Heston.

sonably calculated threat of harm does not. It all goes to intent and clearly Congress had no illegitimate intentions.

Next, the Court rejected the defendants' second argument that the new preventive detention statute allowing for no bail for dangerous defendants violated the Eighth Amendment requirement that "excessive bail shall not be required." In support of this line of argument, Salerno and his associate had cited the *Stack v. Boyle* case [already discussed in this book, just above]. In *Stack*, the Supreme Court held that in order to avoid being excessive, bail should not be set at a "figure higher than an amount reasonably calculated" to ensure defendant's presence at trial. Salerno and his co-defendant argued that one can infer from *Stack* that the only permissible criteria in setting bail is concern regarding possible flight. In other words, *Stack* never suggested that concern regarding future dangerousness was ever a valid criteria in setting bail.

The Supreme Court acknowledged that *Stack* did not address future dangerousness but noted that the above language in *Stack* was "far too slender a reed on which to rest this argument." The Court said that justices in *Stack* never talked about future dangerousness because that had nothing to do with the case before them. The Court went on to say that the government's interest in preventing people like Salerno and his associate from murdering people while waiting for their trials was a compelling one. It also pointed out that nothing in the text of the Eighth Amendment bail clause limits courts to only consider issues of flight in setting bail amounts. Also, of extreme importance was the fact that though the Eighth Amendment forbade "excessive bail," nothing in its language expressly forbids denying bail entirely in the first place. Thus, Congress is constitutionally permitted to require judges to consider relevant, compelling criteria other than flight (such as future dangerousness) in their bail setting endeavors and has the power to require the complete unavailability of bail in certain circumstances.

Two members of the Supreme Court dissented vigorously from the above decision. Writing for them both, Justice Marshall likened the majority's ruling to one more compatible with a "police state" than with our constitutional democracy. He said this "decision disregards basic principles of justice established centuries ago." He mocked the majority's opinion that the intent of Congress to protect rather than punish made the statute acceptable by saying that, "The majority's technique for infringing this right [to bail] is simple: merely redefine any measure which is claimed to be punishment as 'regulation,' and, magically, the Constitution no longer prohibits its imposition." He further blasted the majority's finding that the Eighth Amendment prohibition against "excessive bail" was not offended because Congress was not requiring excessive bail but rather outlawing the availability of any bail in any amount. Justice Marshall said that this was "mere sophistry" on the part of the majority. He said that the majority likes to think that because the Eighth Amendment merely prohibits "excessive bail" and does not literally forbid refusing bail entirely in certain cases, that courts can get around the "excessive bail" prohibition simply by refusing to set bail in any amount. Marshall thought that it was foolish to assume that setting bail at $1 billion dollars might be excessive in a case while refusing to set bail in any amount would be OK. Either way, the result for a defendant would be the same: loss of liberty. Marshall concluded his dissenting opinion by saying that the presumption of innocence, only won after centuries of hard struggle, and buttressed by the right to bail, was in danger of losing much of its meaning.

Types of Bail

People no longer have to post a friend or relative as bail who will serve out their sentence should they fail to appear for court. Nowadays, people post things instead of human beings. There are several options available. **Cash bond** (including physical money or credit cards in some jurisdictions) is one option. This works well for middle class people charged with relatively minor crimes. But, cash is not a serious option to many defendants charged with serous felonies requiring the posting of huge sums of money. Another alternative to posting cash is to post **property bail**, usually in the form of real estate. Under this option, the defendant or a relative pays to have the property's value attested to by a certified assessor. In the case of real estate, a lien is then placed on the property by the court which will not be removed until the defendant shows up for court. Yet another option (quite common when the risk of flight is tiny) is for the magistrate to allow **R.O.R. bail** (release on recognizance) in which the defendant's promise to return is the bail ("his word is his bond"). Finally, defendants can seek out a **bail bondsman** who will post the full amount of the bail on behalf of a client in return for a 10 to 15 percent fee which will be kept as profit if the defendant shows up for court (if the defendant jumps bail the bail bondsman loses the full amount he or she had posted). Bail bondsman obviously have a huge financial incentive to check out the bona fides of anyone they take on as a client, thus assuming the risk analysis role that busy courts are often unable to do themselves.

Legal Rights of Bounty Hunters

Bail bondsmen sometime do get burned by clients who **abscond.** When clients fail to appear for court, a bail bondsman has two options. He or she can "eat the loss" and do nothing, writing if off as a cost of doing business. Or, he or she can hire a bounty hunter to bring the culprit back. Bail bondsmen pay bounty hunters a percentage of the forfeited bail if they are able to produce the defendant for court.

Unlike police officers and other public officials, private bounty hunters are given extraordinary powers in returning bail jumpers to court. Since they are not government officials or even government agents, the Constitution does not limit their actions. Hence, bounty hunters do not have to concern themselves with such things as search warrants, arrest warrants, or formal extradition procedures.[6] This incredible state of law dates back a long time. In most states little has changed since the United States Supreme Court noted in the 1872 case of *Taylor v. Taintor*[7] that:

---

6. See, Drimmer, Jonathan. (1997). "America's Least Wanted: We Need New Rules to Stop Abuses." *Washington Post, September 21, 1997*, at C6.

7. 83 U.S. 366 (1872).

> Whenever they [bounty hunters] choose to do so, they may seize him and deliver him up in their discharge; and if that cannot be done at once, they may imprison him until it can be done ... They may pursue him into another State; may arrest him ... and if necessary, may break and enter his house for that purpose ... The bail have their principle on a string, and may pull the string whenever they please and render him in their discharge.

Since the Fourth Amendment prohibition against unreasonable governmental searches and seizures does not apply to these private actors, bounty hunters sometimes even force their way into homes belonging to people other than the absconder in their apprehension efforts. When Arizona passed a law (the only state yet to do so) forbidding bounty hunters from entering homes without permission,[8] bounty hunters in that state complained that Arizona legislators were helping fugitives because now "they'll be hiding out at Mom's house and not answering the door."[9]

Given the awesome power involved, becoming a bounty hunter is shockingly easy. Though some states (e.g. Nevada and Utah) require some specific training or a certain amount of law enforcement experience, most states only require that new bounty hunters seeking licenses have no prior felony or violent records and a licensed bail bondsman willing to supervise them.[10]

Plea Bargaining

There was a time in America (the first half of the 1800s) when plea bargains were relatively unheard of and most cases were resolved by way of jury trials. This period has been referred to as the **golden age of trials.**[11] True, trials tended to be very short by today's standards (one jury might easily hear several trials or more in a single day). Technical rules of evidence were largely non-existent.[12] But, defendants' cases were decided by juries rather than by attorneys negotiating with one another.

By the late 1800s all of this started to change. In many areas, plea bargaining became entrenched before the end of that century.[13] Yet despite the growing practice of plea bargaining, American lawyers and judges were reluctant to openly acknowledge its existence. It was if it were the dirty little secret of American jurisprudence. Judges and lawyers were not sure what they were doing was constitutional. After all, the Constitution called for a criminal court system based on due process accomplished through

8. Merry, Ann L. (1999). "Comment: S.B. 1257: Arizona Regulates Bounty Hunters." *Arizona State Law Journal* 31: 229–257, footnote 53.

9. Id., citing McCloy, Mike. (1998). "Bounty Hunter Bill Advances: Kin of Slain Pair Testify to Panel." *Arizona Republic, February 26, 1998*, at B1.

10. Merry, *supra* note 8, at 240 (see also article's appendix for a state by state summary of licensing requirements for bounty hunters).

11. Levine, James P. (1991). *Juries and Politics.* Belmont, CA: Brooks/Cole Publishing Company, at 24.

12. Id., at 25.

13. Sanborn, Joseph B., Jr. (1986). "A Historical Sketch of Plea Bargaining." *Justice Quarterly* 3 (June):111–138.

public trials, not guilty pleas. Plea bargaining, on the other hand, involved secret negotiations and arguably coerced guilty pleas. It was one thing for a defendant to voluntarily give up a right to trial and to plea guilty. But could a system which resulted in so many defendants rolling over and admitting guilt be truly said to be non-coercive? After dodging the question for decades, the U.S. Supreme Court finally ruled on the constitutionality of plea bargaining.

The Constitutionality of Plea Bargaining

Santobello v. New York

404 U.S. 257 (1971)

Santobello, a repeat criminal, was charged with various gambling offenses. As part of a plea agreement with a prosecutor, he pled guilty to a lesser included offense in exchange for having the more serious charges dropped. The trial judge accepted Santobello's plea of guilty and scheduled a sentencing hearing. After a series of delays, the sentencing hearing finally took place but by then Santobello had changed his mind and asked permission to withdraw his guilty plea previously entered. The trial judge refused Santobello's request and sentenced him to one year in prison, the maximum sentence for the crime to which he pled guilty.

Santobello appealed this conviction, arguing that he should have been allowed to withdraw his guilty plea. Part of Santobello's complaint was that the prosecutor who had made the initial deal with him had promised to make no recommendation regarding the actual sentence. However, because a new prosecutor had taken over the case, this promise was not followed and the new prosecutor (over defense counsel's objection) argued for the maximum, one-year sentence which the court eventually imposed. The court did say that it was not sentencing the defendant to the maximum sentence because of the prosecutor's recommendation but rather because of defendant's terrible pre-sentence report.

On eventual appeal to the U.S. Supreme Court, Santobello still sought to have his guilty plea nullified. The U.S. Supreme Court agreed that the case had to be remanded because of the district attorney office's failure to live up to its promise not to recommend a sentence. However, the Court also ruled for the first time ever that plea bargaining in and of itself is not inherently unconstitutional. Using what has become often-cited words, the High Court said that,

> The disposition of criminal charges by agreement between the prosecutor and the accused, sometimes loosely called 'plea bargaining,' is an essential component of the administration of justice. Properly administered, it is to be encouraged. If every criminal charge were subjected to a full-scale trial, the States and the Federal Government would need to multiply by many times the number of judges and court facilities (at 260).

The Court did say that in order to stay within the bounds of the Constitution, plea bargaining had to result in an agreement that was entered into voluntarily and knowingly. But, as long they were fairly arrived at, there was nothing inherently wrong with plea bargains.

There was no dissent to the above opinion that plea bargains can be constitutionally tolerated. However, many scholars have condemned the practice as wicked and the Court as negligent in allowing it. For example, Douglas Koski, of the National Center for the Advanced Study of Social Forces, has written,

> What is so bad about plea bargaining? ... Plea bargaining achieves just what the Framers expected the jury trial to prevent, the aggrandizement of state power. Plea bargaining transfers the power of condemnation to a low-visibility decision maker, the prosecutor ... Plea bargaining is also wrong because it is coercive. A legal system that comes to depend upon coercing people to waive their supposed rights is by definition a failed system. The system can no longer function by adhering to its own stated principles. Plea bargaining puts the accused under ferocious pressure to bear false witness against himself.[14]

Whether plea bargaining is the blessing the Supreme Court believes or an abomination like some others suggest, one thing is certain. It is now an American institution.

Types of Plea Bargains

There are three main types of plea bargains. Sometimes all three are used within the same jurisdiction but often local legal culture tends to dictate the use of just one type in most cases. So what type of plea bargain you might expect depends heavily on which state and even county in which you happen to live.

In a **sentence bargain** the prosecutor "recommends" to the court the actual sentence a defendant will receive (in addition to the charge to which he or she will plead guilty). If the court rejects this recommendation, the defendant is free to withdraw his or her offer to plea guilty. In practice, judges rarely reject the prosecutor's recommendation since to do so could very likely produce a time-consuming trial. As long as the prosecutor and the defense attorney are both satisfied with an agreed-upon sentence, the judge normally is happy to go along.

In a **charge bargain** the prosecutor does not negotiate an actual sentence but rather allows a defendant to plead guilty to a lesser charge in exchange for giving up the right to go to trial. For example, a person charged with burglary may be permitted to plead guilty to theft or a person charged with aggravated assault may be permitted to plead guilty to simple assault. The judge is then expected by all concerned to give a sentence appropriate to the reduced (not the original) charge. It would be against the judge's interests to surprise everyone with too severe a sentence given the reduced offense since that would only encourage more trials in the future. In some areas, judges are bound by sentencing guidelines which basically box the judge into a narrow range of potential sentences based upon the crime pled to and the prior record score of the defendant. Hence, attorneys in such areas can very accurately predict what the sentence will be.

---

14. Koski, Douglas D. (2003). "The Declining Importance of the Jury Trial and the Plea Bargaining Problem." Chapter One in, Douglas D. Koski (ed.). (2003). *The Jury Trial in Criminal Justice.* Durham, NC: Carolina Academic Press, at 8–9.

In a **count bargain** the defendant charged with multiple offenses pleads guilty to one or more of them in exchange for the rest being dismissed. For example, a defendant charged with six counts of burglary might plead guilty to one of the burglaries in exchange for the other five counts being dropped. The judge would then be expected to give the burglar a sentence that a person would expect to receive who had only committed one offense, not six.

Judicial Participation in Deal-making

Should judges be allowed to participate with the attorneys in plea bargain negotiations? An argument could be made that they should. After all, they could help break deadlocks by suggesting what they think would be a wise course for defendants and prosecutors to follow. They also have to ultimately accept any plea bargain that is negotiated anyway, so why not let them participate in the process from the beginning?

Despite such potential justifications for judicial participation in deal-making, nearly all states and the federal courts forbid judges from such activities.[15] What are these jurisdictions so afraid of? The main fear is judicial vindictiveness at post-trial sentencing should defendants have been so brazen as to have rejected the judge's "sensible" and "generous" plea bargain guidance. One jurisdiction that bucks this trend is Vermont. The case on point that follows is from that state.

State v. Davis

584 A.2d 1146 (Vt. 1990)

Davis was convicted by a Vermont jury of homicide by vehicle while drunk driving. At sentencing, the trial judge sentenced Davis to serve one to three years in prison. Davis became upset with this sentence because the same trial judge earlier had offered him a sentence of serving just four months (along with some probation) were he to plead guilty instead of insisting on his right to a trial. Davis appealed the sentence (though not the conviction) and alleged improper vindictiveness on the part of the sentencing judge. Davis asked the Vermont Supreme court to vacate the sentence and remand the case for sentencing before a different (and supposedly neutral) judge.

The Vermont Supreme Court denied Davis the relief he sought. The Court admitted that virtually every other state, as well as the federal courts, forbid trial judges from participating in plea bargain negotiations. Those other jurisdictions forbid such involvement apparently out of concern that trial judges may loose their neutrality and become vindictive at sentencing should a defendant turn down the judge's suggestion of how to resolve the case without trial. However, the Vermont Supreme Court said that it refused to adopt this fear of vengefulness possessed by its sister jurisdictions. In its judgment, there is no inevitability of vindictiveness on the part of judges whose proposals have been turned down. The Court pointed to the Vermont

15. See Fed. R. Crim. P. 11(e)(2) which expressly forbids trial judges in federal courts from participating in plea negotiations. See also, *State v. Davis*, 584 A.2d 1146 (Vt. 1990) in which the Vermont Supreme Court recognizes that Vermont is about the only state that allows it.

Standards for Criminal Justice that guarantee, by way of statute, that "The court should not impose ... any sentence in excess of that which would be justified by any of the protective, deterrent, or other purposes of the criminal law because the defendant has chosen to require the prosecution to prove guilt at trial rather than to enter a plea of guilty or nolo contendere." It reasoned that the existence of such a statute clearly instructs trial judges to refrain from vindictiveness should defendants exert their trial rights.

Of course, the Vermont court recognized that trial judges could disobey the above statute and engage in revenge. But, it believed that appellate courts could deal with such impropriety on a case by case basis, especially since state law requires that all negotiations involving a trial judge be placed on the record. Appellate courts could, for example, find proof of vindictiveness whenever it sees in the transcript that a trial judge has complained to a defendant or defense counsel about the "high costs of trials." They could also find proof of vindictiveness where a trial judge has complained to defendants that those who insist on trials "do not show proper repentance." They could also find such proof where a judge has commented that the evidence against a defendant was so strong that he or she would be wasting the court's time by going to trial. But, where the only so-called proof of vindictiveness is that a judge gave a defendant a longer sentence after trial than what the judge was willing to do as part of plea bargain, there is no basis for an appellate court to assume judicial revenge. After all, if judges had to give defendants the same sentence they had originally suggested as part of a plea agreement, there would be every incentive for defendants to "lock in" this sentence and still go to trial.

In short, unless an appellate court can find comments made by a trial judge who has participated in plea discussions that provide real proof of vindictiveness, the mere fact that a sentence imposed after a jury trial is longer than what was offered as part of a plea bargain will not be presumed to show proof of judicial revenge. Vermont likes its judges to participate in plea negotiations because they help the parties to break deadlocks and thus help avoid costly, unnecessary, and time-consuming trials.

What do you think of Vermont's allowing its judges to participate directly in plea discussions? If you are ever arrested would you prefer to be processed in a state like Vermont that allows this practice or would you prefer to be processed in a state that expressly forbids it? Do you agree with Vermont that the vast majority of judges can be trusted to remain professional and not become vindictive when "jilted," or do you agree with most other jurisdictions that apparently have no such degree of confidence in their judiciary?

Guilty Pleas

Our criminal court system is often thought of as a trial-based system but it would be more accurate to think of it as a guilty-plea based system. American courthouses engage in fast food justice, turning out their finished products so efficiently that it would make Colonel Sanders proud to be an American.

As we learned earlier in the *Santobello* case, the Supreme Court had no problem with plea bargains and rapid justice. In fact, it thought plea bargains ought to be encouraged. However, in that same case it did caution that plea bargains (like all forms of guilty pleas) had to be entered into "voluntarily and knowingly." Let us know look at what these words specifically mean.

"Voluntarily and Knowingly Entered" Requirement

Boykin v. Alabama

395 U.S. 238 (1969)

Boykin was charged with five armed robberies in Alabama back in a time when armed robbery in Alabama was still potentially a capital offense. Boykin pled guilty to all of these robberies and the judge subsequently sentenced him to death for each count. The record of the trial court gave no indication whatsoever that Boykin understood what he was doing when he pled guilty or that his guilty pleas were of his own free will.

Boykin appealed his convictions and death sentences to the Alabama Supreme Court but it affirmed what the trial court had done. Boykin then asked the U.S. Supreme Court to hear his appeal and it agreed to do so.

On appeal, the U.S. Supreme Court overturned the death sentences and vacated the guilty pleas. It held that a judge who accepts a guilty plea without asking any questions whatsoever of a defendant violates that defendant's constitutional rights. It ruled that not only did the trial court engage in error by its actions (or lack thereof) but it had engaged in plain error. A judge simply cannot accept a guilty plea without a showing that it was entered into knowingly and voluntarily.

In order to ensure that a plea is **knowingly entered**, any trial court "is best advised to conduct on the record examination of the defendant which should include ... that the defendant understands the nature of the charges, his right to a jury trial, the acts sufficient to constitute the offenses for which he is charged and the possible range of sentences."

In order to ensure that a plea is **voluntarily entered**, courts should make sure through their questioning that the guilty plea is not the product of force or threats or promises other than what was included in the plea agreement.

The Court emphasized that guilty pleas are not just minor events but constitute full-blown convictions just as though someone had been convicted by a jury or a judge. A guilty plea must be taken very seriously by the judge in that it "supplies both evidence and verdict, ending controversy."

Thanks to the case above, many jurisdictions have developed what are referred to as **Boykin forms**, boiler plate documents which defense lawyers must go over with a client before a judge will allow the person to enter a plea of guilty pursuant to a bargain. These forms tell the defendant of his or her right to a jury trial, to confront witnesses, to testify (or not) in one's own defense, and to put the state to its high burden of proof; they then go on to explain the elements of the crimes one is pleading guilty to and the possible range of sentences for these crimes. The lawyer has the client initial each point as the lawyer reviews it and the initialed document is then presented to the judge in court while the guilty plea is being processed. Typically, a judge will show the client the document and ask him or her to verify that certain key points were adequately explained to his or her satisfaction by the attorney.

Sadly, some defendants can be so scared, depressed, crazy, or overwhelmed that they would be willing to admit to anything and to sign any Boykin Form. To guard against this, judges wishing to accept a plea bargain must make sure that there is at least a factual basis for the charges before accepting a guilty plea. Apparently, "factual basis" is something much less than proof beyond a reasonable doubt yet something more than proof provided solely by a defendant's mere willingness to plea guilty. The case that follows discusses this factual basis requirement in the context of an apparent drug lord's initial willingness to forfeit a fortune in supposedly ill-gotten assets as part of a plea bargain about which he later had second thoughts.

Libretti v. United States

516 U.S. 29 (1995)

Joseph Libretti was indicted in federal court on a series of counts involving narcotic trafficking, money laundering, and firearms violations. Libretti apparently had made a fortune in the distribution of cocaine and heroin. So, in addition to alleging his crimes, the indictments against Libretti included a statement (required by Congress) that the federal government intended to seek forfeiture of all of Libretti's assets obtained with his drug profits.

Libretti was brought to trial but after several days of testimony Libretti decided to make a deal with the prosecutors. In exchange for dropping most of the counts against him, Libretti agreed to a twenty year sentence and to forfeit specific property mentioned in the indictments that the government believed was obtained or facilitated by his drug sales. Specifically, Libretti agreed to forfeit his home, automobile, guns, and safety deposit boxes stuffed with cash. The government believed that these assets were fruits of Libretti's criminal career since it was hard to see how Libretti could have possibly acquired them with his modest, legitimate income.

The judge accepted the plea agreement and sentenced Libretti to the twenty years and ordered the assets forfeited to the government. The judge found a factual basis for the plea of guilty to the drug offense but did not bother to find one for the forfeiture of the assets (e.g., were the assets truly Libretti's and not someone else's and did Libretti in fact obtain them illegitimately like the government claimed). Libretti later changed his mind about having agreed to forfeit so many assets and asked the judge to let him take back that part of the plea agreement. When the judge refused to adopt Libretti's argument that the forfeiture aspect of the plea bargain was void because of the failure of this same trial judge to look for a factual basis, Libretti appealed.

The United States Court of Appeals for the Tenth Circuit now considered Libretti's argument regarding a factual basis. It agreed that federal law provides that judges simply cannot accept a guilty plea (pursuant to a bargain or otherwise) without first determining its accuracy. In order to verify its accuracy, a trial court wishing to accept a plea of guilty must indeed first "make such inquiry as shall satisfy it that there is a factual basis for the plea." That said, the circuit court went on to rule that the "factual basis" requirement simply did not apply to forfeiture of drug-trade obtained assets. The court wrote that, "By its plain terms, the [factual basis] rule applies only to a 'plea of guilty.' Our precedent makes clear that this language refers to a defendant's admission of guilt of a substantive criminal offense charged in an indictment ..." and not to any sentencing decision. "Forfeiture is an element of the sentence imposed *following* conviction or, as here, a plea of guilty, and thus falls outside of the [factual basis rule]."

Libretti had made some counter-arguments which the circuit court rejected. First, he argued that criminal forfeiture is "not simply an aspect of sentencing but is, in essence, a hybrid that shares elements of both a substantive charge and a punishment imposed for criminal activity." Libretti based his hybrid argument on the fact that Congress required prosecutors seeking forfeiture to include that fact as part of any indictment. The circuit court however ruled that the fact that Congress gives defendants heightened protection regarding forfeiture by creating a certain procedural rule does not alter the basic nature of forfeiture as a punishment. Prosecutors may include their intent to seek forfeiture in their indictment, but that does not mean that forfeiture is thereby somehow transformed into a substantive crime.

Libretti had also tried to argue that if trial courts did not have to find a "factual basis" for the forfeiture, greedy federal law enforcement agencies could engage in overreaching by coercing frightened, desperate defendants facing long prison sentences to surrender property that they had legitimately obtained. The court acknowledged that this was a concern, especially given the power imbalance that often exists in the negotiating process, but said that it could be addressed separately in a case by case basis if and when it arises. There was no need to require a factual basis for the forfeiture in every case as a matter of routine.

Finally, Libretti raised the specter that criminal defendants seeking to make a deal might agree to forfeiture of assets that they knew belonged to innocent third parties because they could not care less if others were cheated out of their belongings. Requiring trial courts to engage in a factual basis inquiry would protect against this. The circuit court rejected this argument as well. It reasoned that any potential, third party claimants alleging to have been wrongly deprived of their assets could always file a petition later with the court, which would then grant them a hearing on their concerns. This would protect such occasional claimants sufficiently while conserving scarce judicial resources by allowing criminal court judges to swiftly move along the court's business.

In sum, the Tenth Circuit acknowledged the need for trial judges to find a factual basis before accepting someone's apparently voluntary guilty plea to a substantive criminal offense, but did not require trial judges to find a factual basis for criminal forfeiture of assets or any other sentencing decision.

Types of Guilty Pleas

As we have learned, guilty pleas must be "knowingly and voluntarily entered" in order to be valid. The irony here is that despite the requirement of voluntariness, many court observers believe that plea bargaining by its very nature is often necessarily coercive.

Judges want to have it both ways. They want defendants to be scared out of going to trial yet they do not want them to admit that they feel coerced and intimidated.

Entering a guilty plea is not easy for many defendants to do. When push comes to shove, they may be very reluctant to orally admit guilt in court because they in fact feel that they are being coerced into giving up trial rights they do not want to give up. To help "grease the skids," courts have devised several types of guilty pleas.

The first type of guilty plea (one not providing for any greasing of the skids) is a **straight plea of guilty**. A defendant entering this type of plea simply admits to the court that he or she is guilty of the crime to which he or she is admitting. There is nothing fancy here. The judge asks the defendant if he or she did what the government alleges and the defendant owns up to it. Most defendants pleading guilty (by way of plea bargain or otherwise) enter this type of guilty plea.

A second type of guilty plea is the **nolo contendere plea**. Literally, these words mean, "I will not contest it." In effect, a defendant who is entering such a plea is neither admitting guilt nor denying guilt. It is a face-saving mechanism that some have criticized as a foolish concept[16] which some prosecutors and judges resist using. Legally, it has precisely the same effect as a straight plea of guilty without the defendant having to ever say he or she is in fact guilty. In addition to saving face, it also has the advantage of not being admissible as evidence of guilt in any potential subsequent civil lawsuit involving the same set of facts. Trial-level courts are given great leeway by higher courts as to whether or not to allow a defendant to plead "nolo" rather than "guilty." Simply put, courts may accept such pleas as long as it is in the "public interest" to do so.[17] As a practical matter, this type of plea is reserved for special defendants who are sophisticated enough to insist on it and/or who otherwise need extra help in getting through the process.

A third type of guilty plea is the very rare and very strange **Alford plea** which many prosecutors are forbidden by their superiors to use "except in the most unusual of circumstances."[18] Judges also feel uncomfortable with such pleas since they seem to turn the guilty plea hearing into something of a farce. Nevertheless, such pleas are legal and used from time to time, especially in cases in which a defendant absolutely refuses to plead "guilty" or even "nolo contendere." Unlike a "no contest" plea, an "Alford Plea" involves a defendant who is affirmatively asserting that he or she is actually innocent (but will nevertheless accept the punishment). The plea comes from the case of *North Carolina v. Alford*, discussed just below, and is tolerated by the courts for the reasons set forth in the decision.

North Carolina v. Alford

400 U.S. 25 (1970)

Alford was charged in North Carolina with first degree murder. Alford flat out told the trial judge that he was innocent of any crime but that he was willing to plead guilty

16. Herman, G. Nicholas. (1997). "Preparing for Plea Bargaining." Chapter 4 in *Plea Bargaining*. Charlottesville, VA: Lexis Law Publishing, at 125, citing comments of Judge Learned Hand.

17. *United States v. Chin Doong Art*, 193 F. Supp. 820 (E.D. N.Y. 1961).

18. Herman, *supra* note 16, at 118, citing policies of the U.S. Department of Justice.

to second degree murder (as part of a bargain) in order to avoid the threat of the death penalty. The court accepted Alford's plea and sentenced him to thirty years in prison, the maximum sentence for second degree murder. Later at prison, Alford changed his mind about doing the long thirty years and tried to take back his so-called "guilty plea" by pointing out the fact that he never actually had admitted guilt. Indeed, he even had told the court that he was innocent.

In ultimately reviewing this matter, the U.S. Supreme Court ruled that such a plea (in which a defendant protests his innocence but is willing to accept the agreed-upon punishment) was lawful. The Court wrote that it could see no real difference between a "nolo contendere" plea in which a defendant refuses to admit guilt and a plea such as this in which a defendant asserts his innocence. Either way, the defendant is willing to voluntarily submit himself to punishment and to give up his trial rights. Like the standard in accepting any type of guilty plea, a court can accept an Alford Plea as long as it finds that there is a "factual basis" that links the defendant to the crime and as long as the plea is "voluntarily and knowingly entered."

Withdrawing One's Guilty Plea

Like Alford in the case covered just above, many defendants who enter guilty pleas as part of a plea bargain get to prison and change their mind. Prison is hard time. Could you not see yourself quickly changing your mind if you were sent off to prison to begin serving a painful sentence?

Courts want finality. They like it when time-consuming trials have been successfully avoided. They do not want to make it easy for defendants to ruin this success by making it easy for defendants to withdraw their pleas.

Changing one's mind simply is not recognized as a valid basis for withdrawing one's guilty plea (though the occasional sympathetic trial judge might rarely allow it). Legally, there are only seven grounds for which a trial judge must allow the withdraw of a plea of guilty whether the judge wants to or not.[19]

1 One ground is that the plea was not voluntarily entered. This means that the defendant was improperly coerced into pleading guilty. This is a sticky area since nearly everyone who pleads guilty probably experiences some coercion. But, some threats no doubt go beyond the pale.

2 A second ground is that the plea was not knowingly entered. This occurs when a defendant does not understand the nature of the charges that he or she is pleading guilty to, or does not understand the potential range of penalties that he or she is facing before accepting a so-called bargain.

3 A third ground is that the defendant was denied effective assistance of counsel. The fact that one did not get an average lawyer is not good enough. One's lawyers must have been so incompetent as to have been shocking.

19. The seven grounds which follow are found in various legal cases cited in Herman, *supra note* 16, Chapter 11.

A fourth ground is that the sentence the defendant wound up receiving exceeded the legal maximum for the offense. Suppose I plead guilty to misdemeanor theft and the maximum sentence for that crime is 11 months in jail. But the judge sentences me to 22 months. If this were to occur, I must be permitted to withdraw my guilty plea.

A fifth ground to withdraw a guilty plea is the trial court lacked jurisdiction over the offense. Suppose I murder someone in Delaware but plead guilty to the offense in Maryland. Since the Maryland court lacked jurisdiction over this crime, I must be permitted to withdraw my Maryland guilty plea.

A sixth ground is that the criminal statute which I violated attempts to criminalize conduct that is constitutionally protected. For example, suppose I burn an American flag in order to protest U.S. government actions that I hate. If I were to plead guilty to the crime of flag desecration, I could withdraw my guilty plea since there is a constitutional right to burn a flag if done to express my political sentiments.

The seventh and final ground to withdraw a guilty plea is that my conviction constituted double jeopardy. A guilty plea, just like a trial verdict, counts as a conviction. The Fifth Amendment to the Constitution protects us from being twice put at risk of punishment for the same offense. Suppose that I could prove that the simple assault that I plead guilty to last week was a subset of a strong-arm robbery case that I was acquitted of six months ago. Because of double jeopardy, the court would have to let me withdraw my guilty plea to the assault charge since it was really part of that old robbery matter.

Despite the fact that it sounds like there are many ways to force courts to allow one to withdraw a guilty plea, the fact is that very, very few defendants can legitimately raise any of the above grounds. For the vast majority of defendants who plead guilty, the case is forever closed. Unlike a verdict arrived at by way of a jury trial, there is no automatic right to appeal the vast majority of convictions attained by way of a guilty plea.

This completes the chapter on laws associated with bail, plea bargaining and guilty pleas. The next series of chapters that follow take us away from such pre-trial concerns and into the laws associated with trials and their aftermath.

Chapter Seven

Law of Evidence, Part I: Categories of Evidence, Relevancy, and Prejudicial Impact

A Forward to Your Study of the Law of Evidence

This chapter and the next one will expose you to the law surrounding the admissibility of evidence. As a way of introduction to both of these chapters, consider the following.

Imagine that you are placed on an island with a group of 50 people. You are completely cut off from the rest of the world and you want to set up a system to maintain order on your island. Presume that rules (laws) are enacted and you are left with the task of how to fairly determine both civil and criminal disputes as they arise in your community. How would you set up the system to resolve these disputes? What rules would you follow in your "court" to assure that the process is fair and efficient? What information should it consider? Who should be allowed to present it? Should the parties be allowed to compel the appearance of and testimony from witnesses who have information about the case? How should evidence be presented? Is there some evidence that should not be allowed in court because of its unreliability? Are there other reasons to keep evidence from being presented to the decision maker? Will the rules be permitted to change and evolve?

This exercise illustrates the difficulty of setting up rules to govern court procedures. Early in United States history, courts determined the admissibility of evidence based upon ancient rules that evolved from English common law. Under this judicial system, each state had authority over and was responsible for promulgating rules within its own courts. With 50 states and the federal government each having its own courts, it is easy to see the potential for confusion for those practicing or appearing before various courts. Some states codified their rules, but consistency was lacking, even within courts in a single system.

In 1965 Chief Justice Earl Warren appointed a distinguished committee of lawyers and legal scholars to study and draft rules that would apply in the federal system. After a decade of discussion and protracted review, the Federal Rules of Evidence were adopted by Congress in 1975. These rules apply in all federal courts, in both civil and criminal proceedings.

Also during the 1970s, Uniform Rules of Evidence were proposed to the states by the National Conference of Commissioners in an effort to promote consistency and stability in the application of rules across the country. The Uniform Rules of Evidence and the Federal Rules of Evidence are similar to one another, following the same format and numbering system. Forty-two states have adopted the Uniform Rules of Evidence, modifying them to more fully meet their particular needs.[1] Because of their similarity to the Uniform Rules, and their wide application, the Federal Rules of Evidence are primarily studied in American law schools, and will be the basis for study in this chapter as well as the next.

In both the federal and state systems, the rules of evidence continue to be a work in progress. As society changes, and technological and scientific changes are applied in the courtroom, evidentiary rules are challenged and evolve. Courts, legislative and judicial administrative bodies amend rules to meet these demands.

Students who study law either at the undergraduate level or in law school generally spend most of their time reading about and participating in class discussions on legal theory. This is how it should be. But, as any practicing trial lawyer knows, what wins most cases in the real world is not skilled doctrinal argument but rather the presentation of a good set of facts to the jury. It is the evidence, rather than the law, that usually wins or loses a case for most lawyers.

To the chagrin of some grandstanding, manipulative lawyers, the evidence that can be presented at trial is limited. The various rules of evidence see to that. When a lawyer violates ones of these rules during a trial or other proceeding, the lawyer for the other side will (hopefully) object and the judge (hopefully) will sustain that objection. These rules exist in an attempt to "secure fairness" and to eliminate "unjustifiable expense and delay" so that "truth may be ascertained and proceedings justly determined."[2] For example, various rules provide that some evidence is not relevant and simply would waste a jury's time and possibly even confuse the jury. Other evidence is relevant but would so prejudice the jury against a party that it would prevent a fair trial. Both of these topics (relevancy and prejudicial impact) will be covered in this chapter. (The next chapter will cover other important limitations on evidence.) However, let us start with the most basic of basics in our journey into the law of evidence by first considering the four categories of lawful evidence.

Categories of Evidence

There are **four main categories of evidence** that lawyers attempt to introduce at trial in order to help prove their side of things: direct evidence, circumstantial evidence, real evidence, and documentary evidence. Each of these four types of legal evidence is explained and explored below.

1. For a list of the states that have adopted the Uniform Rules of Evidence, and internet links to state rules, see http://www.law.cornell.edu/uniform/evidence.html (retrieved September, 2007).

2. See, Federal Rule of Evidence 102

Direct Evidence

Direct evidence is testimonial evidence which if believed by the jury to be true requires no inferences or guesses to be made on the part of the jury. More simply put, this type of evidence is generally referred to as "eyewitness testimony." But, "eyewitness testimony" is perhaps a bit too simplistic a description since "ear witness," "smell witness," and "taste witness" also qualify as direct evidence.

For example, suppose a police officer testified on the stand that she responded to a domestic violence call and upon arriving at the home saw the husband slam his fist into his wife's nose. If such testimony were given, the jury would not have to infer whether or not the defendant punched his wife. The jury would only have to decide whether or not the police officer was giving truthful testimony. If the jury concluded the officer was telling the truth, then it could directly conclude that the defendant punched his wife.

If, on the other hand, the officer testified that she did not actually see the husband punch his wife, but upon arriving at the home saw blood on the angry husband's fist and the wife with a profusely bleeding nose, the jury would have to infer that the defendant had punched his wife even if the jury believed the officer's testimony to be truthful. Such testimony by the officer would not be direct evidence but merely circumstantial evidence (more on circumstantial evidence later).

Juries love direct evidence, especially from eyewitnesses that they believe would have no reason to lie. Direct evidence is often given heavy weight by juries, sometimes even making a case "open and shut." But, have you ever been mistaken for somebody else in day-to-day life? Perhaps eyewitness testimony is given more weight by juries than it deserves, as the science presented in the case below suggests.

State v. Long

721 P.2d 483 (Utah 1986)

On a March evening in Salt Lake City, just after dark, somebody approached a man who was coming home and walking up to his front door. The homeowner felt a cold metallic object pressed against the back of his neck and heard a voice tell him, "Don't move or I will blow your head off." Just then, the victim's girlfriend happened to open the front door and saw what was happening outside. She slammed the door shut and told the victim's son, Jacob Rocha, that his father was being held up at gunpoint by a black man outside. Jacob quickly retrieved a .357 magnum from a drawer while the victim's girlfriend telephoned the police. As Jacob approached the front door from inside the house, the door suddenly flew open and the armed assailant fired a sawed off shot gun blast into the home. Jacob was hit by the blast and thrown back against a wall. Crying, he returned fire. The assailant then fled. The entire encounter between Jacob and the man shooting the shot gun at him took six seconds. During this period Jacob obviously was under extreme stress and admitted that his eyes were "glossy" from his tears.

Jacob's father and a neighbor saw the armed assailant run away. The gunman was with a second person, who fled with him. Both men ran to an Oldsmobile with the engine running, got into the car, and took off. A high speed chase with the police soon developed, resulting in the police eventually nabbing them. Upon arrest, the police noticed blood on one of the two men, Anthony Long, who also had a gun wound in his abdomen area and a bullet hole in his shirt. The police charged Anthony Long with being the gun-wielding assailant at the house. Specifically, Long was charged with aggravated assault and possession of a firearm by a restricted person.

Following Long's arrest, Jacob was shown a photo array and asked to identify the man who shot him with the shot gun. He was unable to identify Long from the photos. However, Jacob was able to identify Long later on in court as the gunman, both at the preliminary hearing and again at trial.

Long's theory of the defense was that he was merely present at the crime scene, and that Jacob Rocha wrongfully identified him as the gunman. Long claimed that it was the person he was with that was the actual armed perpetrator. To help neutralize Jacob Rocha's eyewitness testimony that Long was indeed the gunman, Long asked the trial judge for a cautionary instruction regarding the inherent fallibility associated with eyewitness testimony. The trial judge refused to give such an instruction and Long was convicted. Long appealed.

The Utah Supreme Court reversed Long's conviction and ordered a new trial. It ruled that a cautionary instruction regarding the inherent potential weakness of eyewitness testimony should henceforth be given "whenever eyewitness identification is a central issue in a case and such an instruction is requested by the defense." It would no longer leave it to the trial court's wide discretion as it had in the past. It noted that by giving trial judges such wide discretion, they almost never elected to give the cautionary instruction. The Utah Supreme Court noted that, "Given the great weight jurors are likely to give eyewitness testimony, and the deep and generally unperceived flaws in it, to convict a defendant on such evidence without advising the jury of the factors that should be considered in evaluating it could well deny the defendant due process of law ..."

So, what are the "deep and generally unperceived flaws" of eyewitness testimony? The court spoke of what the scientific community refers to as the "memory process," which includes three stages: acquisition, retention, and retrieval. There are problems associated with all three stages.

During the first, or acquisition stage, a person can be limited by such things as poor eyesight, poor lighting, length of time, etc. But, in addition to these obvious limitations, is the not so well-known debilitating influence that stress can play. Many lay jurors believe the myth that people under stress actually have their senses enhanced and are better able to perceive what is taking place. Actually, science shows the opposite is true. A person under extreme emotional stress is much less able to accurately perceive what is going on. Jacob Rocha was obviously under a huge amount of emotional stress when he tearfully "observed" Long shooting at him. His ability to correctly identify Long was therefore greatly reduced. In addition to this stress, Jacob Rocha also may have been subject to limitations associated with cross-racial identification. Rocha was white and the armed gunman was black. Studies show that eyewitnesses identifications involving suspects of one's own race tend to be more statistically accurate than those involving suspects of another race.

The second, or retention stage, likewise poses grave risks to accuracy. It is during this stage that a witness stores the events into his or her memory. The problem is that the human mind abhors gaps in knowledge, and tends to unconsciously fill in the gaps with logical theories that the mind creates. With the passage of time, these theories become reality and the witness becomes more certain and more confident of what supposedly took place. What was "seen and heard tend to become more accurate, more complete and less ambiguous in appearance."

The third, or retrieval stage, of the memory process also presents dangers. It is during this stage that a witness is asked to recall and communicate to others what he or she has observed. One danger associated with this stage is that of the witness being asked suggestive questions (sometimes even unconsciously) by the police and others. For example, Jacob Rocha could not pick out Long's picture in the photo array but was able to easily identify him at the preliminary hearing and at the trial. Of course, during those proceedings Long would have been sitting at the defense table right next to his attorney (and was also the only black man in the courtroom at the time).

Because of these grave problems associated with the memory process, the Utah Supreme Court simply did not think that a fair trial could take place whenever eyewitness testimony was central to the case and no cautionary instructions were given. The Utah Supreme Court did not require any formulaic instruction to henceforth be given, but said that it believed it could "trust that trial counsel and judges will be able to produce appropriate instructions that satisfy the concerns expressed here today." It did however give some "guidelines," reflecting the points made above, that courts could use if they so wanted.

Given the great weight that jurors indeed give eyewitness testimony, and given juror ignorance regarding its inherent defects, why do you suppose that so many trial judges refuse to instruct juries about these defects when it is left up to them to decide whether or not to provide the guidance? Do you think that all states should adopt the approach in the case above requiring trial judges to give such instructions on demand?

Circumstantial Evidence

Circumstantial evidence is evidence which even if believed by the jury to be truthful, still requires the jury to infer a conclusion. For example, if I hear a gunshot and run into the room and see you holding a smoking gun over a dead body, I would still have to infer that you shot the victim. After all, it is possible that the victim shot himself and that the individual holding the gun merely picked it up after the fact.

Criminals do not like to wait around for an eyewitness to be present before they commit their misdeeds. Hence, many cases can only be proven by way of circumstantial evidence, if they can be proven at all. A case relying entirely upon circumstantial evidence can properly result in a conviction as long as the circumstantial evidence of guilt is beyond a reasonable doubt. The question in cases that are wholly circumstantial then usually revolves around whether or not the evidence is of sufficient quality to overcome reasonable doubt, as the case that follows indicates.

People v. Basciano

486 N.Y.S. 2d 434 (1985)

An employee of a roller rink in New Paltz, New York came to work one morning to discover a broken front window and several arcade games inside the establishment tipped over on their sides. The coin boxes of each of these machines had been broken into and emptied. The police were summoned, and were able to lift a clear fingerprint from the inside of one of the coin boxes. This coin box, prior to the burglary and theft, had been kept locked and could only be accessed by the six employees of the owner of the game machines.

The police compared the fingerprint they had lifted with those on file at the police station and expertly matched it with that of the defendant, Basciano. Basciano was subsequently charged and convicted of burglary of the roller rink and theft of the coins. He appealed this conviction, claiming that all evidence against him was merely circumstantial and that it was insufficient to support a finding of guilt beyond a reasonable doubt.

On appeal, the New York appellate court sustained the convictions. It agreed that proof involving circumstantial evidence must be beyond a reasonable doubt, which it defined as "excluding to a moral certainty every other reasonable hypothesis." Here, it ruled there could be no other reasonable hypothesis. If the defendant was not the one who broke into the coin box, then how did his print get there? He was not employed by the people who own and service these arcade machines, nor has he ever been employed by them. His fingerprint was recently left there, as evidenced by the fact that there was no dust on it even though there was dust everywhere else within the coin box. The court reasoned that the "only reasonable inference to be drawn from the presence of his fresh fingerprint inside the machine was that he forcibly opened it for the purpose of extracting its cash contents." In sum there was sufficient circumstantial evidence to infer his guilt beyond a reasonable doubt.

Real Evidence

A third type of evidence is known as **real evidence**. Simply put, this consists of tangible physical objects or traces of physical objects (e.g., a gun, torn underpants, burglar tools, blood, semen, etc.). This type of evidence is introduced through a witness on the stand who is familiar with its context and can testify to its relevancy. The side wishing to have the evidence admitted usually first asks the court stenographer or the clerk sitting in the courtroom to mark it as either a state's exhibit or as a defense exhibit (which is usually done with a tag or a little sticker they keep on hand). The moving attorney then usually shows it to opposing counsel as a courtesy so that the other side can examine it up close. Next, the attorney approaches the witness on the stand with the object and asks what it is and how the witness can identify it as such (e.g., the police officer witness might say it is the knife which she found next to the murder victim). Finally, the attorney will ask the judge to allow admission of the object into evidence as "People's exhibit three" or "Defense exhibit three," or whatever number the presenting side is up to at that point. Once admitted, the object will be later sent to the jury room as the jury deliberates the verdict. Juror members will be able to hold it and closely inspect it to their satisfaction.

One ground for objecting to the admissibility of an object involves problems establishing a **chain of custody**, that is, proof that the object is the very one found at the crime scene and that it has not been substituted, altered or tampered with during testing, transportation and/or storage prior to trial. Chain of custody is not critical when an object is so unique that the witness himself can confidently identify it just by looking at it. For example, if a police officer on the stand is shown a knife with the victim's initials peculiarly carved on it, he may be able to recognize it as the same knife found by him at the crime scene. On the other hand, certain physical evidence is **fungible**, meaning it can not be readily identified by a witness unless there is some documented chain of custody to rely on. The same holds true for physical evidence sent by the police to labs for testing. Absent a documented chain of custody, how can one be sure whose blood, semen, hair, etc. has actually been tested by the lab? The case that follows illustrates this type of concern.

Byerly v. Ashley

825 S.W. 2d 286 (Ky. App. 1991)

The Western Kentucky Farm Center (a prison) sought to discipline an inmate for allegedly using a controlled substance while serving his time. The "proof" against the inmate was a "hot urine" which confirmed the presence of a forbidden substance in his system. The inmate objects to this "proof" and asks the reviewing court to grant a declaratory judgment in his favor, thereby preventing the prison from going forth with its desire to subject him to administrative punishment. The reviewing court refused the inmate's motion for declaratory judgment, and the inmate appealed this denial to a Kentucky appellate court.

The inmate's motion for declaratory judgment was based on potential problems associated with the "chain of custody" regarding the urine sample taken from him. Apparently, prison officials who had taken the urine sample from the inmate had attached a form to the urine sample, as was their practice. Everyone associated with the prison who handled the urine sample signed his or her name and the date on the form to show an unbroken chain of custody. However, once the urine sample arrived at the laboratory, the signature trail stopped. Laboratory technicians who handled the urine sample during the testing process simply failed to sign and date the form, which was still attached to the urine sample. Hence, there was nothing on the form to show who, how many, or when people handled the urine sample once it reached the laboratory.

The prison argued that it is not its fault that laboratory workers failed to sign the form. It argued that it had no authority to dictate procedures to an independent laboratory. The appellate court said that this may be true, but corrections officials do not have to take their business to laboratories that refuse to follow proper procedures.

The prison also tried to argue that, even though laboratory officials ignored the form attached to the sample, no fatal defect occurred because the laboratory report clearly provided a statement that the "chain of custody procedure was followed for this specimen." However, the appellate court was not satisfied with this self-serving, summary statement on behalf of the laboratory. The report did not specify what specific steps the laboratory took to guarantee the integrity of the specimen, and so there is no way for a court to confirm that appropriate chain of custody procedures were indeed employed.

The appellate court emphasized that the purpose of a proper chain of custody is to establish that "the sample tested is the same as that taken from a particular individual and that, at the time it is tested, the sample is in the same condition as when taken, free of tampering." Since the laboratory could not show a proper chain of custody, any results implicating the inmate were too unreliable to be of any use. Establishing a chain of custody for urine samples is not a hard or burdensome thing to do: it simply amounts to putting signatures and dates on a form.

The appellate court concluded that even though this particular inmate was not being subjected to new criminal charges, he still was being subject to additional prison discipline. This being the case, due process required that any evidence used against him in a disciplinary matter be reliable. Because prison officials seeking to punish the appellant could not certify with reasonable certainty that the urine tested at the laboratory was in fact his, the trial court below was ordered to grant the declaratory relief that the inmate requested.

Documentary Evidence

One final, major category of legal evidence is known as "documentary evidence." **Documentary evidence** consists of writings or other recordings (including videos and sound recordings). For example, someone in court might wish to prove the contents of a ransom note, a suicide letter, a will, a written contract, or a taped confession. Of course, the best and clearest proof of what is in such recordings would be the original document or recording itself, rather than some reader or listener's interpretation of it. This brings us to the "Best Evidence Rule." The **Best Evidence Rule** maintains that in order to prove the contents of a writing, voice recording, or photograph, the original is required unless it has been innocently lost or destroyed.[3]

Suppose a man and his sister are suing each other over who should inherit their father's estate. The sister wants to testify that she read a will just last month that her father had written leaving everything to her. In addition to her, the sister's husband, son and minister are also prepared to testify that they too had read the will and that indeed everything was left to this sister. Should these witnesses be allowed to bring up what was in the will merely via their sworn oral testimony in court? Or should they be required to produce the will (if in fact it still exists and is in their possession)?

The Best Evidence Rule would cover such a situation. The rule maintains that in order to prove the contents of a writing or other recording, the original is required unless it has been innocently lost, destroyed or is otherwise genuinely unavailable to the party. Oral testimony will not suffice unless the document or recording itself is truly not available. In addition to the innocent loss or destruction of the item, unavailability

3. See, e.g., Fed. R. Ev. 1002

could include the document being in the hands of the opposing party who refuses to produce it (e.g., in the hands of a defiant litigant or in the hands of a criminal defendant who does not have to give it up due to the privilege against self-incrimination).[4]

Of course, despite the Best Evidence Rule, nothing would prevent a person from orally testifying as to what she saw or heard with her own senses even if a recording of the event also existed. For example, if a police officer both concurrently heard and tape recorded a confession, the officer could testify to what he heard with his own ears even though a tape recording is available. Here, the officer would not be testifying about the contents of a recording but rather testifying as to what he heard himself with his own ears. If he were not present during the confession and was relying solely on the tape recording, he would have to produce the recording in order to satisfy the Best Evidence Rule.

The Best Evidence Rule does not apply to physical objects like guns, knives, or hair but rather just to documents or recordings of some kind. The reasons for this rule are obvious: to prevent fraud and to limit innocent misinterpretations of documents or recordings.

It is possible to have more than one original of certain documents. Long ago, courts began ruling that this can happen when the document was made by the "same mechanical act," such as a carbon copy produced by an old-fashioned typewriter or a copy produced by a printing press using the same type set.[5] But, what about photocopies? For a long time they were not allowed. But since they are now so routinely done in the course of modern business (and hence trustworthy), most states and the federal courts allow them as long as "no genuine question is raised as to the authenticity of the original" or unless "it would be unfair to admit the duplicate in lieu of the original."[6]

Another exception to the Best Evidence Rule exists with regards to voluminous writings or recordings. It would be impractical for a judge or jury to listen to recordings or read through documents that are exceedingly long. In such situations, a qualified person (e.g., an accountant) may be permitted to summarize their contents so long as the opposing side has been given a reasonable opportunity in advance to inspect the originals.[7]

The Best Evidence Rule has been around for a very long time. Even so, it continues to present some interesting new issues as our information technology progresses.

United States v. Maxwell

42 M.J. 568 (A.F.C.C.A. 1995)

Air Force Colonel James Maxwell, despite 25 years of otherwise outstanding service, was convicted in a court-martial of using his computer to transmit sexual images of children engaging in sexual acts. He did this early in the internet era (mid 1990s), using his America Online account (which at the time only had 215,000 subscribers). The

4. Fed R. Evid. 1004
5. See, e.g., *Davis v. Williams Bros. Constr. Co.*, 269 S.W. 289 (Ky. 1925).
6. Fed R. Evid. 1003
7. Fed R. Evid. 1006

problem for the appellate court concerned the newness of this emerging technology and its intersection with the venerable, old Best Evidence Rule.

Specifically Colonel Maxwell argued on appeal that the use of pornographic images printed off of a computer by an FBI agent and used against him at his trial violated the Best Evidence Rule. The FBI agent had gone to American Online and, armed with a search warrant, asked them to retrieve transmissions made by Maxwell on their network. Using special software, American Online was able to extract the visual images which the FBI Agent was seeking. These images were put onto high density computer disks from which the FBI printed off hard copies using a computer. These hard copies were used to help convict Maxwell.

Maxwell argued that a computer itself should have been brought to court, and the jury allowed to view the alleged pornographic images on an actual computer screen rather than just a printout of these images. The defense cited the military's version of the Best Evidence Rule which says that, "To prove the content of a writing, recording or photograph, the original writing, recording, or photograph is required, except as otherwise provided in these rules, this Manual, or by an Act of Congress."

The military appellate court, however, sided with the trial court which had convicted Maxwell and ruled that the use of the hard copy printout did not violate either the letter or the spirit of the Best Evidence Rule. Specifically, it found a clear exception to the Best Evidence Rule in Military Rules of Evidence 1001 (3) which provides that, "If data are stored in a computer or similar device, any printout or other output readable by sight, shown to reflect the data accurately is an 'Original.'" Since the printout was in fact "an original," Maxwell's conviction should be affirmed.

Apparently, the Military Rules of Evidence were ahead of Maxwell's game and had already anticipated people like him trying to use the Best Evidence Rule to hamper computer—related criminal prosecutions. Do you feel that such a rule, which turns a computer printout into an "original," could ever violate the spirit of the Best Evidence Rule? Can we trust investigators to print out un-doctored versions of what would appear on screen? If so, should we trust the printouts of criminal defendants as well? What about parties suing one another in civil court? What, if anything, is the potential for abuse here?

Relevancy

Up to this point we have been looking at the four categories of evidence. But not all direct, circumstantial, real, or documentary evidence is admissible. It still has to be relevant. In fact, "Objection, relevancy," is probably one of the most commonly heard utterances made during trials.

The rule with regards to irrelevant evidence is quite simple: it is always and without exception inadmissible. Not all relevant evidence is admissible (e.g., the fruit of illegal searches), but all admissible evidence must be relevant. **Relevant evidence** is that evidence "having a tendency to make the existence of any fact that is of consequence to the determination of the action more probable or less probable than it would be without the evidence."[8] The evidence does not have to make the fact at issue a lot more or a lot less probable, but it does have to contribute something to the truth-finding enterprise. It is possible for evidence to be relevant (in that it technically adds or subtracts something from the probability of some issue) and yet immaterial (in that it adds or subtracts so little as to be a waste of time). Nowadays, most lawyers have forgotten this subtle distinction and equate irrelevancy with immateriality.

One might ask why any lawyer would wish to present irrelevant evidence in the first place, especially criminal lawyers who are paid by the case and not by the hour. Though ethically questionable, there may be strategic advantages to doing so. Lawyers sometimes attempt to introduce irrelevant evidence in order to confuse juries, prejudice juries, rattle enemy witnesses, or unduly prolong the trial in an attempt to cause lack of attention to what is really important.

One obvious example of irrelevancy would be the injection of someone's minority religious status into a trial merely in order to discredit that person. Rule 610 of the Federal Rules of Evidence is on to this scam, and specifically prohibits the pointing out of someone's religious beliefs as a way to discredit that witness. But, suppose a defendant in a criminal trial wants to introduce evidence of his deep religiosity in order to bolster (rather than take away from) his credibility? Are deeply religious people less likely to commit crimes than the irreligious? This was the issue addressed in the case that follows.

United States v. Brown

41 M.J. 1 (1994)

Brown was convicted by a military judge during a court-martial of illegal use of cocaine in violation of the Uniform Code of Military Justice. On appeal, he argued that the trial judge erred when he refused to allow evidence of Brown's strongly held religious beliefs regarding the sinfulness of illegal drugs during the proceedings. The trial judge refused to hear testimony regarding these beliefs on the grounds that any such evidence would be completely irrelevant to the issue of guilt or innocence.

The prosecution's case rested primarily upon Brown's testing positive for cocaine during a urine analysis. Brown, on the other hand, denied having ever knowingly used cocaine. He suggested that either the urine test was a "false positive" or else he must have unknowingly ingested cocaine somehow when he consumed weight-loss medication he obtained from a German pharmacy.

During the trial, Brown, who says that he stopped using alcohol when he accepted Christ as his savior, had wanted to present testimony regarding his strong religious beliefs regarding illicit drugs from both his military chaplain and from his wife.

Apparently, his wife would have testified that her deeply religious husband routinely asks to be excused from social functions in which alcohol will be served (e.g., the manda-

8. Fed R. Evid. 401

tory NCO Ball), and that he, like her, teaches their children as a matter of religious principle to never use alcohol or drugs.

Brown's chaplain evidently would have testified that he could not imagine Brown using cocaine since such behavior would be completely out of character for him in that it would violate his Christian witness. The chaplain was certain that the urine test must have been a "false positive."

The trial judge was not impressed with any of this potential testimony, ruling that Military Rule of Evidence 610 specifically classifies religious belief or lack thereof as irrelevant to the issue of witness credibility, and hence completely inadmissible.

On appeal, the military appeals court reversed Brown's conviction and held that the trial judge did indeed err in refusing Brown to present evidence of his deeply held religious beliefs. It said that Military Rule of Evidence 610 (like its civilian counterparts) likely violates a defendant's constitutional right to present a defense. The court reasoned that the rule might make sense when it is used to protect a defendant from a prosecutor wishing to invade American values of toleration and privacy by bringing up someone's unorthodox religious views (including atheism), but it wrongfully hampers defendants who wish to be proponents of such evidence in developing a critical theory of the defense.

The court ruled that it thought it "self-evident that opposition to drug use on the basis of deeply held personal moral convictions would make appellant less likely to have used drugs than opposition based merely on fear of punishment or disapproval." Given that the evidence was indeed probative and relevant, the military trial judge abused his discretion when he refused to "consider the fundamental premise on which appellant's defense was based."

In a dissenting opinion, another judge expressed his opinion that "it is dangerous and unwise to argue that there is a correlation between general character evidence and a person's religious beliefs." The dissent felt that trial courts should not get into the business of evaluating religious claims, especially given the many unorthodox religions that exist in the community. Such evidence, the dissent believed, offered little probative value while greatly increasing the risk of prejudice.

Prejudicial Impact

Suppose you were a prosecutor trying a defendant for rape. He is asserting his innocence and is swearing that the victim consented to the sex. Suppose further that you happen to know that this defendant had been convicted two times in the past nine years for raping other women. Wouldn't you as the prosecutor want the jury to hear of this defendant's prior bad acts? If you were on the jury, wouldn't you find such information to be interesting if not critical? On the other hand, wouldn't you as the defendant worry about getting a fair trial if such information were presented?

Because of prejudicial impact, not all evidence that is relevant is admissible. Rule 403 of the Federal Rules of Evidence states that, "Although relevant, evidence may be excluded if its probative value is substantially outweighed by the danger of unfair prejudice ..." In other words, **prejudicial evidence** is information that would tend to create more bias than useful knowledge—evidence that on balance would do more harm than good. If evidence will tend to distort the reasoned judgment of the jury, it will be excluded even though it is relevant. Evidence of bad character unrelated to the present case, prior sexual conduct of rape victims, earlier offers by the defense to plea bargain, and prior criminal records all often qualify as evidence too potentially explosive to be admissible despite having some relevancy. The case that follows is a good example of an appellate court attempting to balance relevancy against prejudicial impact.

United States v. Layton

767 F.2d 549 (9th Cir. 1985)

This case involved the murder of a congressman who came down to Latin America to investigate reports of Americans being abused by leaders of a religious sect whose members had emigrated from the U.S. to a new home. While there, the investigating congressman was apparently shot to death by a member of the sect while trying to leave the area on an airplane. Layton was charged with the congressman's murder. Immediately following the congressman's murder, the sect's leader, Jim Jones, fearful that American authorities would return to punish him and his followers for the crime, ordered his people to commit suicide by administering poisoned Koolaid to themselves and their children. Mass numbers of people sheepishly complied.

At the trial of Layton for the murder of the congressman, the prosecution wished to have a so-called "Last Hour Tape," produced by sect leader Jim Jones himself, admitted into evidence in an attempt to prove that Jones and Layton had conspired to have the congressman assassinated. This tape included the rants of Jones acknowledging the fact of the congressman's death along with the sounds of screaming and dying children in the background. But, the defense won a pre-trial motion to have this audiotape excluded, under the theory that any relevant information heard from the tape would be far outweighed by the danger of creating unfair prejudice in the minds of the jury. The prosecution appealed this pre-trial decision of the judge to exclude the tape. (Unlike post-conviction appeals, prosecutors are allowed to appeal pre-trial rulings without violating double jeopardy since the trial has not yet started.)

The issue on appeal was whether the trial court abused its discretion in ruling that the audiotape should be excluded on the grounds that any probative value of its content would be outweighed by its prejudicial impact (the essence of Federal Rule of Evidence 403). The appellate court sided with the trial court and held that the decision to exclude the tape from evidence was a wise one.

In reaching its decision, the appellate court first agreed with the trial court that the probative value of the tape was very low. The issue at trial was whether or not Layton had conspired with sect leader Jim Jones to execute the congressman. Nothing in the tape of screaming, dying sect members helped much in proving any such conspiracy. The appellate court pointed out that Layton's position during trial was that he was only trying to kill "traitors" that were leaving the religious camp with the congressman on the plane. He never personally shot at the congressman himself, so he should not be found guilty of his particular murder.

The prosecution on the other hand had attempted to argue that the audiotape proved that Layton and Jones both understood that the congressman was to die. The appellate court acknowledged that it was true that Jones was heard on the tape saying that, "The Congressman's dead, the Congressman lays dead, many of our traitors are dead, they're all laying out there dead ... I didn't [do it] but my people did ..." But in the appellate court's view, this was at best very wink evidence in establishing that Layton was the one who had killed the congressman pursuant to Jones' orders or otherwise. The tape simply failed to convincingly show that Layton was aware of any plan on Jones' part to see to the congressman's death, or even that Jones was aware in advance that the congressman was among those who were going to die.

This rather weak evidence on the tape linking Layton to Jones' supposed desire to see the congressman dead was coupled with a huge potential for prejudicial impact should the jury hear the recording. The sounds of children screaming and begging for their lives while their parents poisoned them at the direction of Jones shouting out orders in the background would, according to the appellate court, "distract even the most conscientious juror from the real issues in this case." It would be impossible for jurors listening to this tape to not have strong emotional reactions to what they heard. They would find it difficult to concentrate on the substance of what Jones was saying regarding the death of the congressman, while ignoring the heart-breaking and emotionally charged sounds of the children in the background.

Since the probative value of the tape in linking Layton to the murder of the congressman was slight, and the potential prejudicial impact of the tape was very great, the appellate court concluded that the trial judge did not commit an abuse of discretion in ruling that the audiotape was inadmissible. It clearly was inadmissible.

Prior Records

One common category of potentially highly prejudicial evidence is the prior criminal record of a defendant on trial. Suppose, for example, that someone is on trial for drunk driving. She denies being intoxicated and explains her refusal to take the breath test to the jury by saying that she refused out of outrage for being wrongfully harassed by the police. She explains her inability to walk a straight line by testifying that she was so nervous that she felt weak in the knees. Suppose further that she has three prior drunk driving convictions in the last two years. Would members of the jury appreciate learning of such prior convictions in evaluating her various claims? Would it be fair to force the prosecution to keep such information hidden from the jury? Or, would such information unfairly smear the defendant in they eyes of the jury?

Generally speaking, courts will not allow prior records to be used by the prosecution in an attempt to show propensity on the part of the defendant to break the law. In other words, there is a **general rule of inadmissibility of prior records**. Such evidence may have some relevancy (once a drunk driver, more likely to be a drunk driver again), but it is thought that the prejudicial effect will usually outweigh the probative value. (There are some very technical exceptions to this rule but they are beyond the scope of this introductory book.)

Offers to Plea Bargain

Suppose a defendant offers to plea guilty to some crime in exchange for some bargain but the deal falls through. Should the earlier offer on the part of the defendant to plea guilty be used against him at trial? What if the defendant not only offers to plea guilty but makes certain incriminating statements during the negotiation process? Should these statements be admissible at a subsequent trial? The case that follows addressed these concerns.

United States v. Mezzanatto

513 U.S. 196 (1995)

Mezzanatto was caught attempting to sell a pound of methamphetamine to an undercover agent for $13,000 from his car parked outside the front of a friend's house. The friend, who was working for the police to get himself out of trouble, had set Mezzanatto up.

After his arrest, Mezzanatto and his lawyer met with the prosecutor to try to work out a deal of some sort. At the meeting, the prosecutor told the defendant that though he had no obligation to talk, if he did talk he would be required to tell the complete truth. The prosecutor warned the defendant that, as a condition of trying to work out a deal, if the defendant was caught lying during the discussions, the negotiations would end. The prosecutor also made as a condition of bargaining that should negotiations end, any statements the defendant did make during discussions could later be used against him at trial (e.g., if the defendant tried to con the jury by giving statements that contradicted what he told the prosecutor during plea discussions). The defendant agreed to these conditions despite the fact that Federal Rule of Evidence 410 specifically says that "any statement made in the course of plea discussions" is not admissible at trial should the plea negotiations fall through.

During the plea negotiations, the prosecutor got the defendant to admit that he knew the package he was selling to the undercover agent contained methamphetamine. But, the defendant went on to lie to the prosecutor about his degree of involvement in the drug trade (the prosecutor successfully confronted the defendant with a videotape showing the opposite). Because the defendant lied to the prosecutor during the discussions, the prosecutor broke off negotiations and the case proceeded to trial. During the trial, the defendant attempted to convince the jury that he did not knowingly sell methamphetamine to the undercover agent but instead thought something entirely else was in the package. The prosecutor countered this testimony with evidence of the defendant's previous admissions to him during the aborted negotiations that he knew that what he was selling was indeed methamphetamine. The defendant was convicted of selling the drugs and given a 170 months in prison. He appealed.

On appeal, the defendant cited Federal Rule 410 (mentioned above) that seems to say that the right to confidentiality of statements made during plea negotiations is absolute. The defendant argued that even though he agreed that any statements made during the negotiations could be used against him if he took the stand and lied at trial, that such an agreement on his part should not be held against him in light of the clear language of Rule 410 that "any statements made during plea discussions" are "not admissible" should the case go to trial.

The intermediate appellate court agreed with the defendant and reversed his conviction. But, on appeal by the prosecution to the U.S. Supreme Court, the conviction was reinstated. The U.S. Supreme Court ruled that the defendant's rights under Rule 410 could indeed be waived (given up) by him.

The Supreme Court admitted that the plain language of Rule 410 at first glance does not seem to provide for any exceptions (including voluntary waiver by defendants). However, it said common sense must be used when interpreting defendant's rights under it. It said that courts have long held that even "the most basic rights of criminal defendants are ... subject to waiver." For example, the Constitution clearly and in very plain language provides for a right against self-incrimination, a right to a lawyer if charged with a crime, a right to a jury trial, and a right to confront one's accusers. Yet, all of these rights are routinely waived by defendants despite the absolutist-sounding language of the Constitution granting these fundamental rights. If defendants can knowingly and voluntarily waive these fundamental rights, then certainly they can voluntarily waive their rights under Rule 410. Since Mezzanatto knew what he was doing when he agreed to the prosecutor's conditions of engagement, he has no right to insist that statements made during negotiations be kept hidden from the jury when he took the stand and later tried to contradict himself.

Mezzanatto tried to find sympathy with the Supreme Court by suggesting that there was a gross imbalance between him and the prosecutor in terms of bargaining power when he agreed to what he did, and that his waiver therefore should not be used against him. But, the Supreme Court said that a system that tolerates plea bargains inevitably requires many defendants to make some very tough choices (e.g., many defendants feel compelled to give up the right to trial even when offered only long prison terms in exchange). The fact that Mezzanatto had to make a tough choice with a tough prosecutor is just how the game is played in our system of justice.

The dissenting judges disagreed strongly with the majority opinion above. In their written opinion they conceded that defendants give up many basic rights despite language in the Constitution giving them these rights. But they wrote that they believed Congress really meant it when it plainly said that any statements made by a defendant during plea negotiations would be inadmissible at trial. The dissent reasoned that this right could not be voluntarily waived by a defendant because Congress obviously wants to encourage people to enter into plea negotiations. To allow prosecutors to use statements made during plea negotiations against defendants at trial (even if they supposedly consent to this in advance) might discourage people from plea bargaining in the future. Congress knows that this would not be tolerable. Rule 410 is meant to serve the interests not just of defendants but of the government as well by promoting plea agreements. Were defendants to begin taking too many criminal cases to trial, the system would quickly collapse. Congress no doubt meant to encourage plea bargaining when it wrote the clear and absolutist language of Rule 410.

Rape Shield Laws

Rape cases present a tempting situation for the defense to try to smear the reputation of a victim by introducing evidence of her past sexual history into the trial (usually to bolster defense claims that the sex in question was consensual). In the past, victims have often felt that they were the ones on trial rather than the defendant. In an effort to prevent the trial from becoming an opportunity to re-victimize the victim through the introduction of highly embarrassing (and marginally relevant) evidence of past sexual activity, states have generally passed what have become known as **rape shield laws**.

Federal courts also have adopted such a rule. Federal Rule of Evidence 412 provides that "evidence offered to prove that any alleged victim engaged in other sexual behavior" or "evidence offered to prove any alleged victim's sexual predisposition" is generally not admissible in any criminal proceeding. Some exceptions apply. For example, evidence tending to show that someone other than the defendant might have been the source of the semen or evidence of the victim's past sexual practices with regards to this very defendant might be admissible if relevant to the issue of consent.

Federal and state rape shield laws have drastically cut into the traditional practice of smearing victims during rape trials. Yet, there are times when defendants might feel that rape shield laws deny them the constitutional right to present their core defense. The case that follows involves such a concern.

United States v. Withorn

204 F.3d 790 (8th Cir. 2000)

Withorn, a 19-year-old man, beat and raped a 12-year-old girl in a remote location on an Indian reservation. After his arrest, Withorn told an officer that he did have sex with the girl, but that it was consensual. He also said that he thought the girl was 16 years old at the time.

At trial, the jury was presented evidence that showed the girl had suffered swelling, bruises, scratches and other physical traumas that were consistent with her allegations that she never consented to sex with Withorn. Withorn wanted to counter this evidence that suggested force by bringing out the fact that he was not the first male whom the victim accused of forcible rape. Apparently, the same girl had earlier accused Chris Fallis, a teenage friend of Withorn, with rape in a separate incident a few years earlier. That case never went to trial because Fallis committed suicide before the case went to court. Withorn had wanted to bring the matter up in his own trial to suggest that he was not alone in claiming a false accusation of rape (Fallis also had claimed innocence prior to his death).

The prosecution asked the trial judge to forbid Withorn's attorney from introducing any evidence regarding the old, Fallis case. The trial judge granted the state's request, citing the federal rape shield rule. Withorn was convicted of the rape and (having had a prior juvenile record for raping his cousin) was sentenced to twenty years in prison.

On appeal, Withorn asked the court to reverse his conviction on the ground that he had been denied due process when he was forbidden from asserting a key element of his defense (that this female has in the past accused someone else of rape who denied it). In other words, Withorn argued that the federal rape shield law as it was being applied to him violated his constitutional right to a fair trial.

In analyzing Withorn's claim, the appellate court noted that in order to trump the rape shield statute with an appeal to the Constitution, Withorn would have to convince the court that the invocation of the rape shield rule in his trial was "so extremely unfair" as to "violate those fundamental conceptions of justice which lie at the base of our civil and political institutions." The court did not believe that Withorn had met this high burden. It noted that the Congress had a very legitimate desire in protecting rape victims from having to undergo the indignity of having past, unrelated sexual encounters put on display. Congress also correctly wanted to encourage rape victims to come forward and prosecute their attackers by shielding them from smear tactics. Of course, these legislative desires would not be allowed to violate fundamental conceptions of justice, but there is nothing in this set of facts to suggest that the use of the rape shield law to protect this tragic young girl was so outrageous as to deny fundamental fairness.

Leg Irons and Jail Clothes

Should courts permit juries to see defendants who come directly from jail to trial in their jail clothes or leg irons or manacles? Should defendants be given the dignity of wearing street clothes and to be free from other signs of their status as prisoners? Despite the inconvenience, jailers now allow trial defendants to dress in their street clothes before bringing them to court. This is because the U.S. Supreme Court, in the case of *Estelle v. Williams*[9], ruled that, "The accused's condition implicit in such distinctive, identifiable attire may affect a juror's judgment. The defendant's clothing is so likely to be a continuing influence throughout the trial that ... an unacceptable risk is presented of impermissible factors coming into play."

But, what about a situation in which a defendant poses a real risk of escape or assault? Should courts be allowed to require leg irons or handcuffs? This is the issue addressed in the next case.

United States v. Stewart

20 F.3d 911 (8th Cir. 1994)

Hot tempered Alexander Stewart, an Arkansas prison inmate, punched the Deputy Director of the Arkansas Department of Corrections at the end of an evidentiary hear-

9. 425 U.S. 501 (1976), at 504.

ing held pursuant to a civil action which Stewart had filed against the state. The official's nose was broken and required reconstructive surgery.

Stewart was charged with criminal assault and also with retaliation against a witness. During his pre-trial arraignment, Stewart was again disruptive. Later, prior to trial, he fired his court-appointed lawyer and chose to start representing himself. On the day of the trial, Stewart again was disruptive in court when the trial judge tried to make sure that Stewart understood the dangers of representing himself. When the trial judge warned him about his disruptive antics, Stewart responded by being argumentative. He also started making a long series of silly objections, the apparent purposes of which were simply to annoy the judge and to delay the proceedings. Finally, he made a couple of serious objections. He objected to the fact that the jury was about to see him dressed in prison clothes and also that the jury would see him in leg irons. The trial judge refused his requests to have the leg irons removed and street clothes provided.

During the trial, Stewart told the jury that he had punched the official because he wanted to be kept in federal custody and thereby avoid being sent back to state prison where he knew he would be killed by other inmates. The jury eventually found Stewart guilty of assault (but not guilty of retaliation against a witness). Stewart was sentenced to 70 months for the assault.

On appeal, Stewart (now represented by a lawyer) argued that he had been denied a fair trial when the trial judge refused to grant his requests for street clothes and no leg irons. The appellate court ruled against Stewart and upheld his conviction.

The appellate court first discussed the issue of the jury seeing Stewart in leg irons. It agreed with Stewart that ordinarily such a situation would constitute reversible error because a jury's seeing a defendant in leg irons ran the real risk of undermining judicial impartiality. The leg irons might signal to the jury that the defendant is unable to make bail, belongs in jail, and other negative factors. However, the court also held that "in certain extreme situations vigorous measures" might be needed "to handle a particularly obstreperous and disruptive defendant." It said that "the flagrant disregard in the courtroom of elementary standards of proper conduct should not and cannot be tolerated. We believe trial judges confronted with disruptive, contumacious, stubbornly defiant defendants must be given sufficient discretion to meet the circumstances of each case."

In Stewart's case, the trial court acted well within its discretion when it required Stewart to wear leg irons during his jury trial. First, the very reason Stewart was on trial was because he had broken the nose of a witness in an earlier court proceeding. He was therefore dangerous. Second, Stewart had constantly disrupted pre-trial court proceedings by aggressively showing contempt for court decorum at his arraignment and preliminary hearing. He also had been disruptive just before trial when the judge tried to remind him of his right to the services of a free trial lawyer. Because of these antics, the trial judge could have reasonably concluded that Stewart posed a real risk of taking hostile actions during the trial itself. There was no abuse of discretion in requiring leg irons during trial.

The appellate court still had to deal with the issue of Stewart's going to trial in prison clothes. Ordinarily, prison clothes like leg irons can taint the proceedings by prejudicing the jury against the defendant. Defendants have the right to project an aura of dignity by wearing street clothes. However, in this case there was little harm done. Leg irons are much more damaging than prison clothes in creating prejudice. There would be little difference in a jury seeing Stewart dressed in street clothes wearing leg irons than seeing him dressed in prison clothing wearing leg irons. Either way, they would see him in leg irons and realize that he was not at liberty. A jury will not be prejudiced by what it already knows. Since it found no error, the court affirmed Stewart's conviction.

Victim Impact Evidence

Juries can be prejudiced not just during trials but during sentencing as well. In the United States, juries today only typically sentence someone when the issue is death vs. life in prison. Is evidence that the murder of a particular person had a large, negative effect on survivors (a type of so-called **victim impact evidence**—information regarding the lingering effects of a crime on victims) useful and relevant in deciding life vs. death? Or, would such evidence impermissibly prejudice juries by tempting them to conclude that some murder victims' lives are worth more than other murder victims' lives?

This is an issue which the U.S. Supreme Court itself had a very difficult time resolving. In a trilogy of quick cases, the Supreme Court first took one position, stuck with it in a second case, only to then completely reverse itself a short time later. The case that follows, though decided by a Pennsylvania appellate court, does a good job at summarizing the U.S. Supreme Court's ultimate conclusions on the matter.

Commonwealth v. Means

773 A.2d 143 (Pa. 2001)

Means and an accomplice robbed, beat and fatally shot a man who just happened to be walking down a street in Philadelphia. Means and his accomplice then proceeded to a home a couple of blocks away where they encountered a doctor who was planting a tree in his yard. They beat and robbed the doctor, and shot him in the leg. Meanwhile, the police, who had just discovered the dead body of the first victim came upon Means and his accomplice while they were still in the act of attacking the doctor. The two thugs took off in opposite directions while the police gave chase. During the chase, Means tried to shoot at the police officer but his gun misfired. Eventually Means was caught and charged with murder of the first victim, robberies, and related crimes.

A jury convicted Means of murder and lesser offenses and then had to decide whether or not he deserved the death penalty. At this point, Means asked the trial judge to disallow any victim—impact evidence that the prosecution might wish to present during this penalty phase of this capital trial. Means claimed that such evidence would violate both the U.S. and the Pennsylvania Constitutions.

The trial judge agreed with Means and granted his motion by declaring victim-impact evidence in violation of the U.S. and Pennsylvania Constitutions. At this point the proceedings were halted to allow the prosecution time to appeal this decision to the Pennsylvania Supreme Court.

On appeal, the Pennsylvania Supreme Court sided with the prosecution in declaring that neither the federal nor state constitutions were violated by the introduction of victim-impact evidence in death penalty cases. In its opinion it first gave an overview of the U.S. Supreme Court's thinking on the subject relative to the federal constitution.

The Pennsylvania court began by first noting that the U.S. Supreme Court in the case of *Booth v. Maryland*[10] held in 1987 that victim-impact evidence in death penalty cases did indeed violate the U.S. Constitution. It reiterated this conclusion in the 1989 case of *South Carolina v. Gathers*[11]. But then, amazingly, it quickly reversed itself just two years later in 1991 in the case of *Payne v. Tennessee*[12].

The initial reasoning of the Court in the older *Booth* and *Gathers* cases was that the prejudicial effect of such evidence far outweighed any probative value it might have in deciding the appropriate life vs. death decision. Such evidence was thought to have little relevancy. The focus in deciding life vs. death should be on the defendant and his or her characteristics rather than on the characteristics of a victim. In addition to this lack of relevancy, great prejudice could result. Juries learning how a death affected survivors might be easily swayed by emotion and swept away by their passion. Such evidence invited jurors to prejudicially value some human lives more than others, which would not be proper (e.g., is the life of a laborer worth less than the life of a professional person?). Because of these concerns, the Court initially believed that allowing such evidence violated the Eighth Amendment's prohibition against cruel and unusual punishment.

But, then quickly came the Supreme Court's reversal in the *Payne* case noted above (facilitated by the fact that its two earlier decisions were decided by close 5/4 votes). In *Payne*, the U.S. Supreme Court said that nothing in the Eighth Amendment would prohibit victim-impact evidence during capital sentencing. Such evidence is highly relevant without being unduly prejudicial. It is relevant because "such information conveys to the jury that the decedent was a unique individual whose loss affects society." It is not fatally prejudicial because should the jury's passions ever become inflamed, courts can deal with such a problem on a case by case basis. Juries are not so untrustworthy that we have to assume that they will always become blinded with passion and irrationality. Juries can generally be trusted to avoid prejudicially valuing one victim's life more than another's since "juries are not provided with comparisons among victims; in any given trial, the jury is provided a glimpse of only that particular individual victim's life."

The Pennsylvania Supreme Court concluded its analysis by ruling that Means not only fails under the U.S. Constitution but under an appeal to the Pennsylvania Constitution as well. It said it found the U.S. Supreme Court's reasoning in *Payne* very persuasive and would adopt it in interpreting the Pennsylvania Constitution, just as nearly all the other state supreme courts have chosen to do in analyzing their own state constitutions.

---

10. 482 U.S. 496 (1987)
11. 490 U.S. 805 (1989)
12. 501 U.S. 808 (1991)

This completes the chapter on Law of Evidence, Part I. In the next chapter you shall look at some really interesting issues you have heard about all your life in watching courtroom dramas on television. This next chapter will hopefully answer any lingering questions you may have about such topics as attorneys being required to keep naughty secrets, experts giving their opinions on the stand, and hearsay (like lack of relevancy, one of the most common objections raised in trials).

Chapter Eight

Law of Evidence, Part II: Competency of Witnesses, Privileged Communications, Opinion Evidence, Hearsay and Its Exceptions

In this chapter we pick up your study of evidence with more specific rules. We will study the most common form of evidence, testimonial, and the rules regarding lay and expert opinions. If the jury is supposed to be the fact finder and draw its own independent conclusions, should witnesses be able to give opinions or just facts?

One of the primary goals of the rules of evidence is to receive all relevant evidence so that the court may make a fair determination of the issues before it. The rules regarding hearsay and requiring competent evidence and witnesses further this goal by setting standards for the quality of evidence that is available to the court. In stark contrast to this goal, we will study privileges. They have the radical result of keeping relevant evidence from the court in order to further important relationships in our society.

Our study of the rules of evidence is necessarily abbreviated, as entire classes are dedicated to their study. Seek to understand both the content of the rules and the reasons behind them. It will give you a better basis for applying the principles in other areas of evidence that have necessarily been excluded from these chapters.

Competency of Witnesses

Competent evidence is evidence that is legally admissible. A competent witness is one who is allowed to testify in court. Generally, all witnesses are deemed competent unless a rule specifically excludes them.[1] This rule abolishes all common law rules that excluded witnesses from testifying for reasons such as age, mental or moral capacity, or their relationship to a party in the case. It excludes only those witnesses who fall under the specific exclusions listed in the rules, some of which are discussed immediately

1. Fed. R. Evid. 601

below. The party who objects to the witness has the burden of finding another rule that provides a basis to exclude them.

Personal Knowledge

One of the oldest English common law concepts requires a witness have personal knowledge of the matter he testifies about.[2] Rule 602 codifies this rule and requires all non-expert witnesses have personal knowledge about the matter they testify about.[3] This promotes the production of the best and most reliable evidence before the court. Witnesses are allowed to testify about what they saw, heard, smelled, or otherwise perceived with one of their senses. Generally they cannot testify about what someone else told them occurred. This is hearsay and will be discussed further below. The more reliable evidence comes from the person who perceived it testifying directly in court.

Before the witness may testify, the person who presents him has the responsibility to lay a foundation to show that he had the opportunity to perceive the event that is the subject of his testimony. This is generally done by asking the witness questions about the date and time of the event, assuring that he was present, and then asking the witness about the event. For instance, the attorney may ask the witness the following questions to lay a foundation.

Attorney: Mrs. Jones, where were you on June 15th of this year at approximately 5:00 p.m.?

Mrs. Jones: I had gone to the grocery store and was on my way home to fix dinner.

Attorney: Did anything unusual happen?

Mrs. Jones: Yes. While I was at the stop light on Riverdale Road by my home waiting for it to turn green, I saw Old Man Smith's horse run through the intersection right in front of me.

Attorney: How did you know it was the Smiths' horse?

Mrs. Jones: I've lived next door to the Smiths for the past ten years and I have had to put the horse back in their pasture about once a month during the last two years.

Attorney: Were you doing anything that might have distracted you from seeing this?

Mrs. Jones: Well, I wear glasses and I didn't have them on at the time, but I'd know that horse anytime.

In this instance, the attorney laid sufficient foundation to establish that Mrs. Jones had personal knowledge. She was present at the selected location and able to observe the horse run through the intersection. If the witness was not attentive, or her mem-

---

2. 9 Holdsworth, Hist.Eng.L. 211 (1926), cited in *McCormick on Evidence*, Ch.3, § 11, characterizes the rule as having its roots in medieval law.

3. Expert witnesses are discussed separately below.

ory not complete about the event, she might not be able to testify. The judge may exclude the witness, or allow her to testify and instruct the jury that it should only give the weight to the testimony that it deems appropriate based upon the lack of memory.

Oath/Affirmations & Religion

Prior to being allowed to testify, witnesses must be willing and able to declare to the court that they will testify truthfully. This is done by taking an **oath** or **affirmation** calculated "to awaken the witness' conscience and impress the witness' mind with the duty to do so." [4] An **oath** is a "solemn attestation of the truth of one's words or the sincerity of one's intentions, specifically: one accompanied by calling upon a deity as a witness."[5] An **affirmation** is the making of a "solemn declaration under the penalties of perjury in place of swearing an oath to which one conscientiously objects."[6]

The rule is intended to be flexible, allowing for testimony despite religious differences, including testimony from atheists, conscientious objectors, children, or those with mental defects.[7] Further, the fact that a witness is religious is not admissible to show that the witness is more or less credible.[8] The judge or jury should make their determination on the truthfulness of the witness based upon the testimony and demeanor of the witness. Their religious beliefs, or lack thereof, should not bear upon witness credibility.

Judges and Jurors

Judges and jurors have the responsibility to determine what the facts are, based upon the evidence presented to them. It would be awkward indeed if either one were allowed to testify in a case where they were sitting as a fact finder. If the judge is a witness, who rules on objections or compels him to answer? How does a lawyer walk the line of cross-examining or impeaching the judge who is presiding over the case and will in the future rule on motions brought by that lawyer? How can the judge remain impartial in the eyes of the jury or the public?[9] The Federal Rules of Evidence simply prohibit a judge from testifying in any proceeding over which he is presiding.[10] If a judge may be called as a witness, he would step down and allow another judge to preside over the case.

For similar reasons, a juror is not a competent witness in a case where he is sitting as a juror. There are exceptions, but only where the juror is asked to testify regarding irregularities in the proceeding.[11]

4. Fed. R. Evid. 603
5. Merriam-Webster's Dictionary of Law (1996)
6. Merriam-Webster's Dictionary of Law (1996)
7. Note to Fed. R. Evid. 603.
8. Fed. R. Evid. 610
9. Questions raised in the Notes to Fed. R. Evid. 610
10. Fed. R. Evid. 605
11. Fed. R. Evid. 606

Mental Incapacity and Children

Under the Federal Rules of Evidence, even very young children and others with mental deficiencies may be able to testify. If the witness has information that will assist the court in its fact finding process, the age or maturity of the witness does not itself determine his or her competency to testify. The judge must be convinced that the witness understands the difference between telling the truth and telling a lie, and will tell the truth to the Court. This rule has allowed even very young children to testify where they are found to be capable of telling the truth and promise to do so.

No specific language is required for the oath or affirmation, and judges are given wide latitude to form questions based upon the needs of the witnesses. The judge or jury is then left to determine, as with every other witness, the witness' credibility. This was discussed in the following case.

United States of America v. Allen J. (a Juvenile)

127 F.3d 1292 (10th Cir. 1997)

Allen J., a fifteen-year-old juvenile, was charged and adjudicated for raping his twelve-year-old cousin. On appeal, Allen J. claimed that the trial court should not have found the victim competent to testify. He alleged that a formal competency examination should have been completed prior to allowing her to testify because she suffered from "Fetal Alcohol Syndrome or Fetal Alcohol Exposure" and "mild retardation and learning disabilities."

The Court recognized the presumption in Rule 601 that "every person is competent to be a witness," and found that there is no minimum or baseline mental capacity requirements witnesses must demonstrate before testifying. Mental capacity of a witness should be assessed in determining the weight and credibility of his or her testimony, not whether he or she is competent to testify. In federal cases such as this one (it occurred on an Indian Reservation) the Court need only determine whether the child is capable of understanding and answering simple questions, as required by federal statute.

The victim was asked several questions before she was allowed to testify. "These questions included: 'Do you understand what it is to tell the truth?' and 'Do you know the difference between the truth and a lie?' The victim did not respond to the judge's questioning. (The court then asked the prosecutor to try questioning the witness. The prosecutor began with simple questions ('What is your last name?', 'How old are you?', and 'Where do you live?'), which the victim answered. After about thirty questions along these lines, almost all of which the victim was able to answer correctly, the prosecutor shifted to questions relating to the difference between the truth and lies. Among other questions, the prosecutor asked the victim if she understood she had promised to tell the truth in court, to which the victim responded affirmatively. After this series of questions, which established the victim knew the difference between a truth and a lie, knew she was to tell the truth in court, and knew she would be punished if she told a lie, the court directed the prosecutor to proceed to the heart of her case. Defence counsel objected repeatedly throughout this process and throughout the remainder of the victim's testimony."

Allen J based his appeal on the fact that the victim did not respond to the judge's questions, and gave incorrect and nonsensical answers to several questions asked by the prosecutor. Basing the decision on the interpretation of Rule 603, the Court found that the issues raised by Allen J went to the victim's *credibility*, and not her *competency* to testify. The appellate court cited the precedent of an 1895 United States Supreme Court case where a five-year-old was allowed to give critical testimony is a capital case. "Since that time, the trend in the law has been to grant trial courts even greater leeway in deciding if a witness is competent to testify." This is an area where the trial judge is given a great deal of discretion, and there was sufficient evidence here to support the trial court's ruling.

Other Categories of Disqualification

Under the common law rules, several categories of witnesses were not competent to testify. For example, under common law, belief in a divine being who would punish false swearing, was required before a witness could testify. This excluded all but members of the major religions from testifying.[12] Someone who had been convicted of treason, a felony or a crime involving fraud or deceit was likewise not allowed to testify.[13] Parties to a lawsuit and those having a direct interest in the action were disqualified from testifying[14] because of concerns that their self-interest would keep them from being reliable witnesses. For similar reasons, early common law also prevented a party's spouse from testifying either for or against the party in either a civil or criminal case.[15]

As the common law evolved, and finally as the Federal Rules of Evidence have been adopted and codified the rules, most of these prior disqualifications have been abandoned, generally allowing the court to receive evidence. As was seen in the *Allen J.* case above, what would have previously been a basis to disqualify the witness is now simply grounds for impeaching his credibility. To **impeach** a witness is to "cast doubt on, as to challenge the credibility of a witness or the validity of a witness's testimony."[16]

The current rule allows the court to receive the information from the witness, for instance from a spouse of the party, someone convicted of fraud or deceit, or a child witness. The examination or cross-examination of the witness reveals the potential bias the witness has toward the parties, or their incapacity. The jury is ultimately left with the responsibility to determine whether or not to believe the testimony.

Privileged Communications

With few exceptions, rules of evidence facilitate the objective of finding the truth. For instance, requiring the witnesses to have personal knowledge of the event they testify

12. *McCormick on Evidence*, Ch.7, § 63, citations omitted.
13. 2 Wigmore, Evidence §§ 519, 520.
14. 2 Wigmore, Evidence §§ 575–580.
15. 2 Wigmore, Evidence §§ 488, 600–620, 2227–2245.
16. Merriam-Webster's Dictionary of Law (1996).

about, or excluding evidence involving "unfair prejudice," aid the court in the ultimate search for the truth. These and other rules seek to exclude evidence that is likely to mislead or prejudice the court.[17] It is a well established principle that "the public ... has a right to every man's evidence."[18]

In stark contrast to the goal of facilitating the finding of the truth, privileges keep relevant evidence from the court, impeding the fact finding process. Keeping relevant evidence from the court is a high price, requiring the justification for the privilege to be compelling. The rationale for **privileges** is found in the protection of a relationship that is deemed to be of such importance overall that it outweighs that of the fact finding process of the court.

For example, a person confesses to his priest, or tells his attorney during the course of his criminal prosecution, that he robbed a bank. Neither the priest nor the attorney can be compelled to testify to this fact in court. You can see the value of the testimony in a criminal prosecution for bank robbery, yet the jury would not hear the testimony.

As a matter of public policy, the privilege is necessary to encourage communication within these important relationships. In other words, without a privilege protecting the communication, people would not be candid with their attorney, clergy, physician or even spouse. Closely related to the rationale of protecting the relationship, is that of protecting privacy within these relationships.[19]

Because the cost of a testimonial privilege is so high, courts have recognized that "they must be strictly construed and accepted 'only to the very limited extent that permitting a refusal to testify or excluding relevant evidence has a public good transcending the normally predominant principle of utilizing all rational means for ascertaining truth.'"[20] Courts and legislatures continue to review privileges and carefully weigh their costs and benefits. Courts will not enlarge the privilege any more than is deemed necessary to accomplish the purpose for the rule.

That being said, it is interesting to recognize the extent that privileges are used within states. In addition to the ten or so privileges adopted by states specifically following the Uniform Rules of Evidence or those originally proposed by the United States Supreme Court, states add numerous statutory privileges. Nearly 30 years ago when Utah revised its Rules of Evidence, the Advisory Committee noted that in addition to the privileges specifically enumerated in the Rules of Evidence that it adopted, it had compiled a list of over 40 statutes that either directly or indirectly create privileges. It also recognized several other statutes that imposed a professional or institutional obligation of keeping confidences.[21]

The rule protecting against self-incrimination is of constitutional origin, and, when coupled with the exclusionary rule, keeps relevant information from a court. The ra-

---

17. See *McCormick on Evidence*, Ch. 8, § 72.

18. *United States v. Bryan*, 339 U.S. 323, 331 (1950).

19. *Id.*, citation omitted.

20. *Elkins v. United States*, 364 U.S. 206, 234, cited in *Trammel v. United States*, 445 U.S. 40, 50 (1980).

21. Advisory Committee Notes to Utah R. Ev. 501. See also Hutchings, M. L., "Privileges in Utah Law," *Utah Bar Journal* 2:3:34 (Mar. 1989).

tionale for this privilege is not to protect a relationship, but rather to safeguard the integrity of the criminal justice system. If an officer violates your right not to be a witness against yourself, and unconstitutionally compels you to provide a self-incriminating statement, it won't be used against you in court. This is an over-simplification of the rule, but illustrates the privilege. While the confession of a defendant is highly relevant and probative, the higher goal of safeguarding constitutional rights and affirming the government's role in our accusatorial system over-rides the goal of finding the truth in a particular case. This privilege is discussed elsewhere in this book and is therefore not included in the privileges discussion below.

The Federal Rules of Evidence, when proposed to Congress by the United States Supreme Court, contained nine separate privileges. In its debates, Congress became so divided over the issue of privileges that the dispute threatened to sink the entire effort to codify federal evidence law. To avoid that result, Congress rejected the specific privileges proposed by the Supreme Court, and submitted a very broad rule that allows for the "creation, refinement and evolution of federal privileges to the common law process."[22]

Privileges are, therefore, determined by statute, rule, constitution and common law. The Federal Rules of Evidence recognize those privileges recognized at common law.[23] Before a privilege is recognized, at least four prerequisites have been suggested. First, that the communications were in fact made in confidence such that they would not be disclosed. Second, that the confidentiality was essential to maintain the relationship between the parties. Third, that the relationship is one that the community recognizes as important. Finally, that the injury to the relationship if the confidence is disclosed is greater than the benefit gained by the disclosure.[24] Three specific privileges are discussed below.

Attorney/Client

Deeply embedded in our system of justice is the idea that an attorney owes loyalty to her client and should not be compelled to tell her client's secrets to a court. This allows for the free flow of information from client to attorney, allowing her to better represent her client and, in a criminal case, challenge the government forces against him. The **attorney/client privilege** is found in the evidence rules of all states.

The Uniform Rules of Evidence provide that the client, or someone on his behalf including his attorney, may claim the privilege. The privilege only attaches to "confidential" communications between the attorney and client for the purposes of rendering legal services.[25] The communication would not be privileged if the client talked to the attorney about something unrelated to legal representation. For instance, courts have found no privilege where the attorney was doing something that a non-attorney

---

22. Leonard, D. P., "Symposium: Federal Privileges in the 21st Century: Introduction," 38 Loy. L.A. L. Rev. 515 (Winter, 2004). Leonard provides a good discussion of the pros and cons of the development of federal privileges that has occurred with Fed. R. Ev. 501.

23. Fed. R. Ev. 501

24. 8 Wigmore at § 2285 (footnote omitted).

25. Uniform Rules of Evidence (1999) 502(b) & (c)

could do, such as prepare tax returns or conduct a business meeting where minutes were taken. A communication made to a person as a friend or messenger is not privileged just because that person happens to be an attorney.

The privilege is not absolute. No privilege is found under the "**crime-fraud exception**" when a person seeks advice from an attorney concerning a future or ongoing act of crime or fraud. The privilege does apply, however, where a client seeks advice merely to determine whether a prospective course of conduct is lawful.[26] A client would not be able to consult with an attorney on the best way to murder a spouse and keep that communication confidential.

Courts have also found no privilege where the client has a claim against the lawyer. This keeps a client from taking action against the attorney regarding bad representation, then claiming the privilege when the attorney seeks to defend himself against the client. Finally, the privilege belongs to the client and should not be used by the attorney to the detriment of the client.[27]

Communications are confidential only if the people to the conversation reasonably believed that they would be kept confidential. If a client intends the communication to be confidential it must be made outside of the presence of others who are not necessary to the communication. If other people could reasonably overhear the conversation, or where the client anticipates that the attorney will disclose the communication to a third party, no privilege will likely be found. The client holds the privilege, and if he chooses to speak about the communication, he may waive the privilege. The following case illustrates the problems that arise when the client discloses the information to a third person.

In re Grand Jury Subpoena

341 F.3d 331 (4th Cir. 2003)

Appellant, a person of Middle Eastern descent, was questioned by two FBI agents in March, 2002, to determine whether he had information regarding terrorism investigations, and regarding his "green card" application. This noncustodial interview lasted approximately 45 minutes and occurred in the lobby of his apartment.

Appellant was asked about his answer to the following question on his application: "Have you ever, in or outside the United States ... been arrested, cited, charged, indicted, fined, or imprisoned for breaking or violating any law or ordinance, excluding traffic violations[?]" Appellant had answered the question "no," although officers learned that he had a prior shoplifting conviction. When asked about the inconsistency, appellant said, "I answered 'no' to the question ... under the advice of an attorney."

In February 2003, the attorney identified by the Appellant as having given him that advice, was subpoenaed before a federal grand jury. The grand jury was impaneled to investigate the Appellant for making a false statement on his green card application. The attorney answered questions establishing that she was the Appellant's former attorney.

---

26. *United States v. White*, 887 F.2d 267 (D.C. Cir 1989).

27. Uniform Rules of Evidence (1999) 502(d)(1)–(7) provides exceptions where no privilege exists despite the attorney/client relationship.

She declined to answer specific questions regarding whether Appellant consulted with her regarding the application, and whether she advised him to answer "no."

A hearing was later held before the District Court who granted an order compelling the attorney to answer the questions. It concluded that Appellant had waived the attorney-client privilege when he disclosed the information to the FBI. That ruling is the subject of this appeal.

The Court recognized that "[w]hen the attorney-client privilege applies, 'it affords confidential communications between lawyer and client complete protection from disclosure.' However, because this privilege 'impedes the full and free discovery of the truth,' it must be "narrowly construed and recognized only to the very limited extent" that it achieves a higher public good. [28] The privilege applies only if:

(1) the asserted holder of the privilege is or sought to become a client;

(2) the person to whom the communication was made

  (a) is a member of the bar of a court, or his subordinate and

  (b) in connection with this communication is acting as a lawyer;

(3) the communication relates to a fact of which the attorney was informed

  (a) by his client

  (b) without the presence of strangers

  (c) for the purpose of securing primarily either

    (I) an opinion on law or

    (ii) legal services or

    (iii) assistance in some legal proceeding, and not

  (d) for the purpose of committing a crime or tort; and

(4) the privilege has been

  (a) claimed and

  (b) not waived by the client.[29]

The government first claimed that the answers to the questions were not covered by the privilege. The government argued that because Appellant "answered 'no' to Question 1(b) in a publicly filed document, he cannot claim an attorney-client privilege in connection with that answer because he did not intend for it to remain confidential." The Court disagreed with the government, finding that the attorney-client privilege applied to legal advice she may have given her client regarding his response to a question on a document. The Court also disagreed with the government regarding Appellant's "waiver" of this privilege by filling out a government document based upon the legal advice. The attorney-client privilege applies.

The Court agreed with the government, however, that a privilege may be waived either expressly or by conduct. When someone talks to another person about their at-

28. Citing *Hawkins v. Stables*, 148 F.3d 379 (4th Cir. 1998).

29. *United States v. Jones*, 696 F.2d 1069 (4th Cir. 1982).

torney-client communications, they waive their desire to keep it confidential. Appellant argues that there was no waiver because he merely revealed his conduct (that he acted in a certain way) without disclosing the substance of the advice. The Court, however, pointed out that the Appellant gave the substance of the advice when he told the FBI that the attorney had advised him to answer "no."

The Court also found no merit in the Appellant's argument that the FBI agents coerced and deceived him into disclosing the privileged information. He was not in custody, the interview was in the lobby of his apartment building, and lasted less than one hour. The fact that they talked to him about terrorist activities, and then about his answers to the application was of no consequence.

Although the questions asked of the attorney would reveal communications protected by the attorney-client privilege, the privilege was waived when the Appellant disclosed the content of the communication to the FBI agents. The order compelling the attorney to testify was upheld.

Priest/Penitent Privilege[30]

The **priest/penitent privilege** is one of the oldest and least controversial privileges in American law. It has been adopted by nearly every state in the Union,[31] and recognized in federal courts.[32] The privilege protects "communications to a member of the clergy, in his or her spiritual or professional capacity, by persons who seek spiritual counselling and who reasonably expect that their words will be kept in confidence."[33] It "recognizes the human need to disclose to a spiritual counsellor, in total and absolute confidence, what are believed to be flawed acts or thoughts and to receive priestly consolation and guidance in return."[34]

Consistent with the intent of the privilege, it only applies to those cases where the communications are of a religious or spiritual nature. Courts have refused to acknowledge the privilege where the communications with the clergy were to solicit assistance in avoiding tax obligations,[35] and where the defendant had business communications with a priest that he employed in a nonreligious capacity. [36] Who is a clergy can also pose interesting questions. A "clergy" is customarily defined as "a minister, priest, rabbi," or similar religious person, or one reasonably believed to be such a person.[37]

As with other privileges that protect confidential communications, the presence of a third person not necessary to facilitate the communication, can void the privilege. The reasoning for this is that privileges should be "narrowly construed" because they

---

30. Also referred to as the Clergy/Communicant privilege
31. See In re Grand Jury Investigation, 918 F.2d 347 (3rd Cir. 1990), ftnt 10 for a list of state statutes containing the privilege.
32. *Id.*
33. *Id.* at 377
34. *Trammel v. United States*, 445 U.S. 40, 45 (1980) cited *Id.*
35. *United States v. Dube*, 820 F.2d 886 (7th Cir. 1987), cited *Id.* at 382.
36. *United States v. Gordon*, 655 F.2d 478 (2d Cir. 1981), cited *Id.* at 383.
37. Proposed Fed. R. of Evid. 506(a)(1).

keep important information from the court. If a third person is present, the communication is not considered confidential or important enough to the parties involved. The presence of a third party is at issue in the following case.

In re Grand Jury Investigation

918 F.2d 374 (3rd Cir. 1990)

A grand jury was investigating an alleged arson regarding a fire at the home of a black family who lived in an all-white neighborhood in the Forest Hills section of Pittsburgh, Pennsylvania. The targets of the investigation were the next door neighbors, Mr. and Mrs. George Kampich, and Mrs. Kampich's adult son, George Shaw. The Kampichs and Shaw are white, and the investigation was for possible violations of federal law prohibiting racially motivated housing discrimination, and conspiracies to violate civil rights. Days after the fire, those three and Shaw's fiancee, Patty DiLucente, counselled with their Lutheran clergyman, the Reverend Ernest Knoche ("Pastor Knoche").

There were three discussions with Pastor Knoche regarding the fire. At the first one, only Mr. and Mrs. Kampich were present. That discussion was held to be privileged by the trial court and was not appealed by the government. A second discussion, a family counselling session, was held with Mr. and Mrs. Kampich, Shaw and his fiancé. This discussion was found to be privileged by the trial court, and was the subject of the appeal in this case before the Third Circuit Court of Appeals. The government contended that the presence of the fiancé was "neither essential to nor in furtherance of any religiously motivated communications to the pastor on the part of the others present" and therefore no privilege should exist. They further argued the accepted principle that evidentiary privileges should be narrowly construed because they impede the truth finding function of the court. A third discussion involved Pastor Knoche, the four from the prior discussion, and also a police officer. Presumably because of the presence of the police officer, no privilege was claimed regarding that discussion.

The Court addressed the issue as to whether there was a clergy/communicant privilege, and determined that it was well recognized at common law, in federal and state cases, and in state statutes. It looked historically at the rule, and balanced the need for the rule against the need for the information in a court's (or in this case the grand jury's) quest to find the truth. The Court held that the privilege applies "to protect communications made (1) to a clergy person (2) in his or her spiritual and professional capacity (3) with a reasonable expectation of confidentiality." It further found that "the presence of third parties, if essential to and in furtherance of the communication, should not void the privilege." Regarding the first and third discussions with Pastor Knoche, the lack of a third party in the first discussion, and the presence of the police officer in the third discussion, were presumably recognized by the parties as determining whether those conversations were confidential.

The question here was whether the presence of Shaw's fiancé voided the confidential nature of the communication. Was her presence proof that they did not reasonably expect confidentiality in that discussion? This was a family counselling session and she was neither related by blood nor marriage. The Court said that the confidentiality of the communication "depends upon whether the third party's presence is essential to and in furtherance of a communication to a member of the clergy." The appellate court sent the case back to the trial court to take evidence and make a ruling on this issue following the law that it set forth.

Husband/Wife

The **spousal privilege** arose from the ancient rule that prohibited a spouse from testifying either for or against the other spouse. The basis for this rule was two fold. A defendant-husband could not testify for himself because of the obvious bias. Second, because the husband and wife were one, and the wife was not legally recognized, she could not testify. It was not until 1933 that this testimonial disqualification was formally abolished in the federal courts.[38] The Court left in effect the portion of the rule that allowed defendants to keep their spouse from testifying against them. The rule evolved from one of disqualification to a privilege to keep one's spouse from testifying against one.[39]

As with the attorney/client and priest/penitent privileges, the spousal privilege has been in existence for a very long time. Unlike those two privileges, it has encountered strong opposition. The purpose of protecting the marital relationship is a laudable one, but is obtained at the expense of keeping important evidence from the court. In 1958, the United States Supreme Court addressed this issue for application in federal courts. It held that the spousal privilege belonged to both the testifying and the non-testifying spouse. A spouse could not testify against the other unless *both* consented. [40]

If the marriage is no longer in existence, or where the witness spouse wants to testify, the goal of protecting the relationship is not very compelling. Some courts have therefore ruled that in their jurisdictions, the witness-spouse alone holds the privilege. In other words, in these jurisdictions, if the witness-spouse wants to testify, he or she is allowed to do so. Another blow to the privilege came when courts defined confidential communications narrowly. Under this view, the witness-spouse could testify to what he or she saw (since that would not be revealing actual communications), or to communications made when a third-person was present. Only communications made directly between the spouses, during the course of their marriage, are allowed protection under this rule. The United States Supreme Court again took up the issue of who held the spousal privilege in the following case.

Trammel v. United States

445 U.S. 40 (1980)

Otis Trammel and two others were charged with importing, and conspiring to import, heroin into the United States from Thailand and the Philippine Islands. The government alleged that the petitioner and his wife, Elizabeth Ann Trammel, brought heroin into the United States from the Philippines.

---

38. *Funk v. United States*, 290 U.S. 371 (1933).
39. See the discussion in *Trammel v. United States*, 445 U.S. 40, 44 (1980) (citation omitted).
40. *Hawkins v. United States*, 358 U.S. 74 (1958).

Mrs. Trammel travelled to Thailand, purchased a supply of heroin, and brought it back into the United States. A customs search in Hawaii discovered the drugs and she was arrested. She agreed to cooperate with the government and testify against her husband and others. In consideration of her testimony, the government granted her immunity and did not prosecute her for the drug offenses.

When the government called Mrs. Trammel to testify against her husband, Mr. Trammel claimed a spousal privilege to keep her from testifying against him. The Trammels were still married at the time of trial, although Mrs. Trammel had told him, "I would go my way and he would go his." The trial court ruled that Mrs. Trammel could not testify regarding confidential communications between her and her husband. She could, however, testify to any "act she observed during the marriage and to any communication 'made in the presence of a third person.'" Upon the strength of Mrs. Trammel's testimony, Mr. Trammel was convicted of the drug offenses.

The issue before the Supreme Court was whether Mr. Trammel could keep his wife from voluntarily testifying. The Court considered the common law rule, upheld in *Hawkins*,_that a spouse could not testify against the other unless *both* consented to the testimony. It also acknowledged that the purpose behind the Federal Rules of Evidence was to provide the courts with flexibility and leave the door open to change. Consideration was given to the fact that the majority of the states, and the Uniform Rules of Evidence, restricted the defendant-spouse from asserting the privilege and thus keeping the witness-spouse from testifying when the witness-spouse wanted to do so.

The Court reasoned that this spousal privilege not only protected confidential communications between spouses, but went further than any other privilege and allowed a spouse to exclude all adverse spousal testimony. It balanced the cost of the rule (keeping relevant evidence from the court) against the benefit to the relationship of keeping her from testifying. If the spouse wants to testify, reasoned the Court, the "relationship is almost certainly in disrepair; there is probably little in the way of marital harmony for the privilege to preserve. In these circumstances, a rule of evidence that permits an accused to prevent adverse spousal testimony seems far more likely to frustrate justice than to foster family peace."

Balancing the important interests at stake, the Court held that the "witness-spouse alone has a privilege to refuse to testify adversely; the witness may be neither compelled to testify nor foreclosed from testifying. This modification—vesting the privilege in the witness-spouse—furthers the important public interest in marital harmony without unduly burdening legitimate law enforcement needs." Mrs. Trammel's testimony was not prohibited by the spousal privilege.

Other restrictions on the spousal privilege have been recognized. Conversations about or in furtherance of crimes in which the spouses are jointly participating are not covered by the spousal privilege.[41] Likewise, there is no privilege to keep a victim-spouse from testifying about what her spouse did to her or to a victimized child within the home.[42]

41. *United States v. Marashi*, (9th Cir. 1990).
42. *United States v. Bahe* (10th Cir. 1997).

Despite the spousal privilege, courts have refused to find a parent/child privilege. A parent can, therefore, be required to testify against his or her child, or vice-versa, under penalty of contempt. Although a compelling interest in maintaining family peace and relationships can be made, confidential communications in this relationship are not recognized as privileged.

Other Privileges

Numerous other testimonial privileges exist to protect relationships. Doctor/patient privilege, and the closely aligned psychotherapist/patient privilege, have been recognized at common law and by the United States Supreme Court to encourage candor and honesty within those relationships.[43] Courts have found the existence of a privilege for licensed therapists and counselors, but have generally failed to extend the privilege to unlicensed counselors or volunteers. Some states have enacted exceptions to this privilege, requiring disclosure of statements regarding child abuse.

Executive and governmental privileges have been recognized by federal courts. A great deal of deference is given to claims of national security and military secrets. A law enforcement privilege commonly exists to protect law enforcement from disclosing the names of informants. This helps to encourage the free flow of information during an investigation. If the information for a confidential informant is the sole evidence against a defendant, however, the prosecution may not have sufficient evidence to prove its case without having the informant testify directly against the defendant.

Testimonial Evidence

Testimonial evidence is by far the most common type of evidence, and its importance is evident. Any evidence that is used by the judge or jury must have been properly admitted. In other words, it would be improper for a court to consider information it had learned from a source outside of court. At the basis of this principle is a portion of the Sixth Amendment to the United States Constitution called the **Confrontation Clause**. It provides to the criminal accused, in all prosecutions, the opportunity to confront all witnesses against them. With very few exceptions, the confrontation clause requires that witnesses come into an open courtroom, testify, and be subject to cross-examination to challenge their testimony.

Some witnesses come to court voluntarily, but under the **Compulsory Process Clause** of the Sixth Amendment, the accused in a criminal prosecution, has the right to compel the appearance of reluctant witnesses. A **subpoena** is an order issued from the court and served on the witness that compels him or her to appear in court. It may be necessary to require witnesses to appear in court and bring something with them. This may be necessary to obtain medical records from a doctor or photographs from a foren-

43. *Jaffe v. Redmond*, 518 U.S. 1 (1996).

sics witness. A **subpoena duces tecum** is an order requiring a witness to appear and bring something with him or her. That document is served on a witness when there is a need to compel the production of something for the case.

Witnesses act as the eyes and ears for the court. Generally they testify from first hand knowledge regarding what they saw, heard, smelled, or otherwise perceived with one of their senses. **Opinion testimony** is testimony relaying a conclusion or opinion as opposed to direct knowledge of the facts at issue. For example, opinion testimony could testify that ballistics testing concluded that the bullet which killed the victim came from the defendant's gun, or that the blood near the victim did not match that of the defendant. Drawing conclusions or opinions about the facts of a case is primarily a task for the judge or the jury, and opinions by lay witnesses are not allowed with important exceptions discussed below. The rules break down witnesses into two categories: lay and expert witnesses.

Lay Opinions

A **lay witness** is a person who testifies to facts, without particular expertise or specialized knowledge. As discussed above, Rule 602 requires that witnesses have personal knowledge about that which they testify. As the witness testifies about what he perceived, he helps the jury understand the facts surrounding the issue that is before the court. Although an expert who also has personal knowledge may be allowed to speak as a lay witness, a lay witness does not give her opinion on a matter that requires scientific, technical or specialized knowledge. Rule 701 allows a lay witness to give an opinion if it is "(a) rationally based on the perception of the witness, and (b) helpful to a clear understanding of the witness' testimony or the determination of a fact in issue, and (c) not based on scientific, technical, or other specialized knowledge...."

The rule recognizes that some matters are within the bounds of human experience and are not easily explained without drawing an inference or conclusion. A lay witness is allowed to testify to those things that cannot be described factually in words, without the conclusions or inferences such as the "degrees of light or darkness, sound, size, weight [and] distance."[44] Lay witnesses have been allowed to give opinions about the appearance of persons or things. Examples include opinions that the defendant appeared to be unkempt, sleepy, angry, happy or in pain. Identifying a person or thing also requires the witness to give an opinion, but is allowed under the rule. Lay witnesses have been allowed to identify a person on a video surveillance camera, or a voice from an audio recording.

The distinction between lay and expert opinion is that "lay testimony 'results from a process of reasoning familiar in everyday life,' while expert testimony 'results from a process of reasoning which can be mastered only by specialists in the field.'"[45] For instance, a business owner may testify about the projected profits of her business, or damages to the business, without being qualified as an accountant or appraiser.[46] People

44. See the 2000 Amendment Advisory Committee Notes to Fed. R. Evid. 701, citing *Asplundh Mfg. Div. v. Benton Harbor Eng'g*, 57 F.3d 1190, 1196 (3d Cir. 1995).

45. *Id.* Notes to Fed. R. Evid. 701, citing *State v. Brown*, 836 SW2d 530, 549 (Tenn 1992).

46. *Id.* Notes to Fed. R. Evid. 701, citing *Lightning Lube, Inc. v. Witco Corp.* 4 F.3d 1153 (3d Cir. 1993).

with a history of heavy drug use have been allowed to give lay opinion that a substance appeared to be amphetamines.[47] A person with personal knowledge of how people acted when they were intoxicated could testify that the defendant appeared to be intoxicated. An automobile driver with personal experience driving an automobile could testify that the car was speeding. A lay witness with experience could testify that a substance appeared to be blood, but would have to be qualified as an expert to testify that bruising around the eyes is indicative of skull trauma.[48] Finally, a law enforcement officer was allowed to give a lay opinion that the defendant was acting "suspiciously." He was required to be qualified as an expert, however, to give testimony on the code words used to refer to drug quantities and prices which required specialized knowledge.[49]

Expert Opinion

As distinguished from lay witnesses, expert witnesses often have no personal knowledge of the case before the court. **Expert witnesses** possess, however, some scientific, technical, or other specialized knowledge that will help the court understand the evidence or to determine a fact in issue. An expert is qualified because of his or her knowledge, skill, experience, training, or education. Experts are allowed to give an opinion if (1) the testimony is based upon sufficient facts or data, (2) the testimony is the product of reliable principles and methods, and (3) the witness has applied the principles and methods reliably to the facts of the case.[50]

The trial judge becomes the gatekeeper, responsible to make sure that expert testimony is both reliable and helpful to the court. Expert testimony must be the "product of reliable principles and methods that are reliably applied to the facts of the case."[51] It is not enough that an expert presents his or her qualifications and assures the court that his or her opinion is reliable.[52]

The present rule was a response to *Daubert v. Merrell Dow Pharmaceuticals, Inc.*.[53] The *Daubert* case sought to liberalize the admissibility of expert testimony which had required, prior to *Daubert*, the "general acceptance" of the method or theory within the scientific community where it was based. The problem with "general acceptance" as the sole and end-all criteria was that legitimate but cutting-edge technologies would have to be excluded since they might not yet have come to the attention of the slow to catch on, general membership of a relevant scientific community. *Daubert* took the determination of whether to allow the expert testimony from the scientific community and placed it with the trial judge. *Daubert* set forth a list of flexible factors in determining the admissibility of an expert's testimony. First, has the expert's technique or theory been objectively challenged or is it simply a subjective and conclusory approach that cannot be reliably assessed? Second, has the technique or theory been subject to peer re-

47. *Id.* Notes to Fed. R. Evid. 701, citing *United States v. Westbrook*, 896 F.2d 330 (8th Cir. 1990).
48. *State v. Brown*, 836, SW2d 530 (Tenn. 1992).
49. *United States v. Figueroa-Lopez*, 125 F.3d 1241 (9th Cir. 1997).
50. Fed. R. Evid. 702.
51. Advisory Committee Notes on the 2000 Amendments to Rule 702.
52. *Daubert v. Merrell Dow Pharmaceuticals, Inc.*, 43 F.3d 1311, 1319 (9th Cir. 1995).
53. 509 U.S. 479 (1993).

view and publication? Third, what is the known or potential rate of error of the technique or theory? Fourth, are standards and controls in existence and maintained? Finally, has the technique or theory been generally accepted in the scientific community? These factors were not intended to be a rigid or an exclusive checklist. The trial judge is given substantial discretion and encouraged to be flexible in applying the factors the judge in the courtroom deems appropriate to determine the reliability of expert testimony. Appellate courts will generally defer to the trial court's decision regarding the admissibility of expert testimony.[54]

A preliminary question is whether the witness possesses some knowledge, skill, experience, training or education that qualifies him as an expert. If the matter is within the common knowledge of the jury, expert testimony is not appropriate. For example, an expert would not be necessary to give an opinion that when roads are wet they get slippery, or that when an item is released from an overhead location it will fall to the ground.

The requirement for "knowledge, skill, experience, training or education," is broad, allowing a witness to be qualified based upon any one of those areas. The expert may have an educational degree that provides his expertise, or specialized knowledge based upon his experience. To do otherwise would disqualify a witness who has not yet had the opportunity to develop experience, but has training and education in a particular area. In that case, the lack of experience would go to the credibility of the witness, not to her ability to be recognized as an expert. Consistent with the broad wording of Rule 702, courts have generally been reluctant to exclude an expert based upon his or her lack of qualifications.[55]

The applicability of *Daubert* to non-scientific expert witnesses, the deference to be given to the trial judge's determination, and the analysis to determine who is an expert, were at issue in the following case.

Kumho Tire Company, Ltd., et al., v. Patrick Carmichael, et al.

526 U.S. 137 (1998)

"On July 6, 1993, the right rear tire of a minivan driven by Patrick Carmichael blew out. In the accident that followed, one of the passengers died, and others were severely injured." The Carmichaels brought suit against the tire's maker and its distributor, (Kumho Tire), claiming that the tire was defective. A significant portion of Carmichael's case rested upon the opinion of Dennis Carlson, Jr.

Kumho Tire sought to exclude Carlson's testimony arguing that it was unreliable under *Daubert* and Rule 702. The trial court examined Carlson's methodology against the *Daubert* factors to determine whether it "has been a subject of peer review or publication," the "known or potential rate of error," and the "degree of acceptance ... within the relevant scientific community." The trial court determined that these factors argued against the reliability of Carlson's methods and excluded his testimony. The case was appealed to the Eleventh Circuit Court of Appeals who reversed the trial court's deci-

54. *General Electric Company v. Joiner*, 139 L.Ed.2d 508 (1997).
55. *Prince v. Michelin N. Am., Inc. 248 F.Supp2d 900 (WD Mo, 2003).*

sion. It noted that *Daubert* was only applicable in the application of scientific content and principles, rather than in skill- or experience-based observation which was at issue in this case. Kumho then appealed the case to the United States Supreme Court.

The Court reasoned that Rule 702 "imposes a special obligation upon a trial judge to 'ensure that any and all scientific testimony ... is not only relevant, but reliable.'" This gate-keeping function applies not only to "scientific" testimony but to all expert testimony. The factors set forth in *Daubert* are flexible and "do not constitute a definitive checklist or test." They are dependent upon the facts and circumstances of a particular case. The Court further reiterated the deference standard that appellate courts are to pay to the determination made by the trial court.

The Court went on to point out that Carlson had sufficient qualifications to be an expert. He had a masters degree in mechanical engineering, ten years of work for Michelin, and had provided expert testimony as a tire failure consultant in other cases. However, despite this, the Court went on to rule that the testimony must nevertheless be excluded. The testimony was excluded because the Court found the methodology used by Carlson in analysing the data, and the scientific basis for his analysis, to be unreliable. Ultimately, not one of the *Daubert* factors were found to apply. The lesson from this case appears to warn experts that not only must they be qualified, but their methodology must also be sound to be found reliable and therefore admissible.

The Supreme Court ultimately concluded that *Daubert's* general holding that the trial judge has a "gatekeeping" function, applies not only to scientific but also to technical and other specialized knowledge. It also concluded that "a trial court may consider one or more of the more specific factors that Daubert mentioned when doing so will help determine that testimony's reliability. But ... the test of reliability is 'flexible,' and Daubert's list of specific factors neither necessarily nor exclusively applies to all experts or in every case." Finally, the trial court has broad latitude and appellate courts apply an "abuse of discretion" standard to determine whether the trial court committed error. Applying those standards the Court held that the "District Court's decision in this case—not to admit certain expert testimony—was within its discretion and therefore lawful."

Basis for an Expert Opinion

An expert obtains information to form the basis of his or her opinion through three different methods. First, he or she may have personal knowledge of the event that is at issue in the court. For instance, a medical doctor who examined the victim of an aggravated assault has first hand knowledge of the victim's injuries. The doctor may be called to testify as to the extent of the injuries or asked to give his opinion as to the cause of the injuries.

Second, contrary to the rules governing most witnesses, expert witnesses are allowed to give opinions that are not based on firsthand knowledge or observation. An expert may be given facts in court, and asked to draw an expert opinion based upon those facts and her specialized knowledge or expertise. This is often done through the use of a hypothetical question. An attorney restates the facts that have been brought out during the trial, and asks the witness to draw an expert opinion regarding them.

Finally, the expert may have been presented with information outside of court, and asked to draw conclusions about them in the court. This would be the case with an accident reconstruction expert hired to determine the cause of an automobile collision. He would obtain information and test his theories outside of the courtroom, then testify to those before the court. A forensics examiner who tests a green leafy substance outside of court and determined it to be marijuana, and then testifies to that opinion in court would also fall into this category. Rule 703 allows experts to rely upon outside information to form their opinion, even if that outside information would not be admissible in court, so long as it is the type of information reasonably relied upon by experts in their particular field in forming such opinions or inferences. A common example is the reliance of an expert upon hearsay information to form their expert opinion. A medical doctor may rely upon x-rays, lab reports, nurse's notes and narratives from other doctors to form his or her opinion. An accident reconstruction expert may rely upon information he or she has been told by various people, as well as police reports and photographs. Again, the expert's opinion is not conditioned upon the admissibility of each of the items that he or she relied upon.

The jury is not required to give the expert witness' testimony more or less weight than any other witness. An expert's testimony is given the amount of weight that the jury deems appropriate under all of the circumstances.

Opinion of the Ultimate Issue

At common law, witnesses were not able to give opinions regarding the ultimate issue in a case. The witnesses were to provide evidence to the court, and the judge or jury was to draw their own conclusions based upon the facts presented. The "ultimate issue" rule was modified by Rule 703 and "testimony in the form of an opinion or inference ... is not objectionable because it embraces an ultimate issue to be decided by the trier of fact." This is consistent with the purpose of allowing information before the court if it will be helpful to the determination of the matter before it.

One large exception still exists regarding the ultimate issue. Rule 704(b) still prohibits an expert witness from testifying with respect to the mental state or condition of a defendant in a criminal case where it constitutes an element of or defense to the crime. That determination is left to the judge or jury. This exception arose out of the 1981 assassination attempt by John Hinckley, Jr. upon President Ronald Reagan. The federal jury ultimately found Hinckley to be not guilty by reason of insanity. The public was outraged and critics blamed a "battle of the experts" for confusing the jury. By prohibiting experts from giving their ultimate opinion regarding sanity, Congress sought "to eliminate the confusing spectacle of competing expert witnesses testifying to directly contradictory conclusions as to the ultimate legal issues to be found by the trier of fact."[56]

It is argued that the congressional response, as well as the perception among the public due to the publicity surrounding this trial, is misguided. In reality, few crimi-

56. Braswell, A. L., (1987) "Note: Resurrection of the Ultimate Issue Rule: Federal Rule of Evidence 704(b) and the Insanity Defense," 72 Cornell L. Rev. 620, 623 (citations omitted).

nal defendants raise the insanity defense and most such attempts fail. [57] Congress resurrected the ultimate issue rule in this instance, which arguably has not met the goal of avoiding confusion regarding expert testimony.[58]

Hearsay

One of the most frequently used objections in court is hearsay. The term is used by the general public in every day conversation and is highly misunderstood, sometimes even by lawyers. Most people understand "hearsay" as a statement made by someone else. It is usually referred to in a derogatory manner to describe a statement or evidence that is not reliable. In court, hearsay means something much more. The purpose of this section is to define hearsay, describe and provide the basis for the hearsay rule, and discuss several of the exceptions to that rule.

To illustrate the concept of hearsay, imagine the following conversation between a police officer and a woman reporting a crime.

Officer: So, Mrs. Cook, you appear to be very upset. Tell me what happened.

Mrs. Cook: I received a very disturbing telephone call.

Officer: What was so upsetting about the call?

Mrs. Cook: Well I'm certainly not going to repeat what was said. Suffice it to say that it was of the irritatingly offensive, juvenile variety.

Officer: Do you know who made the call?

Mrs. Cook: Yes, it was my young neighbor, Gerald Gault.

When a witness testifies before a court, his credibility is always at issue. If he is not truthful, his testimony has little value. By requiring a witness to appear before the court, under oath and subject to cross-examination, the credibility of the witness is assessed. Did the witness accurately *perceive* what he testifies about? Is the witness's *memory* about the perception accurate? Does the witness's description of the event *accurately reflect* his perception?[59]

Take the exchange between the officer and the citizen above. If the officer were allowed to testify to what Mrs. Cook said, the benefits of cross-examination would never be realized. Gerald would not be able to test whether Mrs. Cook accurately perceived the telephone call. (Could she adequately hear the male's voice on the other end of the phone? Did it appear that he was trying to disguise his voice? Has she talked to Gerald on the telephone before? How long did the telephone conversation last? Why did she believe that it was him?) He could not challenge whether Mrs. Cook's memory was accurate. (How long was it from the time that the telephone call was made until the report

57. The insanity defense is raised in only one to two percent of criminal cases that go to trial, and of those cases, only about ten percent end in a verdict of "not guilty by reason of insanity." *Id.* at 627 (citations omitted).

58. *Id.*

59. *McCormick on Evidence*, § 245 (citations omitted).

was made? Did she make any notes to help her remember what was said? Had Mrs. Cook been awakened or otherwise distracted by other events that were going on in the home at the time of the call?) Finally, Gerald has no way to challenge whether the description of the event accurately reflects Mrs. Cook's perception. In this example, we don't even have a clear description of what was said. (What did the male say to her? Is what was said even a violation of the law? Is she ultra sensitive about matters of this nature and could that impact her description? Could she have thought it was Gerald because of her frustration over his breaking her window earlier that week during a game of neighborhood baseball?)

Hearsay is generally thought to be unreliable because the person who made the statement is not in court and subject to cross-examination where credibility can be assessed. In this example, Mrs. Cook would be required to testify first hand so that the reliability of her statement could be determined.

This example also illustrates another potential problem with hearsay. An accused in a criminal case has a constitutional right under the Sixth Amendment to confront his accusers. While I have taken some liberties with the facts to illustrate hearsay concerns, in *In re Gault*,[60] the United States Supreme Court reversed Gerald's adjudication for a delinquency based upon this hearsay statement made by the officer. Because Mrs. Cook did not testify herself, Gerald was denied his right to confront his accusers under the confrontation clause.

That being said, much hearsay is deemed reliable and admissible in court. Part of the reason for this disparity is that hearsay ranges from untrustworthy rumors on one end, to sworn statements from credible witnesses on the other. The court is left to balance the need for the evidence against the concerns regarding its unreliability and the unfairness to the opposing side in not being able to effectively cross-examine the evidence.

Definition of Hearsay

Rule 801 defines **hearsay** as "a statement, other than one made by the declarant, while testifying at the trial or hearing, offered in evidence to prove the truth of the matter asserted." In other words, it is a statement offered in court, by someone other than the person who made the statement, to prove that the statement is true. A **statement** is an oral or written assertion, or nonverbal conduct of a person intended by the person as an assertion. A **declarant** is a person who makes a statement.[61]

In the example above, Mrs. Cook's statement (Gerald made a lewd telephone call to me) was being offered in court by someone else (the officer) to prove that the statement was true. It is hearsay.

A **statement** could be oral, written or non-verbal, so long as the person intended it to assert something. If declarant Denise told Wilma witness that she saw Jim walking on the side of the road on June 4th at 8:00 p.m., that is a statement. Denise intended

60. 387 U.S. 1 (1967)
61. Fed. R. Evid. 801

to assert that Jim was walking on the side of the road at that time and place. If Wilma testified in court to Denise's statement, it would be hearsay if offered to prove that Jim was in fact walking on the side of the road at that time and place.

An **affidavit** is a sworn statement in writing made under oath or on affirmation before an authorized magistrate or officer.[62] If Denise signed an affidavit that she saw Jim walking on the side of the road on June 4th at 8:00 p.m., that would be as much of a statement as the oral assertion discussed above. If the affidavit is offered in court to prove that Jim was in fact walking on the side of the road at that time and place, it is written hearsay.

People often intend to assert something through non-verbal actions. If Wilma asked Denise if she saw Jim walking on the road and Denise shook her head "yes," that is a non-verbal statement. If Wilma testified to Denise's statement in court, it would be hearsay.[63] Other non-verbal actions such as pointing could also be a statement if intending to assert something.

The rule requires that the statement is offered in court to "prove the truth of the matter asserted." In the examples above, Denise's statement is hearsay because it was being offered for the truth: to prove that Jim was walking on the side of the road at that time and place. The following fact pattern sets forth a statement that would not be hearsay because it is not offered to prove the truth of the matter asserted.

> As a prank, a man falsely shouts "Fire" in a crowded theater. He is prosecuted for the offense, and various witnesses are called who testify that the man did indeed shout the word "fire," but objection is made by the defendant that such testimony is hearsay, i.e., it is testimony about an out-of-court statement introduced for the truth of the matter stated. The proper ruling is that the statement is not hearsay, because it is not introduced to prove that there was a fire in the theater. In fact, it is introduced as part of the prosecution's case designed to prove the opposite, namely, that there was no fire.[64]

In another example, Mrs. Smith calls 911 and reports that a burglary is in progress at her home. An officer is called to the witness stand and asked why he went to the Smith home. He would be allowed to testify that someone identifying themselves as Mrs. Smith made a call and said that a burglary was in progress at her home. The out of court statement was not being made to prove that a burglary was in fact going on (the truth of the matter asserted) but to explain why the officer went to the person's home. It is not hearsay.

You can see how the legal definition of hearsay differs substantially from that used by the general public. Hearsay is a technical rule, not only in how it is defined, but also how it is applied. An exhaustive discussion of the hearsay rules would take much more time and space than we have available. The following discusses several of the more well-recognized exceptions where out-of-court statements are allowed to be made in court by someone other than the declarant.

---

62. Merriam-Webster's Dictionary of Law (1996).

63. This statement could also be characterized as a non-hearsay identification under Fed. R. Evid. 801(d)(1)(c).

64. Saltzburg, S.A., Capra, D.J., and Martin, M.M., Commentary, USCS Fed. R. Evid. 801, Lexis-Nexis Academic World, retrieved on-line October, 2007.

Exceptions to Hearsay and Non-Hearsay

There are so many exceptions to the hearsay rule that the exceptions run the risk of negating the rule. Twenty seven hearsay exceptions, plus areas identified as "non-hearsay" and a catch all exception, are provided for in the Federal Rules of Evidence. With each of the exceptions to the rule, one or both of two policy considerations justify its use: *reliability* and *necessity*. Under the reliability or trustworthiness rationale, the hearsay is intrinsically credible. This credibility makes up for the concerns regarding its inability to be cross-examined. Under the necessity justification, the lack of other evidence makes the hearsay evidence better than no evidence. Many exceptions are justified by both considerations. As you study the exceptions to the hearsay rule, understanding the justification for the rule will help you remember the exception.

1. Prior Statements and Admissions

Two types of statements are categorized as non-hearsay under Rule 801: prior statement by a witness and admission by a party-opponent. Whether they are categorized as non-hearsay or as an exception to hearsay, the outcome is the same. The out of court statement is allowed into court.

It is difficult to justify the exclusion of an out of court statement if the person who made the statement is present in court and able to either adopt or correct the statement. Under Rule 801(d)(1), the declarant testifies in court and is subject to cross-examination. If he testifies inconsistent with a **prior sworn statement**, that statement may be brought up to challenge (impeach) his credibility. If his prior statement is consistent with his testimony, the statement may be offered to bolster a challenge to his credibility.

Suppose, for example, that a defendant in a civil case had given a **deposition** in a police brutality case. A deposition is a statement made under oath by a party or witness in response to oral examination or written questions and that is recorded by an authorized officer (such as a court reporter). The defendant police officer testified in the deposition that he was present when an assault on the plaintiff occurred. At trial, he testifies that he does not recall being present during the assault. His deposition (out-of-court) testimony could be read to support an inference that he was not being truthful in his present testimony. The justification is that it is both reliable (was made earlier as sworn testimony and subject to cross-examination), and he is now present in court and can correct any inconsistency if appropriate.

The other category of non-hearsay allows the **admission** by a party-opponent.[65] The statement must be that of the party, and is offered against him in court. Suppose that a defendant had given a statement to a police officer admitting that he knew illegal drugs were present in his home. At trial the officer could take the stand and tell the court what the defendant said. As with the prior non-hearsay, the declarant is in court and has the ability to set the record straight by explaining or denying the statement. This has some additional concerns, however, because the statement is being used against

65. Fed. R. Evid. 801(d)(2)

a person who has a constitutional right not to testify and the only way he can rebut the out of court statement is to take the stand and subject himself to cross-examination.

The rationale for allowing this statement is two-fold. It is reliable because people generally do not make statements against their own interest unless they are true. It is also necessary to receive the statement because the defendant may exercise his rights under the Fifth Amendment not to be a witness against himself, not take the stand. The only way the court will hear the admission, which is likely very probative evidence, is if the statement is allowed in by someone who heard the declarant make the statement.

In criminal cases, an admission from the accused is likely to also be a confession. The Fifth Amendment right not to be a witness against himself, the Sixth Amendment right to counsel, as well as court cases such as *Miranda v. Arizona*, could also apply. These concepts are discussed elsewhere in the text, but are often considerations when an admission by a criminal defendant is sought to be used in court.

Michael Nowell v. City of Cincinnati, et al.

2006 U.S. Dist. LEXIS 68182, 71 Fed. R. Evid. Serv. (CBC) 251
(S.D. Ohio, 2006)

Plaintiff Nowell claims that he was bouncing a basketball outside his home when a Cincinnati police officer began asking him questions. When Nowell refused to answer, he was taken to the police car and patted down for weapons. A second officer then came but was told that everything was under control. According to Nowell, the second officer then attacked him without warning nor provocation. The officer twisted Nowell's arms, slammed his head into the concrete several times, maced him repeatedly, and beat him with a knight stick. Several officers, including a supervisor, later arrived to investigate the incident. The officers cited Nowell for disorderly conduct.

Nowell filed a complaint against the officers and some eight months later the Cincinnati Police Internal Investigations Section issued a report concerning its investigation. Later, a Citizen's Complaint Authority determined the Officers detained Nowell without reasonable suspicion or probable cause, used excessive force against Nowell and withheld medical treatment. The Cincinnati Police Captain advised Nowell that the officers and their supervisor "used excessive force and violated police procedure when they searched you, slammed you to the ground and sprayed you with chemical irritant.'" Nowell then brought a civil lawsuit for false imprisonment and arrest, excessive force, malicious prosecution and spoilation of evidence. Defendants deny any wrongdoing.

Nowell asked the court to admit the internal investigations report. After discussion, the court admitted the report under the public records exception of Rule 803(8). It next considered whether portions of the report were inadmissible for hearsay reasons. The report included summaries of interviews with four eye-witnesses to the assault. The court defined hearsay under Rule 801 as "a statement, other than one made by the declarant while testifying at the trial or hearing, offered in evidence to prove the truth of the matter asserted." The eyewitness statements are "classic hearsay," and even "double hearsay." The first level of hearsay would be that the statements were not offered by the declarants (eye witnesses), nor even by the officer to whom the statements were given (the second level). For these reasons, the eye-witness summaries were excluded.

If Nowell wants this testimony, he could call the eye-witnesses themselves so they would be subject to cross-examination.

The report also included a statement from Attorney Cosgrove, the Chief Legal Counsel for the police department, that the first officer lacked legal justification to detain or arrest Nowell. Nowell argued that the attorney's statement was admissible hearsay as a statement by a party opponent. The court agreed, finding that the statement was an admission as it was "made against the person to whom it was offered." It was also made within the scope of the attorney's employment as chief counsel of the City's legal department, so he acted as the defendant's representative.

The court then addressed the issue of whether the attorney's statement was an expert opinion, under Rule 702, requiring notice before it may be admitted. It determined that the portion of the report that expressed the attorney's legal opinion regarding the officer's reasonable suspicion to detain or probable cause to arrest, was excluded as expert opinion.

The next piece of the report sought to be excluded as hearsay was the investigator's conclusions contained in the report. They were not based upon her own perceptions but on the unsworn statements of third parties. Further, they were arguably not helpful to the jury but merely told it what conclusion to reach. The court found that the information the investigator relied upon was trustworthy because it came from a number of different sources. The information upon she relied was of the type that experts in her field customarily relied upon, and her findings were admissible as an admission of a party-opponent.

2. Excited Utterances

Another well recognized exception to the hearsay rule occurs when a statement is made regarding a "startling event or condition made while the declarant was under the stress of excitement caused by the event or condition."[66] The spontaneous or **excited utterance exception** generally requires three elements. These are (a) an exciting event (b) an utterance prompted by the exciting event without time to reflect, i.e., dominated by the nervous excitement of the event, and (c) the utterance must explain or illuminate the exciting event. [67] The last element has not been applied with consistency by the courts.

A time element is present, requiring the declarant to still be under the state of excitement from the event. Without time to reflect about the response, the statement is inherently trustworthy and "free of conscious fabrication."[68] Some, however, have criticized this rationale because excitement often impairs our ability to observe.[69] Nonetheless, excited utterances remain a frequently used source of hearsay.

There are instances when the admission of hearsay may conflict with a defendant's Sixth Amendment right to confront his accusers. In *Crawford v. Washington,*[70] the

66. Fed. R. Evid. 803(2)

67. Murphy Auto Parts v. Ball, et al., 249 F.2d 508 (D.C. Cir. 1957), citing Wigmore, Evidence §§ 1750, 1754 (1940).

68. 6 Wigmore § 1747

69. Advisory Committee Notes to Fed. R. Evid. 803(2)

70. 541 U.S. 36 (2004)

Supreme Court barred the admission of "testimonial hearsay" received by the court under an exception to the hearsay rule, where the declarant is not available for cross-examination. Though the Court unfortunately did not clearly define "testimonial hearsay," it apparently believes that if statements made by someone out of court come too close to resembling full-blown, courtroom-style testimony, the statements will be deemed "**testimonial hearsay**" and will not be allowed in as evidence. This will be so even if the attorney wanting to use the out of court statements can point to one of the ordinarily accepted exceptions to the hearsay prohibition.

For example, the excited utterance, and various other forms of hearsay, fall under exceptions that usually allow their admission because they were otherwise deemed to be reliable. The *Crawford* court however cautions that always dispensing away with "confrontation because testimony is obviously reliable," can sometimes be "akin to dispensing with jury trial because a defendant is obviously guilty."[71] In the following case, a rather long, 911 tape by an excited anonymous caller was used by the court as an excited utterance and the Defendant challenged its admission as a violation of the Confrontation Clause of the Sixth Amendment. He argued that these so-called "excited utterances" were so lengthy and meaty as to resemble courtroom testimony. By reading this case you should be able to get a better idea of what courts mean by forbidden, "testimonial hearsay."

United States of America v. Jean Brito

427 F.3d 53 (1st Cir. 2005), cert denied 2006 U.S. LEXIS 5230 (2006)

On February 9, 2003, in Brockton, Massachusetts, during the early morning hours, a man working late at his office, heard gun shots from outside. He called 911 and stated that he saw a black man with a hat load a clip into a gun and walk away. Officers were dispatched to the scene.

Immediately after that the following 911 call was made, from an anonymous woman:

Caller: Listen to me. I just seen a man with a gun in his hand. It's at that club called Boomers. There was a shooting there just a second ago. He has on a black cap with a black leather coat. I can't quite remember the color of his sweater. But I was just saying to my son when I was getting in the car that I didn't come to Brockton to die. And when I was pulling out and backing out driving down the street, he pointed a gun at me and acted like he was shooting at my car.

Operator: Is he a black man?

Caller: Yes, he is a black man. He has on a baseball cap, he looks like he might be between the height of 5'8" and 5'10". But he's there right now, he's standing in between like two buildings. He's basically on Perkins Ave., right beside [the club Boomers].

Operator: Okay, we're on our way down there. I'll tell the officers to look for a guy with a black cap, black leather coat, about 5'8".

71. *Id.* at 62.

Caller: Yes, please do. He has the coat unzipped. And it looked like a nine millimeter. I could be wrong but it looked like a nine.

This new information was relayed to the officers who were on their way to the scene. About a block away, "they saw a 5'8" black male, wearing a black hat and jacket, standing next to the open passenger door of a car. The man's right hand was hidden inside his unzipped jacket, as if he were holding something." A chase ensued during which the man threw a 9 millimeter pistol on the ground. After apprehending the fleeing man, officers identified him as Jean Brito. The gun thrown matched the shell casings and empty magazine clip found near the parking lot.

The Defendant said he had purchased a gold chain from two men in a bar earlier that day. Later, two other men confronted him, one of them claiming to be the owner of the chain, and demanded its return. Defendant offered to sell it to them, but they did not have enough money with them. The owner later showed up with three friends and invited the Defendant into their car. When he refused and started walking away, he heard gunshots. He hid in some nearby bushes until he heard police sirens. He denied being part of a chase or possessing a firearm at any time. Based primarily upon the testimony of the officers and the 911 call, Defendant was convicted of possession of a firearm by a convicted felon and possession of a firearm by an illegal alien. He received a 210 month sentence.

The 911 call from the anonymous woman was categorized as an excited utterance, an exception to the hearsay rule. The Defendant claimed that the admission of that evidence violated his 6th Amendment right to confront witnesses against him. *Crawford* (the case discussed earlier that forbids excited utterances that are so lengthy that they come across looking like courtroom testimony) was decided one month after Defendant's conviction.

So, the issue here is whether or not 911 calls are simply courtroom style testimony masquerading as genuine excited utterances. The Court of Appeals reviewed decisions from other courts regarding this issue. Some courts decided that 911 calls were always an excited utterance made under the influence of a startling event. The caller is not acting in response to interrogation or in anticipation of being a witness. Their statements are "emotional and spontaneous, rather than deliberate and calculated;" a "cry for help" not the equivalent of formal examination.[72] Under this analysis, the calls are not deemed "testimonial" and are allowed under *Crawford.*

Other courts took the view that people calling 911 could reasonably expect their statements of the events would be used for prosecution. This reasonable expectation makes the statements testimonial because the purpose of giving the information is for "investigation, prosecution and potential use at a judicial proceeding."

The Court in this cased adopted the rule followed by a third set of courts which decided to look at each case individually and declined to always allow, or disallow, 911 calls as testimonial. Whether a statement is an excited utterance or testimonial hearsay requires courts to assess the declarant's mind set at the time. "The excited utterance inquiry focuses on whether the declarant was under the stress of a startling event. The

72. Citations to the original cases omitted.

testimonial hearsay inquiry focuses on whether a reasonable declarant, similarly situated (that is, excited by the stress of a startling event), would have had the capacity to appreciate the legal ramifications of her statement."

If a statement is an excited utterance, then the court must look at all the surrounding circumstances to determine whether the person also made a "testimonial statement." Generally, statements made while there is personal danger are not testimonial because they are speaking out of urgency and a desire for a prompt response. They would be admitted as an excited utterance. After the danger has subsided, however, the person who continues to speak, while still under stress of the event, may be more able to comprehend the significance of her statements and be testimonial, triggering the Confrontation Clause.

The court found this case similar to one where "a teenager witnessed a man pointing a gun at a woman, flagged down a passing police cruiser, and reported what he had seen." That was deemed to be an excited utterance, not testimonial, because it was made to obtain immediate assistance for the woman who was in danger. In the case before the court, the 911 caller was urgently requesting assistance to get a dangerous man off from the streets. The Court found the 911 call from the anonymous caller was non-testimonial, and admissible as an excited utterance.

3. *Dying Declarations*

Another category of hearsay is allowed to come into court depending upon whether the person who made the statement is available. There may be several reasons why a declarant is "unavailable." These include instances where the declarant has exercised his or her Fifth Amendment right against self-incrimination and chooses not to testify. The declarant may simply refuse to testify despite court orders. Perhaps the declarant has no memory of the event and is therefore unable to testify. He or she may also be unable to testify because of death or a physical or mental illness. If the party who wants the statement to come in has exhausted all reasonable means to get the declarant into court, they may be deemed "unavailable."[73]

If the person who made the statement is available, and could be subpoenaed into court, he should testify himself because that would be the most reliable thing to do. The quality of that evidence is preferred over the hearsay statement. If the person who made the statement is *not* available, the hearsay statements in this category are allowed to come in. The preference here is that the hearsay statement is preferred over the total loss of the evidence.[74]

Some of the categories of hearsay that are allowed if the declarant is *not* available include former testimony, statements against interest, statements about personal or family history, and statements made under belief of impending death. It is this last category, commonly referred to as the "dying declaration" exception, that we will explore below.

Under the **dying declaration exception**, "in a prosecution for homicide or in a civil action or proceeding, a statement made by a declarant while believing that the declar-

73. Fed. R. Evid. 804(a)
74. Advisory Committee Notes to Fed. R. Evid. 804

ant's death was imminent, concerning the cause or circumstances of what the declarant believed to be impending death" is allowed into evidence.[75] At common law, there was a religious justification for allowing this hearsay. If someone was about to face "God," they would not want the last words spoken in this life to be a lie. The dying statement of the victim of a homicide who said, "George shot me" would be allowed into George's homicide trial. The great need for the statement coupled with the religious justification for the statement, justified the admission of the statement. Under the current rule, the statement can also be used in a civil action.

Dying declarations may also be very close to an excited utterance. For example, suppose that George's victim did not die but as a result of the injuries he was in a persistent vegetative state. Now suppose further that George is charged with aggravated assault. Under the Federal Rules, the dying declaration would not apply because it is not a homicide prosecution. The statement would still likely come in as an excited utterance, discussed in the preceding section, if made while the victim was still under the stress or excitement of the assault.

An important requirement of a dying declaration is that the declarant believed his or her death was imminent. The following case discusses this requirement, and gives us insight into the justification for dying declarations.

United States of America v. Melvin Troy Two Shields

435 F. Supp. 2d 973 (D.N.D. SW Div. 2006)

On January 21, 2006, victim Thomas BuffaloBoy, drove to the home of his sister, Roselyn, in the New Sioux Village of Fort Yates, North Dakota. He was spitting blood into a cup and his face was swollen. Thomas did not know what had happened and Roselyn called for an ambulance, believing that her brother was intoxicated.

EMTs arrived and took the victim to a hospital due to injuries to his face. He continued to state that he could not remember how he was injured. At the hospital it was determined that BuffaloBoy suffered from a concussion and a broken jaw. His blood alcohol content was 0.389% (at 0.08% a driver is considered unsafe to operate a motor vehicle in most states). At this point his condition was "stable."

Other family members arrived at the hospital and attempted to find out from BuffaloBoy how he sustained his injuries. He was specifically asked whether the defendant caused his injuries, to which he shook his head no. When asked if he was trying to protect the defendant, he did not respond. Sometime later, prior to surgery, a list of specific names was given to BuffaloBoy asking about their involvement. Again, he did not answer. BuffaloBoy initially tolerated the surgery well, but the following day he suffered complications and died. The cause of death was listed as "complications of blunt force injuries of face." Defendant was charged with the murder and sought to introduce the negative head shake of the victim in response to the question whether the defendant inflicted the wounds on victim.

Both parties admit that the head shake qualifies as hearsay. It was nonverbal conduct intended by BuffaloBoy as an assertion. Further, it would be offered by someone

75. Fed. R. Evid. 804(b)(2)

other than BuffaloBoy at trial. The issue in controversy was whether the hearsay was admissible under an exception to the rule.

The Court discussed the justification for the admission of dying declarations. The declarant must have spoken "without hope of recovery and in the shadow of impending death." It is not enough that the declarant fears or even believes that an illness will end in death. "There must be 'a settled hopeless expectation' that death is near at hand, and what is said must have been spoken in the hush of its impending presence.... The patient must have spoken with the consciousness of a swift and certain doom."[76] "[T]he sense of impending death is presumed to remove all temptation to falsehood, and to enforce as strict ... adherence to the truth...."[77] Knowledge of the seriousness of ones condition may be inferred from the "nature and extent of the wounds inflicted."[78]

Applying that law to the facts of this case, the Court found insufficient evidence to support a finding that BuffaloBoy believed death was imminent at the time he shook his head "no" to the question of whether the Defendant inflicted the injuries. There was no evidence that BuffaloBoy himself, family members or medical staff believed his injuries were life threatening. Indeed, his death the morning after the surgery was sudden and unexpected. No evidence supports a finding that BuffaloBoy believed that death was imminent at the time he shook his head. Further, his injuries were not of such a nature that impending death could be inferred from his injuries.

4. *Other Exceptions*

Numerous other exceptions to the hearsay rule are contained in the Federal Rules. Present sense impressions; then existing mental, emotional, or physical condition; statements for purposes of medical diagnosis or treatment; records of regularly conducted activity; public records; vital statistics; and family records to name just a few. As stated earlier, becoming familiar with the purposes and justifications for allowing the admission of hearsay statements will help the student identify instances when an exception is likely to occur.

The last two chapters have provided a good introduction to the rules of evidence. Those working in the criminal justice system in identifying, collecting or presenting evidence are strongly encouraged to study the rules of evidence in more detail and identify those rules that apply in their jurisdiction.

---

76. *Shepard v. United States*, 290 U.S. 96 (1933).
77. *Mattox v. United States*, 156 U.S. 237 (1895).
78. *United States v. Peppers*, 302 F.3d 120 (3d Cir. 2002).

Chapter Nine

Proof beyond a Reasonable Doubt

You have likely watched a scene in some movie where the judge or lawyer reminds the jury of its solemn responsibility:

> Ladies and gentlemen of the jury, the defendant is presumed to be innocent until proven guilty by the prosecution. The defendant does not have to prove his innocence. After weighing all of the evidence, you can only convict the defendant if you are satisfied beyond a reasonable doubt that he is guilty. If you have reasonable doubt of guilt, then you must vote to acquit.

As the typical movie continues, the jury disappears into the jury-room to deliberate while the court spectators tensely wait on the edge of their seats for the dramatic reading of the verdict: "We the jury find the defendant guilty (or not guilty) of the charge of murder in the first degree." Upon the reading of the verdict, the courtroom erupts into cheers of joy or outbursts of rage, or both. The judge angrily pounds her gavel, demanding order. The movie ends but the debate continues. Did the jury get it right? Was justice served?

Each day in our criminal courts similar but normally much less dramatic scenes are played out in trials. Most people are surprised to learn that, despite perceptions they get from the media, less than 10% of all cases ever even make it to trial. Voluntary or negotiated guilty pleas are the rule; trials, especially with a jury, are significant exceptions.

In an actual criminal case, reaching a verdict is obviously serious business because a person's life, liberty, or property is at stake. Perhaps a guilty verdict will mean death, 30 years in prison, a large fine, loss of social status, or a combination of various life-changing penalties. A verdict of guilt could mean an innocent person is tragically punished. A not guilty verdict could mean a guilty person will go free. The pressure on the judge or jury (the **fact finders**)[1] to get the decision right is immense. Given the high stakes, it is vital that our justice system has an effective means for sorting out the guilty from the not guilty.

Through centuries of development, one of the chief means for safeguarding justice, in conjunction with the rules of evidence you studied in Chapter 8, has been the high

1. In this chapter, you will see references to fact finders, finder of facts, juries, or judges in different scenarios or discussions. Whether jury or judge, the fact finder in a case is the one who decides what the facts are from the evidence. If the trial has a jury, then the jury is the finder of fact. If there is no jury, then the judge is the finder of fact. In all cases, the judge decides what the law is, what it means, and how it is applied in a case.

burden of proof placed on a prosecutor in each criminal case. The American ideal is that only the guilty will be convicted of crimes after the prosecution proves guilt beyond a reasonable doubt. Fortunately a jury can only convict a defendant when the jury members are nearly certain of guilt based on the proof presented at trial. The burden is high and rightly demanding.

Most adults in the United States are at least generally aware of this burden of proof requirement. But the unfortunate truth is that the public and those involved with our legal system have long struggled to effectively understand and deal with the concept of proving guilt of wrongdoing beyond a reasonable doubt.[2] For example, in March of 2007, the jury in the perjury trial of Lewis "Scooter" Libby, the Chief of Staff for Vice President Dick Cheney, asked the judge to clarify the meaning of "reasonable doubt" as it had been defined in a jury instruction. Libby had claimed as one of his defenses that any inconsistencies in his prior statements to investigators could be blamed on his poor memory and heavy workload but not intentional perjury. So, the jury, in considering the meaning of reasonable doubt, wanted to know if it would have to be "not humanly possible for someone not to recall an event" in order for them to find guilt beyond a reasonable doubt. The jury was confused; the stakes were high. Apparently the jury satisfactorily sorted the question out to suit their needs because it convicted Libby.[3] President George W. Bush, a short time later, partially pardoned Libby by suspending his prison sentence. The Libby case is just illustrative of the reality that the proof beyond a reasonable doubt standard is not easy to grasp in a court of law, especially where someone's freedom is at stake, where numerous evidentiary rules control the flow of information, and when the nation is watching, .

The terms "*proof*," "*beyond*," "*reasonable*," and "*doubt*" are generally abstract anyway, and open to varying interpretations when considered as a whole and in the context of a trial. Thus, courts have struggled to adequately define the concept and jurors have been inconsistent in their understanding and application. The principal of proving guilt beyond a reasonable doubt is usually only covered in criminal justice textbooks in a paragraph or two. Unfortunately, few people learn more than the basics, if they learn that much.

Even if a person does have a fairly solid understanding of the concept, it is still not simple to apply in a real case. What does it mean to actually prove someone is guilty beyond a reasonable doubt? How do you know when your doubts are reasonable or even beyond reasonable? Does the standard mean having "no" doubt whatsoever? What about "some" doubt? How do you know when "some" doubt or "little" doubt is reasonable or unreasonable?

In summary, just what does proof beyond a reasonable doubt mean in the American legal system and why is it important for you to better understand the principle? With the high stakes in each case—the potential loss of life, liberty, or property—it

2. See e.g., Kramer, Geoffrey P. and King, Doreen M., *Do Jurors Understand Criminal Jury Instructions? Analyzing the Results of the Michigan Juror Comprehension Project*, 23 U. Mich. J.L. Ref. 401, 429–433 (summarizing findings regarding general lack of understanding of jurors and impact on attorneys and the system).

3. See e.g., Bohn, K. and Courson, P. (2007). Libby jury asked to explain 'reasonable doubt' question. (March 5, 2007). http://www.cnn.com/2007/POLITICS/03/05/cia.leak/index.html (April 10, 2007).

is vital that those who determine the fate of the accused really understand the seriousness of their duty and the proper application of the burden of proof. The purpose of this chapter is to help answer those questions—to help you better understand the meaning and broad impact of the principle of proving guilt beyond a reasonable doubt, in combination with the inseparable concepts of due process and the presumption of innocence. With such understanding, you can more fully comprehend the big picture of criminal justice in a constitutional system. Interspersed throughout the chapter you will find analysis, examination, and examples that will increase your overall understanding of this concept, what it means, what it does not mean, and how it has been and should be applied in our courts.

Guilty or Not Guilty: You Make the Call

In most cases, the typical individual who appears for jury duty has limited knowledge of the law and how a trial is conducted outside of what he or she has seen in the media. Once in court, jurors listen to the lawyers and all of the legal maneuvering and quickly realize the Hollywood versions of a trial are quite different than reality. A real trial moves a lot more slowly and is not nearly as dramatic. After listening to the witnesses and lawyers for days, weeks, or even months, the judge explains the law to them through dozens of often complex jury instructions. Jurors are told to determine if the defendant is guilty beyond a reasonable doubt based only on the law and evidence. In the best of situations, the job is difficult and the pressure is great.

The following scenario is intended to put you in a similar spot as a typical juror who is trying to apply the facts to the law and understand the jury instructions about the burden of proof. Right now you know few specifics about the concept so you are just going to have to use your best judgment in this hypothetical to decide if the prosecution has met its burden of proof—like jurors do each day in courtrooms around the nation.

Imagine you were selected to be one of twelve jurors in a double murder trial. The trial ends up lasting over eight months. During that time, you were sequestered from family and friends. You had to live in a hotel. You were not allowed to watch television or read newspapers unless the subject was specifically approved by the judge. Day after day, you listened to a seemingly endless parade of witnesses and had to evaluate literally hundreds of pieces of evidence. You were paid less than $20.00 per day for doing your legal duty as an American citizen (and suffered financially, as a result).

Evidence was presented about alleged acts of domestic violence committed by the defendant against his wife, threats he made against her life, and a myriad of other unusual behaviors. Blood samples, DNA tests, time lines, and clothing articles were introduced, all allegedly linking the defendant to the crime in some way.

At long last, the trial ended after months of grueling testimony. The prosecutor summarizes the seemingly endless evidence, followed by the defense attorney's own vision of the truth and faults in the case. Through dozens of jury instructions, the judge explained the law to you and read you the following key instruction defining "reasonable doubt" and explaining the burden of proof:

> [Reasonable doubt] is not a mere possible doubt, because everything relating to human affairs is open to some possible or imaginary doubt. It is that state of the case which, after the entire comparison and consideration of all the evidence, leaves the minds of the jurors in that condition that they cannot say they feel an abiding conviction of the truth of the charge. The prosecution has the burden of proving beyond reasonable doubt each element of the crimes charged in the [criminal complaint] and that the defendant was the perpetrator of any such charged crimes. The defendant is not required to prove himself innocent.... [4]

Exhausted, you retreat into the jury room with the other eleven jurors for deliberations. After spending a few hours going over key facts, the jury foreperson asks what each juror thinks. Six jurors say they are certain the defendant is guilty. Three jurors say they are pretty sure the defendant killed the victims and are, therefore, willing to vote guilty. Two jurors say there is a strong possibility the defendant is guilty and that, though they have some questions about the jury instructions on reasonable doubt, they feel inside their hearts that he is guilty. With some reluctance, they too are willing to vote guilty.

You have thought long and hard about the matter. You want to do the right thing. In your mind, you honestly believe the defendant is guilty but you are not certain the prosecutor proved his guilt. You keep rereading the jury instruction. You were disappointed at the prosecution's efforts and were amazed by the defense attorney's savvy. Without question, the defense successfully poked a few holes in the prosecution's case that leave you wondering about alternative explanations for the murders. It seems possible to you that someone else could have committed the murders. Guilty or not guilty? Reasonable doubt or not? You are torn. You have to make a decision.

Based on the responses of the other eleven jurors and your own viewpoint, is there a unanimous verdict of guilt? Reread the jury instruction above. Based on the opinion of the jurors and your own thoughts, has the jury unanimously determined the defendant is guilty beyond a reasonable doubt or are there reasonable doubts? Can you vote guilty or must you vote not guilty? Do you think the jury instruction defining "reasonable doubt" is clear or does it just confuse matters? The defendant's freedom is at stake; you and the other jurors literally hold his life in your hands and the whole world is watching. Guilty beyond a reasonable doubt or not guilty due to reasonable doubt? If you are unsure, join the crowd.

The above scenario is roughly based on the 1995 case of *State of California vs. Simpson*.[5] The jury instruction is the actual one used in the case but the overview of the jurors' opinions is fictional. O.J. Simpson, the former larger-than-life football star and actor, hero to millions, was charged with the murder of his wife Nicole Simpson Brown and her friend Ronald Goldman. After eight months of trial and just four hours of deliberation, the twelve member jury unanimously found Simpson not guilty of double

4. Schmalleger, Frank. (1996). *Trial of the Century: People of the State of California vs. Orenthal James Simpson*. New Jersey: Prentice Hall, at 221.

5. Numerous books have been written about the trial. For a good overview of the case, see the books referenced in the footnotes immediately before and after this footnote.

murder. The verdict of the most watched case in history created a huge stir and division in the country. Overall, a majority of people thought he was guilty and were stunned by the verdict. Opinions often followed racial lines. A majority of African-Americans, for instance, strongly supported the verdict. One person who had watched the trial on television, summarized the proof as he saw it: "I personally would have reasonable doubt, but it's true there is overwhelming evidence that he is possibly guilty."[6] Possibly guilty (but with reasonable doubts)? What does that mean legally? Probably guilty? While many of the jurors said they believed Simpson killed the victims, their unanimous, not guilty verdict shows that they agreed that the prosecution did not prove guilt beyond a reasonable doubt. The verdict, of course did not prove Simpson was innocent.

In addition to other flaws in the televised trial, many critics blamed the jury instructions for confusing the jurors. Do you agree the jury instructions are confusing? Do you think that confusing instructions could actually impact the outcome of a case?. If so, in what way? Should Simpson have been found guilty because the jury believed he committed the crime regardless of whether they believed the prosecution established proof of guilt beyond a reasonable doubt? We live in a constitutional democracy and are subject to the rule of law. What would the consequence be for our nation if emotions and opinions determined justice rather than due process, precedent, and law?

Introductory, Non-Technical Definition of Reasonable Doubt

Before we get any further and start looking at cases and constitutional law, let's discuss the concept of proof beyond a reasonable doubt from a common sense review of its basic terms. First, what is "**reasonable doubt**?" To keep this simple, we will define "**reasonable**" as sound judgment or what the average person would think was true, right, or appropriate in a given situation. "**Doubt**," for our purposes, means you are unsure of or uncertain about something. Jurors with "reasonable doubt" should be able to explain the reason for their doubt. So, if you are a juror in a rape case who is unsure or doubtful about the defendant's guilt based on your best judgment or specific reasoning after listening to and weighing all the evidence, you cannot vote for a conviction . You have reasonable doubt and under our system, that is not enough for a conviction.

Now, what if your doubt is minimal? You are extremely sure or quite convinced! You recognize that there is always a chance a witness could have lied or that there was a misidentification. Despite a touch of doubt, you are still firmly convinced the defendant is guilty. Therefore, you can vote for a conviction because the level of proof has gone "beyond" reasonable doubt. Any doubts you have are unreasonable (too remote, too unlikely under the facts). It is hard, after all, to be absolutely certain about anything. You have reasonably concluded that the prosecutor has proved guilt. You have reached a level of certainty that eliminated any reasonable doubt and moved you to the required

6. Abramson, Jeffrey. (1996). *Postmortem: The O.J. Simpson Case.* New York: Basic Books, at 160.

higher level of proof. If, for instance, your main doubt was that you heard that there was a one in a million chance that the DNA results could be erroneous or you recognize that there is a possibility that a witness lied even though you believe he told the truth, your doubt is unreasonable so you should vote to convict.

Associate Justice of the Rhode Island Superior Court, Stephen J. Fortunato, Jr., after carefully evaluating the opinions of the United States Supreme Courts on reasonable doubt, evaluating history, and scrutinizing many commentators, has proposed the following jury instruction that clearly encapsulates the key issues discussed so far:

> The government must prove each and every element of the crime beyond a reasonable doubt. This is a very high burden of proof. It means that you may find the defendant guilty only if, after reviewing all the evidence and discussing the evidence with your fellow jurors, you are convinced in your mind that it **is just about certain** — or nearly certain — that the defendant committed the crime. If after reviewing the evidence, your mind is in such a state that you **are not just about certain** — or nearly certain — that the defendant committed the crime, you must return a verdict of not guilty. (emphasis added)[7]

Later in the chapter we will more broadly define the concept of proof beyond a reasonable doubt through other authorities, but ultimately, the above statement is as comprehensive and effective as any definition we will discuss.

Now, for practice, let us suppose you were a juror in a robbery case. An eyewitness testified at trial. She was about 25 feet away from the scene of the crime when the robbery took place. The lighting was good and the witness has good eyesight. You believe the eyewitness is reliable and told the truth when she said she saw the defendant pull a knife on the victim and take his wallet. You learn that the witness has a prior criminal record for theft. Still, her testimony was consistent and given with a level of confidence that impressed you. You and the other jurors all believe the defendant is guilty so he is convicted.

Applying what you have learned so far about proof beyond a reasonable doubt can you explain in your own words why you voted to convict? How sure were you and what kind of doubt, if any, could you rightly have? What if you did not believe the eyewitness and voted to acquit: could you likewise explain the basis for that conclusion? We will now try to better understand the nature of the burden of proof and why it is mandated.

Proof beyond a Reasonable Doubt: A Constitutional Requirement

Though the Constitution makes no specific mention of any burden of proof, there was a long-standing tradition in our criminal courts of using the reasonable doubt stan-

7. Fortunato, Stephen, J. Jr., *Instructing on Reasonable Doubt after* Victor v. Nebraska*: A Trial Judge's Certain Thoughts on Certainty*, 41 Vill. L. Rev. 365, 427 (1996).

dard. It was not until 1970, in the following landmark case, that the U.S. Supreme Court first declared that proof beyond a reasonable doubt was a constitutional requirement in all criminal cases.

In re Winship

397 U.S. 358 (1970)

A twelve year old boy from New York was charged in juvenile court with theft. He was accused of entering a locker room and stealing $112 from a woman's pocketbook. After a hearing, the judge found the boy delinquent (for our purposes that is essentially akin to finding a person guilty in an adult court). The boy was ordered to be placed in a training school for 18 months or possibly until he was 18 years old, if extensions were ordered. The juvenile court judge openly acknowledged that there was not enough proof to find the boy guilty beyond a reasonable doubt. The judge held the common viewpoint that in juvenile court cases the due process clause only required that a court find guilt by a "**preponderance of the evidence**" rather than by the higher standard of proof beyond a reasonable doubt.

According to the juvenile court judge's application of the law, the prosecution's burden of proof was merely the same legal standard applied in civil cases like divorces, personal injury, or malpractice, for instance. Thus, based on the judge's ruling, the prosecution only had to establish guilt by a preponderance of the evidence, or, in other words, guilt by showing that "it was more likely than not" that the boy was guilty. The use of this lower standard of proof is highly significant because it is more susceptible to error than the burden of proof beyond a reasonable doubt.[8] That is so because a judge or jury applying the preponderance standard would merely have to weigh the evidence to see if there was more evidence of guilt than of innocence. If the scale of evidence barely tipped in favor of guilt as opposed to innocence, that would be adequate under the preponderance standard to allow the jury to vote for a conviction— even though reasonable doubt still existed.[9]

The case was appealed and eventually made its way to the Supreme Court. Ultimately, the Court had to decide if guilt could be based on the preponderance of the evidence or whether proof beyond a reasonable doubt was required as one of the "essentials of due process and fair treatment."[10] In other words, was the higher standard of proof-beyond a reasonable doubt—essential in our system of justice in a case where a juvenile committed an act that would be a crime if committed by an adult? The implications of the case reached beyond juvenile court matters, however, because the Supreme Court had never formally declared that any criminal conviction, whether for an adult or a juvenile, required proof beyond a reasonable doubt. The historical use of the standard was based on tradition only. *The Court was finally ready to fully settle the issue.*

The United States Supreme Court, in a 7–2 decision, reversed the conviction of the youth after concluding that the juvenile court incorrectly interpreted the due process requirements of the Fourteenth Amendment. In reversing the juvenile court's decision,

---

8. *In re Winship* at 371 (J. Harlan, *dissenting*).

9. *Id. at 364* (quoting Dorsen & Rezneck, In Re Gault and the Future of Juvenile Law, 1 Family Law Quarterly, No. 4, pp. 1, 26 (1967)).

10. *Id.* at 359.

the Supreme Court held that "the Due Process Clause protects the accused against conviction except upon proof beyond a reasonable doubt of every fact necessary to constitute the crime with which he is charged."[11] The Court unambiguously ruled that the Due Process Clause requires that guilt be established in all criminal cases by proof beyond a reasonable doubt.

In so ruling, the Court traced the concept of proof beyond a reasonable doubt to at least 1798 and even to earlier colonial times. The Court emphasized that the principle was a safeguard against unjust convictions and an essential requirement in our free society to protect citizens from unjust loss of life, liberty, or property. The standard, the Court continued, "plays a vital role in the American scheme of criminal procedure," being the chief means of protecting people from erroneous convictions. In short, the requirement of establishing proof beyond reasonable doubt is "indispensable." Our system values a person's good name and freedom; it simply does not want to condemn anyone when there is reasonable doubt. Without such a high standard of proof, the court emphasized, the criminal justice system would lack "moral force" because people would be left with doubts as to whether innocent people were being convicted of crimes.[12]

In the next section we will more fully explore the meaning of guilt through proof beyond a reasonable doubt as discussed and defined by the Supreme Court. With the understanding you have now, do you agree with the decision in *In re Winship*?

Attempting to Further Define and Understand Proof beyond a Reasonable Doubt

One of the perplexing challenges we have in better understanding this concept is that some scholars believe that the more one delves into the topic the more complicated the topic actually gets. An appellate judge made the following insightful statement: "I find it rather unsettling that we are using a formulation that we believe will become less clear the more we explain it."[13]

Despite the challenges, the purpose of this section is to try to help you better comprehend proof beyond a reasonable doubt by looking at it from different angles. We already looked at the terms from an introductory, non-legalistic, point of view earlier in the chapter and learned it is a constitutional requirement, but now we are going to look more deeply into the subject.

A. What Proof beyond Reasonable Doubt Is Not!

One of the best places to start to really understand the legal meaning of proof beyond a reasonable doubt is to explain what it is not:

---

11. *Id.* at 364.
12. *Id.* at 362, 364
13. McCue v. Commonwealth, 103 Va. 870 at 1002 (1905) as referenced in Jon O. Newman, *Is Reasonable Doubt Reasonable?*, N.Y.U. L. Rev. 979, 984 (1993).

- Proof beyond a reasonable doubt does not mean that defendants have to prove they are innocent. That burden of proof belongs to the prosecution.
- The burden is not proof of guilt to "an absolute or mathematical certainty."[14] It is impossible, some believe, to be absolutely certain about anything.[15]
- It is not "mere possible doubt" and it is not imaginary or speculative doubt because in life everything is open to doubt.[16]
- Reasonable doubt is not "fanciful doubt" stemming from a creative imagination.
- It does not mean that the finder of fact can only find someone guilty after the prosecution has "ruled out every hypothesis except that of guilt beyond a reasonable doubt" for the defendant.[17]

The burden, consequently, does not require the prosecutor to engage in the impossible task of disproving every conceivable theory, possibility, or explanation of who else could have committed the crime or what else conceivably could have happened. For instance, in an assault case the prosecutor would not have to prove that the ex-boyfriend did not do it or that it wasn't a neighbor with whom the victim had been fighting. Where would such an exercise end? The prosecutor must prove who did it—not who didn't do it. Proving a negative (or who didn't do it or what didn't happen) is extremely difficult, if not impossible.[18] Remember, proof beyond a reasonable doubt does not mean "beyond a shadow of a doubt," "absolute certainty" or "beyond any doubt whatsoever."

On the other end of the spectrum, proof beyond a reasonable doubt cannot be based upon guesses, sympathy, personal moral judgments, public opinion, or presumptions.[19] For example, you could not properly presume a defendant is guilty in a particular case just because she has done bad things in the past and is, in your view, a bad person. Standing alone, such a conclusion is not based on evidence and cannot be the basis for a conviction.

It is also important to understand that the burden of proof in a criminal case is not the same burden of proof required in a civil case.[20] As was previously noted, the standard used in civil cases (like divorce or personal injury) is the preponderance of the evidence, which is a lesser standard than proof beyond a reasonable doubt. The government is not involved in the case so there is no presumption of innocence in favor of either party. Because the dispute is personal and society has no legal stake in the matter, it is no more serious that a ruling might favor the defendant than the plaintiff.

The different standards in civil versus criminal cases is intended to communicate the different degrees of confidence expected in the factual conclusions reached in a

14. *Cage v. Louisiana*, 498 U.S. 39, 40 (1990) (per curium).

15. *Victor v. Nebraska*, 511 U.S. 1, 13 (1994)

16. *Cage v. Louisiana*, 498 U.S. 39, 40 (1990) (per curium); *Victor v. Nebraska*, 511 U.S. 1, 7 (1994) (the Court upholds a jury instruction regarding the idea that reasonable doubt is not mere possible doubt).

17. *Holland v. United States*, 348 U.S. 121, 140 (1954).

18. Fortunato, Stephen, J. Jr., *Instructing on Reasonable Doubt after* Victor v. Nebraska*: A Trial Judge's Certain Thoughts on Certainty*, 41 Vill. L. Rev. 365, 410 (1996)

19. *See e.g., Victor v. Nebraska*, 511 U.S. 1, 13 (1994).

20. *In re Winship*, supra at 363.

court."[21] The higher the burden of proof, the higher the degree of confidence or correctness expected in the decision. Proof by a preponderance of the evidence does not meet that level of confidence; proof beyond a reasonable doubt does.

Several high profile civil cases in recent decades aptly demonstrate that the civil standard is lower and, therefore, more easy to satisfy than proof beyond a reasonable doubt. In the oft-referenced O.J. Simpson murder trial we reviewed above, the jury in the criminal case acquitted Simpson because the jury unanimously concluded it had reasonable doubts about whether Simpson was guilty of murder. On the other hand, in the civil case for wrongful death that took place after the criminal case, the jury concluded that there was a reasonable likelihood that Mr. Simpson was responsible for the deaths of Nicole Simpson and Ronald Goldman so the jury awarded the Brown family millions of dollars. The civil jury had little trouble concluding that the plaintiffs had proven by a preponderance of the evidence that Simpson killed the victims. Officially, Simpson was found not guilty of any crime but instead only liable for the wrongful death of two people. Many fail to recognize the difference between the two burdens of proof and, therefore, mistakenly argue that if Simpson is civilly responsible, then he must also be criminally responsible. Do you understand the difference between the two levels of proof and how that difference affected the outcomes of the Simpson civil and criminal trials?

B. Defining Proof beyond a Reasonable Doubt through Case Law

For over a hundred years, many courts in the United States routinely used language from the 1850 case *Commonwealth v. Webster* that required jurors to "feel" guilt was established by the prosecution "to a reasonable and moral certainty." To convict, the jurors had to consider all of the evidence and have an "abiding conviction, to a moral certainty" that the defendant was guilty.[22]

About 120 years after the Webster charge (as it is referred to) first appeared, the United States Supreme Court stated in *In re Winship* that "**reasonable doubt**" is that which "impresses on the trier of fact the necessity of reaching a 'subjective state of certitude' of the facts in issue."[23] The Court further defined the concept by proclaiming that "proof beyond a reasonable doubt" means (1) that a criminal defendant's guilt must be proved in the minds of the jurors to the "utmost certainty" and (2) that there could be no conviction if the trier of fact had reasonable doubt about the accused's guilt.[24] Taken together, the key notion is that the jury or judge must be nearly but not absolutely certain that the defendant is guilty.

If the jury is adequately certain (has a level of utmost certainty), then they can convict the defendant only because they have moved beyond reasonable doubt and now have no reasonable doubt. Some find understanding the idea of proof beyond a reasonable

---

21. *Id.* at 370.
22. *Commonwealth* v. *Webster*, 59 Mass. 295, 320 (1850).
23. *In re Winship* at 364 (quoting Dorsen & Rezneck, In Re Gault and the Future of Juvenile Law, 1 Family Law Quarterly, No. 4, pp. 1, 26 (1967)).
24. *In re Winship at 364.*

doubt more easy if they rephrase the concept to say the proof "leaves you with no reasonable doubt." Any doubts you do have at this level of certainty, you must conclude, are extremely remote, inventive, or simply unreasonable because they can't be explained with sound reason.[25]

As a final matter, some appellate courts have told trial judges to never define reasonable doubt in the first place because of the problems that arise from the definitions. They have told the trial courts to only tell the jury that they cannot convict the defendant unless guilt is proved beyond a reasonable doubt. Many believe that the jury can then figure out the meaning through the deliberation process and apply it properly.[26]

What do you think of the Supreme Court's definition of proof beyond a reasonable doubt as that which leaves a juror in a "subjective state of certainty" or with "proof to an utmost certainty?" Does that definition really differ from the old Webster charge that there must be an "abiding conviction, to a moral certainty? If you have a room with twelve jurors deliberating over a case, is it likely that all twelve will interpret the definitions the same? If so, then wouldn't it just be better to not define the phrase and let the jurors figure it out the best they can?

In 1990, the Supreme Court revisited the issue of proof beyond a reasonable doubt in two murder cases. The court had to determine if the similar jury instructions for reasonable doubt used in the separate trials for the defendants violated their due process rights under the standards set forth in *In re Winship*.

Victor v. Nebraska

511 U.S. 1 (1994) (Companion case *to Sandoval v. California*)

Clarence Victor, in Nebraska, and Alfred Sandoval, in California, were convicted of murder in separate trials and each was given the death penalty. Because the focus of their separate appeals to the Supreme Court was almost identical, the Court joined the cases and wrote a single opinion.[27] We will focus only on the Sandoval case here.

A jury found Sandoval guilty of committing four murders. He killed two people in a gang-related shooting and two weeks later killed the man who had given information to the police, and also killed the man's wife because she witnessed her husband's murder. After Sandoval was given the death sentence, he appealed, claiming the jury was given an unconstitutional jury instruction regarding the government's burden of proof. The jury instruction, among other things, defined reasonable doubt as follows:

> It is not a mere possible doubt; because everything relating to human affairs, and depending on moral evidence, is open to some possible or imaginary doubt. It is that state of the case which, after the entire comparison and consideration of all the evidence, leaves the minds of the jurors in that condition

---

25. Fortunato, Stephen, J. Jr., *Instructing on Reasonable Doubt after* Victor v. Nebraska*: A Trial Judge's Certain Thoughts on Certainty*, 41 Vill. L. Rev. 365, 380 (1996).

26. *Id.* at 950.

27. *Victor v. Nebraska* is a consolidation of two cases: *State v. Victor*, 457 N.W.2d 431 (Neb. 1990) and *People v. Sandoval*, 841 P.2d 862 (Cal. 1993).

> that they cannot say they feel an abiding conviction, to a moral certainty, of the truth of the charge.[28]

Sandoval argued that the jury did not sufficiently understand the instruction, especially the phrase "moral certainty," and consequently, could have based their conviction on insufficient evidence. He argued that the phrase was outdated and confused modern jurors, allowing them to convict him even though guilt had not been proved beyond a reasonable doubt.

After reviewing the above jury instruction in light of the holding in *In re Winship*, the Supreme Court upheld the conviction and ruled that the instructions did not confuse the jury. The Court reiterated that the phrase "moral certainty" meant the same thing as beyond a reasonable doubt.[29] Then the court stated that "taken as a whole, the instructions correctly conveyed the concept of reasonable doubt to the jury."[30] Even though some parts of the instruction may have been unclear, the court was satisfied that the jury instruction, when considered in its entirety, did not mislead the jury.

Is the *Sandoval* definition of reasonable doubt clear to you? Do you think the *Winship* requirement of "**utmost certainty**" is the same thing as the *Sandoval* requirement for "**moral certainty**?" Would that answer vary from person to person depending on one's own sense of morals or values? Both Sandoval and Victor, who faced a similar jury instruction, argued that the definitions of reasonable doubt were unclear and outdated. The Supreme Court disagreed. Both lost their appeals and remained on death row. Some have argued that the Court's holding expanded the definition of proof beyond a reasonable doubt and, arguably, diluted or reduced the burden defined in *In re Winship*.[31]

C. Numerical Quantification

You may better understand the concepts being discussed in this chapter if they are quantified along a scale so that you can at least have a basic numerical or comparative idea in your mind of what the standards mean. Please understand that Courts do not define burdens of proof by reference to percentages of certainty or numbers so this discussion is intended to be explanatory rather than authoritative. Regardless of any reservations about the method, some educators have noted that students often better grasp these comparative concepts by considering them on a scale from 0% to 100% certainty. The following is a summary of key points along that scale and what they mean:

- 0% certainty means no evidence of any kind;
- 51% certainty means more likely than not or the preponderance of the evidence;
- 80% certainty means some strong evidence of guilt but also reasonable doubts

28. *Id.*
29. *Id.* at 12.
30. *Id.* at 22 (quoting *Holland v. United States*, 348 U.S. 121, 140 (1954)).
31. See generally Fortunato, Stephen, J. Jr., *Instructing on Reasonable Doubt after* Victor v. Nebraska*: A Trial Judge's Certain Thoughts on Certainty*, 41 Vill. L. Rev. 365 (1996).

- 95%–99% certainty may be utmost certainty or proof beyond a reasonable doubt
- 100% certainty is hard to obtain but is easily proof beyond a reasonable doubt

Applying this scale to an example, let's assume a person vanishes and the police can find absolutely no evidence of any kind about what happened to the person or where the person might be. You could fairly conclude there is 0% proof of any real crime. Certainly there is not only reasonable doubt of criminal activity but there is essentially complete doubt because there is no real evidence at all.

By contrast, if there is a video tape that clearly shows the husband shooting his missing wife in their bed and then put her body in a dumpster, as well as a voluntary confession by the husband, most would agree that you have something like 99% to 100% certainty that the husband is guilty. You have no reasonable doubt. Because you easily have proof to an "utmost certainty" that goes beyond a reasonable doubt, you could unquestionably vote to convict the husband. Ultimately, opinions differ on the exact number that should be used to represent proof beyond a reasonable doubt. Some will say 90% sure is enough while others will say 99.9% sure is the minimum. The key is that whatever percentage or quantum of proof a juror focuses on, the overriding principal is that the juror must still have no reasonable doubt and be "firmly convinced" or convinced to an "utmost certainty."

In the really tough cases, which would be more typical, the jury would hear witnesses explaining why the defendant is guilty and see evidence tying him to the crime scene in one way or another—like DNA, blood, and fingerprints. The jury would also hear evidence put on by the defense showing why it couldn't have been the defendant, why the police erred in the investigation, and why it was likely someone else. The jury might also learn how much the defendant loved his wife and what an outstanding citizen he is. That kind of case may be up for grabs when it comes to predicting the outcome. Will the jury be 50% sure, 80% sure or 99% sure? No fancy definition of proof beyond reasonable doubt or number system based on percentages of certainty can make that kind of decision easy. The jurors have to look at the witnesses, judge credibility, consider the circumstances, view all the evidence, and do the best they can to decide what the facts are and whether those facts prove the defendant is guilty. If they are only 80% sure based on the evidence, even if deep down inside they think the defendant might have killed his wife, that is likely not enough for a conviction.

Finally, if the family of the deceased wife files a civil lawsuit, they only have to prove that it is 51% likely that the defendant wrongfully killed his wife. Would it be difficult under many fact scenarios, in your view, to show that it is more likely than not that the husband killed his wife? A few strong pieces of evidence, even with some key points of doubt, could still be enough to find liability.

Again, keep in mind that our efforts above to quantify proof beyond a reasonable doubt with percentages of certainty are not utilized in courts. What is required, we know, is "not a mathematical or scientific certainty but, proof beyond a reasonable doubt."[32] There is, nonetheless, value in engaging in the quantitative evaluation.

32. *People v. Malloy* 55 N.Y.2d 296, 300, 303 (1982).

Constitutional Ideals Related to the Burden of Proof

In discussing the prosecution of an individual charged with a crime, it is vital that you recognize the links between three inseparable constitutional principles:

(1) due process of law;

(2) the presumption of innocence; and

(3) proof beyond a reasonable doubt.

You can better understand and appreciate the burdens of proof in our system by seeing the relationships between the three principles and better understanding what they mean in the criminal justice system.

First, you should already understand from this and prior chapters that in our legal system, all people charged with a crime are entitled to **due process of law**. Specifically, the Fifth and Fourteenth Amendments to the U.S. Constitution proclaim that no person can "be deprived of life, liberty, or property, without due process of law." In general, then, the Government cannot convict and incarcerate a person unless those engaged in government systems have adhered to the legally prescribed methods for arrest and prosecution. If the substance of a law or the procedures utilized by law enforcement or a court are found to be defective, then the defendant's due process rights will have presumably been unconstitutionally violated. Consequently, further government action against the person in such case is restricted and all charges could be dropped. For example, if an officer made an arrest without probable cause in violation of the prohibition against unreasonable searches and seizures, then, in most cases, the charges would be thrown out.[33]

Second, as we have already established, the Supreme Court has declared that all citizens facing charges are **presumed innocent** until the government proves them guilty. In our adversarial system where the defendant is presumed to be innocent, the accused is protected against self-incrimination, is entitled to legal counsel to ensure the government meets its burden of proof, and has a right to a public trial where guilt must be proven through admissible evidence. No matter how horrible the alleged acts of the suspect might be or how guilty society thinks the person is, the suspected criminal is indeed innocent until the government proves otherwise.

Finally, it makes sense that if a person who is arrested is presumed to be innocent, then due process requires that guilt be established in a court by some required level of proof. In our system, as you already know, that level or burden is referred to as **proof beyond a reasonable doubt**.

Can you see how the guarantees of **due process** and the **presumption of innocence** are inseparably connected to the concept of **proof beyond a reasonable doubt**? Do you believe that in order for our system to be just and fair, that an accused must be afforded these protections or does our system go too far in protecting those accused of crimes? In 2007, many sports enthusiasts ignored these three vital principles and unilaterally pri-

33. *Terry v. Ohio*, 367 U.S. 643 (1961) (exclusionary rule applicable to state cases).

vately "convicted" Barry Bonds, Major League Baseball's All-Time Home Run Champ, of improprieties relating to alleged steroid use. Without affording him the time-honored protections of due process of law, presumption of innocence, and guilt established by proof beyond a reasonable doubt, he was essentially convicted by self-appointed jurors in the courtroom of public opinion as he pursued and surpassed the coveted home run record. Should we be able to arbitrarily take away someone's life, liberty, or property (or right to peace and dignity) just because it looks like there is some evidence of wrongdoing? If so, what would that say about our system of justice and law? Our criminal justice system could not survive if it let public and media opinions dictate the outcomes of cases in this manner. To do so would debase the Constitution and would strip these key constitutional principles of all real meaning and value.

Guilty Pleas Affected by the Reasonable Doubt Standard

Despite the impressions we get from sensational media cases, few criminal cases actually end in a trial. Virtually none end with last second, surprise witnesses or evidence. In fact, over 90% of all state felony criminal cases, including the much hyped driving under the influence cases involving Hollywood personalities Paris Hilton, Mel Gibson, and Lindsey Lohan, for instance, are resolved before a trial through the entry of a guilty or no contest plea.[34] The vast majority of millions of criminal cases are resolved so quickly that few get any media coverage at all. Why do so few cases go to trial? Is that a good thing or is something wrong with our system?

Your answer to those questions might depend on how much you really understand about the burden of proof the prosecution faces and how that burden impacts the day to day operations of the criminal justice system. In general, the public's sense of what is "going on" in the legal system is overly affected by trials involving a few high profile defendants. Several recent examples have made trials seem to some to be more like circus acts than forums for fairness and truth. Literally hundreds of millions of viewers have followed the relatively recent trials of media celebrities like O.J. Simpson, Martha Stewart, Robert Blake, Michael Jackson, Kobe Bryant, and Scott Peterson, to name only a few. The media's sensationalized coverage of every angle of these trials has put the Hollywood spin and spotlight on our court system. Consequently, many Americans are left skeptical and believe that in most cases freedom or reduced sentences are too easily bought through a crafty band of $500 an hour lawyers.

More citizens might have a better impression of the criminal justice system if they just understood that the sensational cases are not typical of the day to day happenings of the criminal courts. It would be especially helpful if the public really understood the key principles surrounding the burden of proof that are covered in this chapter. Such

34. *Victim Input into Plea Agreement*, U.S. Department of Justice, Legal Series Bulletin 7 (November 2002) 1; Alschuler and Deiss, *A Brief History of the Criminal Jury in the United States*, 61 U. Chi. L. Rev. 867 (1994).

knowledge would answer the question why so few criminal cases actually go to trial or why prosecutors cut so many deals rather than "just" take the cases to trial.

As was previously noted, very few criminal cases ever go to trial. The overwhelming reality based on the statistics is that the vast majority of the time the arrested suspects actually committed a crime. The evidence is so strong that the defendants voluntary plead guilty as charged or plead guilty to a negotiated charge. There are over two million people in American jails or prisons today. As was noted, less than 10% of these inmates were imprisoned after a trial. Where the evidence has some recognized weaknesses or the procedures might have been irregular, prosecutors routinely and necessarily negotiate plea deals, as we learned in Chapter 6. Even in seemingly strong evidentiary cases, plea deals are regularly cut because of the high legal standards or burdens prosecutors face in every case. It simply would not be possible or even a wise use of resources for any prosecutor's office to force every case to trial. Not surprisingly, a prosecutor faced with the heavy burden of having to prove every case beyond a reasonable doubt might see plea bargaining as a practical necessity.

Defendants, especially those represented by counsel, recognize the high burden of proof and try to capitalize on that reality at every opportunity. The burden of proving a seemingly basic case such as theft, for instance, is substantial because the prosecutor has to produce enough admissible evidence to prove beyond reasonable doubt that the accused intended to permanently take another's property. If a woman, for example, were being prosecuted for getting gas and driving off without paying for it, the prosecutor would have to firmly convince the jury that the woman intentionally drove off without paying for the gas. How could the prosecutor prove that the suspect did not accidentally or absent-mindedly get in her car and drive off? Could a skilled defense lawyer get some jurors to believe it was not theft but only an accident, especially if the person had a perfect record? There is a good chance this case will end in some sort of a negotiated plea because the verdict could go either way. Not surprisingly, all the parties involved in a case, facing the high burden of proof, have serious cause to carefully reflect upon and evaluate their actions before they spend the significant time, money, and energy required to take a case all the way through a trial. As you can hopefully see, plea bargaining plays a vital role in the criminal justice mix because of the high burden of proof.

Ordeals: Proof of Guilt from a Historical Perspective

During parts of Medieval-European history, different cultures—with their kings, magistrates, religious leaders, or other officials—used a variety of methods to "prove" guilt or innocence beyond doubt, as we would put it. The accused, unfortunately and against almost insurmountable odds, generally bore the burden of proving his or her innocence. The basic idea for centuries was that some "Divine or supernatural Power" was just and would, therefore, not allow any injustice such as the conviction of an innocent person.[35] Thus, the authorities of the day merely needed to subject an accused

35. John H. Wigmore. (1941). *A Kaleidoscope of Justice.* Washington D.C.: Washington Law Book Co., at 5.

to a series of tests or **ordeals** in order to separate the guilty from the innocent.[36] It was believed that God, to the extent necessary, would miraculously intervene to guarantee the innocent were protected and the guilty were discovered through the different ordeals. The goal of the accused was normally just to survive the physical ordeal with their bodies and lives in tact.

One ordeal, for example, compelled the accused to walk across red-hot steel for a given distance or time period. Other subjects may have been forced to put a hand into a pot of boiling water to remove a stone from the bottom. Those who did not get burned or who were deemed by clergy to have been adequately healed by Divinity were deemed innocent (in essence, beyond doubt), while those who were burned or who had "festering" wounds were found guilty and were punished under the law—often by death.[37]

In other circumstances, the accused suspects were submerged into cold water to see if they would float or sink. Those who sank, and presumably drowned in many cases, were deemed guilty. Interestingly, in some other cultures, a person who sank was deemed innocent (and was hopefully retrieved from the water in time to celebrate their victory over the charge).[38] In an additional example, sometimes the accusers and the accused engaged in trials by battle. The battles were fights to the death. If the accuser died, the accused had proved his own innocence.[39]

Finally, during some historical periods, especially after many of the ordeals were banned in 13th century England, torture became the preferred method for proving guilt or innocence. Over time, as trials, rules of evidence, and juries developed, some societies increasingly recognized that the accused had certain rights and that there might be more effective ways to prove guilt. The concepts inherent in proving guilt beyond a reasonable doubt, which to some degree had actually been utilized in some cultures for centuries, began to be take shape and be applied in English courts in the middle ages and during the colonial period in the American colonies.

What do you think of the historical examples discussed above for proving guilt or innocence? From your current perspective, you may think these historical methods are barbaric and irrational. How often do you think people were punished for crimes they did not commit? If nothing else, this brief review of several historical examples for finding proof should give you a broader perspective and point of comparison, as well as a larger context, for evaluating our present standard of requiring proof of guilt beyond a reasonable doubt.

Gratefully, our criminal justice system today does not rely on the ordeals to establish guilt. Our historical recognition of the worth of individuals in the context of our criminal courts is exemplified in this well known statement: "It is better that ten guilty people go free than one innocent person be convicted."[40] Or, as Supreme Court Justice

---

36. For additional information on the material presented in this section, *see e.g. Id.* at 5–7 9 (for overview of European ordeals) and Sadakat Kadri. (2005). *The Trial, A History from Socrates to O.J. Simpson.* New York: Random House, generally from 25–104.

37. *See e.g.* Wigmore at 7–12 and Kadri at 25–27.

38. *See e.g.* Wigmore at 15–17 and Kadri at 25–27.

39. *See e.g.* Wigmore at 39–42 and Kadri at 30, 37.

40. Fortunato, Stephen, J. Jr., *Instructing on Reasonable Doubt after* Victor v. Nebraska*: A Trial Judge's Certain Thoughts on Certainty*, 41 Vill. L. Rev. 365, 410 (1996) (citing *4 William Blackstone, Commentaries,* 352).

John Marshall Harlan reiterated, the proof beyond a reasonable doubt standard in criminal cases is based on "a fundamental value determination of our society that it is far worse to convict an innocent man than to let a guilty man go free."[41]

The U.S. Supreme Court, as the guardians and interpreters of American constitutional rights and principles, reversed a conviction because of bad jury instructions in the following murder case.

Cage v. Louisiana

498 U.S. 39, 40 (1990) (per curium)

Defendant Cage was convicted of first-degree murder and was given the death penalty.[42] The defendant appealed claiming, among other things, that the jury instruction was defective in his case. If it was defective and somehow mislead or confused the jury, Cage argued, then he was deprived of his constitutional right to due process of law and was not proven guilty beyond reasonable doubt. To decide the issue, the Court looked carefully at the jury instruction to see if the instruction complied with the standards set forth in *In re Winship*. The jury instruction, in key part, is as follows.

> [A] reasonable doub[t] is one that is founded upon a real tangible substantial basis and not upon mere caprice and conjecture. It must be such doubt as would give rise to a grave uncertainty, raised in your mind by reasons of unsatisfactory character of the evidence or lack thereof. A reasonable doubt is not a mere possible doubt. It is an actual substantial doubt. It is a doubt that a reasonable man can seriously entertain. What is required is not an absolute or mathematical certainty, but a moral certainty.[43]

The Supreme Court ruled that the instruction was unconstitutional. It emphasized that even though the jury was instructed to convict only if they had no reasonable doubt, the instruction went on to unconstitutionally equate reasonable doubt with "**grave uncertainty**" and "**actual substantial doubt**" in the context of "**moral certainty.**"[44] The words "substantial" and "grave," the court held, created a standard of proof higher than that required by law. Thus, when considering substantial and grave doubt in the context of "moral certainty," rather than "evidentiary certainty," a jury could have found a person guilty on less than reasonable doubt.[45] Hopefully you can see that the instruction is inappropriate because a juror would be led to conclude that unless her doubt rose to the level of grave uncertainty, her doubt would not be unreasonable so a vote for conviction would be appropriate. That turns the burden upside down.

To date, the *Cage* case is the *only case* in which the U.S. Supreme Court has declared a jury instruction defining reasonable doubt unconstitutional. Compare the *Cage* instruction to the jury instruction from *Victor v. Nebraska* set forth above. Can you see

---

41. *Id*, citing Justice John Marshall Harlan Junior's concurring opinion in *In re Winship*, 397 U.S. 358, 373–74 (1970).

42. *Cage v. Louisiana*, 498 U.S. 39, 40 (1990) (per curium).

43. The jury instruction declared unconstitutional for violating the defendant's Due Process rights for poorly defining reasonable doubt. See *Cage v. Louisiana*, 498 U.S. 39, 40 (1990) (*per curium*)

44. *Id.* at 41.

45. *Id.*

any real or clear difference? Many have criticized the *Victor* case because they see no significant difference between the instructions in that case and those in *Cage*.[46]

The Constitutionality of Non-Unanimous Jury Verdicts

Each example used in this chapter so far has dealt with cases where the Defendant could only be convicted by a unanimous finding of guilt by the jury (usually made up of twelve jurors in criminal cases). What if a state passed a law saying that in death penalty cases a person can be found guilty if 9 out of 12 jurors render a guilty verdict? Based on what you have learned about reasonable doubt and the Constitution, could the prosecutor properly prove guilt beyond a reasonable doubt in such a case? The United States Supreme Court answered that question in the following state criminal case.

Johnson v. Louisiana

406 U.S. 356 (1971)

Johnson was convicted of robbery. The victim of the crime identified Johnson as the robber in a lineup and testified to that fact in court. After the trial, nine jurors concluded that Johnson was guilty while three voted that he was not guilty. Both the Louisiana Constitution and Law provide that in cases where the punishment will be hard labor there must be twelve jurors and at least nine of the twelve must find the defendant guilty. Johnson was found guilty by a vote of 9 to 3. He appealed his conviction, claiming that given the three dissenting votes, his due process rights had been violated. After all, he argued, how could there be proof beyond a reasonable doubt when three jurors said he was not guilty.[47] Didn't that fact alone constitute reasonable doubt?

The Supreme Court rejected Johnson's arguments and ruled that Johnson's due process rights were not violated by the non-unanimous verdict. The Court emphasized that, as required in *In re Winship*, the jurors were properly told that they could only vote for conviction if they were convinced he was guilty beyond a reasonable doubt. There was no indication that the nine who voted for guilt had reasonable doubts. If anything, the court noted, the three who voted not guilty should have considered whether their votes were actually reasonable given the super majority that said he was guilty.[48] Lack of unanimity is not the same thing as reasonable doubt. If dissent were the same thing as reasonable doubt then it would follow that in any case where there was any disagreement as to guilt, a new trial should not be ordered but instead the defendant should be acquitted.

---

46. *See e.g.*, Fortunato, Stephen, J. Jr., *Instructing on Reasonable Doubt after* Victor v. Nebraska*: A Trial Judge's Certain Thoughts on Certainty*, 41 Vill. L. Rev. 365, 410 (1996).
47. *Johnson v. Louisiana*, 406 U.S. 357, 357–58 (1971).
48. *Id.*

Johnson applies only to crimes in states that have passed laws allowing a less than unanimous verdict. Federal crimes must still be proved unanimously. Though some have pushed for modifications to the jury system, the historical requirement of unanimity is still followed in almost all state courts.[49]

Sufficient or Insufficient Evidence?

Courts have had to confront a variety of cases in which the question was whether special circumstances in the case nullified a jury finding that there was evidence of guilt beyond a reasonable doubt. Below, we will explore several of those cases. Please note that these cases are merely representative of a few principles. If facts were changed or if the crime were to take place in another state with different laws, the outcome might have been different. Your focus should be on the general principles that relate to reasonable doubt as discussed in this chapter.

A. Guilt or Mere Presence at a Crime Scene?

Consider the following facts from the case *State v. Vaillancourt.*[50] The defendant was accused of burglary. The only witness saw him and the other suspect standing on the porch of a home conversing and ringing the door bell. The witness, who was a neighbor, became suspicious when the two suspects stayed on the porch for about ten minutes. She then watched the two walk to the side of the house. While the defendant stood by and watched, periodically talking, the other suspect tried to pry a window open. The police appeared at the scene and caught the two while they were fleeing.[51]

The defendant was indicted on an attempted burglary charge for "aiding" in the commission of a crime for "accompanying the defendant" and "watching" him attempt to commit burglary.[52] Vaillancourt appealed the indictment claiming that, even if all of the facts alleged in the charge were proven true beyond doubt, the facts still did not constitute a crime. The appellate court reversed the indictment. In doing so, the court discussed the following issues. First, the court noted that "knowledge and mere presence at the scene of a crime could not support a conviction" for the crime at issue because the claimed acts were not enough to satisfy the legal requirements for the crime.[53] Second, under the law of New Hampshire in affect at that time, the defendant's "mere presence," even though he accompanied and observed the crime, was not enough to

49. Glasser, Michael H., Comment *Letting the Supermajority Rule: Nonunanimous Jury Verdicts in Criminal Trials*, FLA. ST. U L. REV. 659 (1997).
50. 453 A.2d 1327, 1328 (N.H. 1982).
51. *Id.* at 1328.
52. *Id.*
53. *Id.*

constitute the "aid" of a crime.[54] It was not evidence that could create proof beyond a reasonable doubt, based on the indictment.

The key in the *Vaillancourt* case appears to be the inadequacy of the written complaint. In the case *State of Missouri v. Kobel*,[55] the defendant was convicted of assault and other criminal actions. He agreed that he was present at the crime scene but denied any criminal activity. The court agreed that "mere presence" at a crime scene is inadequate evidence to convict someone of a crime but noted that it is one of several "indicia" (indicators) of criminal conduct, along with a show of force, flight, and association with others involved in the crime.[56] Despite the Defendant's sworn testimony that others committed the assault, that he had just showed up at the wrong time, and sprayed mace at the victim to protect himself from an act of aggression against him, the jury believed the testimony of others. The jury had a legal basis to convict the defendant and the appellate court was not going to second guess the conclusion of the jury that the defendant lied on the stand.

Based on the ruling in *Kobel*, do you think that the facts in the *Vaillancourt* case were adequate to prove he was guilty? He was present when a crime was committed, conversed with the defendant periodically, and fled when the police came.

B. Is Mere Flight Enough to Prove Guilt?

What if someone runs from the police or leaves the state because the police are looking for them? Do you think the evidence of "flight" alone should be enough to convict a person beyond reasonable doubt? After all, as has been stated, "the wicked flee, even when no one pursueth."[57] Or, it is commonly believed, if someone runs away from the police, they must be guilty of something.

Courts have concluded that flight alone is not evidence of a crime and that it is only marginal proof of guilt or innocence[58] and of "slight value."[59] There are many legitimate reasons why a person might flee from an officer, such as fear of false accusations, the inability to prove innocence, or an effort to protect someone else.[60] Introducing evidence of flight tends to be highly prejudicial to defendants because jurors may be overly influenced by the information and could reach the wrong conclusion.[61] Flight from the police, whether right after a crime or before a trial, should only be admitted if a court determines that its probative value (its value in proving a fact) outweighs any unfair prejudice. So proof of flight can sometimes be admitted when it has a "tendency to prove guilt",[62] but because it can also be misleading, it should

54. *Id.*
55. 927 S.W.2d 455 (Mo. App. W.D. 1996).
56. *Id.* at 459.
57. *U.S. v. Hernandez-Bermudez*, 857 F.2d 50, 54 (1988) (quoting 2 Wigmore, *Evidence § 276 (Chadbourne rev. 1979))*.
58. *See e.g., Miller v. United States*, 320 F.2d 767, 770 (D.C. Cir. 1963); *U.S. v. Hernandez-Bermudez*, 857 F.2d 50, 53–54 (1988).
59. *Miller* at 771.
60. *Hernandez-Bermudez* at 54.
61. *Hernandez-Bermudez* at 54.
62. *Id.*

only be used with caution. Standing alone, it is not proof of guilt beyond reasonable doubt, but when considered in light of all of the proven surrounding circumstances, it could be a fact that supports a conviction.

C. Mere Confession

Could a jury convict a person of a crime if the only evidence they had of the crime was the confession of the defendant? At first blush, you may think that the answer is obvious. After all, if someone confesses to a crime, then why wouldn't we accept that as the basis for a conviction? This issue was addressed in the following typical case.

Michigan v. McMahan

548 N.W. 2d 199 (Mich 1996)

James McMahan was convicted by a jury of second degree murder. He was convicted of killing Carolyn Kenyon who had left her apartment with McMahan and was never seen or heard from again. No evidence was found to show what happened, why she had disappeared, and what condition she might be in. Five years later, McMahan was being investigated for the murder of a ten-year-old girl. During that investigation, he confessed three different times to killing Ms. Kenyon. He claimed the two had partied together and that he had stabbed the victim in the chest after she made him mad. He claimed to having buried her body in several locations before finally putting her body in a plastic bag that he then placed in a dumpster. The police attempted to substantiate the claims but could not do so. Her body was never found and no evidence of the crime was discovered beyond the confession. Despite that fact, the judge allowed the confession into evidence and a jury returned a guilty verdict.[63] The Michigan Court of Appeals reversed the conviction because there was no evidence of how or whether the defendant died other than the Defendant's confession. The State of Michigan appealed.

The Michigan Supreme Court agreed with the Court of Appeals and affirmed the reversal of the conviction. In so concluding, the court emphasized the necessity of **corpus delicti**, meaning proof other than a confession alone that a crime had been committed. The Court went on to hold that without proof of a crime or cause of the death, a person's confession to the crime is not admissible. Corpus delicti is required in order to prevent conviction of a homicide when there was actually no crime and to minimize the effect of a confession unless there is corroborating or supporting evidence to back up the confession.[64] The general law, then, is that there must be some independent evidence that there was a crime in the first place before a confession can be used as the basis for a conviction. A confession standing on its own, without some proof of a crime, cannot be used to establish proof of guilt beyond a reasonable doubt. While it may seem strange, there are instances where people, whether for attention, out of fear, or perhaps due to illness, have confessed to crimes and were convicted, while later it was discovered there was no crime in the first place.

---

63. *People v. McMahan*, 548 N.W.2d 199, 200 (1996).
64. *Id.* at 201.

Conclusion

After studying this chapter you should know a great deal about our criminal justice system through our study of proof beyond a reasonable doubt. You should recognize that in our system of justice, we have intentionally created a series of hurdles, such as the rules of evidence and procedural laws, to ensure that a person who faces the loss of life, liberty, or property is tried in a fair and just manner. Under the Constitution, all defendants are entitled to due process of law and are presumed to be innocent until proven guilty beyond a reasonable doubt. We value the dignity of the individual so much that we would rather see some guilty people go free than have a single innocent person wrongly convicted of a crime. Sometimes errors are made but every effort is made to demand that prosecutors, judges, jurors, and even defense attorneys who advocate for the accused understand and respect the burden of proof beyond a reasonable doubt..

This burden of proof on the prosecution is high and requires that guilt of every element of a crime be proven to a degree of utmost certainty. It does not require absolute certainty, nor does it allow a verdict to be based upon guesses or public opinion. The lesser standard of proof used in civil cases, which is referred to as the preponderance of the evidence, is not appropriate in criminal cases because it merely requires a jury to conclude that the defendant is more likely guilty than not, regardless of the degree of reasonable doubt. The overall level of confidence in a verdict based upon proof beyond a reasonable doubt is much greater than that of a preponderance of the evidence. Historic methods involving pain, suffering, and torture as the means for flushing out the truth are wholly inadequate and antiquated and have no place in our modern system of justice. Today, guilt must rightly be proved by evidence that is proof beyond a reasonable doubt.

Chapter Ten

Criminal Juries and the Law

I consider trial by jury as the only anchor yet imagined by man, by which a government can be held to the principles of its constitution.[1]

Thomas Jefferson, 1789

At the founding of the United States the right of a person accused of a crime to be tried by a jury was considered to be of great importance. Article III, Section 2 of the Constitution states that "[t]he Trials of all crimes, except in cases of Impeachment, shall be by Jury; and such Trial shall be held in the State where the said Crimes shall have been committed." Moreover, the Sixth Amendment provides that a person charged with a crime has the right to trial "by an impartial jury of the State and district wherein the crime shall have been committed."

In *Duncan v. Louisiana*[2], the Supreme Court held that the right to trial by jury in criminal prosecutions to be a **fundamental right** and applicable to state prosecutions via the 14th Amendment. In the majority opinion, Justice White eloquently and famously explained the place trial by jury holds in the American system of justice.

> A right to jury trial is granted to criminal defendants in order to prevent oppression by the Government. Those who wrote our constitutions knew from history and experience that it was necessary to protect against unfounded criminal charges brought to eliminate enemies and against judges too responsive to the voice of higher authority. The framers of the constitutions strove to create an independent judiciary but insisted upon further protection against arbitrary action. Providing an accused with the right to be tried by a jury of his peers gave him an inestimable safeguard against the corrupt or overzealous prosecutor and against the compliant, biased, or eccentric judge. If the defendant preferred the common-sense judgment of a jury to the more tutored but perhaps less sympathetic reaction of the single judge, he was to have it. Beyond this, the jury trial provisions in the Federal and State Constitutions reflect a fundamental decision about the exercise of official power—a reluctance to entrust plenary powers over the life and liberty of the citizen to one judge or to a group of judges. Fear of unchecked power, so typical of our State and Federal Governments in other respects, found expression in the criminal law in this insistence upon community participation in the determination of guilt or innocence.[3]

1. Thomas Jefferson (1789) ME 7:408, Papers 15:269.
2. 391 U.S. 145 (1968).
3. *Id.* at 155–156.

Despite the tremendous value placed in trial by jury, or perhaps because of it, specific aspects of the Sixth Amendment's protections have presented themselves to the nation's courts. This chapter will consider some of these items, including the types of offenses that do not come with a right to a jury trial, how citizens are selected to serve as jurors, limitations on who may or may not sit on a jury, and what a trial court may do in controlling a jury and focusing its duties and obligations. After reading and considering cases involving these issues you will have a better understanding of the importance and limitations of the trial jury in the criminal justice system.

Limitations on the Right to Trial by Jury

The Constitution and Sixth Amendment explicitly provide for trial by jury in *all* criminal prosecutions. Despite the apparent clarity of this language, courts have consistently ruled that not all criminal trials necessitate the use of a jury. In the seminal case of *Duncan v. Louisiana*, the Supreme Court held that the right to jury trial exists only for cases involving **serious offenses** and not for **petty offenses**. In *Duncan*, the Court did not define what is a serious or petty offense, holding only that the case before it, where the defendant faced up to two years in prison, involved a serious offense.

A few years later, the Court clarified the matter somewhat. In *Baldwin v. New York*[4], the Court ruled that "no offense can be deemed 'petty' for purposes of the right to trial by jury where imprisonment for more than six months is authorized."[5] Subsequent to *Baldwin*, courts consistently applied this bright line standard, giving consideration only to the maximum potential imprisonment for a particular offense. In the 1989 case of *Blanton v. City of North Las Vegas*, the Court reopened the question of how to determine if an offense is serious or petty.

Blanton v. City of North Las Vegas
489 U.S. 538 (1989)

In 1987 Melvin Blanton was charged with driving under the influence of alcohol in North Las Vegas, Nevada. In Nevada, DUI was punishable by a minimum term of two days' imprisonment and a maximum term of six months' imprisonment and a maximum $1000 fine, or in the alternative, 48 hours of community service. Following his arrest, Blanton requested a jury trial, arguing that DUI was a serious rather than petty offense. This request was denied by the municipal court. On appeal the Nevada Supreme Court held that pursuant to *Baldwin v. New York*[6] the Constitution does not guarantee a right to a jury trial for a DUI because the maximum term of incarceration is only six months and the maximum possible fine is $1,000. The United States Supreme Court granted *certiorari* to consider the question of whether all crimes with a potential pun-

4. 399 U.S. 66 (1970)
5. 399 U.S. 66 (1970)
6. 399 U.S. 66 (1970)

ishment of incarceration for six-months or less are petty and therefore do not necessitate trial by jury.

In a unanimous opinion written by Justice Marshall the Supreme Court affirmed the decision of the Nevada Supreme Court. The analysis provided by the Court, however, clarified what standards lower courts should use in deciding if a trial for an offense must be before a jury. After discussing the development of the case law involving the right to trial by jury, the Court noted that lower courts have been misinterpreting the Supreme Court's plurality opinion in *Baldwin v. New York*. Justice Marshall wrote that the Court "did not hold in *Baldwin* that an offense carrying a maximum prison term of six months or less automatically qualifies as a 'petty' offense."[7] Rather, *Baldwin* stands for the proposition that a potential sentence of longer than six months is sufficiently severe to raise it to a level above a petty offense. Importantly, the Court went on to hold that an offense that has a potential penalty of six months or less in prison should not automatically be considered a petty crime.

The Court explained that the maximum potential sentence for a crime as laid out by a statute is the primary basis for determining if a crime is petty. There are, however, other possible authorized penalties associated with an offense other than incarceration that may be of such severity that they indicate that a crime is serious rather than petty. Justice Marshall laid out the standard to be applied when characterizing an offense as a petty or serious for Sixth Amendment purposes as follows:

> A defendant is entitled to a jury trial in such circumstances only if he can demonstrate that any additional statutory penalties, viewed in conjunction with the maximum authorized period of incarceration, are so severe that they clearly reflect a legislative determination that the offense in question is a "serious" one. This standard, albeit imprecise, should ensure the availability of a jury trial in the rare situation where a legislature packs an offense it deems "serious" with onerous penalties that nonetheless "do not puncture the 6-month incarceration line."[8]

The Court went on to explain that only penalties mandated in the statute should be considered in this analysis. Unfortunately, the Court did not elaborate on what such punishments might be. Rather, it only applied the facts presented in the case before it to the standard announced. The possible sanctions under Nevada's DUI statute, a 90-day license revocation, imposition of community service, and a $1,000 fine, were not of sufficient severity to rebut the presumption that an offense with a potential prison sentence of six months or less is a petty offense for Sixth Amendment purposes. Accordingly, the Court held that Blanton was not entitled to a jury trial.

As is often the case when it announces a rule, the Supreme Court gave limited guidance on how the rule should be applied. Specifically in this instance, what types of sanctions may render an offense with a short maximum period of incarceration serious rather than petty? Since 1989, state and federal courts have continued to simply use the bright line standard announced in *Baldwin*. Are there any sanctions other than incarceration that you believe are severe enough to have an offense classified as serious?

---

7. *Blanton* at 543.
8. *Id.*

A Jury of One's Peers

It is a commonly held belief that a criminal defendant has a right to a trial before a jury of his or her peers. Just as the Constitution states one has a right to a jury trial for all crimes, the right to a jury of one's peers is not a reality. In *Taylor v. Louisiana*,[9] the Supreme Court held that a jury selection system violates the right to a jury of one's peers if the system does not draw jurors from a **fair cross-section of the community**. While this too seems reasonable, in practice questions have frequently arisen regarding how to determine whether a jury represents a fair cross-section of the community. This fact is illustrated in the following case.

United States v. Shinault

147 F.3d 1266 (10th Cir. 1998)

On July 11, 1995, Michael Shinault robbed two stores while armed with a semi-automatic pistol. He was arrested shortly thereafter and charged with multiple federal crimes. He was tried before a jury in the Wichita-Hutchinson division of the District Court of Kansas. At trial, a jury returned guilty verdicts on all counts, and Shinault was sentenced to 562 months in prison. Shinault appealed to the Tenth Circuit Court of Appeals on the grounds that the jury selection procedures utilized in the District of Kansas denied him his Sixth Amendment right to a jury drawn from a fair cross-section of the community.

After noting that the Sixth Amendment and the Jury Selection and Service Act of 1968,[10] guarantee a defendant the right to trial before an impartial jury drawn from a cross-section of the community, the court of appeals discussed the method used by the District of Kansas for selecting juries.

> The plan adopted by the District of Kansas provides for the random selection of prospective grand and petit jurors from the official lists of actual voters in each of the counties in the six divisions in Kansas.... The names of individuals selected from the actual voter lists are placed on a "Master Jury Wheel" for the division in which the individuals reside. The clerk of the court draws names as needed from the divisional master wheel and mails a jury qualification form to the selected individuals. The form asks the potential jurors to identify their racial and ethnic background. All individuals who return the forms, are eligible for service, and are not excused from service, are placed on the "Qualified Jury Wheel."[11]

Shinault argued that this method, particularly reliance on lists of actual voters, systematically excluded Asians, Blacks, and Hispanics from jury service in the Wichita-Hutchinson Division of the District of Kansas.

The court proceeded to explain that to establish a *prima facie* case that a jury selection system violates the Sixth Amendment's fair cross-section requirement, a defendant must demonstrate three items:

---

9. 419 U.S. 522 (1975)
10. 28 U.S.C. §§ 1861
11. 1271

1. That the group alleged to be excluded is a "distinctive" group;
2. That the representation of this group in venires from which juries are selected is not fair and reasonable in relation to the number of such persons in the community; and
3. That this under-representation is due to systematic exclusion of the group in the jury-selection process.[12]

If a *prima facie* violation is proven, the government then bears the burden of proving that attainment of a fair cross-section is incompatible with a significant state interest.

After noting that the prosecution conceded that the three groups identified by Shinault as being under-represented in the jury pool—Asians, Blacks, and Hispanics—are distinctive groups for Sixth Amendment purposes, the court of appeals addressed the issue of what is the appropriate method for showing statistically that a group is under-represented in relation to its numbers in the community. As it is impossible to measure the percentage of any group of actual voters due to the secrecy of the ballot, the court decided the analysis should be done by comparing the percentage of the minority group on the qualified wheel to the percentage of the groups among the entire voting age population in the appropriate area.

The court then evaluated the facts for under representation under absolute disparity and comparative disparity analyses. The court explained the differences between the two methods as follows:

> **Absolute disparity** measures the difference between the percentage of a group in the general population and its percentage in the qualified wheel. For instance, if Asians constitute 10% of the general population and 5% of the qualified wheel, the absolute disparity is 5%. **Comparative disparity** measures the *decreased likelihood* that members of an underrepresented group will be called for jury service, in contrast to what their presence in the community suggests it should be. This figure is determined by dividing the absolute disparity of the group by that group's percentage in the general population. In the example above, the comparative disparity is 50%: Asians are half as likely to be on venires as they would be if represented in proportion to their numbers in the community.[13]

Table 10-1
Population Data for the District of Kansas

Distinctive Group	Asian	Black	Hispanic
Percentage of voting age population	1.27%	5.11%	2.92%
Percentage of qualified veniremen	.51%	2.55%	1.50%
Absolute Disparity	.76%	2.56%	1.42%
Comparative Disparity	59.84%	50.09%	48.63%

12. Id.
13. Id. at 1272.

In examining the statistics relevant to the case before it (presented in Table 10-1) the court found that Shinault had failed to establish a Sixth Amendment violation. While some absolute disparity is present, the absolute disparity for the three groups ranged from .76% to 2.56%. These levels do not rise to the level needed to establish a constitutional violation as previously established by the court (generally greater than 10%). In considering comparative disparity, the court noted that the high numbers are an artifact of the small overall population in the area and dismissed the notion that they showed systematic discrimination. Accordingly, the court held that Shinault's right to a jury made up of a cross section of the community was not violated.

Note that the right to have a jury drawn from a cross section of a community involves the examination of the entire jury pool as opposed to jurors sitting on a particular trial. So long as jurors are assigned to sit on specific cases at random, the use of a racially unbalanced jury in a particular case does not violate the Constitution.

Juries in Death Penalty Cases: The Death Qualified Jury

At the core of the jury system is having unbiased citizens to decide a person's guilt or innocence based on the facts presented to them. In an effort to identify potential jurors who may have a bias for or against a defendant or prosecution based on individual characteristics of the defendant or victim in a given case or the nature of the crimes involved in the case, the judge and attorneys will conduct what is known as *voir dire* as part of the jury selection process. **Voir Dire** involves the judge and attorneys asking jurors questions designed to learn about potential biases individual jurors might possess. If such bias is found to exist in a juror, that juror will be excused for cause.

Issues surrounding challenges for cause due to bias are especially prevalent in cases involving capital punishment. Given the nature of the punishment, cases involving the death penalty are the most serious faced by the justice system. As such, jury selection in capital cases is often done individually (one juror at a time) and can be very time consuming and detailed, often taking weeks to complete. A primary reason for this is the need to select a "death qualified jury."

A **death qualified jury** is a jury made up of people not categorically for or against the imposition of capital punishment for murder. The standard for selecting a death qualified jury was initially set by the Supreme Court in *Witherspoon v. Illinois*[14]. *Witherspoon* held that individuals could not be excluded from a jury "simply because they voiced general objections to the death penalty or expressed conscientious or religious scruples against its infliction."[15] This standard was further clarified somewhat in a footnote to the Court's opinion:

14. 391 U.S. 510 (1968).
15. *Id.* at 522.

> The most that can be demanded of a venireman in this regard is that he be willing to consider all of the penalties provided by state law, and that he not be irrevocably committed, before the trial has begun, to vote against the penalty of death regardless of the facts and circumstances that might emerge in the course of the proceedings.... We repeat, however, that nothing we say today bears upon the power of a State to execute a defendant sentenced to death by a jury from which the only veniremen who were, in fact, excluded for cause were those who made unmistakably clear that they would *automatically* vote against the imposition of capital punishment without regard to any evidence that might be developed at the trial of the case before them.... [16]

This standard, which required the trial judge to find the juror would automatically vote against the death penalty under all circumstances, was followed by courts for a number of years. In the 1980s a more conservative Supreme Court revisited the standard used in death qualification. The following case essentially eliminated the *Witherspoon* standard for a much more restrictive approach.

Wainwright v. Witt

469 U.S. 412 (1985)

While hunting in a wooded area in Florida, Johnny Witt and a friend came across an eleven-year-old boy riding by on his bicycle. As the boy rode by, the men hit him on the head, rendering him unconscious. The two men gagged the boy, placed him in the trunk of Witt's car, and drove to a deserted grove. While in the trunk, the boy suffocated. At the grove the two men committed various violent and sexual acts on the boy's body before burying it in the grove. Witt was subsequently arrested and charged with first-degree murder.

Since the state was seeking the death penalty against Witt, the jury needed to be death qualified as required by *Witherspoon v. Illinois*.[17] During *voir dire*, the following exchange took place between the prosecutor and a prospective juror, Mrs. Colby:

> " [Q. Prosecutor:] Now, let me ask you a question, ma'am. Do you have any religious beliefs or personal beliefs against the death penalty?
>
> " [A. Colby:] I am afraid personally but not—
>
> " [Q]: Speak up, please.
>
> " [A]: I am afraid of being a little personal, but definitely not religious.
>
> " [Q]: Now, would that interfere with you sitting as a juror in this case?
>
> " [A]: I am afraid it would.
>
> " [Q]: You are afraid it would?
>
> " [A]: Yes, Sir.
>
> " [Q]: Would it interfere with judging the guilt or innocence of the Defendant in this case?

---

16. *Witherspoon, supra.* footnote 21 at 592.
17. 391 U.S. 510 (1968)

" [A]: I think so.

" [Q]: You think it would.

" [A]: I think it would.

" [Q]: Your honor, I would move for cause at this point.

" THE COURT: All right. Step down."[18]

Mrs. Colby was excluded from the jury. Eventually a jury was empanelled, and Witt was found guilty and sentenced to death. Witt appealed on the grounds that the trial court erroneously excluded Mrs. Colby from the jury because of her opposition to the death penalty in violation of *Witherspoon*. The Florida Supreme Court affirmed his conviction and sentence on appeal. Witt then filed a petition for a writ of habeas corpus in federal court. After the district court denied his petition, the United States Court of Appeals for the Eleventh Circuit reversed, holding that the exclusion of Mrs. Colby from the jury was erroneous because she did not state that she would automatically vote against the death sentence. The United States Supreme Court granted the State of Florida's petition for a *writ of certiorari*.

Justice Rehnquist, writing for the majority, stated that since 1968, courts have been misconstruing what the Court actually held in *Witherspoon*. He noted that courts routinely have followed the language in *Witherspoon* which stated, "A sentence of death cannot be carried out if the jury that imposed or recommended it was chosen by excluding venire men for cause simply because they voiced general objections to the death penalty or expressed conscientious or religious scruples against its infliction."[19] The majority went on to state that courts have placed too much reliance on the following language contained in footnote 21 of *Witherspoon*:

> The most that can be demanded of a venireman in this regard is that he be willing to consider all of the penalties provided by state law, and that he not be irrevocably committed, before the trial has begun, to vote against the penalty of death regardless of the facts and circumstances that might emerge in the course of the proceedings.... We repeat, however, that nothing we say today bears upon the power of a State to execute a defendant sentenced to death by a jury from which the only veniremen who were, in fact, excluded for cause were those who made unmistakably clear that they would *automatically* vote against the imposition of capital punishment without regard to any evidence that might be developed at the trial of the case before them.... [20]

Justice Rehnquist wrote that these statements do not reflect the actual holding in *Witherspoon*. Stating that the Court was now explicitly clarifying the proper standard for determining when a prospective juror may be excluded for cause because of his views on capital punishment, the Court held that a court should only consider whether the juror's views would *prevent or substantially impair the performance of his duties as a juror in accordance with his instructions and his oath*. The Court noted that it was not

18. *Wainwright v. Witt*, at 415–416.
19. *Witherspoon, supra*. at 592, quoted in *Witt* at 418.
20. *Witherspoon, supra*. footnote 21 at 592.

overruling *Witherspoon*, but merely modifying and clarifying what it stood for. Justice Rehnquist explained that this standard is proper because it is in harmony with traditional reasons for excluding jurors and with the circumstances under which such determinations are made. He went on to explain that selecting a death qualified jury under the standard announced in this opinion furthers the state's interest in trying capital cases fairly, which may be frustrated by jurors who will not follow the law due to their beliefs regarding capital punishment.

As the Court of Appeals did not apply the standard announced by the Court, the Supreme Court reversed its decision and remanded the matter.

The standard laid out in *Witt* makes it much more likely that a person with strong feelings for or against the death penalty will not be permitted to sit as a juror in a capital case. *Witherspoon* required removal only if a juror would automatically vote against imposition of the death penalty in every case. Individuals generally opposed to the death penalty, but who would consider voting to have it imposed under some circumstances would be acceptable as jurors under *Witherspoon*. Under *Witt*, however, if the judge determines that a juror's attitude toward the death penalty would *substantially impair* his or her ability to deliberate and render a verdict based on the law and the evidence, the juror will not be death qualified. This standard has the effect of removing many people generally opposed to the death penalty from sitting on juries in capital cases because they honestly state that this belief may (although would not definitely) affect their decision.

Anonymous Juries

The Sixth Amendment guarantees a criminal defendant the right to a public trial. This right is designed to ensure fairness to the defendant, maintain public confidence in the criminal justice system, and ensure that judges and prosecutors fulfill their duties responsibly. Although the Constitution establishes a strong presumption in favor of transparency, the right to a public trial is not absolute.

A component of a public trial is public disclosure of the identities of members of the jury. In recent years, however, courts have increasingly used "anonymous juries" in high-profile cases. Anonymous juries are a relatively new phenomenon. The first anonymous jury to be empanelled in the United States was in the 1977 trial of a drug kingpin, Leroy Barnes.[21] Since 1977 courts have increasingly used varying levels of anonymity in limited instances.

Anonymous juries are most commonly used in criminal prosecutions involving organized crime figures, gangs, or drug kingpins. They are employed primarily to protect jurors from being threatened during the trial or harmed following the delivery of a verdict. The use of anonymous juries comes into conflict with a defendant's right to a pub-

---

21. *United States v. Barnes*, 604 F.2d 121 (2d Cir. 1979), *cert. denied*, 446 U.S. 907 (1980)

lic trial. In the following case, the Court of Appeals for the Eleventh Circuit explains how trial courts should determine if the use of an anonymous jury is appropriate.

United States v. Ross

33 F.3d 1507 (11th Cir. 1994)

Alan Ross was indicted, along with fourteen other individuals, by a federal grand jury on conspiracy charges relating to marijuana and cocaine trafficking, and several murders related to the drug trade. Prior to trial, the government requested that the trial court empanel an anonymous jury. The court granted the motion, and ordered that the jurors' names, addresses, places of employment, and spouses' names not be disclosed during jury selection or at any time thereafter. Following a month of testimony, Ross was convicted on all counts and sentenced to three life terms in prison and a ten million dollar fine. Ross appealed his conviction to the Court of Appeals for the 11th Circuit, arguing, among other things, that the use of an anonymous jury violated his rights under the Fifth and Sixth Amendments.

In most cases, the parties know the names, addresses, and occupations of potential jurors, as well as those of any spouses. This information is used by attorneys to formulate questions for prospective jurors during *voir dire* (jury selection) which will help the search of potential biases, prejudices, or any other considerations.

The court noted that use of an anonymous jury is a drastic measure. An anonymous jury may raise the specter that the defendant is a dangerous person from whom the jurors must be protected, an impression which could have a negative effect on a defendant's constitutional right to a presumption of innocence. Accordingly, anonymous juries should be undertaken only under limited circumstances. Specifically, the court held that an anonymous jury should be used only when the trial court concludes that there is strong reason to believe the jury needs protection, and if the judge takes reasonable precautions to protect the defendant's rights and minimize any prejudicial effects.

In determining whether or not to empanel an anonymous jury, courts should look to the totality of the circumstances. Items to be considered include the defendant's involvement in organized crime, the defendant's participation in a group with the capacity to harm jurors, the defendant's past attempts to interfere with the judicial process, the potential punishment facing the defendant, and extensive publicity.

When an anonymous jury is used, a defendant's right to an unbiased jury is sufficiently guaranteed by the court's conduct of a voir dire that can uncover any bias toward issues in the case or to the defendant himself. Additionally, when the trial court gives the jurors a plausible and nonprejudicial reason for hiding their identities, any danger that the jury might infer that the need for anonymity was attributable to the defendant's character is minimized.

In the case before it, the court held that the trial court did not abuse its discretion in ordering an anonymous jury. The court noted that Ross was the leader of a large-scale group that was actively involved in organized crime, that had the means to harm jurors, and that had in fact committed prior acts of violence. Additionally, Ross had previously attempted to interfere with the judicial process by ordering the death of a potential prosecution witness and three relatives of other witnesses for the prosecution. Lastly, Ross was facing a life sentence if convicted at trial.

The court also noted that the trial judge took reasonable steps to minimize any prejudicial effects on the defendant and to ensure that his fundamental rights were protected. The judge told the jury that it wanted to insulate them from improper communication from either side and that its decision was no reflection on the defense.

Based on the circumstances present in the case, and the actions of the trial judge, using an anonymous jury did not violate Ross' rights under the 5th and 6th Amendments.

Was anyone harmed by the use of the anonymous jury? Do you think a defendant would ever be harmed due to having an anonymous jury hear his or her case?

Jury Nullification and the Sanctity of Jury Deliberations

It has often been stated that the jury in a criminal trial serves as the conscience of the community. Rather than the government having the final say regarding if a person has violated a criminal law, it is the jury, made up of average citizens, that has the responsibility of finding a defendant guilty of a crime. As stated by Justice White in *Duncan v. Louisiana*, "If the defendant preferred the common-sense judgment of a jury to the more tutored but perhaps less sympathetic reaction of the single judge, he was to have it."[22] The use of lay people, who may have sympathy and common sense as they enter into their deliberations and return a verdict, is a foundation of the jury system. It has also caused problems for the courts in the form of "jury nullification."

Jury nullification occurs when a jury, based on its sense of justice and fairness, refuses to abide by law and convict in a particular case even though the defendant is unquestionably guilty under the law. It occurs when a jury refuses "to apply a law in situations where strict application of the law would lead to an unjust or inequitable result."[23] What makes jury nullification so troubling for courts is the fact that the exercise of this authority is unreviewable due to the constitutional prohibition against "double jeopardy" — the retrying of an acquitted defendant for the same offense.

While jury nullification is often viewed negatively, there are times when the exercise of the nullification power by a jury is desirable. Examples include juries refusing to convict in cases involving northerners violating fugitive slave laws by harboring runaway slaves in the 1800s, Vietnam War protesters, and battered women who kill their batterer in a situation not falling under the doctrine of self-defense. The use of nullification by a jury is rare, but it does occur.

In spite of its occasional benevolent and appropriate use, jury nullification is viewed harshly by American courts. A defendant is not entitled to inform a jury about jury

---

22. *Duncan v. Louisiana*, 391 U.S. 145, 156 (1968).
23. Alan Scheflin & Jon Van Dyke, "Jury Nullification: The Contours of a Controversy", 43 *Law & Contemporary Problems* 51, 54 (1980).

nullification power, nor will judges instruct juries about their nullification power. The following case deals with an issue that has faced courts a number of times in recent years. What should a judge do if he or she learns that a juror may be partaking in jury nullification during deliberations?

United States v. Thomas

116 F.3d 606 (2nd Cir. 1997)

Grady Thomas and several other individuals, all African Americans, were indicted and tried for numerous narcotics charges. During their trial one juror (the only African American on the jury) posed repeated problems for the court. Several jurors complained that Juror No. 5 engaged in distracting conduct during closing arguments, including squeaking his shoe against the floor, rustling cough drop wrappers in his pocket, and slapping his knee in agreement while verbally voicing his assent during defense arguments. After meeting with counsel to discuss possible courses of action, the court decided to interview the jurors to ascertain the extent of the distractions. Only one juror felt that there would be problems deliberating with Juror No. 5. Based on these interviews and after strenuous argument by defense counsel, the court decided to let Juror No. 5 remain on the jury.

Problems with Juror No. 5 escalated during deliberations. Several other jurors reported to the judge that Juror No. 5 "hollered" at other jurors, refused to participate in deliberations, and even pretended to vomit while other jurors were eating lunch. After receiving these reports, the trial judge conducted a second round of interviews with the jurors. During these interviews, several jurors stated that Juror No. 5 refused to follow the law or to consider the evidence presented by the government and that he was predisposed toward acquittal and refused to discuss the evidence.

Not all of the jurors shared this opinion about Juror No. 5's behavior during deliberations. Several jurors told the court that Juror No. 5 did consider the evidence and the law and was simply not convinced as to the defendants' guilt. Several recalled his stating that the prosecution's evidence was insufficient and unreliable. For his part, Juror No. 5 told the court "that he needed 'substantive evidence' establishing guilt 'beyond a reasonable doubt' in order to convict."

The prosecution moved for the court to dismiss Juror No. 5 from the jury pursuant to Rule 23(b) of the Federal Rules of Criminal Procedure. Rule 23(b) provides that after the commencement of deliberations, a juror may be removed from the jury if there is "just cause." Rule 23(b) also states that "if the court finds it necessary to excuse a juror for 'just cause' after the jury has retired to consider its verdict, in the discretion of the court a valid verdict may be returned by the remaining 11 jurors."

After considering interviews with the jurors and meeting with counsel, the trial judge, over the objections of defense counsel, dismissed Juror No. 5 from the jury pursuant to Rule 23(b). While the court considered the alleged improper conduct (the "hollering" and feigned vomiting), the primary reason, or "just cause," behind the dismissal was the court's belief that Juror No. 5 was ignoring the evidence and the law provided in the court's jury instructions in favor of his own, preconceived ideas about the case. In other words, the judge believed Juror No. 5 was partaking in jury nullification.

Pursuant to Rule 23(b) the remaining eleven jurors continued their deliberations. Shortly thereafter, they convicted the defendants on nearly all of the charges presented. Six of the defendants appealed to the Second Circuit Court of Appeals on the ground that Juror No. 5 was improperly dismissed from the jury.

In considering the appropriateness of dismissing Juror No. 5, the court of appeals spent a good deal of time discussing the history of jury nullification and its place in the justice system. Jury nullification takes place when a juror, for whatever reason, refuses to follow the law when deliberating and reaching his or her individual verdict. The court noted that "the very institution of trial by jury in a criminal case, as Judge Learned Hand observed, 'introduces a slack into the enforcement of law, tempering its rigor by the mollifying influence of current ethical conventions.'"[24] In the end the court concluded that while jury nullification is a *de facto* power possessed by jurors, it is a violation of a juror's sworn duty to apply the law as interpreted by the court. Moreover, the court stated that a trial court has a duty to remove a juror partaking in jury nullification from the jury.

Having reached this conclusion, the court was faced with the more difficult question of what standard of proof is required before a nullifying juror can be dismissed from a deliberating jury. In deciding this question, the court had to determine how to reconcile a trial court's duty to dismiss a nullifying juror and the importance of protecting the secrecy and sanctity of jury deliberations. On the one hand, if the court set a low evidentiary threshold for removing a juror where the trial judge believed the juror was not following the law, jurors who "hold out" from the majority could be removed by the judge based solely on other jurors' statements. On the other hand, if the court set a high standard of proof, proving that a juror was nullifying would be very difficult without intruding on the jury's deliberations.

In examining the evidence of nullification in front of the trial judge, the court was extremely troubled by the trial court's investigation into Juror No. 5's behavior. The court began its analysis by stating that in general "no one—including the judge presiding at a trial—has a 'right to know' how a jury, or any individual juror, has deliberated or how a decision was reached by a jury or juror."[25] The court explained that once a jury begins deliberations, "the presiding judge's duty to dismiss jurors for misconduct comes into conflict with a duty that is equally, if not more, important—safeguarding the secrecy of jury deliberations."[26] In cases where the alleged misbehavior is a purposeful disregard of the law, this conflict is particularly prominent since it is a difficult allegation to prove. In such a case it is possible that a juror, probably one who disagrees with a majority of the jury, may not be nullifying, but rather is making a good faith effort to apply the law to facts as required. Due to the importance of protecting the secrecy of jury deliberations, the court concluded that:

> Where the duty and authority to prevent defiant disregard of the law or evidence comes into conflict with the principle of secret jury deliberations, we are compelled to err in the favor of the lesser of two evils—protecting the se-

24. *Thomas* at 615, citing *U.S. ex rel. McCann v. Adams*, 126 F.2d 774, 776 (2nd Cir. 1942).
25. *Thomas* at 618.
26. *Id.*

crecy of jury deliberations at the expense of possibly allowing irresponsible juror activity.[27]

With this in mind, the court set a very high standard for determining whether a juror should be dismissed under *Rule 23(b)* for refusing to follow the law: "'If the record evidence discloses any possibility that' a complaint about a juror's conduct 'stems from the sufficiency of the government's evidence, the court must deny the request.'"[28]

Analyzing the facts before it under this standard, the court found that there was insufficient proof that Juror No. 5 was nullifying. When asked if he was following the law, Juror No. 5 said he was and was basing his decision on the evidence presented and his opinion of the credibility of the state's witnesses. While other jurors may have disagreed with this statement, their opinions were insufficient to disprove his statement. Accordingly, the court vacated the convictions and remanded the cases for a new trial.

Note the tension between protecting the privacy and secrecy of jury deliberations and the goal of removing a juror partaking in jury nullification. Do you agree with the standards announced by the court? Do they go too far or not far enough?

Breaking Deadlocked Juries: The Use of Dynamite Charges

In all federal trials, and in a vast majority of states, jury verdicts must be unanimous. If a jury is unable to reach unanimity, the court is faced with a **hung jury**, and a mistrial is declared. While a hung jury is generally viewed as a victory for the defense, it is viewed quite negatively by prosecutors and judges. Following a hung jury the prosecution has the option of retrying the defendant or dropping the case. As is readily evident, hung juries create great financial expenses and time costs to the government and the court system. These expenses create large incentives to have a jury reach unanimity.

In an effort to assist the jury in reaching a unanimous verdict, courts will often give an apparently deadlocked jury a supplemental jury instruction, commonly referred to as a **dynamite charge** (also known as an **Allen charge**), in an attempt to free the jury from its blocked progress. The following case examines the appropriate use of dynamite or *Allen* charges in criminal trials, and also illustrates one way such a charge might be worded to a jury.

United States v. Arney

248 F.3d 984 (10th Cir. 2001)

On June 15, 1999, David Arney was indicted on four counts of bank fraud. At Arney's first trial the jury in that case was unable to agree on a verdict, forcing the court to de-

27. *Id.* at 623.

28. *Id.* at 622, quoting *United States v. Brown*, 823 F.2d 591, 596 (D.C.Cir. 1987).

clare a mistrial. Mr. Arney's retrial took place several months later. Following less than two days of testimony the jury began deliberations. Shortly before 5:00 p.m., having deliberated for approximately four hours, the jury sent a note to the judge that said, "Your Honor, we have been unable to reach a unanimous decision. It does not appear that this will change. What should we do now?" In response to this question the district court then gave the following *Allen* charge to the jury:

> This is an important case. The trial has been extensive. Your failure to agree upon a verdict will necessitate another trial and require the parties once again to undergo the investment of time and effort and the stress of trial. The court is of the opinion that the case cannot be again tried better or more exhaustively than it has been on either side. It is therefore very desirable that you should agree upon a verdict.
>
> The court does not desire that any juror should surrender his or her conscientious convictions. Each juror should perform his or her duty conscientiously and honestly according to the law and evidence. The verdict to which a juror agrees must, of course, be his or her own verdict, the result of his or her own convictions and not a mere acquiescence in the conclusions of his or her fellow jurors. However, in order to bring 12 minds to a unanimous result you must examine the questions submitted to you with candor and with a proper regard and deference to the opinion of each other. You should consider that the case must at some time be decided, that you are selected in the same manner and from the same source from which any future jury must be, and there is no reason to suppose that the case will ever be submitted to 12 men and women more intelligent, more impartial or more competent to decide it; or that more or clearer evidence will be produced on one side or the other. You may conduct your deliberations as you choose, but I suggest you now retire and carefully consider again the evidence in this case.

The judge then sent the jury back to continue deliberating. Approximately one hour later, the jury returned its verdict finding Arney guilty on all charges. Arney appealed to the Court of Appeals for the 10th Circuit claiming that the Allen charge given to the jury by the court violated his rights under the 5th and 6th Amendments.

The court explained that an "*Allen* charge,"often referred to as a "dynamite charge," is frequently given to a jury that is having difficulty reaching a unanimous verdict. Its name is derived from the supplemental jury instruction approved by the Supreme Court in *Allen v. United States.* [29] An *Allen* charge, whose specific language may vary from case to case, encourages each juror to review and reconsider the evidence in the light of the views expressed by other jurors. Jurors are encouraged to strive to conscientiously search for truth and not act with dogged determination to have one's way in the outcome of the case.

A concern often raised when an *Allen* charge is given is that it may have a coercive effect on jurors, particularly holdout jurors who are blocking efforts to reach a unanimous verdict. The court stated that it would review an *Allen* charge such as the one given

29. 164 U.S. 492 (1896)

in this case for coerciveness "in its context and under all the circumstances" as required by the Supreme Court.[30] Factors considered by the court in this analysis included the language of the instruction, the timing of the instruction, and the length of the jury's subsequent deliberations.

In considering whether the specific language in the *Allen* charge was improper, the court noted that a trial judge has the right and a duty to assist the jury in reaching a fair and impartial verdict so long as he or she does not coerce the jury into reaching a verdict. Some language in the *Allen* charge, such as telling the jury that a verdict was "very desirable" and stating that the case could not be tried better by either side caused the court some concern. This concern was alleviated, however, by the trial court's telling the jurors that they should not surrender their "conscientious convictions" and that they should consider their own opinions with a proper regard and deference to the opinion of other jurors. The court also noted that the instruction was directed at all of the jurors and not just those in the minority. This balanced instruction decreases the likelihood of coercion.

The court also considered Arney's argument that the timing of the *Allen* charge, which was given between 5:00 and 5:30 in the evening, made it inherently coercive. Arney argued that giving the instruction to a deadlocked jury at the end of the day, would coerce jurors into reaching a verdict so as to prevent them from returning for another day of deliberations. The court found that there was no merit to these arguments and summarily dismissed them.

Lastly, the court considered the length of deliberations after the giving of the *Allen* charge. The court noted that a jury reaching a verdict shortly after receiving an *Allen* charge may indicate coercion. In this case the jury returned with a verdict approximately one hour after receiving the *Allen* charge. The court found that this length of time was not unusually brief and was not indicative of any feelings of coercion on the part of any jurors.

The court concluded that the *Allen* charge was appropriately given and affirmed Mr. Arney's conviction.

Does it seem fair for a court to give an *Allen* charge to a jury? Would eliminating the need for unanimous verdict remove the need to give a dynamite charge? Why not?

Conclusion

Juries are a critical aspect of the criminal justice system. Although a small percentage of criminal prosecutions involve jury trials, the fact that the right exists is an important statement about the operation of a democracy and the power of its citizens. Courts often have the task of balancing the rights of a defendant related to jury trials and the criminal justice system's desire for efficiency and finality. As we saw in this chapter, this conflict has arisen in varied areas. This pattern in likely to continue for generations to come.

30. *Lowenfield v. Phelps*, 484 U.S. 231, 237 (1988).

Chapter Eleven

Law of Sentencing; Cruel and Unusual Punishments

It is exceedingly likely that the vast majority of people accused of crimes are in fact guilty of wrongdoing. Sadly for most of them, the state can prove that they are guilty. For this large group of factually guilty people, the ultimate sentence that they will receive is probably a much more significant legal event than their inevitable conviction by way of jury trial or guilty plea. Hence, for the attorneys representing the vast majority of those charged with crimes, sentencing law is (or at least should be) a very fascinating subject indeed.

The sentencing decision can be a crucial one. Imagine yourself being sent off to prison for a relatively minor felony (e.g., burglary of a tool shed). You quickly compare notes with your new cell mate and learn that he is doing half the time that you are even though he committed a much more serious crime (e.g., forcible rape). You both have similar prior criminal records and were both convicted by way of a jury trial. How could this grossly unfair sentencing disparity have come about? Welcome to the "fascinating" subject of sentencing law.

Let us begin our discussion of sentencing law by first considering the classical goals of punishment. What is it that sentencing judges are trying to accomplish through the intentional infliction of pain on their fellow human beings?

Four Classical Goals of Punishment

Traditionally, there are **four classical goals of criminal sentencing.** These are rehabilitation, deterrence, incapacitation, and retribution.[1]

Rehabilitation assumes a medical model of crime. Crime is seen as a social illness which can be treated and cured. Under this theory, the goal is to do what is necessary to change errant attitudes, to make "true believers" out of former rebels.

---

1. There are many discussions regarding the goals of criminal sentencing. For one such discussion, see LaFave, Wayne R. and Austin W. Scott, Jr. (1986). "Purposes of the Criminal Law—Theories of Punishment." In (same authors) *Criminal Law (2d ed.)*, pp. 22–29.

Deterrence has as its goal the convincing of people that crime is not in their own best interests. It assumes that people are rational and can intelligently do a costs/benefits analysis. Deterrence works best when the penalty is swift, severe and certain. But there can still be a deterrent effect for many people even when the ideal conditions of swiftness, severity and certainty are not all guaranteed. Have you ever found yourself reluctantly clicking on your seat belt even though the penalty for not doing so is rather small and the risk of being caught rather low?

Deterrence has two sub-sets. **Specific deterrence** seeks to convince the actual, individual offender to refrain from repeating the misconduct in the future (e.g., a judge might give a shoplifter ten days in jail so that she is scared out of ever shoplifting again). **General deterrence** seeks to convince the general public to avoid committing a crime (e.g., the friends and acquaintances of the shoplifter hear what happened to her and hopefully will think twice before shoplifting themselves).

Incapacitation has as its goal the removal of an offender from society so that the offender cannot do any more harm, at least as long as the term of imprisonment lasts. Incapacitation does not seek to rehabilitate or to deter, it simply seeks to isolate the offender from society and thus provide relief. This relief can be temporary or (in the case of life imprisonment, execution or banishment) permanent.

Retribution is (to be blunt about it) revenge. A more politically correct term for this is **just deserts.** Retribution has as its goal the settling of a score: "an eye for an eye, a tooth for a tooth." Retribution assumes that criminals are not mere captives of bad biology or slaves to a corrupting environment but rather have the free will to choose right from wrong (and they have chosen wrong).

Some people believe that retribution is a primitive, unenlightened and unethical basis for punishing someone. However, American courts refuse to see it that way. They acknowledge that retribution can be a legitimate consideration in creating a proper sentence. But, if just deserts is the basis for a sentence, must the sentence at least be proportionate to the crime? The case that follows addresses this issue.

Harmelin v. Michigan

501 U.S. 957 (1991)

Harmelin was convicted of possessing about a pound and a half (672 grams) of cocaine. Michigan law required that anyone convicted of possessing more than 650 grams of a Schedule 2 controlled substance (like cocaine) must be sentenced to life in prison without the possibility of parole. Harmelin was sentenced to life in prison and appealed the constitutionality of this long and hard drug sentence. He argued that his sentence was so disproportionate to the harm that he had done that it violated his Eighth Amendment right not to be subjected to cruel and unusual punishment.

The U.S. Supreme Court eventually considered Harmelin's argument. It confessed that prior decisions it had rendered regarding the relationship between allegedly disproportionate sentences and cruel and unusual punishment were all over the map.

For example, it noted that in the case of *Rommel v. Estelle*, 445 U.S. 263 (1980), it had ruled that the imposition of a life sentence on a repeat offender under a recidivist statute for obtaining $120.75 by false pretenses did not constitute cruel and unusual punishment. This was so because the punishment was not clearly disproportionate to the crime. It said that the length of a prison sentence for any crime "is purely a matter of legislative prerogative." However, a footnote in that same decision did say that "this is not to say that a proportionality principle would not come into play in the extreme example ... if a legislature made overtime parking a felony punishable by life imprisonment."

Then, just three years later, the U.S. Supreme Court appeared to flip-flop when it ruled in *Solem v. Helm*, 463 U.S. 277 (1983), that a sentence of life imprisonment for three burglaries imposed under a recidivist statute was disproportionate and thus violated the prohibition against cruel and unusual punishment.

Now, the court hopes in the present case involving Harmelin's possession of 672 grams of cocaine to clear this confusing mess up. Writing for the majority, Justice Scalia held that Harmelin's life sentence for the possession of the 672 grams of cocaine did not constitute cruel and unusual punishment. He wrote that the *Solem* case striking down life imprisonment for three burglaries "was simply wrong." He said that "the Eighth Amendment contains no proportionality guarantee" at all. Relying on old English traditions, he reasoned that the American Eighth Amendment was only meant to forbid cruel modes of punishment (e.g. tortuous punishments) and does not speak at all to length of prison sentences. He wrote that, "While there are relatively clear historical guidelines and accepted practices that enable judges to determine which modes of punishment are 'cruel and unusual,' proportionality does not lend itself to such analysis." In true Scalia form, he questioned what right the Supreme Court could have in judging the length of a prison sentence to be disproportionate when elected representatives of the people of Michigan judged it to be fair and proportionate. As he put it, "Who are we to say no? The Members of the Michigan Legislature, and not we, know the situation on the streets of Detroit."

So, it would appear that *Harmelin v. Michigan* has cleared everything up: that the Eighth Amendment only forbids cruel modes of punishment and does not protect at all against overly long periods of incarceration. However, the matter is unbelievably once again in a state of confusion! In *Lockyer v. Andrade*, 538 U.S. 63 (2003), the U.S. Supreme Court noted that its line of close-shave, 5/4 decisions involving constantly shifting alignments of justices continues to constitute a "thicket of Eighth Amendment jurisprudence." But the High Court said that, despite all of the apparent contradictions, "One governing legal principle emerges ... A gross disproportionality principle is applicable in a sentence for terms of years." While refusing to clarify just what that **gross disproportionality principle** exactly entails, the Court in *Lockyer* simply stated — in dashing the hopes on highly technical grounds of a Three Strikes defendant sentenced to life for stealing some blank videos from K-Mart — that, "The gross disproportionality principle reserves a constitutional violation for only the extraordinary case."

It did make it clear that life in prison for an offender with a serious criminal record stealing a few blank videos did not constitute an "extraordinary case." But in resolving the matter on those technical grounds it did not feel it necessary to explain what an extraordinary case would be. How generous or stingy do you think you would be in finding an extraordinary case?

Sentencing Guidelines

Traditionally, a judge about to sentence a defendant convicted of a crime had tremendous discretion. The judge basically could give the defendant anywhere from probation to the maximum sentence allowed by statute for the category of crime involved. For example, a burglar before a certain judge might get probation for his burglary while a burglar who committed a very similar crime and who had a similar prior record might get three years in prison before a different judge. This lack of consistency caused many in the legal community to call for reforms. These critics thought that judges had too much power. What sentence a defendant received often depended more on which judge he or she landed before at sentencing than on the crime that was committed.

To remedy this situation many states and the federal government came up with "sentencing guidelines" for judges to use in their courts. **Sentencing guidelines** are sentencing grids issued by a legislature which indicate to a sentencing judge the penalty that the state legislature (or Congress in the case of federal courts) deems appropriate for a particular crime in light of a defendant's particular criminal history.

How Guidelines Work

To understand how sentencing guidelines typically work, picture a graph produced by X and Y axes just like you were exposed to in a high school geometry lesson. The X-axis (the horizontal one) represents the seriousness of the current offense on a scale of (say) one to ten—with shoplifting being a one, burglary of a non-residence a five, armed robbery an eight, and murder a ten. One can look up the score for any crime by looking at a detailed list of "crime scores" also published by the legislature.

The Y-axis (the vertical one) on this graph represents the prior record score of the defendant, often on a scale of one to six or so. Each prior felony conviction might generate (depending upon the state) one point towards the overall prior record score, while every two misdemeanors together might generate one point (for a maximum score of up to six points).

Once having determined both numbers, the scorer (e.g., the sentencing judge) plots the defendant's position on the graph included in the sentencing guidelines materials provided by the legislature (e.g., go five positions to the right on the horizontal X-axis and up two points vertically on the Y-axis). This effort will land the defendant in a cell (a box on the graph) with numbers in the cell. These numbers (e.g. 13 to 18 months) represents the presumptive range of months in jail or prison which the legislature deems appropriate for this perpetrator (in this case, the legislature is saying it believes a sentencing judge should give the perpetrator somewhere between 13 and 18 months of actual incarceration time, the precise number of months to be "left" to the judge in what little remains of his or her discretion). In other words, the judge still has some discretion at sentencing, but if he or she follows the legislature's wishes, not very much. Obviously, the farther a defendant's score proceeds horizontally and vertically from the "0,0" point of origin, the longer one's incarceration will be.

Mandatory vs. Non-mandatory Guidelines

In some jurisdictions, legislatures over the years have developed **mandatory sentencing guidelines**, meaning that judges absolutely must follow them. In these states, almost all sentencing discretion is transferred away from judges to the state legislature. This is generally very displeasing to judges who tend to feel like "rubber-stamp bureaucrats" or "judicial accountants."[2] They want to tailor sentences to the individual but instead must do the legislature's lock-step bidding (some judges have been known to weep on the stand as they pronounce "draconian sentences" which they feel grossly exceed the seriousness of the crime).

In some other jurisdictions, legislatures have developed **non-mandatory sentencing guidelines**, which judges must consider before passing sentence but which they are then free to deviate from as much as they feel is appropriate.

In still other jurisdictions, state legislatures have not developed any type of sentencing guidelines whatsoever, leaving it completely up to judges to use their **traditional sentencing powers** to give any sentence they feel is justified as long as the statutory maximum sentence allowed for a particular offense is not exceeded.

Constitutionality of Guidelines

The U.S. Congress in the 1980s adopted a mandatory sentencing guideline approach for the federal criminal courts. But, because of recent U.S. Supreme Court decisions, these federal sentencing guidelines are now (by Supreme Court order) only "advisory." Federal judges must consider them before crafting a sentence but are not bound by them. The companion cases that follow explain why.

Blakely v. Washington

542 U.S. 296 (2004)

and

United States v. Booker

543 U.S. 220 (2005)

Blakely and *Booker* are something of companion cases that were decided on the heels of one another. In *Blakely v. Washington,* Ralph Blakely was charged with the kidnapping of his estranged wife. Blakely, who had psychological problems and was "a difficult man to live with," abducted his wife at gunpoint from her home, placed duct tape over her mouth, and forced her into a wooden box in the bed of his pickup truck. While thus held captive, Blakely pleaded with her to drop the divorce suit against him. The

2. See, Berman, Douglas A. (1999). "A Common Law for this Age of Federal Sentencing: The Opportunity and Need for Judicial Lawmaking." 11 Stanford Law & Policy Review 93, at 101.

wife escaped when the couple's son learned what was going on and went to a friend for help, which friend then called the police.

Blakely was charged with first-degree kidnaping but pursuant to a charge bargain entered a plea of guilty to second-degree kidnaping involving domestic violence. Washington state sentencing guidelines required the sentencing judge to impose a sentence somewhere in the range of 49 to 53 months given this offense and Blakely's prior record. However, the guidelines allowed the sentencing judge to depart from this narrow "standard range" and impose a much greater sentence if the judge finds "substantial and compelling reasons justifying an exceptional sentence." One such "substantial and compelling" reason in a domestic violence case could, by statute, include a finding of "deliberate cruelty." Though Blakely himself during his guilty plea admitted only facts that would place him in the standard range of 49 to 53 months, the judge departed from this range and sentenced him to 90 months after listening to the victim's account of how the kidnaping took place. Blakely objected to the judge having given him more than three years over what he had expected, but the judge adhered to his decision. Blakely appealed and the case wound its way to the U.S. Supreme Court.

The issue before the U.S. Supreme Court was whether a finding by a sentencing judge of "deliberate cruelty" constituted a conviction of sorts that should have been decided by a jury. The U.S. Supreme Court agreed with Blakely that it did. It ruled that such a critical finding of fact by a judge rather than a jury violated Blakely's Sixth Amendment right to a trial by jury. It said that in order to find "deliberate cruelty," a court would either have to first have a set of corresponding facts admitted to by the defendant during his guilty plea or else a finding made by a jury of his peers.

Even though the *Blakely* case involved Washington state sentencing guidelines, many in the legal community immediately began to wonder whether the federal sentencing guidelines (which allowed federal judges to find critical "sentencing facts" greatly affecting the length of sentences) were still constitutional. It did not take long for them to find out. In the case of *United States v. Booker*, the U.S. Supreme Court had to directly grapple with this concern.

Freddie Booker was found guilty by a jury of having possessed 92.5 grams of cocaine. Federal mandatory sentencing guidelines, given this crime and Booker's prior criminal history, called for a sentence of 262 months in prison. However, the sentencing judge found by a preponderance of evidence (all that was required to establish a "sentencing fact") that Booker really had possessed an additional 566 grams of cocaine. This much larger amount of cocaine possession called for a guideline sentence of not 262 months but rather 360 months in prison, which the judge imposed. Booker appealed this sentence all the way up to the U.S. Supreme Court.

The U.S. Supreme Court had to now decide whether the federal sentencing guidelines which provided for an enhanced sentence based on judicially determined facts such as the amount of cocaine that Booker really possessed violated the Sixth Amendment right to trial by jury. The Supreme Court found such a constitutional violation.

The prosecution had attempted to distinguish the Washington state sentencing guidelines from the federal sentencing guidelines by advancing various technical arguments. But the Supreme Court rejected all of them by stating that such arguments attempted to "elevate substance over form." It said that the federal guidelines, just like those of the state of Washington, calculate a normal sentencing score based on just two factors: current offense seriousness and prior record score. Both sets of guidelines also allow judges to depart from a standard sentencing range by permitting the sentencing judge to find certain critical facts only by a preponderance of the evidence. Because the federal sentencing guidelines are so similar to those of the state of Washington, the *Blakely* decision applies not just to Washington's guidelines but to the federal guidelines as well.

The Court said any sentencing facts as important as the amount of cocaine a defendant possessed must be decided upon by a jury using the reasonable doubt standard and not by a judge using a preponderance of evidence standard. The Court (adopting language it had used before in an unrelated case which it thought would apply well here as well) said that the "Federal Constitution requires that any fact (other than a prior conviction) which is necessary to support a sentence exceeding the maximum authorized by the facts established by a plea of guilty or a jury verdict must be admitted by a defendant or proved to a jury beyond a reasonable doubt."

Since the Supreme Court found that the federal sentencing guidelines' allowance of a judge to find "sentencing facts" without a jury's concurrence to be unconstitutional, it had to decide what to do with the federal sentencing guidelines. It ruled that it either had to abolish the Guidelines entirely or else make them merely advisory. It decided that Congress would rather the Court make them advisory than to eliminate them completely and so it ordered that henceforth the federal sentencing Guidelines would be non-mandatory guidelines rather than mandatory ones. This means that federal sentencing judges would still have to use the grid to compute the sentence score but after having then considered it could do as they thought best. They would have to contemplate Congress' desire but could follow their own best judgment.

So, unless and until Congress fixes the current federal Sentencing guidelines, they will remain only advisory. State guidelines (like those of Washington State) also cannot be currently enforced. Guidelines of other states may or may not be constitutional depending upon the degree they allow judges to decide critical "sentencing facts" that so enhance the sentence that they should more properly be decided by juries.

Cruel and Unusual Sentences

Thus far in this chapter we have considered the four classical goals of sentencing and who (judges or legislatures) should decide how long prison sentences should be. But, judges and legislatures have not always limited themselves to sentences involving incarceration in attempting to achieve rehabilitation, deterrence, incapacitation or retribution. Sometimes they have wished to be more creative. Hence historically we have witnessed floggings, disfigurements, dismemberments, castrations, drawn and quarterings, brandings, stocks and pillories, banishments, and even live burials.

A lot can be learned about a society by the way it sentences its criminals. As Winston Churchill once said, "The mood and temper of the public with regard to the treatment of crime and criminals is one of the most unfailing tests of the civilization of any country."[3]

In Singapore, minor mischief makers are sometimes beaten with a cane.[4] In Saudi Arabia, a thief's offending hand is cut off, and people who engage in premarital sex can receive a hundred lashes.[5] As recently as 1997, a Yemeni court sentenced two murderers to be publicly crucified.[6]

Fortunately for those of us who misbehave in the United States, overly enthusiastic sentencing judges are restrained by the Eighth Amendment, which of course prohibits "cruel and unusual punishments." But, what constitutes cruel and unusual modes of punishment must at times be determined by the appellate courts.

Torture

Torture is clearly out of bounds. The founders of our democracy wanted no part of it. Ironically, torture apparently includes corporal punishment of any kind, with the very notable exception of putting someone to death. But even those being put to death have Eighth Amendment rights, as the case that follows well illustrates.

Dawson v. State

554 S.E.2d 137 (Ga. 2001)

This appeal is actually two cases consolidated by the Supreme Court of Georgia into one, since both involve the same issue: whether or not death by electric chair violates the Georgia Constitution's prohibition against cruel and unusual punishment. Both cases involve defendants who murdered. Timothy Dawson was convicted of four murders and was sentenced to die by way of electrocution. Carzell Moore murdered and raped a woman and was also sentenced to die in the same way. Challenges were made in both cases regarding the propriety of the electric chair as a means of execution. One lower court ruled in the Dawson case that use of the electric chair violated the Georgia Constitution while another lower court ruled in the Moore case that its use was permissible. The Georgia Supreme Court agreed to decide the issue for both Dawson and Moore.

The Georgia Supreme Court held that death by electrocution did indeed violate the Georgia Constitution's prohibition against cruel and unusual punishment. It began its reasoning by pointing out that even though the U.S. Supreme Court has never found electric chairs to violate the U.S. Constitution, such lack of a ruling is of no real consequence to Georgians. This is so because the U.S. Constitution, though

3. Krantz, Sheldon and Lynn S. Branham. (1991). *The Law of Sentencing, Corrections and Prisoner's Rights*. St. Paul, MN: West Publishing Co., p.2.

4. Older readers may recall the celebrated news story of the 1990s in which an American teenager caught vandalizing cars in Singapore was sentenced there to be beaten with a cane.

5. Souryal, Sam S., Dennis W. Potts, and Abdullah I. Alobied. (1994). "The Penalty of Hand Amputation for Theft in Islamic Justice." *Journal of Criminal Justice*, 22(3):249–265.

6. "Yemeni Court Upholds Crucifixions." (1997). *Associated Press Wire Service, August 31.*

binding upon Georgians, sets a minimum standard of what is acceptable, not a maximum standard. The Georgia Constitution, as well as the U.S. Constitution, prohibits cruel and unusual punishment, and in interpreting the Georgia Constitution's version of this right, "the applicable standard is the standard of the people of Georgia, not the national standard."

So, what in a nutshell is the standard that the Georgia Supreme Court should use in deciding what is and is not cruel and unusual? Citing language often used in cruel and unusual punishment cases, the Georgia Court emphasized that, "Whether or not a particular punishment is cruel and unusual is not a static concept, but instead changes in recognition of the evolving standards of decency that mark the progress of a maturing society." It believed that there were several factors that suggested that death by electrocution violated the evolving standards of decency of a maturing Georgian society.

First, it noted that the Georgia legislature itself seemed to be haunted by the possibility that the electric chair would be found cruel by future Georgia courts. Why else would it pass a recent law that designated lethal injection as the mode for executions should Georgia courts ever rule that the electric chair violated either the U.S. or the Georgia Constitutions? Such fear of future action on the part of Georgia courts shows a certain consciousness of guilt on the part of the Georgian legislature that ought to be highlighted.

Next, the Georgia High Court took note of the gruesome way the electric chair works in ending human life. Experts had testified that electric chairs do not produce instantaneous death. Because the brain is shielded somewhat from the electricity by the thickness of the skull, the procedure often takes two minutes or longer to produce death. In the meantime, the alternating currents are believed to possibly cause "excruciating pain and a sense of extreme horror." During this process the brain apparently becomes "cooked" as it reaches temperatures between 135 and 145 degrees.

Even if one is not convinced that excruciating pain is a necessary by-product of electrocution (as the prosecution attempted to suggest with its own questionable experts), it is undeniable that mutilation occurs to the body. This mutilation to the corpse would alone constitute cruel and unusual punishment. Charring and burning to the body always occur even when protocols are correctly followed, and the condemned have a right to avoid such indignity to their remains.

The Georgia Supreme Court recognized that modern technology has provided, through lethal injection, a "less painful, less barbarous means for taking the life of condemned prisoners." To the extent possible, executions should involve nothing more than the extinguishment of life. They should not involve anything extra. For this reason, the use of the electric chair in Georgia must henceforth be discontinued.

There was a dissenter on the court to the above ruling. In protesting the above decision, Justice Thompson argued that it was not up to the courts to decide what are evolving standards of decency but up to the people of Georgia themselves, through their elected representatives. If the legislature does not believe the electric chair is barbaric, who is the court to decided otherwise? Justice Thompson wrote that, "In a democratic society legislatures, not courts, are constituted to respond to the will and the moral values of the people." Justice Thompson noted that we no longer have the guillotine. This is not because of any court decisions but rather because the voice of the people against it has been heard by the legislature. Until the people of Georgia speak out against the electric chair, it should not be deemed by courts to be too cruel for decent society.

Would you favor use of the electric chair in your state? What about the gas chamber? The firing squad? Is lethal injection humane or does it too have serious problems?

Shaming

You may think that court-sponsored shaming is a thing of the past, an artifact of Colonial America. Not so. Modern shaming takes place all the time. For example, sex offender registries complete with photos and addresses are available in many states on government-sponsored web sites for all to see. On many such sites, a web page visitor need only type in a zip code to see all of his or her neighbors convicted of various sex crimes pop up. The official intent may be societal protection (a noble goal), but one cannot deny that shaming — whether by intent or as collateral damage — undeniably occurs. Other types of "scarlet letter justice" also frequently take place around the country thanks to inventive judges. The case that follows illustrates just one example.

United States v. Gementera

379 F.3d 596 (9th Cir. 2004)

Shawn Gementera and his accomplice were caught by a police officer in the act of stealing mail from mail boxes along a street in San Francisco. Gementera pled guilty in federal court to mail theft in exchange for the dismissal of a second count of receiving a stolen U.S. Treasury check. It was up to the federal district court judge to craft the appropriate sentence for the mail theft charge.

The judge sentenced Gementera to two months of incarceration followed by three years of supervised release (probation). As part of the conditions of probation, Gementera was ordered by the court to stand outside a post office (to be selected by the probation officer) for eight hours while wearing a two-sided sandwich board type sign that would read, "I stole mail; this is my punishment." Gementera appealed this condition of his probation to the 9th Circuit Court of Appeals

Gementera advanced several arguments in support of his appeal, including the assertion that such a condition violated the Eighth Amendment prohibition against cruel and unusual punishments. In rejecting this (as well as Gementera's other arguments), the court allowed the unusual probation condition to stand.

The court began its cruel and unusual punishment analysis by noting that far more severe examples of shaming commonly occurred in the Colonial era than what was to happen to Gementera. What Gementera was expected to undergo was much less dramatic than what the drafters of the Eighth Amendment apparently were willing to tolerate.

Of course, the court had to acknowledge that what might not constitute cruel and unusual punishment in the 18th Century might indeed constitute it today. Hence, it agreed with the oft-cited rule that the Eighth Amendment must draw its meaning from the "**evolving standards of decency** that mark the progress of a maturing society." So, the real question here was whether forcing someone to stand outside a post office for eight hours with a sign labeling him as a mail thief would violate modern norms of decency.

The court could find no evidence that such a probation requirement would violate modern norms of decency. It said that, with the exception of a few instances in which defendants (unlike Gementera) were to be shamed in high crime areas subjecting them to the danger of physical harm, it could find "no case holding that contemporary shaming sanctions violate our Constitution's prohibition against cruel and unusual punishment." This was so despite many examples of shaming sanctions imposed around the country. For example, it noted that various state courts have rejected Eighth Amendment attacks on such things as: forcing a DUI defendant to place a bumper sticker on his car acknowledging his transgression; requiring someone convicted of DUI to acknowledge such in an newspaper advertisement; mandating a purse thief who silently approached his victim in tennis shoes to henceforth wear tap shoes in public; and the common requirement of probationers wearing embarrassing uniforms while collecting roadside litter as part of court-ordered community service. In the view of many of the courts that have considered the matter, various shaming experiences are constitutional because of one unavoidable reality: they are much less painful and burdensome than the inevitable alternative of imprisonment.

The court concluded its analysis by providing a nice summary. "In the absence of evidence to the contrary, and particularly in comparison with the reality of the modern prison, we simply have no reason to conclude that the sanction before us exceeds the bounds of civilized standards or the evolving standards of decency that mark the progress of a maturing society."

Judge Hawkins, also a member of the 9th Circuit, dissented. He argued that requiring Gementera to wear a sign would serve none of the three official, statutory goals of federal sentencing: deterrence, rehabilitation, or societal protection. Rather, its sole purpose would be to humiliate and dehumanize Gementera. Humiliation in and of itself is not a proper goal of sentencing. As this dissenter put it, "The purpose behind the sandwich board condition was not to rehabilitate Gementera, but rather to turn him into a modern day Hester Prin" (referring of course to the protagonist in the classic novel, *The Scarlet Letter*, who was forced for life to wear the letter "A" for her adultery). Judge Hawkins concluded his dissent by saying that if it were up to him, the circuit court would "remand for sentencing, instructing the district court that public humiliation or shaming has no proper role in our system of justice."

What do you think of shaming as a tool of justice? Is it proper? Should we do much more of it than we currently do? What ideas, if any, do you have for more effectively shaming individuals into complying with our criminal laws?

Banishment

As we have seen, shaming is a Colonial-era punishment that still has life. Another Colonial-era punishment that some believe is making a come back is **banishment** —

the expelling of someone from a community. Does banishment exist as a form of punishment in modern day America? Read the following case and see what you think.

Doe v. Miller

405 F.3d 700 (8th Cir. 2005)

John Doe (obviously not his real name) represented a large group of other "John Doe's" who filed a class action lawsuit against the state of Iowa challenging a new law that prohibited certain categories of sex offenders from residing within 2000 feet of either a school or a child care facility. Among other arguments advanced, the John Doe's maintained that this new law constituted punishment for their crimes and therefore was unconstitutional both as an ex post facto law (since it punished conduct engaged in prior to the passing of the law) and as a law that violated the Eighth Amendment prohibition against cruel and unusual punishment (since, among other things, it constituted banishment). The U.S. District Court agreed with the John Doe's that this law constituted unconstitutional punishment and issued a decree prohibiting the state attorney general and the ninety-nine county attorneys from enforcing the law. The state attorney general appealed this decision to the federal 8th Circuit Court of Appeals.

The 8th Circuit reversed the decision of the lower court and found that the sex offender residency law did not constitute either an ex post facto punishment nor a cruel and unusual punishment. The main reasoning behind this decision was that in its opinion, the law simply did not constitute punishment at all but was merely a civil measure meant solely to protect the health and safety of children.

The John Doe's had agreed that the law was meant to protect children rather than to punish them, but argued that despite the legislature's intent, the practical result of the law was punishment. They cited case law that held that a civil law becomes a criminal penalty whenever the effect of the law is "so punitive either in purpose or effect as to negate the State's intention to deem it civil."

Among other things, the John Doe's offered evidence which they believed proved cruel and unusual banishment. They presented maps showing that entire small towns and majority portions of larger cities in the state were off-limits to them due to the 2000-foot rule. Many of them were unable to return to their homes after prison or capable of finding relatives who did not live within the restricted zones and who could thus take them in. One John Doe who could afford to live without relatives testified that he had looked at 40 different possible residences in his city but was unable to find even one that would comply with the residency restrictions. For many of these offenders, the only available areas to live were rural areas which had few housing options available (even when an option could be found, the landlord often refused to rent to them).

Despite these arguments, the circuit court found the residency restrictions did not impose a punishment of any kind. Speaking to the banishment argument, it said that this was a false analogy. It said that true banishment compelled a criminal to "quit a city, place, or country." Historically it prevented a person from ever returning to their original community in that they were expelled from the area. Unlike true banishment, Iowa's residency law merely narrowed the range of options an offender had within various communities. He or she had options, even though admittedly some might require some hard work in discovering. Additionally, unlike true banishment, Iowa's law simply addressed residency. The offender could still work, shop and recreate virtually anywhere that he or she wished to do so. Since this law was unlike banishment in too many important ways, the circuit court did not find that it constituted punishment either in its express intent or as a practical matter. Since it did not constitute punishment, the U.S. Constitutional prohibitions against ex post facto punishments and cruel and unusual punishments would simply not apply.

In a dissent, Judge Melloy wrote that he believed that this Iowa residency restriction constituted effective banishment and thus punishment. He wrote that the law " effectively results in banishment from virtually all of Iowa's cities and larger towns." True, the law did not constitute complete banishment. But, it was close enough to become very punitive in nature. Because it was punitive, the ex post facto provision of the U.S. Constitution was clearly violated. (And, though this dissenting judge did not specifically address the cruel and unusual punishment clause, one might assume that he would find the punishment of banishment a form of it as well.)

Do you have any sympathy for the John Doe's in the above case? Would you want one of them living near your child's school or day care center? How far would you go in restricting their choice of residence? Would it depend on the specific nature of their crime? What about concerns that some people have that such residency restrictions funnel offenders into those few areas of town that are not off limits? How would you like to be living with your children in those areas flooded with offenders seeking a lawful place to live?

Crafting a Sentence

Other than presiding at trials, one of the most important jobs judges arguably have is crafting appropriate sentences which they will impose following a guilty verdict or a guilty plea. Though most sentences involve matters routine enough that even sensitive judges can avoid second-guessing themselves, there is always those non-routine, very serious cases that put the sentencing judge in the awkward position of having to play God with people's lives. Big cases calling for the possibility of long prison sentences should (and probably do) cause most judges to become very reflective and self-aware of their frightening power. They wish to be neither too harsh nor too lenient in their search for justice. In crafting an appropriate sentence judges should appropriately consider "legal factors" and avoid considering "extra-legal factors." These will be discussed below.

Legal Factors in Crafting a Sentence

Legal factors in crafting a sentence include any facts or information that a judge might lawfully use in deciding a proper sentence (as opposed to a defendant's race, religion, etc. which should be irrelevant). The list of legal factors is long, and necessarily so, since the sentencing judge should consider the "whole person," that is, every important facet of a defendant's life so that the judge can avoid turning the sentencing decision into a mere game of chance.[7] Legal factors judges typically use to decide sentences are generally provided to them in a **pre-sentence report** drafted by a specialized unit of the local probation office ahead of the sentencing hearing. Legal factors provided sentencing judges in such reports typically include:

> Age, education, employment history, prior record, drug and alcohol issues, family background, medical condition, probation/parole history, past attempts at rehabilitation, defendant's version of crime, victim's version of crime, victim impact, acceptance of responsibility, remorse, cooperation with law enforcement, current rehabilitation efforts, compensation efforts, degree defendant's conduct was induced by another, sentencing guideline recommendations if any.[8]

One (formerly) gray area of concern was whether or not it was legally proper for a sentencing judge to consider a defendant's apparent false testimony at trial when he or she elected to exercise the constitutional right to testify in one's own defense. The case that follows grapples with this.

United States v. Grayson

438 U.S. 41 (1978)

While serving time in prison on drug charges, Grayson escaped from custody. He was apprehended and charged with escape, which crime he was convicted of by way of a jury trial. During his trial, he had elected to take the stand to testify in his own behalf. In his testimony he attempted to convince the jury that his escape was necessary and justified because he was about to be viciously attacked by a fellow inmate to whom he owed a gambling debt, who was wielding a large stick with a nail protruding through it. The jury rejected the defendant's testimony and instead chose to believe the Government's evidence which cast serious doubts on crucial aspects of the defendant's story.

Following his conviction, the trial judge explained to Grayson why he was sentencing him to two years for the escape, to be served in addition to the time he was currently serving on the drug charges. The federal trial judge told Grayson that, "It is my view that your defense was a complete fabrication without the slightest merit whatsoever. I feel it is proper for me to consider that fact in the sentencing and I will do so."

Grayson appealed his sentence to the 3rd Circuit Court of Appeals who vacated the sentence on the grounds that the trial court improperly considered Grayson's alleged perjured testimony in crafting a sentence. The Circuit Court ordered the trial court to re-sentence Grayson, this time without giving any consideration to false testimony he may have given in his own defense.

The prosecution appealed this decision to the U.S. Supreme Court who agreed to hear the matter. The U.S. Supreme Court reversed the 3rd Circuit Court of Appeals and reinstated the original sentence of the trial judge.

---

7. See, *United States v. Grayson*, 438 U.S. 41 (1978).
8. Source: Author's professional recollection and Chapter 25 ("Sentencing") in F. Miller, R. Dawson, G. Dix and R. Parnas. (2000). *Prosecution and Adjudication (5th ed.)*, New York: Foundation Press.

The issue of course before the U.S. Supreme Court was whether a trial judge can properly sentence a defendant more severely because he took the stand in his own defense and apparently lied. The prosecution's position was that a "defendant's truthfulness or mendacity while testifying on his own behalf, almost without exception, has been deemed probative of his attitudes toward society and prospects for rehabilitation, and hence relevant to sentencing."

Grayson's lawyers made several counter-arguments to the above. First, defense counsel suggested that lying on the stand in such a situation is no big deal. They cited the "peculiar pressures" placed upon defendants during trials, and suggested that, "It is indeed unlikely that many men who commit serious offenses would balk on principle from lying in their own defense." Defense counsel suggested that even people who feel genuine sorrow for what they have done are usually nevertheless driven by an overpowering urge to remain free and thus lie on the stand.

Grayson's attorneys next argued that defendants have a constitutional right to testify in their own defense. If sentencing judges were allowed to give extra time for false testimony, there would be an impermissible "chilling effect" on this constitutional right.

Grayson's counsel also argued that their client is being punished for the crime of perjury for which he had never been indicted, tried or convicted. This would violate his right to due process.

In rejecting all of Grayson's arguments, the U.S. Supreme Court said that sentencing judges properly should consider the defendant's "whole person," and that a willingness to commit perjury at trial is an important part of that "whole person." The Court dismissed the idea that there would be an impermissible chilling effect on defendant's right to testify in his own defense. The Court said there is no constitutional right to lie in one's own defense. If there is a chilling effect on people's desire to lie then that is a good thing and such a chilling effect would be "entirely permissible." In short, "there is no protected right to commit perjury."

The Supreme Court was careful to acknowledge that defendants who do not take the stand still have a noble right to force the state to prove its case against them. Even if they are ultimately found guilty, judges cannot punish defendants extra who force the state to go through its steps since that is there right. Defendants may permissibly hold the state to its burden of proof but should do so without taking the stand in order to commit perjury.

Justices Stewart, Brennan and Marshall dissented from the above holdings. Writing for all three of them, Justice Stewart had this to say:

> In essence, the Court holds today that *whenever* [italics in the original] a defendant testifies in his own behalf and is found guilty, he opens himself to the possibility of an enhanced sentence. Such a sentence is nothing more or less than a penalty imposed on the defendant's exercise of his constitutional and statutory rights to plead not guilty and to testify in his own behalf.

Do you agree with the majority or with the dissent in the above case? When I was a young assistant district attorney I remember the first time I witnessed a trial judge punish a defendant extra for having testified in his own defense at trial. The judge (and apparently the jury who convicted him earlier) believed the defendant had committed perjury on the stand. The defense attorney was outraged at the trial judge, forcefully accusing him of producing a "chilling effect" on all future defendants' rights to testify at trial in his courtroom. Though I remained silent, I must confess that at the time I was sympathetic to my opponent's position. What do you think?

Extra-legal Factors in Crafting a Sentence

Though sentencing judges should indeed consider the "whole person" when sentencing someone, certain facts about people are out of bounds. Such **extra-legal factors in crafting a sentence** (meaning factors outside the law and hence impermissible to consider) include such things as race, gender, religion, social class, physical attractiveness, accent, etc. Some judges no doubt consider some of these factors—at least unconsciously—but it is almost always improper to do so.

Sentencing Factors vs. Elements of a Crime

Every sensible person agrees that a person should not get more time merely because of one's race or less time because of one's good looks. Still, not everyone should be treated the same. For example, almost everyone would think that a repeat burglar should get more time than a first time burglar. But, who decides whether or not a person has a prior conviction for burglary? This is a job for the sentencing judge, not the jury. In our system, juries decide whether or not the **elements of a crime** (the statutory components of the crime) have been proven. For example, in the case of a burglary the jury will be asked to determine three elements: whether or not the defendant entered a building, whether this was done without permission, and whether he or she entered with intent to commit a crime inside. If the jury finds all of the elements and convicts the defendant, then it is up to the judge to determine the many various **sentencing factors** (background information relevant to the sentencing decision) that can now come into play (see discussion on "Legal factors in crafting a sentence" above). For example, the judge will determine such things as a defendant's prior convictions, educational level, employment history, remorse for crime, etc. But (and here is the point all of this is leading up to), sometimes this gets tricky: the difference between what constitutes "elements of a crime" vs. "sentencing factors" can get murky. The next case examines this problem, a concern introduced earlier in this chapter when discussing the constitutionality of the federal sentencing guidelines. This concern will now be revisited in a broader context.

Apprendi v. New Jersey

530 U.S. 466 (2000)

Charles Apprendi was accused of firing several shots into the home of an African-American family allegedly because he did not want a family of that race living in his neighborhood (he allegedly made statements to that effect which he later denied). Apprendi was indicted for the shooting as well as for various weapons offenses and other related counts. Apprendi and the prosecutor negotiated a plea bargain in which Apprendi pled guilty to the weapons offenses (the ultimate sentences of which were to all run concurrently) in exchange for all other counts being dropped. This charge bargain left the actual sentencing for the weapons offenses up to the judge. It is important that in his guilty plea, Apprendi never admitted that racial hatred was the basis for his crime.

Normally, the maximum that a judge could give Apprendi for such weapons offenses was ten years in prison. However, following Apprendi's plea of guilty, the prosecutor filed a motion with the sentencing judge asking him to enhance Apprendi's potential, maximum sentence due to the alleged racial hatred behind the crime. Apparently New Jersey had a "hate crimes" statute that authorized sentencing judges to give extra time —that is, time beyond the normal maximum—for various crimes if the judge found by a preponderance of the evidence that hate was the motive behind the crime. (Many states now have such "hate crimes" legislation. For example, if a perpetrator is found guilty of certain crimes on a list such as assault, rape, arson, vandalism, etc., he or she can be given an enhanced penalty when the motive for the particular crime is found to be based on hostility towards a victim's race, gender, religion, sexual orientation, or ethnicity.) In the case of Apprendi, the New Jersey sentencing judge did find that Apprendi's crime was motivated by racial hostility and so sentenced him to twelve years in prison (two years beyond the ten year maximum ordinarily allowed for his crime).

Apprendi appealed this sentence to the Appellate Division of the Superior Court of New Jersey and then to the New Jersey Supreme Court claiming that his Constitutional right to due process had been violated when a judge rather than a jury determined that race was the motivation behind his crime. Both of these higher courts rejected his claims. Apprendi appealed to the U.S. Supreme Court which granted him permission to present his case before it.

The U.S. Supreme Court ruled in favor of Apprendi and reversed the decisions of the New Jersey courts. The prosecution had contended that motive is traditionally a mere "sentencing factor" determined by judges (by preponderance of the evidence) rather than by juries (beyond a reasonable doubt). Since a finding of racial "hate" goes to motive, the prosecution contended that this determination had been properly made by the sentencing judge. The High Court did not buy this. It said that though motive might ordinarily be a mere "sentencing factor," all bets are off when the finding of hatred as a motive "bumps up" the potential penalty for the crime beyond the statutory maximum penalty ordinarily designated for the offense. When the motive can cause someone to get more than the maximum, motive then becomes the "functional equivalent of an element of a greater offense." Since racial hate in this context is in reality an offense "element" rather than an ordinary sentencing "factor," a jury rather than a judge must determine it (and the proof therefore must be beyond a reasonable doubt rather than by a mere preponderance of the evidence).

Again, central to the Supreme Court's ruling was its reasoning that the sentencing judge wound up sentencing Apprendi to a period of years that exceeded the maximum statutory penalty generally provided for the crime to which he pled guilty. That, then will be the key: If the so-called "sentencing factor" produces a sentence that can exceed the maximum penalty generally provided for a certain crime, then this "sentencing factor" is in reality an "element" of a *different* crime. Since the finding will create a conviction for what amounts to be a totally different crime, then the defendant has the right to a jury rather than a judge to decide it.

The sentencing judge, in finding racial hatred, took it upon himself to find a fact that in this and similar cases will sometimes be very "hotly disputed." To allow sentencing judges to give more than the maximum sentence ordinarily provided for a crime in such an easy manner would allow the government to cut juries out of the loop by masking true elements of crimes as mere sentencing factors.

Because Apprendi was in effect "convicted" by a judge of a crime to which he neither pled guilty nor was convicted of beyond a reasonable doubt by a jury, his constitutional right to due process had been violated. In other words, his liberty was taken away without his first having been given basic, fair procedures like trial by jury and proof of guilt beyond a reasonable doubt. The case was reversed and remanded to the trial court to give him his due process rights.

This completes our discussion of Sentencing Law. The next chapter will cover what logically should be discussed next: Inmate Rights (also known as "Correctional Law").

Chapter Twelve

Inmate Rights

By definition the imprisonment of an individual includes the loss of liberty and freedom. It also entails the loss of many rights guaranteed to other citizens in the Constitution and Bill of Rights. While the forfeiture of some rights, such as the right to travel, the right of assembly, the right to bear arms, are obviously necessary when dealing with incarceration, the Supreme Court has stated that prisoners do not forfeit all constitutional protections.

This was not always the case. From the founding of our nation until the middle of the twentieth century, individuals incarcerated in the United States had very few legal protections. Inmates were widely considered to be "**slaves of the state**"[1] and were therefore not entitled to rights guaranteed to free citizens under the Constitution. Moreover, as prisons were under the control of the executive branch of government, courts took a "**hands-off approach**" to complaints regarding prison operations and treatment of inmates.

It was not until the 1970s that the existence of rights and protections provided by the Constitution was widely recognized and accepted by the nation's courts to apply to prison inmates. Using the Supreme Court's statement from *Trop v. Dulles*[2] that the Eighth Amendment's cruel and unusual punishment clause draws its meaning from "the evolving standards of decency that mark the progress of a maturing society," the nation's courts began to take an active interest in the way inmates in American prisons were being treated (or mistreated). In this chapter we will examine what rights are maintained by inmates, specific limitations on these rights, and the legal and logical bases for these limitations.

Eighth Amendment Rights

The Eighth Amendment to the Constitution, in seemingly simple language, states, "Excessive bail shall not be required, nor excessive fines imposed, nor cruel and unusual punishments inflicted." While its very language seems to imply that it would apply to situations in which an inmate is incarcerated under conditions that are cruel and unusual, the Supreme Court did not use the 8th Amendment to consider the consti-

1. *Ruffin v. Commonwealth*, 62 Va. 790, 796 (1871).
2. 356 U.S. 86, 101 (1958).

tutionality of the conditions of confinement or treatment of inmates in prisons until 1976. In the passing years since applying the 8th Amendment to evaluating the constitutionality of prison conditions and treatment of inmates, the Court has used the 8th Amendment to consider a wide range of issues including: the number of inmates permitted per cell; the medical, dental, and mental health treatment provided to inmates; the use of corporal punishment against inmates; the segregation of inmates; and the protection of inmates from one another.

This portion of the chapter will examine cases that arose due to several of the items listed above. It is important to remember that in each of these cases the ultimate question is whether the inmate was subjected to cruel and unusual punishment: punishment inflicted or caused by the government. Regardless of the claim, absent an act or omission on the part of prison officials, the government cannot be held responsible and no constitutional violation exists. More specifically, the 8th Amendment prohibits the unnecessary and wanton infliction of pain. As we will see in the following cases, exactly when the infliction of pain is unnecessary and wanton varies depending on the type and severity of the pain, and the mental state possessed by the person permitting or inflicting it. The following cases, which involve the failure to provide a safe environment, the existence of substandard conditions of confinement, the use of force by prison staff, and the standard of medical care owed to inmates, will illustrate how standards related to a seemingly clear constitutional amendment can differ greatly in how they are defined, analyzed and applied.

Safe Environment

While it would be nice if prisons were able to rehabilitate offenders, rehabilitation of inmates must always take a back seat to two more critical responsibilities faced by prison administrators: keeping inmates from escaping and keeping inmates safe. The first of these items is self-evident and will likely never give rise to a claim of an 8th Amendment violation (inmates that are allowed to leave a prison rarely complain). The second item, keeping inmates safe while incarcerated, is a much more difficult, complicated issue. While all would agree that inmates should be kept safe, disagreements arise when considering what prison officials must do to achieve this. This is especially true when prison officials are accused of not doing enough to protect an inmate from other inmates. In *Farmer v. Brennan*, the Supreme Court considers when, if ever, the acts of prison officials which led to the assault of an inmate by other inmates, rise to the level of an 8th Amendment violation.

Farmer v. Brennan

511 U.S. 825 (1994)

Dee Farmer, a preoperative-transsexual, was serving a federal prison sentence for credit card fraud at FCI-Oxford, a relatively low-security correctional institute for nonviolent offenders. Prior to his incarceration, Farmer, who is biologically a male, underwent estrogen therapy, received silicone breast implants, and submitted to unsuccessful "black market" testicle-removal surgery. In response to a disciplinary infraction, Farmer was transferred to the United States Penitentiary in Terre Haute, Indiana, in March 1989. The Indiana prison had a significantly higher security level than existed at FCI-Oxford and housed primarily violent offenders. Although he was initially placed in administrative segregation, Farmer was soon integrated into the general population. Within two weeks of the integration, he was beaten and raped in his own cell by another inmate.

Farmer filed a civil suit in federal court against prison officials alleging a violation of his Eighth Amendment right not to be subjected to cruel and unusual punishment. Specifically, the complaint alleged that prison officials placed him in the general population of USP-Terre Haute despite their knowledge that the penitentiary had a history of violent inmate assaults and that Farmer, as a transsexual who exhibited "feminine characteristics," would be particularly vulnerable to sexual attack by other inmates. The United States District Court granted the prison officials' motion for summary judgment, finding that the prison officials did not possess sufficient knowledge of the potential danger to render them liable under the Eighth Amendment. The Seventh Circuit Court of Appeals affirmed, and the United States Supreme Court granted *certiorari.*

The Supreme Court held that the Eighth Amendment mandates prison officials to take reasonable measures to guarantee the safety of inmates. This duty includes protecting inmates from other prisoners. Prison officials, however, will be liable for violating an inmate's right to be kept safe only if two conditions are present. First, it must be proven that the inmate was placed in a situation that posed a "substantial risk of serious harm." The Court found that there was no dispute that the beating and rape suffered by Farmer met this requirement.

The second requirement for an Eighth Amendment violation for failing to provide a safe environment is that there must be proof that prison officials acted with **deliberate indifference** to the inmate's health or safety. The Court explained:

> A prison official cannot be found liable under the Eighth Amendment for denying an inmate humane conditions of confinement unless the official knows of and disregards an excessive risk to inmate health or safety; the official must both be aware of facts from which the inference could be drawn that a substantial risk of serious harm exists, and he must also draw the inference.[3]

Under this standard a prison official's failure to lessen a significant risk that he or she should have perceived but did not is not a violation of the Eighth Amendment. On the other hand, an inmate does not have to prove that prison officials had actual knowledge that harm would fall upon the inmate, only that there was knowledge that there existed a substantial risk that the harm would occur.

In considering the facts before it, the Court held that there were insufficient facts to determine if prison officials were deliberately indifferent to the risks posed by placing Farmer in the general population. Accordingly, it remanded the matter to the District Court for further consideration of evidence regarding the amount of knowledge prison officials possessed regarding the risks.

---

3. *Farmer* at 837.

The standard an inmate must meet to have prison officials held liable for injuries caused by a third person is extremely high. Not only must an inmate be able to prove that prison officials knew of a substantial risk of harm and ignored the risk, it must also be shown that the action of the officials was unreasonable from the perspective of prison administrators after giving due deference to their decisions. So, while Farmer was victorious at the Supreme Court, the rule announced by the Court led to his eventually losing his case at the district court.

Farmer does not require prison officials to take unreasonable steps to insure the safety of inmates. It only requires them to act if they are aware of a specific danger and it would be unreasonable for them not to act given the specific circumstances. A different question involves the use of force against an inmate by correctional officers and prison guards, rather than by fellow prisoners.

Use of Force

As we are seeing throughout this chapter, inmates do not lose all of their rights and liberty interests because they are in prison. Among these retained rights is the right to be free from being assaulted by agents of the government; particularly the police and in the case of inmates, correctional officers unless justified by particular circumstances. In the prison context, it is easy to see that there may be times when the use of force against an inmate is necessary and justified. It is also possible that the use of violence against an inmate may be inappropriate or excessive. In *Hudson v. McMillian* the Supreme Court set forth standards for determining when the use of force against an inmate ceases to become necessary and instead becomes an 8th Amendment violation.

Hudson v. McMillian

503 U.S. 1 (1992)

On October 30, 1987, Keith Hudson, an inmate at the Louisiana state penitentiary in Angola, got in an argument with a prison guard named Jack McMillian. After the argument, McMillian, with assistance of fellow guard Arthur Woods, placed Hudson in handcuffs and shackles, and moved him from his cell to the prison lockdown area. According to Hudson, McMillian and Woods punched and kicked him numerous times. Hudson also stated that the on-duty supervisor, Arthur Mezo, not only observed the beating but reacted only by directing the officers "not to have too much fun." As a result of the incident, Hudson suffered minor bruises and swelling to his face, mouth, and lip. The assault also loosened Hudson's teeth and cracked his partial dental plate.

Hudson sued the three corrections officers in Federal District Court alleging a violation of the Eighth Amendment's prohibition on cruel and unusual punishments. The District Court ruled that McMillian and Woods used unnecessary force and that Mezo approved their actions as their supervisor. Hudson was awarded $800 in damages.

On appeal, the Fifth Circuit Court of Appeals reversed. Applying its own precedent, the court held that for a violation of the Eighth Amendment to exist due to the use of excessive force, a prisoner must demonstrate: (1) a significant injury; (2) resulting "directly and only from the use of force that was clearly excessive to the need"; (3) that the use of the excessive force was objectively unreasonable; and (4) that the use of force constituted an unnecessary and wanton use of force. The court ruled that since Hudson did not suffer a "significant injury," his Eighth Amendment claim must be denied.

The United States Supreme Court granted certiorari. Writing for the majority, Justice O'Connor explained that for a violation of the Eighth Amendment to be present, there must be a showing of an "unnecessary and wanton infliction of pain." Importantly, the majority stressed, what constitutes an infliction of unnecessary and wanton pain will vary depending on the nature of the alleged constitutional violation. For example, inmates alleging a lack of medical care must show that prison officials acted with deliberate indifference.[4] On the other hand, when authorities use force to put down a prison disturbance, the Court has held that "the question whether the measure taken inflicted unnecessary and wanton pain and suffering ultimately turns on 'whether force was applied in a good faith effort to maintain or restore discipline or maliciously and sadistically for the very purpose of causing harm.'"[5] While acknowledging that courts must give prison officials wide deference in the adoption of practices that in their judgment are needed to maintain institutional discipline and security, this deference is not absolute. The majority concluded that the facts of the present case are somewhat analogous to *Whitley*. Accordingly, the Court held that the *Whitley* standard, "whether force was applied in a good-faith effort to maintain or restore discipline, or maliciously and sadistically to cause harm," should be used in all cases where prison officials are accused of using excessive force.

The majority next considered whether an inmate must demonstrate a significant injury to prove an Eighth Amendment violation. The Court said no. Justice O'Connor stated that there are a number of items a court can consider in determining if the use of force was wanton and unnecessary in a given situation. Items such as the need for the use of force, the amount of force used, the threat "reasonably perceived by the responsible officials," and any efforts made to limit the force used. Moreover, "the absence of serious injury is therefore relevant to the Eighth Amendment inquiry, but does not end it." It is one item to be considered in determining if the alleged wrongdoing was objectively harmful enough to establish a constitutional violation. Even absent serious injury, there may still exist sufficient other items to categorize a use of force as wanton and unnecessary. Applying this standard, the Court held that the lack of serious injury was not a proper basis for the dismissal of the action by the court of appeals.

Once again, we see that so long as prison officials act in a good faith effort to maintain prison order and discipline, there is no 8th Amendment violation. Under the standards set forth in *Hudson*, courts will consider all of the circumstances surrounding uses of force against inmates. Do you think this has the effect of putting correctional officers on trial every time they need to use force? Does it give too much deference to prison officials to justify any act they commit?

---

4. *Estelle v. Gamble*, 429 U.S. 97 (1976), discussed below.
5. *Whitley v. Albers*, 475 U.S. 312, 320 (1986) quoted in *McMillian*.

Medical Care

For an 8th Amendment violation to exist there must be some form of punishment that is deemed cruel and unusual. Moreover, for something to be considered punishment, it must be deliberately inflicted upon an inmate by the state or a state actor. The Court has explained that this is necessary because without action on the part of a state actor there is no "punishment," and if a condition, however repugnant, does not involve punishment, it cannot be considered to be *cruel and unusual punishment* protected under the rubric of the 8th Amendment.

This way of thinking explains why prior to 1976, the 8th Amendment was not used by the Court to address claims of unconstitutional conditions of confinement in a prison. In fact, the first case in which the 8th Amendment was used by the Court to address the treatment of inmates in prison did not involve conditions of confinement at all, but rather the right of inmates to receive needed medical treatment.

Estelle v. Gamble is a critical case for several reasons. First of all, as noted above, it was the first case in which the Supreme Court applied the 8th Amendment to the treatment of inmates and the conditions of their confinement. Secondly, it established the standard which is used in examining 8th Amendment claims in a variety of contexts: deliberate indifference. As you read *Estelle v. Gamble*, ask yourself if the Court came to a just and fair conclusion, and whether the standard set forth is workable for courts and prison administrators.

Estelle v. Gamble

429 U.S. 97 (1976)

J.W. Gamble, an inmate of the Texas Department of Corrections, was injured during a work assignment when a bale of cotton fell on him while he was unloading a truck. Gamble was given a pass to the hospital where doctors checked him for a hernia and then sent him back to his cell. Over the next three months Gamble continued to complain about lower back pain as well as chest pains and high blood pressure. Prison medical staff, which he saw on 17 occasions during this three-month period, treated his back injury with muscle relaxants, pain relievers, and bed rest. He also received medication for the chest pains and high blood pressure. During this period Gamble refused to work because of his ailments. He was referred for discipline for refusing to work. The prison disciplinary committee determined that he was in "first class" medical condition, and placed him in solitary confinement.

Gamble, believing he had received inadequate medical treatment, brought an action against the Department of Corrections, the prison warden, and the medical director of the Department of Corrections. In the suit Gamble alleged that the medical treatment he received was inadequate and "more should have been done by way of diagnosis and treatment," and the prison's failure to provide such treatment constituted cruel and unusual punishment in violation of the Eighth Amendment.

In an opinion written by Justice Marshall, the Supreme Court stated that the Eighth Amendment proscribes conduct that constitutes "an **unnecessary and wanton inflic-**

tion of pain" or that is "repugnant to the conscience of man." The Court explained that the failure to provide treatment for the medical needs of inmates, individuals completely reliant on prison officials for their maintenance, may violate the Eighth Amendment as the "the infliction of ... unnecessary suffering is inconsistent with contemporary standards of decency."

The Court noted that not all failures to provide requested treatment would be unconstitutional. Acts of mere negligence on the part of prison doctors or staff do not rise to the level of cruel and unusual punishment. Rather, the Eighth Amendment is violated only if prison officials act with "**deliberate indifference** to the serious medical needs of prisoners."

Deliberate indifference may be exhibited in several ways. It may be evidenced by prison doctors in refusing to provide reasonable medical care in response to a prisoner's needs, or by prison guards in intentionally denying or delaying access to medical care. Examples of deliberate indifference cited by the Court included doctors refusing to reattach an inmate's severed ear and instead choosing to perform the "easier and less efficacious treatment" of throwing away the prisoner's ear and stitching the stump,"[6] and the actions of prison doctors in injecting an inmate with penicillin with knowledge that the prisoner was allergic, and refusing to treat the allergic reaction.[7]

In considering the treatment of Gamble, the Court held there was no evidence of deliberate indifference. He was able to see prison medical staff on 17 occasions. His chest pains and high blood pressure were successfully treated. While his back pain continued to persist, this was at most medical malpractice and not deliberate indifference. As such, the Court found that his Eighth Amendment rights were not violated.

Since *Estelle*, courts have found that in addition to medical care, inmates have the right to reasonable dental, optical, and mental health care. This includes not only treatment for ailments, but preventive care as well. It does not, however, include complete medical care and treatment. Prisons are only required to provide reasonable and necessary treatments performed in a reasonable manner. An inmate having a tooth pulled, while he or she would have the right to Novocain, would not have the right to nitrous oxide. An inmate with a headache would have a right to aspirin, but would not have a right to ibuprofen. An inmate being treated for a laceration would have a right to have the wound stitched, but there would be no right to plastic surgery to prevent scarring.

Just as inmates do not have a right to premium medical treatment of their own choosing, neither do they have a right to comfortable conditions of confinement. As will be discussed in the next section, they do, however, have some rights when it comes to the manner in which they are housed and treated in prison.

Conditions of Confinement

We have seen a recurrent theme in this chapter: courts will grant prison administrators vast discretion in the operation of prisons if their actions are done for the purpose of

6. *Williams v. Vincent*, 508 F.2d 541 (2nd Cir. 1974)
7. *Thomas v. Pate*, 493 F.2d 151, 158 (7th Cir. 1974)

maintaining order and security. We have also seen there are limits to this discretion. One area where there has been widespread debate involves how involved courts should become in considering whether the conditions of confinement faced by inmates constitute cruel and unusual punishment. While courts have frequently acknowledged that prison by its nature is an unpleasant place to reside, and it would be unreasonable for an inmate to expect comfortable conditions, some conditions of confinement may be unconstitutionally poor. In *Wilson v. Seiter* the Supreme Court considered what standard should be used in considering not only what conditions are violative of the 8th Amendment, but also what role prison officials must have in the creation and presence of these conditions before they are declared unconstitutional.

Wilson v. Seiter

501 U.S. 294 (1991)

In 1986 Pearly Wilson, an inmate at Hocking Correctional Facility in Nelsonville, Ohio, filed suit against prison officials under Section 1983 of the Civil Rights Act alleging that the conditions at the prison violated the Eighth and Fourteenth Amendments of the United States Constitution. Wilson's complaint alleged overcrowding, excessive noise, insufficient locker storage space, inadequate heating and cooling, improper ventilation, unclean and inadequate rest rooms, unsanitary dining facilities and food preparation, and housing with mentally and physically ill inmates. In addition to describing the conditions in detail, Wilson's affidavits charged that the Ohio authorities, after notification, had failed to take remedial action. In response, the prison officials denied that many of the alleged conditions existed and explained that efforts were being made to improve those poor conditions that did exist.

The district court granted summary judgment in favor of the prison officials, opining that Wilson failed to prove wantonness on behalf of the prison officials. The Court of Appeals for the Sixth Circuit affirmed the district court's decision. In its opinion, the court of appeals held that prison officials' culpable states of mind should be evaluated by whether their behavior was "marked by persistent malicious cruelty." Because Wilson had not shown that the conditions at the Ohio state prison were motivated by maliciousness on the part of the prison officials toward inmates, the court of appeals affirmed the summary judgment in favor of the prison officials.

The United States Supreme Court granted certiorari, and with Justice Scalia writing for a five-member majority, reversed the court of appeals. The majority agreed with the court of appeals that a prisoner claiming that the conditions of his confinement violate the Eighth Amendment must show a culpable state of mind on the part of prison officials. The Court, however, refused to require that an inmate show that prison officials acted with persistent and malicious cruelty. Rather, the Court held that in cases involving conditions of confinement, courts should apply the "**deliberate indifference**" standard to claims involving challenges to conditions of confinement. This requires that an inmate demonstrate that prison officials know of and disregard an unconstitutional condition of confinement.

The Court further held that regardless of a prison official's state of mind, only conditions of confinement that produce deprivations denying " 'the minimal civilized measure of life's necessities"' are serious enough to form the basis of an Eighth Amendment claim. Justice Scalia, quoting from *Rhodes v. Chapman*, stated that, since the Constitution "'does not mandate comfortable prisons,"' poor prison conditions amount to an infliction of suffering "sufficiently grave" to violate the Eighth Amendment only when the conditions result in the deprivation of an "identifiable human need such as food, warmth, or exercise."[8]

As the lower courts did not use the appropriate standards for considering whether Wilson's rights were violated, it remanded the matter for further consideration.

Once again we see that an inmate claiming that conditions of confinement are unconstitutional must show that prison officials acted with a culpable mental state to prove a violation of the 8th Amendment. In the final sections of this chapter we will see how other constitutional guarantees apply in the prison context.

Fourth Amendment Rights

The 4th Amendment to the Constitution provides in part that, "The right of the people to be secure in their persons, houses, papers, and effects, against unreasonable searches and seizures ... shall not be violated." You may recall from Chapter 3 that the Fourth Amendment prohibits searches only if a person has a **reasonable expectation of privacy** concerning the subject of the search.[9] Obviously, there must be some limits placed on an inmate's expectation of privacy over his cell and belongings. In *Hudson v. Palmer* the Court was asked for the first time to consider whether the 4th Amendment provides any protection against searches and seizures within an inmate's cell.

Hudson v. Palmer

468 U.S. 517 (1984)

Russell Palmer was an inmate at the Bland Correctional Center in Virginia. On September 16, 1981, Hudson, a correctional officer, conducted a "shakedown" search of Palmer's prison locker and cell for contraband. During the search a ripped pillowcase was discovered in Palmer's cell. Additionally, several of Palmer's belongings were destroyed during the search. Palmer was charged with violating prison rules by destroying property. After a hearing, Palmer was found guilty and ordered to reimburse the State for the cost of the material destroyed, and a reprimand was entered on his prison record.

Believing his rights had been violated, Palmer filed suit in the United States District Court. Palmer alleged that Hudson had performed the shakedown search of his cell and had brought a false charge against him solely for harassment in violation of the Fourth Amendment prohibition against unreasonable searches and seizures. Palmer also claimed that the destruction of his personal property similarly violated the Fourth Amendment. Lastly, Palmer claimed that his Fourteenth Amendment right not to be

8. *Rhodes v. Chapman*, 452 U.S. 337, 347, 349 (1981).
9. See *Katz v. United States*, 389 U.S. 347 (1967)

deprived of property without due process of law was violated by the intentional destruction of his permitted personal property during the search.

Hudson filed a motion for summary judgment which was granted by the district court. On appeal the Fourth Circuit Court of Appeals reversed the district court's decision, holding that prisoners are entitled to protection under the Fourth Amendment against searches conducted solely with the intent to harass or humiliate the inmate.

The Supreme Court disagreed. In very strong and definitive language Chief Justice Burger held that "the Fourth Amendment has no applicability to a prison cell." The Court explained that this is because prisoners do not possess a reasonable expectation of privacy in their prison cells which would entitle them to the protection of the Fourth Amendment against unreasonable searches. While prisoners enjoy many rights and protections under the Constitution, some rights are fundamentally inconsistent with imprisonment itself or incompatible with the objectives of incarceration. Realistically, the loss of many rights is necessary to accommodate the institutional needs and objectives of prison facilities, particularly the unavoidable objectives of internal security and safety. The Court noted that it would be practically impossible for prison administrators to prevent weapons, drugs, and other contraband from entering a prison if inmates retained a right of privacy in their cells. It is the very unpredictability of random searches of cells that makes such searches indispensable and necessary for the safe and effective operation of a prison. Accordingly, the Court held that the search of Palmer's cell and destruction of his property within the cell did not violate the Fourth Amendment.

In reaching the conclusion that any right to privacy is incompatible with the necessary close and continual surveillance of inmates, the Court balanced the security needs of prisons against the interest of the prisoner in privacy within his cell. The Court concluded that by being convicted of a crime an inmate forfeited his or her right to privacy over his or her cell.

First Amendment Right to Religious Exercise

The First Amendment states, "Congress shall make no law respecting an establishment of religion, or prohibiting the free exercise thereof; or abridging the freedom of speech ..." For many years the tension between individual rights guaranteed by the 1st Amendment and the efficient, safe operation of prisons has confronted American courts. In the final section of this chapter we will consider one component of the 1st Amendment: freedom of religion.

The right to practice one's religion freely without fear of repercussions has been a hallmark of American freedoms for hundreds of years. In 1972 the Supreme Court considered what limits may be placed on the religious practices of prison inmates for the first time. In *Cruz v. Beto*[10] the Supreme Court held that inmates who hold unconventional reli-

10. 405 U.S. 319 (1972).

gious beliefs must not be denied a reasonable opportunity to practice their faiths comparably to that offered to inmates following more traditional faiths.

The years following *Cruz* saw an increasingly conservative Supreme Court limit prisoner's rights in all areas, including the exercise of religious practices. In 1987 the Court held that a prison regulation that infringed upon an inmate's practicing his or her religion is constitutional so long as there is a logical connection between the prison regulation and the penalogical interests of security and safety.[11] As nearly every prison regulation can have a logical connection to prison security, prison officials were given great latitude in limiting religious practices of inmates.

Congress, in response to this limitation on religious freedoms, passed the Religious Land Use and Institutionalized Persons Act (RLUIPA). The **RLUIPA** provides that

> No government shall impose a substantial burden on the religious exercise of a person residing in or confined to an institution ... even if the burden results from a rule of general applicability, unless the government demonstrates that imposition of the burden on that person—
>
> (1) is in furtherance of a compelling governmental interest; and
>
> (2) is the least restrictive means of furthering that compelling governmental interest.

The requirement that a restriction on religious exercise further a compelling interest in the least restrictive manner is a much higher standard to meet than a mere logical connection. The following case illustrates how courts have applied the RLUIPA.

Spratt v. Rhode Island Department of Corrections

482 F.3d 33 (1st Cir. 2007)

Wesley Spratt is serving a life sentence for murder in the maximum security unit of the Rhode Island Adult Correctional Institution (ACI). While in prison, Spratt underwent a religious awakening, and began attending Christian services at the ACI. Over time, the prison chaplains began allowing Spratt to preach to inmates during weekly services. In 2000, Spratt was ordained as a minister by the Universal Life Church. From 1996 until 2003, prison officials did not interfere with Spratt's religious activities or weekly preaching, nor were there disciplinary problems arising from his preaching during this seven-year period.

In 2003, a new warden was placed in charge of ACI. On October 15, 2003, Spratt was informed that he was no longer allowed to preach in the chapel because preaching by prisoners was against prison policy. Spratt filed a written complaint with the warden about the policy which was rebuffed. Spratt proceeded to file suit against the warden and Rhode Island Department of Corrections (DOC) alleging violation of the 1st and 14th Amendments and the Religious Land Use and Institutionalized Persons Act. Spratt requested the court order declaratory and injunctive relief, and damages of $40.29 (the cost of legal paper and copies). The DOC denied any wrongdoing and filed a motion for summary judgment which was granted.

---

11. *O'Lone v. Estate of Shabazz*, 482 U.S. 342 (1987).

The United States Court of Appeals for the First Circuit reversed. The court noted that a claim under RLUIPA includes four elements. The plaintiff inmate has the burden of satisfying the first two elements: that an inmate's religious exercise has been burdened and that the burden is **substantial.** If an inmate has established that his or her religious exercise has been substantially burdened, the burden then shifts to the government to show that the burden furthers a **compelling governmental interest** and that the burden is the **least restrictive means** of achieving that compelling interest.

It was not disputed that prohibiting Spratt from preaching placed a burden on his religious exercise and that the burden was substantial. As such the court easily found that Spratt had made a *prima facie* (sufficient) case that his religious exercise had been substantially burdened. The burden of proof therefore shifted to the prison officials to prove that the restriction was needed to further a compelling interest and there was no less restrictive alternative available to the prison to achieve this interest.

The only evidence submitted to the court by DOC evidencing the need to prohibit inmate preaching was an affidavit from an administrator. The affidavit, which was not supported by any underlying evidence, stated:

1. Permitting Spratt to preach could be dangerous because "placing an inmate in a position of actual or perceived leadership before an inmate group threatens security, as it provides the perceived inmate leader with influence within the administration"; and
2. "There is no less restrictive manner to accommodate Spratt's desire to preach to an inmate congregation, other than an outright ban."

The court of appeals was very troubled by the lack of evidence supporting the conclusory statements contained in the affidavit. As courts generally do, and as Congress stated courts should do, the court of appeals stated that it would give "due deference to the experience and expertise of prison and jail administrators" in determining prison policy.[12] The court, however, noted that the Congressional sponsors of the RULPIA stated, "inadequately formulated prison regulations and policies grounded on mere speculation, exaggerated fears, or post-hoc rationalizations will not suffice to meet the act's requirements."[13]

DOC's only evidence that the restriction on preaching was necessary to maintain prison security was the administrator's affidavit. While the court agreed that DOC has a compelling interest in maintaining prison security, it stated that there was no evidence presented establishing that barring Spratt from preaching furthered this interest. Merely asserting that Spratt's preaching caused security problems, absent any evidence that such problems have existed or are likely to occur in the future, is insufficient to meet its burden under the RLUIPA.

The court also held that DOC had not met its burden of showing there were not any less restrictive alternatives besides the absolute prohibition of inmate preaching. A prison "cannot meet its burden to prove least restrictive means unless it demonstrates that it has actually considered and rejected the efficacy of less restrictive measures be-

12. *Cutter v. Wilkinson*, 544 U.S. 709, 717 (2005).
13. 146 *Congressional Record* at S7775 (July 27, 2000).

fore adopting the challenged practice."[14] DOC admitted that it had not considered if there were any less restrictive means of fulfilling its security interests than a total ban on inmate preaching. Rather, DOC argued that any amount of preaching would be "dangerous to institutional security under any circumstances." The court rejected this contention. Noting that inmates are permitted to preach in federal and a number of other prisons, that inmates are permitted to be "leaders" under other circumstances, and that there were no security problems during the seven years Spratt had been permitted to preach, the court found the assertion by DOC to be without merit.

In the end, the court of appeals reversed the granting of summary judgment, and remanded the case to the District Court for additional testimony and consideration of evidence needed to support the claims of Spratt and DOC.

How do you think this case would have been decided prior to RLUIPA? Is this what Congress intended?

Conclusion

The rights possessed by prisoners is a complex area of the law that forces courts, and to some degree society, to balance competing interests. While we accept that individuals, even convicted criminals have certain rights, it is also natural to feel that people found guilty of a crime deserve to be punished and forfeiting constitutional protections is part of that punishment. When all is said and done, absent a clear constitutional violation, the Supreme Court has generally resolved this conflict by giving due deference to corrections administrators so that they have the ability to operate a safe and secure prison. In the next chapter, we look at an even more controversial and complex area as we explore legal aspects of capital punishment.

14. *Spratt* at 41, quoting *Warsoldier v. Woodford*, 418 F.3d 989, 999 (9th Cir.2005).

Chapter Thirteen

Death Penalty Law

What do you think about the death penalty or **capital punishment,** as we also call it? Do you support it or oppose it in the United States or anywhere in the world for that matter? There is a good chance that you have already formed an opinion. You may be strongly and morally in favor of it, believing a life for life is the best form of justice. You might advocate some of the following positions. "I would love to pull the switch and let the monster fry." "Justice demands that killers be killed." You may even celebrate when you get news of an execution.

On the other hand, you may be absolutely against and appalled by the death penalty. You may feel that we lower ourselves to the level of the killer when we kill, arguing two wrongs do not make a right. You may take part in a candlelight vigil at a prison prior to an execution where you sing songs of love, pray, and hold hands with a stranger. You might carry a sign that says: "The death penalty is barbaric!" "This is suicide by state."

The purpose of this chapter is not to change your mind or personal beliefs about capital punishment. Instead, it is to provide an overview of the topic in a historical, national, and international context and give you an opportunity to confront the issues and explore the pros and cons at greater depth. However you end up feeling about the death penalty in the end is not as important as the fact that you took the opportunity to learn more about it from a broader perspective and considered the issues surrounding it that are so divisive in the world today.

The Spotlight and Infamy through Execution

On December 30, 2006, a newspaper headline read: "Saddam hanged: The ex-dictator goes to the gallows before sunrise, executed by vengeful countrymen after a quarter-century of brutality."[1] Another headline read: "Saddam is the King of Swing: Bye-Bye to the Butcher of Baghdad as Diabolical Dictator is Hanged Before Dawn to Delight of Oppressed Iraqis."[2] Photographs taken just before the hanging grimly showed the seemingly calm ex-dictator with a rope around his neck. The pictures were published around

1. The Salt Lake Tribune, Dec. 30, 2006, at A1.

2. *See e.g., Lathem, Niles and Gittens, Haslam. "Saddam is the King of Swing." New York Post* on the Web December, 30 Dec. 2006, http://www.nypost.com/seven/12302006/news/worldnews/saddam_is_the_king_of_swing by Niles Lathem and Hasam Gittens, December 30, 2006.

the world. Additionally, a secretly recorded video that was posted on the Internet captured portions of the actual hanging.

Saddam Hussein was executed by the Iraqi government just two months after he was formally convicted by a jury of his Iraqi peers and only six days after he lost his appeal. Justice was swift and final. Officially, he was executed for "crimes against humanity," stemming from his role in the 1982 killings of the 148 men and boys.[3] Though his formal convictions stemmed from killings that took place more than two decades ago, he was implicated in the deaths and misery of hundreds of thousands of his countrymen during his dictatorial reign.

Reactions to Hussein's execution were mixed around the world. He was both mourned and hailed as a martyr — "a Holy Warrior."[4] Libyans flew flags at half-mast and thousands of Muslims protested and staged anti-American rallies. Human rights activists were outraged by the hanging. Others celebrated in the streets, some jubilantly firing guns into the air in celebration. Many Iraqi, Iranian, Kuwaiti, British and French citizens supported the execution given Hussein's history.[5] A strong majority of Americans favored the hanging, even with the swirling division and politics over the war in Iraq. Since the Nuremberg trials that followed World War II, where high-level Nazi war criminals were hanged for their roles in the deaths of millions in the Holocaust, no other single execution has likely received such worldwide attention and been the cause of so much reaction — both positive and negative.

As an additional example, one of the most significant and high-profile American executions in recent times involved another infamous mass killer, Timothy McVeigh. He killed scores of fellow citizens due to his own depraved sense of justice. No one old enough to remember will ever forget that moment in 1995 when they learned about the unfathomable bombing of the Murrah Federal Building in Oklahoma City. One hundred and sixty-eight innocent victims, including children, were brutally murdered that day, with hundreds more wounded by the powerful bomb blast. The media images of that event are forever ingrained in the minds of people around the world.[6]

With the bombing, McVeigh was the perpetrator of the single worst act of terrorism on American soil at that time. When he was caught, many literally wanted his blood. He received death threats. He was even often forced to wear a bullet proof vest when he was exposed to the public when moving back and forth from jail to the courtroom. In federal court, McVeigh was convicted of mass murders by a jury and sentenced to die for his heinous crimes.

For a strong majority of Americans, who demanded nothing less than death, justice was not served until June 11, 2001, when McVeigh was executed by lethal injection. Not long after eating his last meal, which consisted of two pints of mint chocolate ice

---

3. Santora, Marc (guest from The New York Times), *Troops on alert, worried about violent reaction,* The Salt Lake Tribune, Dec. 30, 2006, p. A15, col 6.

4. *See generally,* Walters, Tom. " *Reaction to Saddam's death mixed around the world.*" CTV News on the Web. 30 Dec. 2006. http://www.ctv.ca/servlet/ArticleNews/story/CTVNews/20061230/execution_reaction_061230/20061230?hub=CTVNewsAt11.

5. *Id.*

6. *See generally, "McVeigh execution: A 'completion of justice."* CNN on the Web. 11 Jun. 2001, August 10, 2007. http://www.archives.cnn.com/2001/LAW/06/11/MCVeigh.02/index.html.

cream, McVeigh was declared dead at 7:15 a.m., five minutes after he received the first of three injections that progressively and, most believe, painlessly killed him.[7] Ten family members of some victims watched the execution in person, while hundreds of others watched by closed circuit television. About 35 people gathered outside the prison with signs to show their support for the execution. About two hundred people showed up to protest the execution and the death penalty, in general. Signs were displayed, candles were lit, and prayers were offered. One sign read: "God said don't kill (even him)." Another read: "America doesn't need closure, it needs forgiveness."

McVeigh was the first person executed by the federal government since 1963. He was defiant and unapologetic to the end. He did not give any last verbal statement, but did leave a written one that read as follows: "I am the master of my fate: I am the captain of my soul."[8] Shortly after the completion of the "captain's" execution, President George W. Bush stated that McVeigh "met the fate he chose for himself six years ago" and "[u]nder the laws of our country the matter is concluded."[9] McVeigh caused unfathomable pain and suffering in the nation through his horrendous actions; he paid with his life. Was the taking of his life by lethal injection as **retribution** for his crimes enough? He presumably suffered no pain and died peacefully. Or, was the death penalty even necessary in order for justice to be adequately served?

Around the world and in the United States, thousands of murderers have been executed. Most of these executed felons may not be as well known as Hussein and McVeigh but, to the victims they left in their wakes, the effects of their crimes are every bit as significant. The circumstances and means of execution may vary, but the end — death by execution — was the same.

Thousands of convicted killers sit on death row today, awaiting their government sanctioned day of execution, if it ever arrives given the appeals process and evolving law. Meanwhile, the authors of thousands of books and websites continue to argue in favor of the time-honored penalty, while thousands more press for the end of what they view as a relic of a barbaric human history. The harm caused by many convicted death row inmates is unquestioned but the "proper" path society should take in this century to achieve justice is hotly disputed around the world. Should killers be killed by governments as payback or retribution? A life for a life? If so, under what circumstances and in what ways? If not, then what will satisfy justice? Finding a consensus for such an emotional, complex, and divisive topic may be impossible to achieve in this nation and around the world.

General Overview and Data on the Death Penalty

According to Gallup Poll surveys, a significant majority of Americans favor the death penalty. In 1994, 90% of Americans favored it while in 2006, 67% were in favor.[10] How-

---

7. Gillespie, Kay L (2003). *Inside the Death Chamber: Exploring Executions.* Boston: Pearson Education, Inc., at 94–97 (citation from the poem "Invictus").
8. Id.
9. Id.
10. Gallup Poll. *Death Penalty.* 12 Aug. 07, http://www.galluppoll.com/content/default.aspx?ci=1606.

ever, 2002 Gallup Poll surveys showed that 75% of U.S. Citizens oppose the death penalty for the mentally ill, 62% for the mentally retarded, and 69% for juveniles.[11]

The following figures show how capital punishment has been used in the United States:

- Since 1976, about 1,089 people have been executed, including 920 by lethal injection, 153 by electrocution, 11 by gas chamber, three by hanging, and two by firing squad.
- As of January 2007, there were 3,350 people on death row.
- Since 1976, 398 people have been executed in Texas, compared to 13 in California, three in Pennsylvania, and one in Connecticut.[12]
- Nationally 317 convicts were executed in 1996, 128 in 2005, and 53 in 2006.[13]
- Since 1890, more than 4,300 inmates in 26 states were executed in the electric chair alone.[14]

In the United States thirty-eight states and the federal government have legalized the death penalty.[15] The following twelve states have banned it as a form of punishment: Alaska, Hawaii, Iowa, Maine, Massachusetts, Michigan, Minnesota, North Dakota, Rhode Island, Vermont, West Virginia, and Wisconsin.[16] The following data shows that since 1976 there has been limited application of capital punishment in many states that have legalized it:

- Four states, including Kansas, New Hampshire, New Jersey, and New York, have had no executions.
- The United States Military has not had an execution.
- Six states executed only one person while another ten states executed more than one but less than eight people.[17]
- Several states, like Illinois and Florida, have placed moratoriums on executions in recent years because of concerns regarding evidence, false convictions, and botched executions.

Based on the above data, even though about 32 states legally allow the death penalty, a strong majority of the 50 states rarely if ever use it for punishment.

Internationally, about 69 countries maintain some form of the death penalty, while about 128 countries have banned it in practice or law. The following countries, for example, are considered anti-death penalty: Canada, Australia, Germany, Costa Rica,

---

11. *Id.*

12. *See* Death Penalty Information Center. *"Death Penalty Fact Sheet. Document: Facts About the Death Penalty August 1, 2007."* 10 Aug. 07, (For the first three bullet points), http://www.d.eath-penaltyinfo.org/FactSheet.pdf [hereinafter Death Penalty Fact Sheet].

13. U.S. Department of Justice, Bureau of Statistics. *"Capital Punishment Statistics."* August 12, 2007, http://ojp.usdoj.gov/bjs/cp.htm [hereinafter Capital Punishment Statistics].

14. Gillespie, *supra* note 7, at p. 62.

15. Capital Punishment Statistics, *supra* note 13.

16. *See e.g.*, Mannheimer, Michael J. Zydney, *When the Federal Death Penalty is "Cruel and Unusual."* U. Cin. L. Rev 819, 825 (2006).

17. Death Penalty Fact Sheet, *supra* note 12 (for the first three bullets).

Venezuela, Finland, France, Greece, United Kingdom, Mexico, Portugal, Spain, Poland, Norway, Ireland, Italy, Namibia, and South Africa. Some of the countries that maintain the death penalty include: United States, China, Iran, Afghanistan, Iraq, Vietnam, North Korea, South Korea, Ethiopia, Sudan, Somalia, and Egypt.[18]

The international trend since 1976 has clearly been toward the elimination of death penalty laws. Virtually all of our nation's closest allies have banned these laws, as have a large number of what might be regarded as predominantly Judeo-Christian countries. It appears from the list that the U.S. position is more consistent with the position of many nations we often oppose ideologically or politically. Do you think it should matter to us what other countries think about the death penalty? Or, should we just do what we want to without regard to others?

Pros and Cons

Thousands of pages, hundreds of books, and endless articles have been written by proponents and opponents of the death penalty. Data and reasoning of all sorts are invoked to "prove" which side is right. An overview of arguments from 1978 that is still commonly used in many textbooks sets forth some of the key arguments for and against the death penalty:[19]

Arguments for Capital Punishment

- ✓ It is a deterrent.
- ✓ It prevents recidivism.
- ✓ It is a moral duty.
- ✓ It is more economical than life imprisonment.
- ✓ It is kinder than life imprisonment.
- ✓ Those executed are the worst offenders and beyond rehabilitation.
- ✓ Those executed are less than human

Arguments against Capital Punishment

- ✓ It is not a deterrent.
- ✓ Murderers rarely murder again.
- ✓ It is morally wrong.
- ✓ It is less economical than life imprisonment.
- ✓ It is cruel and unusual punishment.
- ✓ Those executed are not beyond rehabilitation.
- ✓ Those executed may have some potential as humans, at least in some areas.

You will note that the pro and con statements above are really just parallel arguments.[20] One argues the death penalty is this, while the other says it is the exact opposite. You could go onto the Internet or into most libraries and find support and opposition for each issue. For you to really form your independent judgment, you would literally

18. The information in this paragraph comes from Death Penalty Information Center, *International. Document: Abolitionist and Retention Countries*, 10 Aug. 07, http://www.deathpenaltyinfo.org/article.php?scid=30&did=140.

19. Lester, David (1978). *The Death Penalty: Issues and Answers* (2nd ed.). Springfield, IL: Charles C. Thomas Publisher, citing Turnbull, C. (1978), *Death by Decree.* Natural History 87(5), 51–66).

20. *Id.*

need to take each position, read the different sides of the argument, and then make your decision based on your own weighing of each factor. The key to your overall decision would likely be the relative importance you place on one or more of the particular factors. Could your moral viewpoint alone override any other evidence you might find?

Rather than take each topic one by one, supported with randomly selected "proof," it will be more effective for you to read the following two statements on the topic. The opposing statements generally follow the checklist of arguments listed above. The goal of this exercise is to help you evaluate the death penalty by (1) presenting an intentionally biased but feasible argument written by an average, hypothetical citizen who favors the death penalty; (2) presenting the same type of argument opposing the penalty; and then (3) allowing you to compare the statements so you can reach your own conclusions. Your reaction to what you read may give you a general indication of your position or your general leanings on this issue. You might find yourself loving one position and hating the other, or you might conclude that both sides have their good and bad points, leaving you unsure what you think is best or right overall.

Why the Death Penalty Is Right (Hypothetical Argument for Study)

> Regardless of the costs or what the rest of the world does, the death penalty is the right and best thing for the United States. When the government holds people accountable for murder by taking away their lives, it sends the right message and deters others from committing murders. The following points summarize this position:
>
> - Because of the death penalty, people think twice about what they are doing and hopefully do not kill at all. If people aren't deterred and still kill someone, then killing the murderer is best because it rids the world of bad people.
> - Statistics show that lives are saved because of the death penalty; murder rates go down.
> - Executed inmates obviously won't be a future problem for society. There will be no recidivism (re-offending).
> - More important than all of the other arguments is the fact that the death penalty is simply the right thing to do morally. When people kill another human, moral law says they must pay with their own lives. Retribution requires a life for a life.
> - It is expensive to keep prisoners locked up for decades. With time in prison, inmates get common ailments associated with age, stress and lack of exercise—so costs increase dramatically. It will cost $30,000 or more per year to house murderers for life. Execute them, quickly if possible, and save millions of dollars.
> - Right now there are simply too many appeals and too many lawyers involved. The government needs to be more efficient by shortening the appeals process.

- The death penalty is not cruel and unusual punishment. First, the punishment fits the crime. Second, we have always had the death penalty in our nation (other than a few years in the early '70s for technical reasons). Third, those executed essentially die pain free, which is more than most people will get. Finally, it is more cruel to make someone sit in a tiny cell 23–24 hours a day for years on end.
- Those who are on death row are the worst kind of people. They committed crimes that are despicable and unforgivable. They don't deserve to live.

Once a person crosses the murder line, they have proven they are unworthy of life. There is no point in even trying to rehabilitate them. How could society ever trust them? We know some states are soft on crime and may let one of these crazed killers off on parole. Why take that chance? If they have killed once they can and likely will kill again. Execute them now so we do not have to take any chances and never have to fear them again. It's the right and best thing to do.

Now, compare that statement to the following anti-death penalty statement. The basic order of this argument parallels the first.

Why the Death Penalty Is Wrong (Sample Argument for Study)

The death penalty in the United States is immoral and outdated. It should be banned completely. The civilized world and many states have banned the death penalty because it violates the fundamental principles of human decency. When the government kills it dehumanizes people and sends the wrong message to society, especially kids who thought we were not supposed to kill. The following points summarize this position:

- All the major studies prove the death penalty does not deter future murderers. Most murders result from out-of-control passion, not planning. In fact, there is some research that shows a temporary increase in murder rates after an execution due to the **brutalization effect**.
- Murderers have one of the lowest recidivism rates of any criminals. If they get out of prison, they rarely re-offend and present little or no risk.
- If an innocent person is convicted and executed, the mistake is irreversible. More than one hundred people on death row have been exonerated or freed since the early 1970s. There is strong evidence that innocent people have been executed. Also, there is still too much discrimination in sentencing.
- Most important, the death penalty is morally wrong and lowers society to the level of the killers. It is not right to kill murderers when punishment in prison is adequate. Taking a life for a life is an outdated concept. Two wrongs do not make a right.
- Most killers have special circumstances that contributed to their actions. That does not excuse them but it should be a basis for recognizing that they are humans and worthy of forgiveness at some point.

- Spending many years in prison is retribution and a high price for killing someone. The loss of freedom, perhaps the greatest human right, is no small matter and is certainly not getting off easy.
- It is more expensive to execute murderers than to lock them up for life. After all the appeals and lawyers, it will take over a decade and cost millions of dollars to complete an execution. Given the irreversibility of an execution and the due process rights of our Constitution, taking shortcuts is not the answer. Ending the death penalty is.
- The death penalty is cruel and unusual punishment in the modern world. There have been too many cases where after-death photos and autopsies show that the death was painful. Electrocutions have caught people on fire and lethal injections have taken more than thirty painful minutes to work.

In conclusion, murderers must pay for their serious crimes but killing them is not the answer. It is inhumane and immoral. Many convicts on death row become model inmates, go through substantial changes, get treatment for mental illness, and help other inmates in need. They have human value and dignity even though they lose their freedom. Vengeance by death belongs to God.

This exercise is not a perfect method for studying the positions in this chapter, but through the sample arguments you can at least see the parallelism of each position and get a sense how some of the positions might be applied beyond reading a mere checklist of general arguments. Did you have any emotional reaction to some of the statements? It is now up to you to decide which factors are most important, which ones make the most sense to you, and, ultimately, which position you support. You might ultimately conclude that some factors, such as your own moral judgment or the practical issue of cost may be so significant to you that no amount of reason or evidence can change your view. Difficult issues generally require careful study and some difficult decision-making. Many people feel this is one of those difficult topics.

Historical Background for the Death Penalty

The death penalty or, capital punishment, is the formal term for a public authority, like government, to punish a person for a crime with death. The Latin phrase **"capitalis"** means "of the head." So "capital punishment," it appears, became the common phrase used to refer to punishment by death since beheading was amongst the most common forms of punishment used to carry out the penalty.

The death penalty has been a common feature around the world throughout known history. Through the centuries, criminals have been executed for committing such crimes as "bearing false witness, kidnaping, sexual immorality, witchcraft, idolatry, blasphemy, and sacrilege," as well as homicide, military crimes, and most felonies.[21]

21. "Capital punishment" in Walker, David (1980). *The Oxford Companion to Law.* Oxford: Clarendon Press, *at p.* 184.

The methods for causing death have been as varied as the reasons for the impositions of the ultimate penalty. Whether through drowning, stoning, poison, strangulation, exposure to wild beasts, decapitation, burning at the stake, crucifixion, torture, gas chamber, electrocution, and a myriad of other means, the end was the same—death.[22] People were executed in recent centuries under English Common law for such offenses as treason, murder, rape, and arson of a dwelling.[23] In 1688, under English law, about 50 offenses carried the death penalty. By 1820 there were about 240 capital offenses.[24] Since the colonies were under English rule, the use of the death penalty usually reflected the English common law. Over time, the number of offenses that qualified for the death penalty declined, the methods used to carry out the sentence became less cruel, and the court procedures utilized became more effective.

The Eighth Amendment

Because the Eighth Amendment prohibition against cruel and unusual punishment is the only statement in the U.S. Constitution directly dealing with punishment, it is the centerpiece for discussions about the death penalty. Is it cruel for the government to execute convicted felons and, if so, for which crimes and under what circumstances? Further, when is government sanctioned homicide, referred to as justifiable homicide, usual and accepted?

One thing that is clear from the preceding section is that from colonial days to the present, punishment by death has been a common feature of American justice. Men, women, and children have been executed for a multitude of offenses and by various methods, most of which would not be acceptable today.

The Bill of Rights, which contains the Eighth Amendment, was ratified in 1791. In typical fashion, nowhere does the Constitution contain definitions of "cruel" or "unusual" (just as it does not define due process, probable cause, and other key phrases). But given the historical context of the Eighth Amendment and statements of the Supreme Court, the phrase was never intended to mean there could be no death penalty. The Eighth Amendment was written during a period in history when the death penalty was common place. In fact, the Fifth Amendment's prohibitions against the loss of "life" without due process of law, together with the Eighth Amendment's prohibition against cruel and unusual punishment, imply that the death penalty is acceptable so long as the trial is fair and there is no more pain than necessary to kill the guilty.[25]

During the 19th Century, U.S. Supreme Court cases focused not on the question of whether it was constitutionally permitted to use the death penalty but instead on which methods were permissible.[26] The following is a summary of the first case in

---

22. *Id.*

23. "Capital punishment" in Black's Law Dictionary, (8th ed. 2004), at 223.

24. *Id.*

25. Barry Latzer (1998). *Death Penalty Cases: Leading U.S. Supreme Court Cases on Capital Punishment.* Boston: Butterworth-Heinemann, at 2.

26. *Id.*

which the Supreme Court ruled on the cruel and unusual punishment clause in a death penalty case.

Wilkerson v. Utah

99 U.S. 130 (1879)

In about 1877, the Defendant Wilkerson was convicted by a jury in the Utah Territory for the first degree murder of William Baxter. The trial judge ordered that the defendant "be safely kept" until he was to be "taken from [his] place of confinement to some place within this district ... [to[be publicly shot until ... dead."[27]

The Supreme Court reviewed the case to determine if the death sentence was appropriate. The Territorial law in effect at the time read that a person convicted of first degree murder "shall suffer death" or in some cases "hard labor in a penitentiary for life."[28] A prior law in effect until 1876, just prior to the murder at issue, provided that punishment by death could be carried out by shooting, hanging, or beheading, as directed by the court or as chosen by the Defendant. A law that was enacted shortly before this case, unfortunately, did not specify how the person should be killed. The Defendant, therefore, argued to the Supreme Court that the trial court improperly chose the method for his execution.

After reviewing different historical methods for executing guilty murderers, the Supreme Court evaluated the territorial law in this case. It concluded that the usual methods for punishment in cases when the law was silent about the method for the execution were by hanging or shooting. The territorial legislature, the Supreme Court continued, had the right to decide how a convicted murderer should die so long as the method was not "cruel and unusual." Then the Court added that it would be difficult to exactly define the boundaries of cruel and unusual punishment "but it [was] safe to affirm that punishment of torture, ... [is] forbidden by [the Eighth Amendment]."[29] Of interest, the Court went on to state that executions such as being "drawn or dragged to the place of execution," embowelled alive, beheaded or quartered, burned alive for treason committed by a female; or dissected or other "atrocities" would be unnecessarily cruel and would violate the Eighth Amendment.[30] With that the Court held that execution by shooting for the crime of murder in the first degree did not violate the Eighth Amendment.

Remember, in the *Wilkerson case* there was never any question about whether the government could execute a convicted murderer. The only questions were regarding the method and who would choose. Today, should the Supreme Court even consider whether the Eighth Amendment allows the death penalty in the first place or is that issue forever resolved in your mind? Some of the cases discussed below may affect your viewpoint on this issue.

---

27. *Wilkerson v. Utah*, 99 U.S. 150, 151 (1878).
28. *Id.* at 152.
29. *Id.* at 135–36.
30. *Id.*

Proportionality and Cruel and Unusual Punishment

It was not until 1910 that the Supreme Court first ruled that a particular punishment was "cruel and unusual." That case was *Weems v. United States.*[31] In *Weems*, the Court held that punishment with heavy chains and painful labor for twelve years was disproportionate for falsifying government documents. The punishment was too harsh and, therefore, was not proportionate, meaning it did not fit the crime.

Over the decades after *Weems*, the concept of **proportionality** became more important in death penalty cases. Under the proportionality law, a Court would have to look at the nature of the crime and then decide if the penalty of death fit the crime. For instance, is the death penalty proportionate or disproportionate for the crime of rape? For a long time courts held that the death penalty for rape was proportionate, so many rapists were executed. In a 1977 case reviewed below, the court finally said otherwise. While the *Weems* case was not a death penalty case, it did establish the main standard the court would utilize over the next 100 years in weighing the constitutionality of the death penalty.

Abolishment and Re-Birth of the Death Penalty

For years, many had complained that the death penalty was handed out arbitrarily and, more often than not, in a discriminatory fashion. Many, as well, argued that the penalty constituted cruel and unusual punishment and should be banned altogether in our "evolving society." On the heels of the tumultuous 1960s and in the midst of the conflicts over the Vietnam War that was growing increasingly unpopular, the Court issued an important opinion that stopped further use of the death penalty at that time. It also changed the sentences of hundreds of convicts from death to life sentences. The following case was an important turning point in death penalty law in America.

Furman v. Georgia

408 U.S. 238 (1972)

In this 1972 case, the United States Supreme Court for the first time ruled that the death penalty, as was being implemented in the country at that time, violated the Eighth Amendment prohibition against cruel and unusual punishment. Because the opinion was a 5–4 decision (meaning five Justices voted one way and four the other) and one in which the five Justices could not clearly agree upon the exact rationale for the opinion (called a ***per curiam*** decision because no single justice wrote the main opinion), the exact ruling is essentially impossible to sort out.

31. 217 U.S. 349 (1910)

Some of the Justices argued that the death penalty itself was **per se** unconstitutional under the Eighth Amendment as cruel and unusual punishment. Others argued that the only problem was the way courts were handing out death sentences. Judges and juries, they contended, were given too much discretion or latitude in deciding who got the death penalty and who did not. Such **arbitrary death sentences** violated the Due Process Clause of the Constitution. They presented data, which they concluded, proved there was serious discrimination in the justice system, especially against minority groups and the poor. Justice Potter Stewart poignantly observed: "I simply cannot tolerate the infliction of a sentence of death under legal systems that permit this unique penalty to be so wantonly and so freakishly imposed."[32]

In the end, it was clear that, at a minimum, the Supreme Court was demanding that before the death penalty could be reinstated in the United States, a more fair, consistent, legislatively controlled, and predictable system had to be instituted in the states. In other words, the states had to clean up their acts before they could use the death penalty again. After a hiatus of several years, the Court reviewed the issue and reinstituted the death penalty in the following case.

Gregg v. Georgia

428 U.S. 153 (1976)

Four years after the *Furman* case the Supreme Court was ready to readdress the constitutionality of the death penalty in the United States. In an effort to get the death penalty reinstated, Georgia went to extensive effort to create new laws for the death penalty that got rid of the arbitrary and discriminatory methods used in the past.

The new law established concrete procedures and set forth a list of characteristics that had to be present in a case in order for a convicted murderer to face the death penalty. There had to be two separate trials—one to first determine if the defendant is guilty. If found guilty, another trial was held to decide if the person should receive the death penalty under the law.

In the second trial, before the jury could recommend the death penalty, it had to look at (1) the **aggravating factors**, generally listed in the law but defined as those that made the murder worse than usual and (2) the **mitigating factors**, meaning those which tended to excuse or minimize the defendant's behavior to some degree and reduce the effect of the aggravating factors. For instance, aggravating factors might be a killing that was a planned, intentional act against a child and which included rape and torture. These specific acts or circumstances were specifically listed in the law as aggravating factors, taking discretion away from the jury. Mitigating factors might be such things as the fact that the person had never been in trouble before, was sexually abused by his father, had turned himself in, and showed sincere remorse. In summary, a jury would have to look at a list of aggravating factors in the law, decide if any were present in the case, and then determine if the guilty person merited the death penalty due to those aggravating factors, despite any mitigating factors that might exist.

---

32. *Id.* at 310. ; See, e.g., Latzer, Barry. (1998). *Death Penalty Cases: Leading U.S. Supreme Court Cases on Capital Punishment.* Boston: Butterworth-Heinemann, at 19.

The Supreme Court was satisfied with the new Georgia law. It, therefore, essentially reversed the *Furman* case and reinstituted the death penalty. The Court's one clear holding in the divided opinion was that capital punishment was not, per se, unconstitutional under the Eighth Amendment as cruel and unusual punishment. As long as the procedures for imposing the penalty at least met the level of the new rigorous standards of the Georgia law, then the death penalty could be carried out. During this period in the mid-1970s, thirty-five states changed their laws. The Georgia statute became the model.

Shortly after that case, the first execution took place in the U.S. since *Furman* (actually since about 1968). In 1976, Gary Gilmore killed a motel manager and a service station attendant. He was convicted for the separate murders and sentenced to die by a Utah court. He requested execution by firing squad and claimed his punishment was proper.[33] He was quoted as saying: "You can't take someone's life or do something wrong and then start to sniffle because you are punished."[34] He dropped all of his appeals and essentially taunted the State of Utah to "just do it."[35] He wanted to die—he tried to commit suicide twice and called the Utah Board of Pardons "cowards" for not quickly enforcing his death sentence.[36] Despite vigorous protests from around the world Gilmore was shot by a firing squad in 1977. Books were written about Gilmore, one by Norman Mailer called *The Executioner's Song*, and a movie was made about his life. His was no ordinary case because with his execution, the death penalty was officially reinstated in the United States. Opponents lamented the return to what they viewed as our old barbaric ways. Proponents of the death penalty were relieved to have such an important tool back. The death penalty was back but the landscape in the nation had changed and a legal trend away from the death penalty slowly began to grow.

Race and the Death Penalty

Frederick Douglass, a former slave, scholar, and leader, once said:

> Justice is often painted with bandaged eyes. She is described in forensic eloquence, as utterly blind to wealth or poverty, high or low, white or black but a mask of iron, however thick, could never blind American justice, when a black man happens to be on trial.[37]

If he were living today, Mr. Douglass, among other things, would likely argue that Lady Justice is still not blind when it comes to the death sentence for African Americans and other minorities.

33. Stettler, Jeremiah. *Shots heard 'round the U.S.*, *The Salt Lake Tribune*, January 20, 2007, at B1 and B5.

34. *Id.* at B5.

35. Gillespie, *supra note 7, at 70.*

36. Stettler, *supra* note 33, at B1 and B5.

37. Ogletree, Jr., Charles, *Black Man's Burden: Race and the Death Penalty in America*, 81 Or. L. Rev. 15, 15 (2002) (quoting Douglass' April 16, 1883 speech found in 4 *The Life and Writings of Frederick Douglass, Reconstruction and After*, 357 (Philip S. Foner ed., 1975).

Like most other topics covered in this chapter, you could find research supporting both sides arguing whether discrimination is an issue in death penalty cases. Some researchers insist that there is no clear evidence that minorities are being discriminated against in capital cases. Others exclaim that the data prove otherwise. Of the 3,350 people on death row in 2005, 42% were Black, 56% were White, and 2% were from other races.[38] So, even though Blacks make up only about 13% of the U.S. population,[39] they make up 42 out of every 100 death row inmates. One study concluded that there was some discrimination in 96% of the states where race issues have been studied.[40] As the Supreme Court noted in the *Furman* case that declared executions unconstitutional in 1972, there was evidence of arbitrary and discriminatory decisions that negatively affected minorities and the poor. Justice Thurgood Marshall, the first African American on the United States Supreme Court, made the following statement in 1992, summarizing the issues of race in death penalty cases: "I wish I could say that racism and prejudice were only distant memories ... and that liberty and equality were just around the bend."[41] The data suggest that discrimination is still an issue in death penalty cases.

Mentally Disabled Subjects and the Death Penalty

What if the mental capacity of convicted murderers is such that they have impaired judgment or limited reasoning ability. Should the law still hold them to the same standards as others? Historically, the answer has generally been—yes. For instance, Jerome Bowden was mentally retarded with an I.Q. of 65. He was convicted of murder and sentenced to die. Despite public uproar, he was executed in Georgia in 1986. The Board of Pardons had determined that despite Bowden's mental deficiencies, he understood the nature of his crime and punishment.[42]

In the 1989 case *Penry v. Linaugh*,[43] the U.S. Supreme Court ruled that the Eighth Amendment did not necessarily preclude the execution of a mentally retarded person like Penry, who had the mental capacity of a six-year-old. A convicted person's mental limitations, the Court explained, could be considered in the big picture as one of the factors a jury could take into consideration in deciding whether to sentence a mentally challenged person to death. But, standing on its own, the mental limitations of the person were not enough to categorically prohibit such executions.[44] Thirteen years later, the U.S. Supreme Court, with a few new faces and some changing attitudes about the death penalty, readdressed the issue and changed its interpretation of the law in the following case.

---

38. U.S. Department of Justice, Bureau of Statistics. "*Capital Punishment 2005,* August 12, 2007," at http://ojp.usdoj.gov/bjs/abstracts/cp05.htm.
39. U.S. Census Bureau. "*The Black Population in the United States,*" (at link "The Black Alone or in Combination Population in the United States"). 15 Aug 2007. http://www.census.gov/population/www/socdemo/race/black.html, at Table 1.
40. Ogletree, *supra* note 37, at 16.
41. Id. at 27.
42. *Atkins v. Virginia*, 536 U.S. 304, 313 n.8 (2002).
43. 492 U.S. 302 (1989)
44. *Penry v. Lynaugh*, 492 U.S. 302, 340 (1989).

Atkins v. Virginia
536 U.S. 304 (2002)

Daryl Atkins and William Jones, with a loaded handgun, robbed Eric Nesbitt of his money and then forced him to drive to an automated teller machine where they stole additional cash. After the robbery, Atkins and Jones took the victim to an isolated area and killed him by shooting him eight times. Atkins was caught, tried, and convicted of murder. He was given the death penalty because it was believed that his prior felony record proved he posed a significant risk of future danger and because of the "vileness" of the crime. He was given the death penalty, despite evidence that he was mildly mentally retarded.[45]

The Court noted that starting in 1988, largely in reaction to the *Bowden* case that was discussed above, Congress passed legislation reinstating the death penalty, but specifically prohibiting it upon persons who are mentally retarded. Thereafter, many states followed suit. Because of those changes, the Supreme Court concluded there was a "consistent pattern of change" toward ending such executions. In the Court's view, there was now a "national consensus" against executing the mentally retarded.[46]

In addition to the issue of a consensus, the Court emphasized that given the mental disabilities of a mentally retarded person, the purposes for the death penalty would not be served. Death imposed on people who may not have understood the nature and consequences of their actions or who could not control their impulses would not deter future crimes nor meet the purposes of retribution required in death penalty cases. The death penalty, if it should be used at all, should be reserved for the most blameworthy individuals and not those who most "face a special risk of wrongful execution."[47] The Court did not give an exact definition of "mentally retarded" but, instead, left that up to the states and science to develop or define.

The Execution of Juvenile Murderers

For more than 200 years, our nation allowed the execution of people who committed capital offenses as minors. From the beginning the death penalty could have theoretically been imposed on anyone over age seven. At least 281 juveniles under age eighteen and 126 under seventeen years old had been executed in the United States.[48] Is it cruel and unusual punishment to execute a juvenile for horrible crimes committed under the age of eighteen? Do juveniles know enough or have they developed mentally enough to be held accountable to such a degree? What do you think? The death penalty for juveniles was reaffirmed in the following 1988 case, *Stanford v. Kentucky* but was reversed just over a decade later in *Roper v. Simmons*, which you will also find below. Both cases cover the same issue but the results were totally opposite. In the end,

45. 536 U.S. 304, 308 (2002).
46. *Id.* at 315–16.
47. *Id.* at 319–21.
48. *Id.* at 368.

hopefully you will understand the current law, but also realize the possible implications of the Supreme Court's flip-flop on precedent in future death penalty cases.

Stanford v. Kentucky

492. U.S. 361(1988)

In 1981, seventeen-year-old Kevin Stanford was convicted of killing 20-year-old Barbel Poore.[49] Stanford and an accomplice robbed Poore's workplace. The two criminals raped and sodomized her repeatedly and ended up shooting Poore point blank in the face and the back of the head. The robbery netted the pair a few hundred cartons of cigarettes, two gallons of gas, and a little cash. Because his crimes were brutal and he had a bad juvenile record, Stanford was tried as an adult. He was convicted, and sentenced to death.

After his sentence was handed down, public clamor was significant because Stanford was a minor when he committed the crimes. For many, his age was irrelevant; he was a cold-blooded killer. Stanford argued that as a society we had evolved to such an extent that the execution of minors should no longer be constitutionally permissible. He also argued that the Constitution should be interpreted flexibly and that executing him or any other person for acts committed as a minor was contrary to the "evolving standards" of our modern society.[50] Stanford also argued that since kids under 18 do not carefully or intelligently drive, drink or vote, they are simply incapable of understanding the seriousness of murder and should be held less accountable.

Unfortunately for Stanford, the Supreme Court voted 5–4 to uphold his death sentence and held that the death penalty for a person who murders someone while 16 or 17 years old did not "offend" the Eighth Amendment.[51] Stanford remained on death row for over 20 years until 2003 when the Governor of Kentucky **commuted** his death sentence, largely in reaction to the Court ruling in the Atkins case discussed above (regarding the execution of the mentally retarded). The Governor changed his sentence to life without the possibility of parole.

Only about 15 years after the *Stanford* case and after a few changes in the make-up of the Supreme Court, the same issue was brought back before the Court for a new look in the Twenty-First Century. The Court changed its Constitutional interpretation in the following case.

Roper v. Simmons

543 U.S. 551 (2005)

Christopher Simmons was a seventeen-year-old junior in high school when he told two of his friends that he wanted to commit murder, which he thought they could get away with since they were minors. Two of the three boys followed through with the plan.

---

49. *Stanford v. Kentucky*, 492. U.S. 361, 365 (1988) (because the issue was the same, the Court combined this case with the case *Wilkins v. Illinois*, 487 U.S. 1233 (1988)). Only *Stanford* is covered in this chapter.

50. *Id.* at 369 (quoting *Trop v. Dulles*, 356 U.S. 86, 101 (1958).

51. *Id.* at 380.

They killed the unfortunate victim, Shirley Crook, by tying her up with duct tape and throwing her off a railroad trestle. The victim, a wife and mother of two, was drowned. Afterwards, Simmons bragged to his friends that he had killed a woman. He was arrested and ended up confessing to his crime. Given the nature of the depraved crime, Simmons was tried as an adult and after a short trial was convicted of murder. The prosecution sought the death penalty.[52]

During the sentencing phase of the trial, defense counsel argued that given the fact Simmons was only 17 when he committed the murder, he should not receive the death penalty. Much like Stanford had done in his case, Simmons argued that the legislature had "wisely" determined that juveniles are just not responsible enough to drink, be a juror, or see certain movies. Simmons was shown to be very impulsive, immature, and susceptible to outward influence, as well as being from a broken home that contributed to many of his problems.[53] The trial court did not buy his excuses and sentenced him to death. Eventually the case made its way to the United States Supreme Court.

The Supreme Court reiterated the long-held views that punishment cannot be excessive and that it should be proportionate to the crime committed. Significantly, the Court noted the following: "By protecting even those convicted of heinous crimes, the Eighth Amendment, reaffirms the duty of the government to respect the dignity of all persons."[54] The meaning of cruel and unusual punishment, the court continued, must take into account "the evolving standards of decency that mark the progress of a maturing society."[55]

After reviewing changing public sentiments about executing juvenile offenders, the Supreme Court held that the juvenile death penalty was a disproportionate penalty in violation of the Eighth Amendment protection against cruel and unusual punishment.[56] The court noted that 30 states prohibited executions in such cases and that in the 20 that still allowed it, executions were rare. Since the 1989 *Stanford* case, only six states had executed prisoners for crimes they committed as juveniles. The court also noted that the U.S. was the only nation on earth that still officially sanctioned juvenile death. The Court overruled *Stanford* because the Court was convinced that society now viewed juveniles as "categorically less culpable than the average criminal."[57] The Court saw a clear trend toward the abolishment of the practice of executing those who committed the crime as juveniles and concluded that the character of juveniles was less developed.[58] The fact that juveniles are "immature and irresponsible" gives them greater claim to forgiveness than adults, the Court ruled, and makes their conduct less morally reprehensible. To the Court, death is not warranted for a person who is less culpable and just an immature and irresponsible kid who is not likely to be deterred by fear of the death penalty.

Do you agree with the *Stanford* opinion more or the *Simmons* opinion? Should those who commit murder in their teens be categorically shielded from the death penalty?

52. *Roper v. Simmons*, 543 U.S. 551, 556–57.
53. *Id.* at 558–59.
54. *Id.* at 560–61.
55. *Id.*
56. *Id.* at 575.
57. *Id.* at 567.
58. *Id.* at 567–58.

What if someone commits murder on her 18th birthday? What changed besides age to automatically make that person eligible for the death penalty? What are the implications of these opposite rulings for other death penalty precedents?

Death Penalty for Rape as Cruel and Unusual Punishment

In U.S. History many men, especially minority men accused of raping a white woman, were executed. The Classic book and movie, *To Kill a Mockingbird* addresses that issue. As case law developed in the 1970s after *Furman*, it was the right time for the court to determine if a death penalty for rape was proportionate to the crime. It did so in the following case.

Coker v. Georgia

433 U.S. 584 (1976)

The Defendant Coker was a career criminal. He had served various sentences for murder, rape, kidnaping, and aggravated assault. He escaped from prison and raped Elnita Carver after committing armed robbery against the victim's husband and tying him up. He was convicted of raping a woman during the commission of a robbery. Georgia law read that "a person convicted of rape shall be punished by death or by imprisonment for life...." Under the newly revised Georgia death penalty laws, discussed under *Gregg* above, the jury had to find at least one of the statutory aggravating circumstances to warrant the death penalty. The jury easily found two aggravating circumstances: Coker had committed the rape while committing an armed robbery and he had a prior conviction for a capital felony. He was sentenced to die by electrocution. Coker appealed claiming that the penalty of death was not proportionate to the crime of rape and was, therefore, an unconstitutionally disproportionate penalty.

In reviewing the case, the Court emphasized that it had consistently stated that punishments can't be "barbaric" or excessive in relation to the crime charged. An excessive punishment, the Court explained, appears to be "the purposeless and needless imposition of pain and suffering" or "is grossly out of proportion to the severity of the crime."[59] In the end, the Court held that the death penalty for the rape of an adult woman was grossly "disproportionate and excessive." The Court looked at national legislative trends away from making rape a capital offense. Only sixteen states allowed death for rape. The Court emphasized that "without doubt" rape was a serious crime and that the convict should be punished seriously but refused to compare it to murder.[60]

---

59. *Coker v. Georgia*, 433 U.S. 584, 592 (1976).
60. *Id.* at 592.

Errors and the Death Penalty

Once a person has been executed, the action is obviously irreversible. That is why it is so important to ensure that the legal proceedings and appeal's processes are thorough in order to eliminate jury errors. There are some death penalty proponents who maintain that there is no clear proof that any innocent people have ever been executed. You cannot universally prove a negative so cases have to be reviewed individually.

There is strong evidence to support the view that innocent people have been sentenced to death and executed. The authors of *In Spite of Innocence* claim, for instance, that they have documented more than 400 cases where innocent people were sentenced to death and at least 24 were executed.[61] It is known that at least 120 people have been released from death row since 1973, including 35 from 2000–2004, after new evidence **exonerated** or freed them.[62] In 2000, the Governor of Illinois stopped further death penalties after reviewing what he called Illinois' "shameful" record and declaring: "I can't support a system which in its administration has proven so fraught with error and come so close to the ultimate nightmare—the state's taking an innocent life."[63] The Governor admitted to at least 13 mistaken convictions since 1977.[64]

Despite the possibility of errors, most Americans still favor capital punishment. Others, seeing errors and inconsistency, continue to argue against the death penalty. In a revealing statement, Justice Harry Blackmun said the following just before retiring from the Court:

> From this day forward, I no longer shall tinker with the machinery of death. For more than 20 years I have endeavored — indeed, I have struggled — along with a majority of this Court, to develop procedural and substantive rules that would lend more than a mere appearance of fairness to the death penalty endeavor. Rather than continue to coddle the Court's delusion that the desired level of fairness has been achieved and the need for regulation eviscerated, I feel morally and intellectually obligated simply to concede that the death experiment has failed.[65]

Conclusion

The death sentence has a long and storied history in our nation. In colonial times, several hundred different capital offenses and various means of execution existed. Since the passage of the Eighth Amendment in 1791, the death penalty has been commonplace and, overall, not viewed as cruel and unusual punishment. The issue for much

---

61. Gillespie, *supra* note 7 at 114–15.
62. Death Penalty Fact Sheet, *supra* note 12.
63. Gillespie, *supra* note 7 at 114.
64. *Id.*
65. Ogletree, *supra* note 37, at 15.

of our history has not been whether the death penalty was cruel and unusual but rather which methods should be allowable.

A strong majority of Americans support the death penalty. Despite that fact, there has been a decline in the number of executions in recent years and in the number of states and nations that allow it. In the early Seventies, the Court banned the death penalty altogether largely because the Court found that it was being implemented in an arbitrary and discriminatory fashion. In 1976, after many states modified their laws to make the court procedures more uniform and less arbitrary, the death penalty was reinstated in the nation.

Since that time, over 1,000 people have been executed across the country. Through a series of cases, the Supreme Court has ruled that the execution of rapists is disproportionate to the crime committed, and that the death penalty for those who are mentally retarded and who committed their capital offenses when they were minors is cruel and unusual punishment. The Court has been highly influenced by national and international trends against the death penalty.

Finally, it is apparent that over the past centuries, mistakes have been made. There is strong evidence that the death penalty has been used in discriminatory fashion and that innocent people have been sentenced to death and executed.

In conclusion, like most topics, especially those with so many moral, cultural, or legal implications, any person can come up with a long list of pros and cons to support his or her viewpoints. Ultimately, you have to look at the key issues and decide for yourself which factors are most important to you in the 21st Century.

Chapter Fourteen

Juvenile Law

The American juvenile justice system is distinct from its adult counterpart, yet enjoys many of the same underlying principles. It is often approached with skepticism or misunderstood by those who lack a fundamental understanding about its origins, development, purposes, procedures and practices. This chapter will review the American Juvenile Justice System from a legal perspective, exploring the laws, rules and United States Supreme Court cases that have molded its development. After studying this chapter you should have a basic understanding of juvenile court history, the differences and similarities between the juvenile and the adult systems, current processing and procedures and current trends.

Part I: Development and Evolution

Common Law through 19th Century

Under English common law and through much of the 19th century in the United States, children under seven years old were not capable of forming criminal intent and therefore could not be held accountable for their actions in court. Between the ages of seven and fourteen, there was a presumption that juveniles could not form criminal intent, but that could be rebutted by evidence of intent. In other words, if the government could present sufficient evidence that the juvenile was capable of forming the mental intent necessary for the offense, a seven- to fourteen-year-old could be tried, convicted and sentenced in the adult criminal system. At age fourteen, children were presumed capable of forming criminal intent and held accountable for their actions as adults.

As the United States changed from an agrarian to a more industrialized nation during the 19th century, the labor system of youth likewise transformed. Children as young as four were reportedly working in factories. During the early 1800s, children composed 47 to 55% of the labor force in the cotton mills of New England.[1] The use of child labor depressed the wages of adults, and weakened family ties due in part to long work hours. Along with the growth of factories, large numbers of immigrants contributed to the numbers of homeless and impoverished children in urban centers of the United States. Traditional familial control over children suffered, and children engaged in unlawful behavior were treated, under the common law, as adult offenders.

1. Krisberg, Barry (2005). *Juvenile Justice: Redeeming Our Children*, Sage Publications, at 25.

Houses of Reform

The New York House of Refuge opened in 1825 and is recognized as the first reform institution for juveniles in the United States. It was quickly followed by similar reform institutions in Boston (1826) and Philadelphia (1828) and by 1868 an estimated 40,000 to 50,000 youths were housed in over 20 such institutions across the country.[2] Reform institutions addressed concerns that delinquent children were being placed with more seasoned adults in adult correctional facilities, increasing their likelihood of becoming adult offenders. On the other side were concerns that judges and juries would not punish or intervene with delinquent children because the only option was use of adult courts and correctional facilities.

Houses of reform sought to teach children through a structured daily regime, often consisting of eight hours of work, then four hours of school and religious study and prayer. Corporal punishment was among the forms of control used on the children.[3]

State Establishment of Juvenile Courts

The next step in the evolution of juvenile justice occurred in Cook County, Illinois, in 1899, where the first official juvenile court was established. Other states quickly followed its lead, and by 1923, all but Connecticut and Wyoming had adopted a court system for the adjudication of juvenile offenders that was completely separate and independent of the adult system. By the early 1940s, all states had adopted a juvenile court system.[4]

The early reformers were appalled by the condition of adult correctional facilities and by the adult procedures and penalties inflicted upon children. They believed society's role with delinquent children should not be confined to determining their guilt or innocence. The adult goal of retribution was replaced with those of treatment and rehabilitation. The child was perceived as criminal only because he had not received the appropriate moral training and education that was available to the non-criminal child. With treatment, he could be cured of this ill and become a productive member of society.[5] Society had a duty to ascertain, "What is he, how has he become what he is, and what had best be done in his interest and in the interest of the state to save him from a downward career." The child—essentially good, as they saw it—was to be made "to feel that he is the object of the state's care and solicitude," not that he was under arrest or on trial. The rules of criminal procedure were therefore altogether inapplicable. The apparent rigidities, technicalities, and harshness which they observed in both substan-

---

2. Rowe, Julie (2006). "Note: Mourning the Untimely Death of the Juvenile Death Penalty: An Examination of Roper v. Simmons and the Future of the Juvenile Justice System," 42 Cal. W. L. Rev. 287, 291 (Spring).

3. For a detailed description of the forces that led to the reform movement and a careful explanation of the routines and impact of that movement see Krisberg, id at note 1, Chap 3, "The Historical Legacy of Juvenile Justice" and supporting scholarship.

4. Kamenstein, Adam D. (1977). "Note: The Inner-Morality of Juvenile Justice: The Case for Consistency and Legality," 18 Cardozo L. Rev. 2105, July, (citations omitted).

5. *Id.* at 2111 (citations omitted).

tive and procedural criminal law were therefore to be discarded. The idea of crime and punishment was to be abandoned. The child was to be "treated" and "rehabilitated" and the procedures, from apprehension through institutionalization, were to be "clinical" rather than "punitive."[6]

Under this rehabilitative approach, the state stepped into the shoes of the parent to provide necessary protection and rehabilitation of the child. This concept of **parens patriae** originated in England as the Crown acted as the legal guardian of those unable to protect themselves. It was used by the American juvenile courts as a basis for a system that sought to cure juveniles of the ills that led them to engage in socially unacceptable behavior. Through structured treatment and education, the state sought to rehabilitate the juvenile into becoming a productive member of society. The court procedure was relaxed, without the formality of the adult criminal system. A child was not entitled to liberty as an adult would be, but was entitled to custody. His parents could make him go to school and follow laws and rules. If the parent defaulted in performing these "custodial" functions, the state would intervene. Because the child had no liberty rights, the state was merely providing a custodial function which was "civil" and not "criminal" in nature.[7]

The difference between a juvenile "civil" proceeding and an adult "criminal" proceeding meant the difference between being rehabilitated as opposed to punished. A youth may not appreciate the difference, however, when his liberty could be taken under the guise of rehabilitation for an even longer period of time than it would have been if he were an adult.

In the best interests of the child, the judge's options ranged from warnings, to probation supervision, to training school confinement. The sentences of the juvenile court were indeterminate, and the length of the jurisdiction or authority of the juvenile court lasted generally until 21 years of age.[8]

The judge, acting as a concerned paternal figure providing guidance and acting out of concern for the child's best interests under the concept of parens patriae, was given a great deal of discretion in disposing of the child's case. One of the early criticisms of juvenile courts was the inconsistency in treatment due to the wide discretion of the judge. Procedures that would have been followed in the adult criminal courts gave way to an informal paternalistic process, claiming that procedural due process would irreparably impair the ability of the juvenile court to function.

Due Process Era

By the mid-1960s, several civil rights cases were decided by the United States Supreme Court, signaling constitutional changes in various areas.[9] Sweeping changes

6. *In re Gault*, 387 U.S. 1, 15–16 (1967) (citations omitted).

7. *Id.* at 17 (citations omitted).

8. Snyder, Howard N. and Stickmund, Melissa (2006). *Juvenile Offenders and victims: 2006 National Report*, at 96. Washington, DC: US Department of Justice, Office of Justice Programs, Office of Juvenile Justice and Delinquency Prevention.

9. For example, *Mapp v. Ohio*, 367 U.S. 643 (1961) imposed the exclusionary rule on state law enforcement for 4th amendment violations; *Miranda v. Arizona*, 384 U.S. 436 (1966) imposed now

in the juvenile justice system started with *Kent v. United States* (1966) requiring procedural safeguards in juvenile waiver proceedings. The following year, the landmark case of *In re Gault* (1967) provided due process protections for juveniles in cases where the juvenile's liberty was at stake. While juveniles were not granted all rights guaranteed to adults, the right to counsel during the adjudication process significantly changed the process, formalizing it and leading to other reforms. Following *Gault*, states revamped their statutes and administrative rules, incorporating the constitutional requirements in the adjudicatory process, from arrest through corrections. Several cases have subsequently come before the Supreme Court, addressing more specific constitutional rights for juveniles.

A. Treatment of Juveniles as Adults

The first big case during this era, *Kent v. United States* (featured below), addressed juvenile rights during the transfer process from the juvenile to the adult system. The process is known by various names: certification, transfer, and (perhaps most commonly) **waiver.** Prior to *Kent*, juveniles generally did not have attorneys to represent them in juvenile court, and the procedure once they got into court seldom involved rights to discovery and cross-examination that would occur in the adult system. Unfortunately, the consequences for waived juveniles were as serious as if they were adults and they ended up getting the worst of both systems. They did not receive the benefits of the more gentle, rehabilitative juvenile justice system, nor the constitutional protections of the adult system. Such was the case with Morris Kent, which gave the United States Supreme Court the opportunity to address which constitutional rights applied to juvenile waiver proceedings.

Kent v. United States

383 U.S. 541 (1966)

Morris A. Kent Jr., age 16, was taken into custody for the house breaking, robbery and rape of a woman in her home. During a seven hour interrogation without warning of the right to remain silent or consult with counsel, he admitted his involvement in that offense, and volunteered information regarding other similar offenses. Once Kent's mother was informed of his confinement, she retained an attorney to represent her son. Counsel was informed of the possibility that Kent would be waived into the adult system and he informed the juvenile authorities of his intent to oppose the waiver. Kent was detained for almost a week, during which time there was no arraignment and no probable cause determination by a judge who would have informed him of his constitutional rights.[10]

Mental health professionals examined Kent, and his attorney filed a motion requesting a hearing in the juvenile court on the issue of waiver. He also asked to examine Kent's social service file, which would be available to the judge in making the waiver decision.

---

familiar 5th amendment restrictions on law enforcement during custodial interrogations; and *Gideon v. Wainwright*, 372 U.S. 335 (1963) imposed a 6th amendment right to appointed counsel in felony cases.

10. Had Kent been an adult, he would have been entitled to an arraignment in front of a judge to determine probable cause and inform him of his constitutional rights.

The juvenile court did not respond to Kent's motions, held no hearing, did not confer with Kent's attorney or his parent, did not provide the social file to Kent's attorney, made no findings nor gave any reasons for its decision. An order was entered stating that "after 'full investigation, I [the juvenile judge] do hereby waive' jurisdiction of petitioner" to be held for trial before the U.S. District Court for the District of Columbia.

Kent was later indicted on two counts each of housebreaking, robbery and rape, and one of housebreaking and robbery. After several motions were heard, the adult court determined that Kent was competent to stand trial. A jury ultimately found Kent guilty of six counts of housebreaking and robbery. The jury found him not guilty by reason of insanity on the rape. He was sentenced to a total of 30 to 90 years in prison, to be started with a mandatory commitment to St. Elizabeth's Hospital, a mental institution, until mental health was restored.

On appeal, the United States Supreme Court addressed several concerns regarding the waiver, stating that "there is no place in our system of law for reaching a result of such tremendous consequences without ceremony—without hearing, without effective assistance of counsel, without a statement of reasons." Had Kent remained in the juvenile system, his maximum disposition would have been confinement until his 21st birthday, about five years. By transferring him to the adult system he was exposed to the possibility of the death penalty for the rapes, and transferred from a juvenile receiving home for children to an adult jail.

The Court did not require that juvenile court provide all of the adult protections to juveniles. The court expressed concerns, however, that juveniles received the "worst of both worlds: that he gets neither the protections accorded to adults nor the solicitous care and regenerative treatment postulated for children." The Court held that juveniles are entitled to the following rights before a valid waiver order may be entered:

1) counsel to represent them;
2) a hearing;
3) access by counsel to the social records and probation or similar reports considered by the court; and
4) a statement of the reasons for the decision.

B. Due Process Rights during Adjudication

Kent v. United States signaled a change in the constitutional rights available to juveniles at least when the state was seeking to hold them accountable as an adult. The following year the landmark case of *In re Gault* provided sweeping changes and rights to juveniles throughout the adjudicatory, or trial, stage of the juvenile court proceeding.

In re Gault

387 U.S. 1 (1967)

Fifteen-year-old Gerald Francis Gault and his friend were taken into custody by the sheriff as a result of a neighbor's, Mrs. Cook's, complaint that the boys had made "lewd or indecent remarks to her" over the telephone. No steps were taken to notify Gerald's parents that he had been arrested. Once his parents learned that he was being held in the detention home, they were informed of a hearing the next day. The petition filed against Gerald was never served on his parents, and alleged in very broad terms that he was a "delinquent minor."

No record of the first hearing was made. The judge later recalled he had questioned Gerald about the call. There was some conflict in recalling what the boys testified to at the hearing.[11] The neighbor never testified and was not subject to cross examination. The judge said he would "think about it" and continued Gerald's detention.

Three or four days later, Gerald was sent home without explanation and further hearing was set. At the second hearing, further testimony was taken but again, no verbatim record was kept. Gerald denied making any lewd remarks and Mrs. Cook did not testify. A probation report was received by the judge but was not disclosed to Gerald nor to his parents. The judge found against Gerald and committed him to the State Industrial School until his 21st birthday or sooner lawfully discharged. If Gerald had been an adult convicted of this same offense, the maximum penalty would have been "$5 to $50, or imprisonment for not more than two months." The judge also found him to be "habitually involved in immoral matters." No appeal was permitted under Arizona law in juvenile cases. Gerald's advocates filed for habeas corpus relief to get appellate review of the decision.

Arguments were made in the appellate courts that juvenile courts had different goals than the adult courts. Constitutional protections available in the adult system would interfere with the rehabilitative goals of the juvenile system. A juvenile was not entitled to liberty but to custody, to have someone take care of him, and if his parents did not afford him this custodial privilege, the law would do so. A benevolent judge or juvenile system would step into the shoes of the parents and provide them with the care and supervision they were not otherwise receiving. The state argued that constitutional and procedural protections would not work in the juvenile system any better than they would in a home with these same rehabilitative and supervision goals.

Ultimately the case ended up in the United States Supreme Court which held that the due process clause of the 14th Amendment applies to juvenile proceedings and specifically that when juveniles are subject to having their freedom taken away, they are entitled to:

1) notice of the charges against them;
2) an attorney;
3) confront and cross-examine the witnesses against them; and
4) the privilege against self-incrimination.

After examining the juvenile justice system, the Court found that the lack of constitutional protections had neither reduced crime nor rehabilitated youth. It used strong

11. There had been no verbatim record kept at the juvenile hearing, so the judge and others at that hearing had to reconstruct what had happened from the minute entries and their own memories.

language to impress the need for due process. "Juvenile Court history has again demonstrated that unbridled discretion, however benevolently motivated, is frequently a poor substitute for principle and procedure." It went on to say that "due process of law is the primary and indispensable foundation of individual freedom. It is the basic and essential term in the social compact which defines the rights of the individual and delimits the powers which the state may exercise." It cited with approval a quote comparing the powers of the Star Chamber[12] as a "trifle" in comparison with those of the juvenile courts. Further, it stressed the importance of procedural due process by asserting that "[p]rocedure is to law what 'scientific method' is to science."

This landmark case resulted in sweeping legislative and administrative changes across the country to comply with the newly found constitutional requirements. Other problems with the case, such as no record nor right to appeal, not specifically ruled on in this case, were also addressed legislatively by states. *In re Gault* ushered in the **due process era** of the juvenile courts, restricting the near unbridled discretion previously administered by probation departments and juvenile courts.[13] It is insightful to address each of the rights guaranteed by the court in this case, and apply them to the Gault facts. If Gerald had been afforded the due process rights required by the Court, how could it have made a difference in the ultimate outcome?

The United States Supreme Court has had subsequent opportunities to address procedural rights of juveniles. These cases made juvenile courts function more like adult criminal courts, while still recognizing that there were substantial differences between the two systems, citing the rehabilitative aspects of the juvenile court. While the courts were becoming more structured in granting due process rights to juveniles, Congress passed legislation that moved the juvenile justice system into a more deinstitutionalized, less structured correctional system.

Deinstitutionalization Era

The shift into the **deinstitutionalization era** was first pushed by Congress with the Juvenile Delinquency Prevention and Control Act of 1968. Congress recommended that states handle non-criminal "status offenses" (acts that are forbidden only due to youthful age) outside of the juvenile court system. Congress put still more teeth into the shift by later passing the Juvenile Justice and Delinquency Prevention Act of 1974, requiring states not place status and other non-criminal offenders in an institutional setting. It also required housing juvenile offenders separately from adult criminal offenders. Federal funding was tied to deinstitutionalization re-

12. The Star Chamber was an "old English court abolished in 1641 that exercised wide civil and criminal jurisdiction under rules of procedure suited to the prerogatives of the king and that was marked by secrecy, the absence of juries, self-incrimination, and an inquisitorial as opposed to accusatorial system of justice." *Merriam-Webster's Dictionary of Law* (1966).

13. The *Gault* Court stated that " ... unbridled discretion, however benevolently motivated, is frequently a poor substitute for principles and procedure."

sulting in sweeping changes in the juvenile correctional system across the country. Large institutions were replaced with much smaller housing facilities, and offenders were released to community based programs or placed under supervision in a home setting.

"Get Tough" Era—Waiver, Certification and Automatic Transfer

During the 1980s there was a wide spread perception of growing juvenile crime and a lack of sufficient response by the juvenile justice system to curb this tide. States responded during the 1980s and 1990s with legislation requiring juvenile authorities to treat certain classes of serious juvenile offenders in the adult system where more punitive measures could be given. Between 1992 and 1997, all but three states passed statutes ensuring more punitive treatment of serious youthful offenders. **Transfer** or **waiver statutes** were changed in 45 states, making it easier to try juveniles in the adult system. Juvenile and adult court sentencing options were expanded in 31 states. Further, 47 states modified their laws relaxing the traditional confidentiality of juvenile court proceedings.[14]

The result was that during this **get tough era** many youths who would have been adjudicated in the juvenile system, ultimately ended up in the adult courts and correctional system. The assumptions underlying the changes in the state statutes were that the adult system would be more punitive than the juvenile system, and thereby better protect society from the perceived increase in juvenile crime.

Juvenile courts traditionally had authority, when requested, to transfer serious offenders into the adult system. Two primary factors to determine the appropriateness of a transfer to the adult system are the age of the juvenile and the seriousness of the offense charged. Once a juvenile's case is handled in the adult system and there is a conviction, the juvenile is generally treated thereafter as if he or she were an adult, even for future offenses.

Age

Of the states that set forth a minimum age for transfer into the adult system, the greatest number of states (16) follow the common law rule of age 14. In 23 states, however, there is no minimum age, leaving this decision up to the judge to determine whether the juvenile was sufficiently mature to form the required mental state required for the offense, and the maturity needed for transfer to the adult system. Eleven states specify an age less than 14, with Kansas and Vermont specifying the lowest age at 10. New Mexico, on the other side, requires a minimum age of 15.[15] Table A sets forth the minimum ages by state, for waiver into the adult system.

---

14. Snyder & Strickland, *supra* note 8, 96–97.
15. *Id.*

Table A
Minimum Age Allowing Transfer into Adult System
Collected after 2004 Legislative Session

Age	States
No Minimum Age	Alaska, Arizona, Delaware, DC, Florida, Georgia, Hawaii, Idaho, Indiana, Maine, Maryland, Nebraska, Nevada, Oklahoma, Oregon, Pennsylvania, Rhode Island, South Carolina, South Dakota, Tennessee, Washington, West Virginia, Wisconsin
10	Kansas and Vermont
12	Colorado, Missouri, Montana
13	Illinois, Mississippi, New Hampshire, New York, North Carolina, Wyoming
14	Alabama, Arkansas California, Connecticut, Iowa, Kentucky, Louisiana, Massachusetts, Michigan, Minnesota, New Jersey, North Dakota, Ohio, Texas, Utah, Virginia
15	New Mexico

© 2000 (original copyright); © 2006 (most recent copyright) National Center for Juvenile Justice Griffin, Patrick. 2006. "National Overviews." State Juvenile Justice Profiles. Pittsburgh, PA: National Center for Juvenile Justice. Online. Available: http://www.ncjj.org/stateprofiles/.

There are three main categories of transfer statutes:

1. **Judicial Waiver.** Judicial waiver statutes are the most common form of waiver statutes, found in 46 states.[16] Also called transfer, certification, remand or a bind over, these statutes generally give a judge the most authority to review and determine the appropriateness of the transfer into the adult criminal system. Statutes generally set forth factors to be considered in determining waiver, including age, seriousness of the offense, prior record, prior services rendered to the juvenile, likelihood of rehabilitation in the juvenile system, and time during which the juvenile system may maintain jurisdiction.

Judicial waiver statutes are divided into three subcategories. **Discretionary waiver** statutes give the judge the most discretion to look at a variety of factors to determine the appropriateness of transfer to the criminal system. **Presumptive waiver** statutes provide a presumption in favor of waiver which must be overcome by evidence presented by the juvenile. **Mandatory waiver** statutes require a juvenile be waived if specified factors are found by the judge. In these cases the judge's role is limited to determining whether the statutory criteria is present.

2. **Concurrent jurisdiction.** Other statutes provide for both the adult and juvenile courts to have jurisdiction over certain offenses and offenders. These

16. Griffin, Patrick (2003). *Trying and Sentencing Juveniles as Adults: An Analysis of State Transfer and Blended Sentencing Laws.* Pittsburgh, PA, National Center for Juvenile Justice.

statutes, also referred to as **prosecutorial waiver, prosecutorial discretion** and **direct file statutes**, give prosecutors the discretion to determine whether to file the charges in the adult or the juvenile system. The discretion given to prosecutors in these statutes has given rise to some concern over disparity in treatment between jurisdictions. After the 2004 legislative session, 15 states have concurrent jurisdiction statutes.[17]

3. **Statutory or legislative exclusion.** Under these statutes, the juvenile court is divested of jurisdiction, generally for the most serious offenses committed by juvenile offenders. The age of the juvenile is also often a factor. These statutes limit the juvenile court's authority to try these cases, automatically placing them in the adult court and correctional systems. A judge does not determine whether transfer is appropriate, rather statutory criteria determines the jurisdiction of the court. After the 2004 legislative session, 29 states have statutory or legislative exclusion statutes. [18]

Although not generally categorized as statutory exclusion, in the 13 states where juveniles are treated as adults at age 15, 16 or 17, a large number of cases that would be handled in juvenile court in another state, are processed through the adult courts of those states as criminal offenses. It is estimated that if 16 and 17 year olds in those 13 states were processed in adult courts at the same rate that 16 and 17 year olds in other states are processed through the juvenile courts, more juveniles are tried in adult courts through this transfer mechanism than through all other methods combined.[19]

Characteristics of Waiver Statutes

State statutes often provide for **reverse waivers**, where adult court judges are allowed to reverse a case back to the juvenile court for adjudication, disposition, or the utilization of juvenile correctional facilities. Reverse waiver provisions are found in 22 of the 36 states that provide for statutory/legislative exclusion or concurrent jurisdiction. The factors for reversal are often the factors that would have been considered if the case had gone through a judicial waiver hearing before being transferred to the criminal from the juvenile court.[20]

In most jurisdictions, when a juvenile's case is handled in the adult court, it has adult sentencing options available after conviction. Likewise, when a juvenile court adjudicates a case, it has the juvenile correctional options available for disposition. These juvenile sentencing options, however, end and the juvenile is released when the juvenile reaches a specified age set forth by statute.

Blended sentencing is a dispositional option which gives the court additional sentencing options in both the adult and juvenile correctional systems that would not have been available to adult offenders. For example, a juvenile who was waived or automat-

---

17. Snyder & Stickmund, *supra* at note 8, 113.
18. Snyder & Stickmund, *supra* at note 8, 114.
19. *Id.*
20. *Id*, at 110.

ically filed upon in the adult court, would traditionally go into the adult correctional system for sentencing and thereafter be treated as if he were an adult for all purposes. In a state with a blended sentencing option, the adult court judge may utilize the juvenile correctional system for sentencing, taking advantage of the more rehabilitative aspects of that system. If the youth failed to perform satisfactorily under that option, the juvenile could be transferred back into the adult facility.

Blended sentencing also refers to juvenile courts which have options to utilize adult correctional facilities as part of their dispositions. Blended sentencing options vary widely among jurisdictions.

Consistent with the changes in waiver laws that occurred across the country during the early 1990s, the country saw large increases in waived cases, spiking in 1994. The number of delinquency cases waived to criminal court increased 83% from 1985 to 1994. By 2002, however, cases had decreased to 1% below the 1985 level. Juveniles are most likely to be waived into criminal court for committing offenses against persons. Waivers for crimes against persons increased 130% from 1985 to 1994, then decreased 47% to 2002, making those crimes the most likely subject of waiver cases. Prior to 1993, property cases outnumbered person offenses as the subject of waivers, sometimes by a ratio of nearly 2 to 1.[21]

Part II: Current Juvenile Justice System

Juvenile courts are created by statute, with state legislatures adopting rules and procedures, consistent with constitutional requirements, they deem appropriate for their state. While they share common goals and have similarities, we are able to speak only in generalities about the procedures and terminology of courts across the country. Where the United States Supreme Court has spoken, interpreting the United States Constitution, those rights apply to all juveniles within the United States. Students working with their juvenile court or correctional systems are encouraged to become familiar with the specific laws, procedures and customs within their jurisdiction.

Jurisdiction

Juvenile courts generally have **jurisdiction**, or authority, over delinquencies, status offenses and family services cases. Each of these terms will be discussed below.

A. Offenses which would be criminal offenses in the adult system are called **delinquencies** or **delinquent acts** when committed by juveniles who go through the juvenile system. For delinquencies, most juvenile courts have jurisdiction over those who were under the age of 18 when they violated the law.[22] Ten states have jurisdiction until the

---

21. *Id.*, conclusions based upon data collected from Stahl, A., Finnegan, T., and Kang, W. (2005). *Easy Access to Juvenile Court Statistics: 1985–2002* [online analysis]. Updated September 13, 2005. <www.ojjdp.ncjrs.gov/ojstatbb/ ezajcs>.

22. The data for this section relies heavily upon Snyder and Stickmund, *supra* at note 8, 103–104.

age of 17, and in three states the jurisdiction ends at age 16. To state it another way, violations of the law are treated as criminal offenses in the adult system after the offenders attain specified statutory ages. See Table B for a state by state breakdown of jurisdiction by age.

Table B
Oldest Age for Original Juvenile Court Jurisdiction over Delinquency Cases (2004)

Age	States
15	Connecticut, New York, North Carolina
16	Georgia, Illinois, Louisiana, Massachusetts, Michigan, Missouri, New Hampshire, South Carolina, Texas & Wisconsin
17	Alabama, Alaska, Arizona, Arkansas, California, Colorado, Delaware, District of Columbia, Florida, Hawaii, Idaho, Indiana, Iowa, Kansas, Kentucky, Maine, Maryland, Minnesota, Mississippi, Montana, Nebraska, Nevada, New Jersey, New Mexico, North Dakota, Tennessee, Utah, Vermont, Virginia, Washington, West Virginia & Wyoming

Snyder, Howard N. & Stickmund, Melissa, 2006. *Juvenile Offenders and Victims: 2006 National Report*. Washington, DC: US Department of Justice, Office of Justice Programs, Office of Juvenile Justice and Delinquency Prevention. Online Available: http://ojjdp.ncjrs.gov/ojstatbb/nr2006/downloads/NR2006.pdf

Some state statutes provide for dual or concurrent jurisdiction with the adult court dependent upon the age of the offender, offense and prior record. In these instances the prosecutor is given the discretion to determine the court where they will file the charge. Categories of lesser offenses where this often occurs include traffic, fish and game and boating violations.

As discussed earlier, many states also have statutory exclusion laws where juveniles who are charged with certain serious offenses must be charged in the adult system.

Most states allow the common law (historical tradition) to determine the lower ages of delinquency jurisdiction. Sixteen states, however, set a minimum age for delinquency jurisdiction starting at age 6 in North Carolina, age 7 in Maryland, Massachusetts and New York, age 8 in Arizona, with the balance of those who have set a lower age setting it at age 10.

The jurisdiction of the juvenile system for purposes of imposing sanctions and services generally lasts past the upper jurisdictional age discussed above. For instance, assume a juvenile is charged with joyriding in his neighbor's vehicle in a state where the upper age of jurisdiction is age 18. In most states, the juvenile court and juvenile correctional systems would retain jurisdiction for purposes of providing sanctions and services to him until his 21st birthday. Otherwise, a juvenile could escape sanctions if they were close enough to the upper age limit when they committed the offense. Eight state statutes limit jurisdiction at the 19th and 20th birthdays. Nine state statutes extend jurisdiction later than the 21st birthday, with three of those states extending jurisdiction until the juvenile court sanction is completed. See Table C for a state by state explanation of the upper age limits for juvenile court jurisdiction.

Table C
Oldest Age Juvenile Court May Retain Jurisdiction for Dispositional Purposes in Delinquency Matters (2004)

Age	States
18	Alaska, Iowa, Kentucky, Nebraska, Oklahoma, Tennessee
19	Mississippi & North Dakota
20	Alabama, Arizona*, Arkansas, Connecticut, Delaware, District of Columbia, Georgia, Idaho, Illinois, Indiana, Louisiana, Maine, Maryland, Massachusetts, Michigan, Minnesota, Missouri, Nevada**, New Hampshire, New Mexico, New York, North Carolina, Ohio, Pennsylvania, Rhode Island, South Carolina, South Dakota, Texas, Utah Vermont, Virginia, Washington, West Virginia, & Wyoming
21	Florida
22	Kansas
24	California, Montana, Oregon, & Wisconsin
Until full term of disposition order	Colorado, Hawaii, New Jersey

Note: Extended jurisdiction may be restricted to certain offenses or juveniles
*1979 state case law restricts jurisdiction to age 18.
**Until full term of disposition for sex offenders
Snyder, Howard N. & Stickmund, Melissa, 2006. *Juvenile Offenders and Victims: 2006 National Report*. Washington, DC: US Department of Justice, Office of Justice Programs, Office of Juvenile Justice and Delinquency Prevention. Online Available: http://ojjdp.ncjrs.gov/ojstatbb/nr2006/downloads/NR2006.pdf

Generally, when juveniles reach these upper age limits, juvenile courts and juvenile correctional facilities have no more authority to act over the juvenile for their juvenile offenses, and they must be released. This may place pressure on prosecutors to look at waiver proceedings into the criminal courts for juveniles who could not be held long enough in the juvenile system to satisfy the correctional needs for the severity of the offense they committed. In a partial response to that problem, some states provide for a **blended disposition** where juvenile courts have the authority to impose adult correctional options.

B. **Status offenses** are offenses like consuming alcohol or tobacco, truancy and curfew, which are unlawful only due to the age of the offender. These offenses are generally processed the same as delinquency cases, however in some states they are treated more like dependency or family services cases. Juvenile status offenders are viewed as being in need of supervision and may be referred from social services agencies as well as law enforcement. Dispositions for status offenses may also be limited by statute, taking away the option of detention or institutionalization.[23]

C. Juvenile courts also exercise **family services** jurisdiction over juveniles who have been **neglected** or **abused** as defined by state statutes. In these cases, the juvenile courts seek to protect children, rehabilitate families, and provide protective and supervisory services to meet those goals. They may also initiate criminal court proceedings against the adults who engaged in the conduct against the child. Criminal proceedings may continue at the same time as the juvenile court proceedings. Depending on the state, the proceedings may be in the same court or in different courtrooms with different judges. Because juvenile court is a civil proceeding, courts have held that the dual procedures do not violate double jeopardy rights. While they may have overlapping goals, juvenile courts focus and act in the best interests of the child while the criminal courts focus on the adult with punitive measures including incarceration as an option.

"Family services" jurisdiction also occurs in **dependency proceedings** in which the juvenile court acts to protect a juvenile who is in need of services or supervision even where the parents are not at fault. This may include runaways or ungovernable children. As with other family services cases, the juvenile court takes jurisdiction to operate in the child's best interests.

Terminology

Juvenile courts use different terminology than that used in the adult system. The origin of the terminology differences can likely be traced back to the rehabilitative model that the court was founded under. Labeling a child as **delinquent** as opposed to **criminal** could be viewed as more rehabilitative. While different areas of the country use terminology in various ways, the following illustrates common and general differences.

The names of juvenile courts vary across the country. While **juvenile court** is generally used, it is known by various other names including district, superior, circuit, county, family, or probate court. Sometimes the court with adult or general jurisdiction has a separate division for juvenile matters. In other states, the juvenile court is completely separate from the adult court.[24]

Juveniles are not arrested, but are **taken into custody**, primarily by law enforcement officials who initiate most cases that are referred to juvenile court.

Juveniles are taken to **receiving** or **detention centers**, *not* jails. States generally have laws that prohibit juveniles from being taken to adult jails except in limited circumstances.

A law enforcement officer will **refer** the juvenile to juvenile court, providing the court with a **referral** (request) and documentation of the alleged offense, asking the court to take **jurisdiction** or authority over the child.

---

23. Snyder and Stickmund, *supra* note 8 at 107.
24. Snyder and Stickmund, *supra* note 8 at 106.

The charging document (an "information" or "indictment" in the adult system) is generally a **petition** in the juvenile system. That document is brought "*In the Interest of...*" as opposed to "State vs. John Doe."

The **petition** alleges a violation of the law deemed to be a **delinquent act** or **delinquency**, not a crime.

If the case is petitioned, the child will appear in front of a judge and plead **true** or **not true** to the petition (rather than guilty or not guilty.)

If the child admits the allegations in the petition, or the allegations are found to be true after a trial, the case is deemed **adjudicated**. In the adult system this would be a conviction.

Following adjudication, the child could have a **dispositional hearing** or the judge could proceed with the **disposition** of the case without such a hearing. In the adult system this would be a sentencing.

For a quick summary of some of the differences in terminology between the juvenile and adult courts, please see Table D.

Table D
Common Terminology Differences —
Juvenile and Adult/Criminal Systems

Terminology Chart

Juvenile Terminology	Adult Terminology
Delinquency or delinquent act	Crime
Taken into custody	Arrest
Receiving or Detention Centers	Jails
Referral	No direct corollary
Petition	Information or Indictment
True or Not True (Plea)	Guilty or Not Guilty
Adjudication	Conviction
Disposition	Sentence
Non-judicial closures	No direct corollary
Civil proceedings	Criminal proceedings

Processing through the Juvenile Justice System

A juvenile who is processed through the juvenile justice system has many opportunities to be **diverted** or treated outside of the formal court. It starts with the law enforcement officer who is called to respond to a violation of the law by a juvenile. The officer may arrest juveniles and take them to detention, cite or release them to their parents and refer them to juvenile court for later prosecution, release and divert them into a non-judicial program, or simply release without action.

A juvenile taken into detention is generally processed more quickly through the system than is a juvenile who is not in custody. Prosecutors, often in conjunction with juvenile court probation officers, will review cases which are referred to juvenile court for prosecution. They must determine whether the juvenile falls within the jurisdiction or authority of the court. Under some instances statutes will require that the juvenile be sent into the adult system for prosecution due to age or the seriousness of the offense.

The juvenile court probation intake division will also review the case. One of the biggest differences between the juvenile and adult systems is its use of probation officers in this **intake** function. In the juvenile system, probation officers engage in both the traditional supervision function after adjudication and also an intake function, reviewing a juvenile's actions and working with juveniles prior to their adjudication. Sometimes this is done even before a prosecutor sees the case.

As part of intake, probation officers are often given the authority by statute or court rule to divert or **non-judicially close** a case, which would be unheard of in the adult correctional system where adults generally do not even see a probation officer until after conviction. The ability to non-judicially close the case is generally governed by statute or court rules, giving probation officers authority to divert the case for handling outside of juvenile court if deemed appropriate.

To illustrate the use of a non-judicial closure, take the common example of a 14 year old referred to the court for breaking his neighbor's window. A probation officer would be assigned to the case, and meet with the child and parents. The probation officer takes social history from them and becomes familiar with the facts and surrounding circumstances. He finds out that the child was tossing a baseball with a friend and that they were in the victim's yard. The victim was a man who had been upset with the children in the past for playing in his yard. On this occasion he came out of his house and yelled at the children, calling them a racial name that was very hurtful to the children. One of the children took his baseball and threw it at the victim's big picture window, at which time they both ran. Their parents and police were immediately summoned to the scene.

After the neighbor and children had both calmed down, the child recognized that physical violence is not justified by even hurtful words. The victim also acknowledged his contribution to the situation. The victim was elderly and had difficulty mowing his lawn and tending to his yard. The children agreed to mow the victim's lawn for the rest of the summer and to help him with yard work to pay for the broken window. The children's parents were supportive of the plan.

This would be an appropriate case for a non-judicial closure by a probation officer, or a non-arrest by a police officer. As long as the children kept their end of the bargain, the case would be closed without a formal juvenile court record. If, however, the children were involved in further conduct of this nature, or failed to work off their obligation to the victim, the case could still go through juvenile court. This case also illustrates why this would work with a 14 year old child, but not a 24 year old adult.

If the case is not diverted out of the system by the prosecutor, probation officer or police officer, it proceeds with formal charging and processing in the juvenile court. A formal petition charging the juvenile with an offense is filed, asking the juvenile court to take jurisdiction over him. If the prosecutor asks the judge to waive or transfer the juvenile into the adult system, the court must rule on that issue. If the case goes forward through the juvenile court, the judge will assure that the juvenile's constitutional rights are followed. The constitutional rights that a juvenile is entitled to during adjudication were set forth in *In re Gault*, and discussed above. Other rights which have been addressed by the United States Supreme Court will be discussed in the following section. The adjudication process is very similar to that of an adult charged with a crime.

After adjudication the juvenile may be released and the case dismissed. If the petition is found to be true, the juvenile court takes jurisdiction over him and orders a disposition that is in the juvenile's best interests. The judge has juvenile correctional options available, from long term residential services all the way down to supervision services in the child's own home.

Specialty Courts

Specialty courts have arisen over the past couple of decades and are an integral part of the current judicial landscape. Arguably, juvenile courts were the first "specialty" courts, set up to handle a specific need that was not being otherwise adequately addressed through traditional courts. That footnote aside, juvenile courts across the country have adopted their own drug courts, mental health courts, domestic violence courts, and others, to meet their individual needs. These "courts" vary widely, but are generally cases that are grouped together to receive particular attention, review and treatment within the traditional juvenile court. Cases are reviewed frequently, and tracked closely so that any problems or violations can be addressed quickly by the court.[25]

Youth Courts, also called "teen" and "peer" courts, are an up and coming part of juvenile justice in this country. They are often discussed as a specialty court within the juvenile system, however they may or may not be a part of the local juvenile court. Youth courts may be a formal diversion directly from the juvenile court, or they may be run by local law enforcement, schools, communities or non-profit organizations.

In youth courts, other youth occupy the positions held by adults in the court system. A volunteer youth may act as a judge, attorney, bailiff, clerk or juror. Youth courts involve volunteer youth in an active civics lesson, enabling them to assist offending youth to conform their conduct in socially acceptable ways.[26] Offending youth who go through youth court generally do not have a formal record kept of the proceedings. They are able to learn from the experience by engaging in community service, restitution, classes or treatment, and other appropriate sanctions. Statutes govern the jurisdiction and procedures of youth courts in some states.[27] Youth courts are an increasingly important part of the juvenile justice system in the United States.[28]

---

25. Further information about specialty courts in general, and juvenile specialty courts in particular, may be found at http://www.courtinnovation.org and http://www.ndci.org or http://www.nadcp.org.

26. More information about youth courts may be found at http:/www.youthcourt.net

27. For a state by state analysis of statutes regarding youth courts see Heward, Michelle (2006), *An Update on Teen Court Legislation*, OJJDP, DOJ; Washington, D.C., available online at http:/www.youthcourt.net, then follow the links; and Heward, Michelle E. (2002). The Organization and Operation of Teen Courts in the United States: A Comparative Analysis of Legislation, *Juvenile and Family Court Journal*, (Winter) pp. 19–35.

28. According to the National Association of Youth Courts, there were 1,139 youth courts in 49 states and the District of Columbia at last count. Retrieved from http:/www.youthcourt.net August, 2007.

Adjudication Rights of Juveniles

The Court in *In re Gault* extended important constitutional rights to juveniles (notice of charges, counsel, cross-examination and confrontation, and the privilege against self-incrimination). The court stopped short, however, of extending all adult rights to juveniles. How closely should the juvenile system mirror the adult system? If all rights are extended to juveniles, will the juvenile court loose the ability to work quickly and in the child's best interests? If all rights are not extended the juveniles, will the court have too much discretion and introduce arbitrariness into the process? The balance needed to act in the child's best interests continues to be debated and argued throughout our country.

As we will discover, the juvenile court has been either constitutionally or statutorily required to provide juveniles *most* of the procedural rights guaranteed to adults charged with similar offenses in the adult system. Several specific cases are discussed below.

A. Preventative Pretrial Detention

Schall v. Martin

467 U.S. 253 (1984)

Martin, a 14-year-old juvenile, was arrested and charged with first degree robbery, second degree assault and possession of a dangerous weapon. It was alleged that he and two others hit another juvenile over the head with a loaded gun, then stole his jacket and shoes. Martin had the gun in his custody when he was taken into custody late on that date and he lied to police. Because of his age, he fell under the jurisdiction of the Family Court in New York.

Under the New York Family Court Act, a juvenile could be detained prior to trial based on a finding that there is a "serious risk" that the child "may before the return date commit an act which if committed by an adult would constitute a crime." Due to the allegations, Martin's possession of the gun when he was taken into custody, the lateness of the hour, and his lie to police regarding his address, Martin was detained. A probable cause hearing and then a trial were held where Martin was adjudicated and ordered to two years of probation. This all occurred within 17 days of when he was taken into custody.

Martin brought a class action suit with other similarly situated juveniles, alleging that pre-trial detention violated due process rights, constituting punishment prior to conviction. The Court of Appeals affirmed a lower court ruling in favor of the juveniles, finding the pre-trial detention statute was not used for preventative means, but was primarily used as punishment for unadjudicated acts.

The United States Supreme Court recognized that while juveniles have many of the same rights as adults, they have tried to strike a balance, respecting the informality and flexibility of the "fundamentally different" juvenile proceedings. Two conclusions were made by the Court. First, it determined that the pre-trial detention statute served a legitimate state interest in protecting both the juvenile and society from delinquent activity. It considered, while not conclusive, the fact that every state in the country had a preventative detention statute. Second, the court concluded that preventative detention was not intended nor used as a punishment, but was an incident of a legitimate state interest. The statute provided the juvenile with expedited hearings, and more formal judicial fact finding determinations. Further, the place of detention was found to be appropriate and not overly harsh.

Finally, the procedural safeguards required for preventative detention were found to be constitutionally adequate to protect against erroneous and unnecessary deprivations of liberty. These procedures included notice, a statement of facts and reasons prior to any detention, a formal probable cause hearing within three days, and a formal trial in an expedited time period.

B. Burden of Proof

In re Winship

397 U.S. 358 (1970)

Winship, a 12 year old juvenile, was adjudicated for entering a locker and stealing $112 from a woman's pocketbook. The judge acknowledged that the proof might not establish guilt beyond a reasonable doubt, but rejected Winship's contention that the criminal standard of proof beyond a reasonable doubt was constitutionally required. Winship was placed in a training school for an initial period of 18 months, subject to annual extensions until his 18th birthday, six years in his case.

The court discussed the need for proof beyond a reasonable doubt in order to maintain confidence and respect in the application of *criminal* law. It characterized the requirement of proof beyond a reasonable doubt as a prime instrument for reducing the risk of convictions resting on factual error. Although the right to proof beyond a reasonable doubt is not specifically stated in the Constitution, the Court determined that the Due Process Clause protects the accused adult against adjudication except upon proof beyond a reasonable doubt of every element of the offense.[29]

The issue in this case, however, was whether the standard applies to juveniles adjudicated for delinquent conduct. The state argued that a delinquent adjudication is not a criminal conviction, but is civil in nature. Further, juvenile proceedings are confidential, more informal and flexible by design, to determine what is in the child's "best interests." The majority of the court was not persuaded by the state's arguments. Dissenting Justices Burger and Stewart tried to convince the majority that the court's decision could "spell the end of a generously conceived program of compassionate treatment intended to mitigate the rigors and trauma of exposing youthful offenders to a traditional criminal court...." These dissenters felt the court was moving backwards in transforming the juvenile courts into criminal courts. Despite these concerns, the majority nevertheless concluded that the Due Process Clause of the 14th Amendment requires proof beyond a reasonable doubt when the juvenile's liberty is at stake.

29. This applies to juvenile adjudications for delinquency offenses, but is not constitutionally required in other cases such as family services cases which come before the juvenile courts.

C. Right to a Jury Trial

McKeiver v. Pennsylvania

403 U.S. 528 (1971)

Several cases were consolidated in this case, asking whether the Due Process Clause of the Fourteenth Amendment assures the right to jury trial in the adjudicative, or trial, phase of a state juvenile court delinquency proceeding. The juveniles argued that their cases were essentially criminal in nature, where a jury would be required, and that the rehabilitative benefits of the juvenile system would not be changed by inserting a jury requirement.

The Court found that a jury trial is different in nature from the other rights granted juveniles in *Gault, Kent, Winship* and other cases. A jury was deemed *not* essential to the juvenile fact finding process, citing other proceedings such as probate, workers compensation and deportation cases which do not require juries. Interestingly, the court had, only two years earlier, found that juries were a "fundamental right, essential for preventing miscarriages of justice and for assuring that fair trials are provided for all defendants" in adult criminal cases.[30] The court recognized that juries have an important place in the fact finding process and, while not constitutionally required, states may find it desirable to provide juveniles with juries. Few states though have provided this right statutorily for juveniles. This case signaled a retreat by the Court from its previous cases which had equated the rights of juveniles with the rights of adults in criminal proceedings. It further reaffirmed the role of the juvenile court as protectionist and rehabilitative, making this a significant case for that aspect alone.[31]

D. Double Jeopardy

Breed v. Jones

421 U.S. 519 (1975)

In this case the Court addressed the question of whether a juvenile court delinquency adjudication placed a defendant in jeopardy which would forbid a subsequent adult criminal conviction on the same offense. In February, 1971, a juvenile court petition was filed against Jones, then 17 years of age, alleging he had committed a robbery with a deadly weapon. An adjudicatory hearing was held, testimony taken from two witnesses and the respondent, after which the juvenile court found the allegations in the petition were true. A dispositional, or sentencing, hearing was later held where the juvenile court placed respondent on notice of its intent to transfer him into the adult system. Jones claimed surprise and the matter was continued for one week. At that subsequent hearing, he was waived into the adult system.

---

30. *Duncan v. Louisiana*, 391 U.S. 145, 158 (1968). Cited by Geimer, William S., (1986). "Ready to Take the High Road? The Case for Importing Scotland's Juvenile Justice System," 35 Cath. U.L. Rev. 385, Winter.

31. Geimer, *id.* at 393, found *McKeiver* to be more significant than *In re Gault* for this reason.

A preliminary hearing was held in the adult court, Jones was formally charged, and ultimately, the court found him guilty of first degree robbery in the adult system. In December, 1971, the appellate process began, raising the issue of whether the initial juvenile court adjudication constituted jeopardy under the Double Jeopardy Clause of the 5th Amendment, which would prohibit a subsequent trial and conviction in the adult system.

The court acknowledged that double jeopardy in this case had not subjected the defendant to more than one *punishment* for the offense, but that the Double Jeopardy Clause was set up to protect against more than just punishment. Jones was twice subject to the risk of trial and conviction, had to defend himself twice against the state's allegations and the accompanying psychological, physical and financial strains. The court found insignificant the differences between the juvenile and adult court processes for purposes of double jeopardy, and held that once a juvenile had been adjudicated as delinquent in a juvenile court, jeopardy attached, and he could not then be subject to a subsequent trial in the adult system for the same offense.

E. Death Penalty

Several cases have been decided by the United States Supreme Court over the last twenty years regarding the death penalty for those who were juveniles at the time they committed the crime. Cases illustrating Supreme Court jurisprudence in this area have already been presented in Chapter Thirteen (the chapter dealing with "Death Penalty Law"), so only a brief summary review will be repeated here.

The Eighth Amendment to the United States Constitution prohibits cruel and unusual punishments. That amendment has been the focus of death penalty challenges and is interpreted by using national standards of decency to determine what is cruel and unusual. The Court has determined that these standards evolve over time, placing the Court in a difficult position to rule on current standards of decency.

In *Thompson v. Oklahoma* (1988)[32], the court set aside a death penalty that had been pronounced on a 15 year old defendant. A divided court determined that national standards of decency did not permit the execution of any offender who was under age 16 at the time he or she committed the crime. The court argued, among other things, that the reasons society does not pass all of its privileges and responsibilities to juveniles also help to explain why we do not view their conduct as morally reprehensible as an adult's.

The next year, in *Stanford v. Kentucky* (1989)[33], a 5–4 Court was asked the same question as in *Thompson*, but applied to a 16 year old offender. Again, the court sought to determine whether there was a national consensus regarding contemporary standards of decency, this time for the execution of a 16-year-old offender. It noted that 22 of 37 death penalty states permitted execution for 16-year-old offenders, and 25 permitted it for 17-year-olds, thereby indicating there was no national consensus. Without a national consensus, the Court was not willing to find the execution of 16 or 17 year old offenders as "cruel and unusual."

32. 487 U.S. 815 (1988)
33. 492 U.S. 361 (1989)

Using parallel reasoning, and on the same day as the *Stanford* case was released, the Court reached the same conclusion regarding the execution of a mentally retarded person convicted of capital murder. It looked at the number of states that allowed the execution of mentally retarded individuals and held that there was no national consensus which would make their execution "cruel and unusual" in violation of the Eighth Amendment. See, *Penry v. Lynaugh*, (1989).[34]

In 2002, the United States Supreme Court again was asked to rule on the question of the appropriateness of executing a mentally retarded person. In *Atkins v. Virginia*, (2002)[35] the court reversed its position in *Penry*, holding that the Eighth and Fourteenth Amendments prohibit the execution of a mentally retarded person. That case set the stage for a request to readdress the issue of whether executing 16 and 17 year old juveniles was also cruel and unusual.

In 2005, (a relatively short period of time for the Court to readdress an issue) the matter was indeed before the Court, in the case of *Roper v. Simmons*.[36] In this landmark case, the Supreme Court ruled that it would now be considered cruel and unusual punishment to execute anyone under the age of eighteen. With reasoning parallel to that used in *Atkins*, it found that a national consensus had developed against the death penalty for 17 year old juveniles. Most states no longer allowed it (including five that had abolished it since the *Stanford* decision), and the few that did rarely used it. The Court noted that a lack of maturity and underdeveloped sense of responsibility characterize juveniles and it would be wrong for the Court to continue to allow their executions.

Conclusion

The juvenile justice system within the United States arose from a perceived need to treat juveniles differently from their adult counterparts in the judicial and correctional systems. It evolved, and continues to do so, from social and systemic needs as they arise. Statutes and rules in each individual state have set up the frame work within which the juvenile justice system operates, tempered by constitutional restraints. While juvenile justice is the subject of entire courses of study, this chapter should give students an overall perspective of the history, current procedures and practices used in this country.

34. 492 U.S. 302 (1989)
35. 536 U.S. 304 (2002)
36. 543 U.S. 551 (2005).

Chapter Fifteen

Appellate Law

Criminal justice practitioners make mistakes: lawyers make mistakes; judges make mistakes; jurors make mistakes. Even legislators drafting statutes make mistakes. The system needs to have some mechanisms for fixing bad mistakes. One such critical mechanism is the appeal.

Almost all Americans instinctively believe that there should be such a safeguard as the appeal. Imagine how scary it would be if there were absolutely no such chance to have "botched-up" justice corrected. And, all of us know that justice can indeed become "botched up."

This chapter will explore important issues in "Appellate Law." No other country on the planet gives more power to appellate courts than does the United States. Let us look at how these incredibly powerful courts operate. We will begin with the basics: the purposes behind appeals.

Purposes of an Appeal

Appeals are permitted in order to achieve one of two important goals: error correction or policy review. **Error correction** typically involves fixing mistakes made during a trial that may have caused a wrongful outcome. In other words, the trial was broken somehow. Perhaps the trial judge overruled a critical objection that should have been sustained or perhaps the jury returned an absolutely preposterous verdict despite the evidence presented to it. In other words, a judge did not follow the rules or a jury ignored common sense and we cannot accept the outcome.

As important as error correction is, policy review is something much more profound. **Policy review** involves an appellate court striking down legislation or practices as violating a constitution (either state or federal). It goes way beyond fixing normal, course-of-business mistakes that judges and juries inevitably make. It basically amounts to the court using its nuclear option: trumping other branches of government with a declaration of unconstitutionality.

Most appeals do not involve the creation of newly discovered constitutional doctrine. For example, if a judge fails to suppress illegally obtained evidence that should have been suppressed, an appellate court will fix this error by overturning the verdict and ordering a new trial. Or, if a jury convicts somebody on evidence so weak that no reasonable jury could possibly have found guilt beyond a reasonable doubt, the appellate court will overturn the verdict and set the defendant free. In other words, most appeals involve error correction.

On the other hand, sometimes appellate courts go beyond merely correcting human error and engage in substantive constitutional review. Policy review is exemplified by such cases as *Roe v. Wade* (the famous abortion rights case) or *Miranda v. Arizona* (which gave us the famous "Miranda rights" that police recite during arrests). Judges in such cases actually use a constitution to create new legal doctrine rather than correct ordinary error. Any appellate court can engage in policy review, but constitutional issues of national importance often are ultimately decided by the U.S. Supreme Court.

Let us look more closely at important concepts behind error correction and policy review. We will begin with the former and then move on to the latter.

Error Correction

American criminal trials are great contests and like all fair contests are governed by certain rules. These rules regarding what is admissible at trial and what is not are known collectively as the **Law of Evidence**. Most of these rules exist to facilitate the work that lay jurors have in rendering accurate decisions. For example, many of the rules (e.g., prohibitions against hearsay, lay opinions, and irrelevant testimony) prevent the use of evidence that is unreliable or that would waste a jury's time. Some of the rules actually hinder the truth-finding mission of the jury but exist to accomplish other worthy goals. For example, some rules exist to discourage police from violating constitutional rights (e.g., the suppression of evidence from illegal searches), while others help preserve certain relationships by protecting confidences (e.g., husband-wife privilege regarding testifying against one another). Of course, it would be much easier in some respects to do away with these rules of evidence entirely. Trials could then become much simpler and the need for lawyers lessened. On the other hand, it is likely that the dozen of "witches" condemned in the rough and tumble trials of colonial Salem would have fared much better in a system with more elaborate rules.

Whether we are grateful for the modern rules of evidence or wish that they could just all be eliminated, the fact is that they exist and must be honored. So, what happens if they are not honored?

It is common knowledge that in the case of an unfair conviction, an appellate court will overturn the conviction. But what if trial error resulted in an unfair acquittal? Suppose, for example, a defense lawyer is asking a witness a question that violates a very important rule of evidence and the prosecutor wisely objects. Suppose further that the judge foolishly or maliciously overrules the prosecutor's objection and allows the witness to respond. As a result, highly inflammatory and unreliable evidence likely caused the prosecution to lose its case. Can the prosecutor appeal this wrongful acquittal? No. Why not? Let us look at the concept of "double jeopardy."

A. Error Correction: Double Jeopardy

Should a judge or jury find a criminal defendant not guilty, the state may not re-prosecute for any reason. There simply are no exceptions to this rule.[1] The Fifth Amendment to the U.S. Constitution states that no "person [shall] be subject to the same offense to be twice put in jeopardy of life or limb." (Life or limb is construed to include any criminal punishment.) The reason behind this right is that Americans need protection from the fear and expense that successive trials can produce. Even more importantly, people need protection from the oppression that could occur were the government free to try defendants over and over again until it got lucky.

But, suppose the prosecution is not seeking to oppress anybody but is rather the clear victim of a miscarriage of justice—of obvious error made by judge or jury. For example, suppose a racist judge demonstrates flagrant bias against a minority victim in favor of a white defendant throughout the trial. Because of this racist's help, the white defendant is acquitted. Or suppose in another trial that it is learned (after an acquittal) that two key alibi witnesses had committed perjury. Or suppose in yet a different trial that a jury shows its contempt for justice by finding some bad actor not guilty despite proof of guilt to a near mathematical certainty. Under any of these nasty scenarios, double jeopardy would prevent a re-trial of the case. Some legal scholars find such conclusions repugnant. For example, Thomas DiBiagio wrote in a law review article that:

> Because an acquittal that is defective in some fundamental respect seriously affects the fairness, integrity, or public reputation of the judicial proceeding, the Supreme Court should interpret the Double Jeopardy Clause to permit judicial review and retrial following reversal based on plain error, intimidation, tampering or misconduct.[2]

Though DiBiagio's view is not unreasonable, it does not conform to legal precedent. Even proof that a trial judge took a bribe or that a jury was tainted would not legally allow for a retrial. On the other hand, suppose a case went to trial but ended with a **hung jury**, that is, a jury that was hopelessly deadlocked and unable to agree on a verdict of guilty or not guilty (this can easily happen since many states require unanimous verdicts). Would double jeopardy bar a prosecutor from trying again with a different jury? This issue of hung juries was something the U.S. Supreme Court had to struggle with in the early years of the nation.

In the 1824 case of *United States v. Perez,*[3] the High Court was confronted with a case of first impression. Josef Perez was tried in a capital case but the jury was unable to agree on an outcome. The court ultimately dismissed the jury without being asked to do so by either the prosecution or the defense. Perez then argued that he could not be retried because of double jeopardy. In ultimately deciding the matter, the U.S. Supreme Court noted that it was "aware that there is some diversity of opinion and practice on this subject in the American Courts; but after weighing the question with

---

1. *United States v. Ball,* 163 U.S. 662 (1896).
2. DiBiagio, Thomas M. "Judicial Equity: An Argument for Post-Acquittal Retrial when the Judicial Process is Fundamentally Defective." 46 Cath.U.L.Rev.77, 77 (1996).
3. 22 U.S. 579 (1824).

due deliberation, we are of the opinion that such a discharge constitutes no bar to further proceedings" (22 U.S. at 580). It based its decision on the fact that the trial judge had no choice but to dismiss the deadlocked jury. It further reasoned that not allowing a retrial would merely defeat justice rather than uphold the spirit of the double jeopardy prohibition.

Generally speaking, **jeopardy attaches** once a trial jury is empaneled and sworn in. That is the point of no return for the prosecutor. He or she must proceed and hope either for a favorable verdict or at least a hung jury. Of course, if a trial jury has not yet been empaneled, double jeopardy has not yet attached. This is why prosecutors who fail to get an indictment before a grand jury can try again when they get new evidence.

Sometimes, enterprising prosecutors will try to get around the spirit of double jeopardy by bringing new and different charges based on old fact patterns that had previously been litigated. The case that follows illustrates the Supreme Court's attitude regarding such mischief.

Ashe v. Swenson

397 U.S. 436 (1970)

The defendant and several other masked gunmen allegedly burst into a poker game and robbed all six poker players of their money. The robbers then fled in one of the victim's car and were subsequently arrested by the police while walking down the highway near the point where the car was abandoned. The defendant was brought to trial for the robbery of just one of the victims (a man named Knight) but for some reason was not tried for the robbery of the other victims.

The case against the defendant for robbing Knight was weak. Only two of the poker players could identify the defendant as one of the robbers and their identifications were shaky: one of the two could only recognize the defendant by his voice and the other only by his size, height and mannerisms. The jury felt obliged to find the defendant not guilty.

Six weeks later the prosecution tried again. This time, they charged the same defendant with the robbery of one of the other victims present at the poker game, a man named Roberts. The prosecution claimed that this did not violate double jeopardy since it was alleging the robbery of somebody other than the victim named in the first trial. The trial judge allowed the new trial. This time the prosecution put on a much better case. Consequently, the defendant was convicted and sentenced to 35 years in prison. He appealed.

The U.S. Supreme Court ultimately heard the case and reversed the conviction. It ruled that prosecutors cannot try someone in piecemeal fashion. They have to bring all of their charges at once. The Fifth Amendment guarantee against double jeopardy was meant to protect people from having to "run the gauntlet a second time." The Court said that the question was not whether the poker players were all robbed (they clearly were) or whether the state could have properly charged the defendant with six separate offenses of robbery at the first trial (it clearly could have done so). But, when it decided to bring just one count of robbery to trial initially, it essentially asked a jury to decide whether or not the defendant could be proven beyond a reasonable doubt to have been present at the robbery scene. That jury found that this could not be proven. As such, the prosecution is forbidden to ask another jury to revisit that same issue.

The Court noted that the prosecution apparently used the first trial merely as a "dry run" for the second. And, like any good lawyer, the prosecutor learned from his mistakes and did a better job the second time around. While this is what any competent lawyer would do if given the chance, it is also something that the Constitution's double jeopardy provision protects against. The judgement was reversed and the defendant freed.

B. Error Correction: Lawyer's Duty to Object and the Plain Error Doctrine

It is not just judges and juries who make mistakes in trials. Lawyers too can drop the ball when they fail to object when they should. Should lawyers be allowed to argue violations of the rules of evidence on appeal if they failed to raise the violations during the trial in the first place?

A long-established rule held dear in the federal courts as well as in all fifty states is that one cannot complain on appeal about errors made during the trial unless these errors were objected to during the trial itself. The existence of this deeply annoying rule keeps every trial lawyer intensely focused, if not outright stressed, during trials. The reasons for the rule creating a **lawyer's duty to object** are several: an objection made during the trial allows the judge to correct the error in an efficient and timely manner; an objection allows the party who is ruled against to try to get the evidence admitted via a different and lawful manner; and requiring lawyers to assert objections forces attorneys to pay attention and to competently do their jobs. The bottom line is (with the sole exception to be noted in the paragraph below) that by failing to object in a timely and specific manner, an attorney fails to preserve an issue for a future appeal. The right to complain to a higher authority is lost forever. So, in order to **preserve an issue for appeal**, an attorney must **protect the record** by making an objection during trial even when the attorney has little hope of getting a favorable ruling from a particular trial judge.

The sole exception to the above rule (adopted by most state courts and the federal courts) is that an appellate court may review a non-preserved issue (meaning one not raised during trial) if the matter constituted "plain error." To qualify as **plain error**, the error must have been "obvious" and "clear" and will result in a "gross miscarriage" of justice if not allowed to be corrected in an appeal.[4]

Thus, rules governing federal criminal trials provide that "plain errors or defects affecting substantial rights may be noticed although they were not brought to the attention of the [trial] court."[5] Similarly, New York by statute authorizes appellate courts in that state to review "an error or defect ... not duly protested at trial ... [which] deprived the defendant of a fair trial."[6]

---

4. *United States v. Keys*, 67 F.3d 801, 809 (9th Cir. 1995).
5. Federal Rules of Criminal Procedure 52 (b).
6. N.Y. Crim P. Law 470.15 (1994).

So, should an attorney wish to appeal a matter not protested at trial, his or her only chance is to argue "plain error." Of course, what constitutes plain error in real-life cases is something that can be debated. The case which follows struggles with this.

United States v. Young

470 U.S. 1 (1985)

Billy Young was vice president of an oil company in Texas. Young had contracted to sell "sweet crude" oil to another company for a certain amount of money but instead delivered inferior grade oil to them which he certified as "sweet crude." Despite his claims that he thought his cheaper grade of oil was the equivalent of "sweet crude" so no harm intended, he was charged with fraud and convicted pursuant to a jury trial.

During the appeal of his conviction he wished to argue prosecutorial trial misconduct but was prohibited from doing so because he failed to object to this alleged misconduct during the trial itself. Thus, by failing to make a timely objection during the trial, he and his lawyers had not preserved the issue for appeal and the federal circuit appeals court ruled that it was prevented from reviewing the issue.

The alleged prosecutorial misconduct at trial involved the prosecutor expressing his personal opinion during his closing argument that the defendant was guilty. Lawyers are forbidden by case law as well as by the ethical cannons of the legal profession from ever expressing their personal opinions about the guilt or innocence of a criminal defendant. Hence, a prosecutor can make a statement in closing argument that "I suggest to you that the evidence clearly shows proof beyond a reasonable doubt" or some such hypothetical, but could never flat out say something like, "I personally am convinced that the defendant is guilty." Defense lawyers similarly have to be careful with how they make their closing arguments by never directly stating their personal convictions regarding guilt or innocence.

During Young's trial for fraud, the prosecutor told the jury during closing argument that, "I don't know what you call that, I call it fraud ... I think it's fraud." He also told the jury that, "If you feel you should acquit him for that it's your pleasure. I don't think you are doing your job as jurors" if you do that. He also said that his "personal impression" was that Young committed the fraud. The defense attorney never objected to any of these forbidden statements nor even asked for a curative jury instruction to be given at the end of the trial.

Perhaps the reason the defense attorney did not think to object to the prosecutor's statements was that he started things by unethically telling the jury in his closing argument (he got to go first) that the prosecutor had tried to "poison" their minds during the trial and that the case had been "presented unfairly by the prosecution." He even pointed at the prosecutor who was sitting at his table and said to the jury that, "I submit to you that there's not one person in this courtroom including those sitting at this table who think that Billy Young intended to defraud Apco."

Young eventually appealed the intermediate appellate court's refusal to even consider his charge of prosecutorial misconduct to the U.S. Supreme Court. Young argued that the prosecutor's statements to the jury constituted plain error and that plain error was an exception to the rule requiring a lawyer to object at trial in order to preserve an issue for later appellate review.

So, was the prosecutor's misconduct plain error? The Supreme Court did not think so. It noted that the prosecutor had indeed behaved badly. But, the defense lawyer to a certain degree invited a personal response from the prosecutor when it had labeled him an abuser of his office who did not believe in his own case. It said that the prosecutor made a mistake in the heat of battle because he had been provoked.

The issue was not whether the prosecutor had made an error in responding in a personal manner to the defense lawyer's provocations, but whether he had committed plain error. The Court noted that plain error involves "particularly egregious errors" that "seriously affect the fairness, integrity or public reputation of judicial proceedings." It said that the plain error doctrine should be "used sparingly, solely in those circumstances in which a miscarriage of justice would otherwise result." To label too many errors as plain errors would ruin our court system's desire to have mistakes made during trials promptly addressed. It would also result in lawyers' getting lazy by not having to worry too much about making objections which serve to call the court's attention to mistakes as they happen.

The Supreme Court concluded by ruling that since the defense attorney basically invited a response from the prosecutor when he had attacked him in such a personal way, the prosecutor's remarks did not cause a miscarriage of justice nor did they create a fundamentally unfair trial. Seeing both sides' antics, the jury was probably not unduly influenced by what the prosecutor had said and could thus remain fair and open minded.

In his dissent from the above decision, Justice Brennan (joined by two others) wrote that the prosecutor's statements to the jury did indeed constitute plain error. Brennan said that two wrongs do not make a right and that the prosecutor could not be justified in departing so far from ethical codes of conduct. Brennan said that even though both sides were at fault, the greater fault lay with the prosecution because prosecutors are held to a higher standard than defense attorneys. Unlike defense attorneys, prosecutors are expected not only to zealously represent their side of a case but, as a representative of the sovereign, to always see that justice is done. Brennan concluded by remarking that "I believe the Court trivializes these high standards by suggesting that a violation may be overlooked merely because the prosecutor decided sua sponte [on his own] that he has to right the scale."

Even though the plain error doctrine exists in the federal courts and most state courts, not all states recognize such a doctrine. These "purist" states simply refuse to allow their appellate courts to consider issues on appeal that were not raised by the attorney during the trial. Pennsylvania is traditionally one such state for reasons the Pennsylvania Supreme Court outlined in the case that follows.

Commonwealth v. Clair

326 A.2d 272 (Pa. 1974)

Clair was convicted by a Pennsylvania jury of murdering his wife. He appealed to the Pennsylvania Supreme Court arguing several errors made during the trial, including allegations that the judge went too far when he provided an oral review of the testimony to the jury at the end of the trial. However, Clair's lawyer failed to object to this alleged error or to the other errors he now wished to raise on appeal. Clair claimed that his lawyer's failure to object should not be an impediment to appellate consideration of these errors because these errors constituted plain errors.

The Pennsylvania Supreme disagreed with Clair's contention that he had the right to pursue his unpreserved claims on appeal by invoking the doctrine of plain error. The Pennsylvania Supreme Court said that Pennsylvania courts simply do not recognize the plain error doctrine.

The Court acknowledged that people who champion the plain error doctrine are basically asserting that some errors are so "basic and fundamental" that appellate courts sensitive to justice must review them even absent an objection made at trial. But, the Court was not persuaded by this line of thought. It noted that it would be "difficult to determine what is a basic and fundamental error." It said that the whole doctrine was silly because convictions are overturned on appeal all the time on matters that probably would not be characterized as plain error. Yet these supposedly lesser mistakes (requiring objections to have been made at trial) are large enough to require the extreme relief of granting a new trial. Could it not therefore be said that these common, reversible errors are every bit as "basic and fundamental" as the so-called plain errors are?

The Court said that to recognize the plain error doctrine in Pennsylvania would lead to a host of evils. It said that the plain error doctrine "removes the professional necessity for diligent preparation; penalizes the opposing party; denies the trial court the opportunity to correct the error; erodes the finality of trial court holdings; [and] encourages unnecessary appeals ..." Because of all of this "no longer will allegations of basic and fundamental error serve to enable parties in criminal matters to seek reversal on alleged errors not properly raised below." Clair's murder conviction was affirmed.

In a Dissent, Justice Pomeroy emphasized that "it is never proper to think of our advocacy system merely as a game to be won or lost according to how well the players know the rules ..." Justice Pomeroy pointed out that, "In the stress of trial, what lawyer has not erred? But the doctrine of basic and fundamental error in criminal cases was not designed to reward the unprepared and incautious attorney; rather, it was to insure a basically fair trial to every defendant, many of whom, of course, have no choice in the selection of their lawyers."

Like Pennsylvania, a minority of states continue to reject the plain error exception to the general rule that trial errors will not be preserved for appeal unless timely objection was made during the trial itself. In refusing to recognize the plain error doctrine in Iowa, the Iowa Supreme Court stated that, "nothing is more basic in the law of appeal and error than the axiom that a party cannot sing a song to us that was not sung in trial court."[7] Are states like Iowa and Pennsylvania unenlightened or does their refusal to recognize the plain error exception make a lot of practical sense? If you believe that

7. *Iowa v. Rutledge*, 600 N.W.2d 324, 324 (Iowa, 1999).

the plain error exception is wrong because professionals should be expected to make timely objections at trial, do you think it is fair to deny public defender clients (who have no choice in the selection of their attorneys) the right to appeal plain errors not objected to during trial?

C. Error Correction: The Harmless Error Doctrine

Lawyers do make mistakes in failing to make timely objections during trials, but judges can also make mistakes while fielding objections that are properly made. Even the most intelligent and conscientious of judges will sometimes err during the ordeal of trials by sustaining or over-ruling objections incorrectly. When this happens, inadmissible evidence may be heard by the jury. Conversely, admissible evidence may be wrongfully kept from the jury. It is likely that few trials of any substantive length are totally error-free. The rules of evidence are very complex and judges considering objections have only a few seconds to make a ruling before looking indecisive or incompetent. It is inevitable that some of their rulings will be flat wrong.

While working as a public defender and later as a prosecutor I always suspected that judges sometimes guessed while ruling on my own or my opponent's objections. Later, while serving as a judge in collegiate mock trial competitions, my suspicions were confirmed. I often found myself unsure and stressed while ruling on objections even though I was an experienced trial attorney who taught courses at the university on the rules of evidence!

The "Harmless Error Doctrine" exists due to the realities of human imperfection and the need to avoid what would otherwise be the automatic granting of new trials after nearly all convictions. Simply stated, the **harmless error doctrine** provides that small errors resulting from judges' poor rulings which very likely did not affect the final outcome do not necessitate a new trial. In order to be considered harmless, there must be no reasonable possibility that the error might have altered the final verdict.[8]

The following two cases illustrate two extremes of the harmless error doctrine. In the first case, decided before the harmless error doctrine was adopted, a ridiculously petty error was held to necessitate a new trial. In the second, much more recent case, the majority renders an opinion on coerced confessions and harmless error that many feel has disturbing implications.

State v. Campbell

109 S.W. 706 (Mo. 1908)

Campbell was convicted of rape of a domestic servant by a Missouri criminal jury in the early 1900s. Apparently, he had assaulted and ravished the young woman while the wife was away with her young daughter on a visit to the wife's sister in a neighboring town. In addition to the victim's testimony, there was physical evidence of the rape.

---

8. *Chapman v. California*, 386 U.S. 18 (1967).

However, in appealing the conviction, Campbell brought up an extreme technicality. Apparently, Section 38 of Article 6 of the Missouri Constitution states that all indictments shall conclude with the phrase, "against the peace and dignity of the state." But Campbell's indictment read, "against the peace and dignity of state" (leaving out the word "the" before the word "state"). Campbell asked that his conviction be reversed because of this alleged failure to comply with a state constitutional requirement.

Amazingly, the state appellate court agreed with Campbell and reversed the conviction. Not yet having developed a harmless error doctrine, the Missouri appellate court felt that it had no choice but to follow the letter of the law. In its opinion, the Court said that, "While it may be conceded that the word 'the' is a small one and in many instances of little importance ... we see no escape from the conclusion that the definite article 'the' preceding the word 'state' is absolutely essential in order to designate the particular State against which the offense is charged to have been committed." The Court said that the word "the" was essential to make perfectly clear that the state in question was Missouri and not some other state. The Court conceded that one could probably safely infer that Missouri was the state being referred to and that all of this might to some seem like form over substance. However, it ruled that "Constitutional requirements are not ordinarily to be regarded as mere matters of form." Hence, the problem confronting the Court was "not what the pleader meant to say, but what he did say, and do the terms used in concluding the indictment in this case substantially conform to the requirements prescribed by the Constitution?" Since the definite article "the" was left out of the indictment, and hence a failure to particularly designate what state was bringing the action resulted, a reversal of the conviction was unavoidably necessary.

If you were the rape victim in this case, how would you feel about the Missouri court system after learning of the above opinion? What kind of personality do you suppose the opinion writer had? How might this personality affect other areas of his life?

In the Middle Ages contracts were considered null and void if certain stock legal phrases and jargon were not included word for word. These ritual phrases were known only to lawyers who jealously guarded their secrecy in order to protect their guild. Can any case at all be made for ever requiring ritualistic, verbatim legal phrases in today's world?

Arizona v. Fulminante

499 U.S. 279 (1991)

The issue in this case was whether or not a jury's hearing a coerced and wrongfully admitted confession to a crime could ever be harmless error. Fulminante allegedly raped, strangled, shot and killed his 11-year-old stepdaughter while he was caring for her during a period that her mother was in the hospital.

Fulminante's first contact with the police occurred when he telephoned the Mesa, Arizona police department to report the girl missing. Two days later, the little girl's body was found in the desert east of town. It was obvious that she had been shot and strangled but because of the decomposition of the body, it was impossible at that time to ascertain that she had been raped as well. The police immediately suspected Fulminante of the murder but, despite inconsistencies in his statements regarding the girl's disappearance, did not feel that they had enough evidence to charge him with the crimes.

Time passed and Fulminante moved to New Jersey. While there he got into some trouble and started serving a prison sentence for weapons' violations (a felon possessing a firearm). Rumors soon started circulating in the prison that Fulminante had murdered a little girl out in Arizona. Such rumors did not make Fulminante popular with his fellow inmates. In the meantime, Fulminante was befriended by a fellow inmate named Sarivola who was acting as an undercover agent for the police. Sarivola told Fulminante that his life was in real danger from the hostile inmates but since they were friends Sarivola would protect him. Sarivola however said "You have to tell me about it. You know, I mean, in other words, For me to give you any help." Fulminante then admitted to Sarivola that he had strangled and shot the girl after having raped her and forced her to beg for her life.

Prior to his trial in Arizona on the rape and murder charges, Fulminante asked the Arizona trial judge to suppress his confession to Sarivola, the undercover government agent, on the grounds that it had been coerced. This request was refused and the case went before a jury who heard the confession, along with other evidence, and convicted Fulminante of all charges.

On appeal to the Arizona Supreme Court, Fulminante's conviction was overturned. Fulminante argued that it was error to allow the jury to hear his confession. The state counter-argued that it was error but harmless error, supposedly because of other, overwhelming evidence the jury was presented. The Arizona Supreme Court ruled that coerced confessions wrongfully admitted at trial could never constitute harmless error no matter what other evidence was introduced at trial. The prosecution appealed the decision of the Arizona Supreme Court to the U.S. Supreme Court.

The U.S. Supreme Court ordered that Fulminante be given a new trial with his confession suppressed. However, it was not because a majority of the justices believed that wrongfully admitting a coerced confession could never constitute harmless error. Five of the nine justices thought that coerced confessions could conceivably constitute harmless error depending upon the case. If evidence against a defendant was otherwise overwhelming, the mere fact that an illegally obtained confession was heard by the jury would not probably have altered the inevitable guilty verdict. These five justices thought that only two errors should never be thought possible to amount to harmless error: being deprived a lawyer at trial or having a judge who was biased. When someone is denied a lawyer or a neutral judge, the whole structure of the trial is ruined. However, admission of an improperly obtained confession does not necessarily destroy the very structure of the process. The bottom line is that every error other than deprivation of counsel or lack of an unbiased judge is fair game for potential harmless error analysis, including admission of an illegal confession.

These five justices who believed that illegally obtained confessions might constitute harmless error admitted that, "Of course an involuntary confession may have a more dramatic effect on the course of a trial than do other trial errors—in particular cases it may be devastating to a defendant—but this simply means that a reviewing court will conclude in such a case that its admission was not harmless error; it is not a reason for eschewing the harmless-error test entirely."

So, if five justices thought that admission of an illegally obtained confession could possibly be harmless error, then why did the Supreme Court order Fulminante a new trial? Because some of these five went on to apply harmless error analysis to Fulminante's case and when they did so concluded that admission of his particular confession was not harmless error after all. They pointed out that the police had no solid case against Fulminante prior to his coerced prison confession and only brought the matter to trial after he confessed to the undercover agent. When these justices' votes for a new trial were added to the votes of the four justices who thought that admission of an illegally obtained confession could never constitute harmless error, there were enough votes to order that Fulminante be provided a new trial without use of any confession.

The four justices who believed that admission at trial of illegally obtained confessions could never constitute harmless error constituted a dissent of sorts (even though they luckily wound up in the majority ordering Fulminante a new trial) and their insightful reasoning should be covered. Prior to this case, courts had always ruled that admission of illegally obtained confessions of trials always hopelessly tainted juries to a degree that rendered any conviction totally unreliable. These four justices felt that "no one can say what credit and weight" a jury might give to a confession admitted in a trial. Such evidence is so powerful that it would "defy analysis by harmless-error standards." They argued that use of a coerced confession "aborts the basic trial process and renders a trial fundamentally unfair." They are disturbed that five justices feel differently and do not believe that they offered "any convincing reasons for overturning our long line of decisions" automatically requiring a new trial whenever a coerced confession was used to help convict someone.

Fulminante got his new trial but only because he got lucky with how the votes technically stacked up in his favor. He did not convince a majority of the justices that illegally obtained confessions put into evidence always leads to a miscarriage of justice. Which justices do you agree with: those who think the admission of a coerced confession is not subject to harmless error analysis because it can never be harmless error; those who think it may be harmless error in theory but not in Fulminante's particular case; or those (like Chief Justice Rehnquist) who think that it may be harmless error in theory and in fact was harmless error beyond a reasonable doubt in Fulminante's particular case? Absent evidence of the coerced confession, how much evidence would you as a juror need in order to find Fulminante guilty upon re-trial?

Policy Review

Thus far, in discussing concepts like the plain error doctrine and the harmless error doctrine we have been acting as if the only potential purpose of an appeal is error correction: that some judge wrongfully admitted evidence or some other big mistake by the trial court was made. But, there is a second purpose for the existence of the appeal: policy review. As mentioned at the beginning of the chapter **policy review** (also known as **judicial review**) involves an appellate court striking down legislation or executive branch actions as violating a constitution. So, whereas a trial judge allowing hearsay evidence to be used to get a conviction would require an appellate court to engage in error correction, a legislature attempting to make inter-racial marriage a crime again would require an appellate court to engage in policy review.

A. Policy Review: The Historic Case of Marbury v. Madison

We Americans take the right of judges to have the final say on what the Constitution requires for granted. But, such a right was not always so obvious. After all, Congress or the President might want to protect the Constitution by seeing that it is being correctly followed. Do they not take oaths of office to "defend the Constitution?" Who says it is the right of the judicial branch to have the last word on what the Constitution really means? The two-hundred-year-old case which follows is one in which the U.S. Supreme Court first asserted its right to have this final say, a custom still followed to this day.

Marbury v. Madison

1 Cranch 137 (1803)

The presidential election of 1800 caused the Federalist party to loose control of both Congress and the presidency. Just before leaving office, lame duck President Adams appointed his political friend Marbury as a justice of the peace for the District of Columbia. But Marbury's commission was not delivered to him because it was mistakenly left (along with several other commissions) on the desk of the outgoing secretary of state who was supposed to have delivered it. When Jefferson, the new president, assumed office he found Marbury's commission still on the desk of the former secretary of state and, angry about this and other "midnight" patronage appointments, forbade everybody in his administration from delivering it. Marbury heard about this and went directly to the U.S. Supreme Court. Marbury asked the High Court to order the new administration to deliver his commission.

Put simply, the issues before the Supreme Court eventually became whether or not the Supreme Court had the power to correct officials of the executive branch who were supposedly failing to do their constitutional duties and whether it could rule on the constitutionality of acts of Congress. Today, we take it for granted that the courts have such powers, but back in 1803 it was not so clear. The U.S. Constitution grants no specific power to the Supreme Court to correct the supposed unconstitutional acts of the two other equal branches of government.

Writing for the majority, Chief Justice Marshall ruled that when it comes to interpreting the Constitution, it is the "province and duty of the judicial department to say what the law is." Marshall wrote that those who argue that the courts must simply uphold legislation without any consideration of whether or not the legislation violates the Constitution would "be giving to the legislature a practical and real omnipotence" that would "subvert the very foundation of all written constitutions." Basically the Court ruled that the Constitution was the Supreme law of the land, that the Supreme Law must be followed, and that for the Supreme Law to have any significance the courts had to see to it that its meaning was correctly articulated.

The bottom line was that the Supreme Court held that the new President had to do his constitutional duty and deliver the commission to Marbury making him a justice of the peace. Chief Justice Marshall, however, was a realist. What could he do if the powerful and popular President Jefferson stood up to the Supreme Court and simply refused to obey? Fearing that Jefferson might indeed ignore its ruling and cause the Court to loose its credibility and future influence, the clever Justice Marshall wrote that although the president had a constitutional and moral duty to deliver the commission, the Court was not going to force him to actually do so. In effect, Justice Marshall got what he probably really was after: a ruling that went unchallenged by President Jefferson or anybody else that the Court would henceforth have the final say on what the Constitution does or does not require of the other branches of government. Over the years that followed, this tentative ruling creating the power of "judicial review"became ratified through other constitutional-level, judicial rulings that also went unchallenged by the president or Congress. Today, nobody questions the authority of the courts to engage in judicial review of legislative acts or executive behavior. But, if it were not for *Marbury v. Madison,* things might have evolved quite differently. America might have become a country where the President and Congress, as well as the Supreme Court, might all claim an equal right to protect, defend and ultimately interpret the Constitution.

As late as World War II, only two countries in the world (the U.S.A. and Norway) gave its judges the power to strike down legislation. Today, more than 80 countries give their judges such power. Thus, the principle of judicial review seems to be expanding quite rapidly.[9]

B. Policy Review: Strict Construction vs. "Living Constitution"

Marbury v. Madison, as discussed above, may have created the principle of judicial review but it completely left unanswered how courts should actually go about interpreting the Constitution. Should judges engage in **strict construction** (seeking to discover and follow the original intent of the Constitution's drafters) or should they be proponents of a so-called **living constitution** (one that evolves with society's changing values)? This question has never been settled and even today the debate rages on.

Current U.S. Supreme Court Justice Stephen Breyer is clearly one in the "living constitution" camp. He has written that, "Since law is connected to life, judges, in applying a text in light of its purpose, should look to consequences, including contemporary conditions, social, industrial, and political, of the community to be affected."[10] For example, the drafters of the Fourth Amendment prohibition against unreasonable searches and seizures could not have foreseen the tremendous technological assaults on

9. Goldstein, Leslie Friedman. (2004). "From Democracy to Juristocracy." *Law & Society Review* 38:611–624, at 612–613.

10. Breyer, Stephen. (2005). *Active Liberty*. New York: Alfred A. Knopf, at 18.

our privacy that would occur from such innovations as electronic listening devices, thermal imaging equipment, computer tracking of personal information, etc. So, constitutional interpretation should be flexible enough to allow modern judges to "look for new legal bottles to hold our old wine."[11] According to Justice Breyer, the need to adapt to the times goes way beyond search and seizure law. For example, the equal protection clause (which mandates that the government should treat all citizens as equals) was not originally thought to be a prohibition against racially segregated public schools. But we have evolved as a people to the point that nobody today could seriously argue that officially segregated public schools are in harmony with "equal protection."[12]

On the other hand, former law professor and current U.S. Supreme Court Justice Antonin Scalia, sees things dramatically differently. He finds great danger in the notion of a "living constitution." For example in his dissent in *Lawrence v. Texas*[13] (the 2003 case ruling that statutes criminalizing homosexual acts are unlawful in that there is a constitutional right to engage in gay sex), Scalia wrote some strong words. He wrote that, "Today's opinion is the product of a Court, which is the product of a law-profession culture, that has largely signed on to the so-called homosexual agenda ... What Texas has chosen to do [in criminalizing homosexual acts] is well within the range of traditional democratic action, and its hand should not be stayed through the invention of a brand new 'constitutional right' by a Court that is impatient of democratic change."

Scalia echoed his strict constructionist sentiments in yet another dissenting opinion. In this different case he lamented,

> What secret knowledge, one must wonder, is breathed into lawyers when they become Justices of this Court, that enables them to discern that a practice which the text of the Constitution does not clearly proscribe, and which our people have regarded as constitutional for 200 years, is in fact unconstitutional? ... Day by day, case by case, [the Court] is busy designing a Constitution for a country that I do not recognize.[14]

No doubt, Scalia would agree with former U.S. Solicitor General (and one-time Supreme Court nominee) Robert Bork who has written that secular, societal elites looking for "meaning in life" have captured the judiciary (just as they have captured the media and the universities) and are twisting the principle of judicial review to advance moral agendas that they know they could never win through the democratic process. Feeling completely free to jettison original intent and impose values driven into them by well-meaning, out-of-touch law school professors, activist judges "arrive at results by announcing principles that were never contemplated by those who wrote and voted for the law. The law in question is usually a constitution, perhaps because the language of a constitution tends to be general and, in any event, judicial overreaching is then

11. Id., at 68.
12. Id., at 119.
13. 123 S.Ct. 2472 (2003).
14. *Board of County Commissioners v. Umbehr*, 518 U.S. 668, 711 (1996) (Scalia, J. dissenting), as cited in Bork, note 15 below, at 52.

virtually immune to correction by the legislature or by the public."[15] Bork believes that using personal judicial values rather than looking to original intent to interpret a written constitution will lead to mischief, judicial despotism, and a gutting of democracy.

Both the idea of an evolving constitution and the idea of original intent has its virtues and vices. The societal debate continues as to which approach on balance is better.

C. Policy Review: The Stare Decisis *Doctrine*

Even though judges engage in judicial review and use constitutions to declare legislative acts unconstitutional, they are restrained by a number of practical factors from being completely free-wheeling in the exercise of their power. One of the more powerful restraints on judges as they interpret constitutions (state or federal) is that of *stare decisis.* **Stare decisis** (Latin for "let the decision stand") is the idea that courts should practice restraint in overturning their own precedents too rapidly even if they think the precedent should now be abandoned. One reason behind *stare decisis* is that flip-flopping causes the public to loose respect for the courts and for constitutional interpretation (making law seem bogus). Another reason for *stare decisis* is that flip-flopping makes it difficult for people who depend on the law to plan their lives.

Of course, courts should not allow the rule of precedent to tie their hands forever. The 1954 case of *Brown v. Board of Education*[16] overturned the 1896 case of *Plessy v. Ferguson*[17] by ruling that official, racially segregated public schools are not acceptable. But note that over a half century passed between these two contradictory decisions, helping to avoid the appearance of flagrant flip-flopping.

On the other hand, *stare decisis* is not an insurmountable hurdle if courts are really itching to change their minds fast. In the 2003 case of *Lawrence v. Texas,*[18] the U.S. Supreme Court ruled that there is a constitutional right to gay sex (and hence laws criminalizing it are forbidden) despite the fact that in the recently decided 1986 case of *Bowers v. Hardwick*[19] it had announced a completely opposite position.

One of the most contentious societal debates today centers on the propriety of laws seeking to criminalize elective abortions. Most people are familiar with *Roe v. Wade,*[20] the famous 1973 case announcing a woman's constitutional right to choose abortion. Fewer are familiar with the case that would have overturned *Roe* but for the principle of *stare decisis* (which principle caused swing-voter Justice Sandra Day O'Connor to vote for its retention). The case that follows is that case.

---

15. Bork, Robert H. (2003). *Coercing Virtue: The Worldwide Rule of Judges.* Washington, D.C.: The AEI Press, at 8–9.
16. 349 U.S. 294 (1954).
17. 163 U.S. 537 (1896).
18. 123 S.Ct. 2472 (2003).
19. 478 U.S. 186 (1986).
20. 410 U.S. 113 (1973).

Planned Parenthood of Southeastern Pennsylvania v. Casey

505 U.S. 833 (1992)

By 1992, *Roe v. Wade*, the famous abortion rights case was two decades old and some believed the time had come to ask the U.S. Supreme Court (which had undergone some personnel changes) for a reversal. The state of Pennsylvania had passed some legislation which, though not outlawing elective abortion outright, imposed limits on elective abortions that seemed to clearly contradict parts of the *Roe v. Wade* decision. The Pennsylvania legislature said that abortions to be performed in the state would henceforth require: informed consent; a twenty-four-hour waiting period; spousal notice; parental consent (in the case of minors under 18); and elaborate record keeping (doctor's name, age of the patient, number of past abortions woman had, etc.).

Before this new Pennsylvania law went into effect, five abortion clinics challenged its constitutionality and the case eventually landed before the U.S. Supreme Court. Many believed that the Court would use this case to completely undo *Roe v. Wade*. However, by a slim 5/4 vote, the "central holding" of *Roe v. Wade* finding a right to an abortion was upheld even though some of Pennsylvania's new, tough restrictions were also upheld. *Roe* was weakened but not obliterated.

In upholding the right to an elective abortion, the majority wrote that prior to "viability" (the point at which a fetus could survive outside the mother), "the state's interests are not strong enough to support" a complete prohibition of the right to an elective abortion or the "imposition of a substantial obstacle" to an elective abortion. That said, the Court went on to rule that requiring informed consent, a 24 hour waiting period, and detailed reporting and record-keeping all were constitutional in that they did not constitute "substantial obstacles" or "undue burdens" to an abortion. A substantial obstacle or an undue burdens exists when it is "calculated [not] to inform the woman's free choice [but to] hinder it."

Hence, by allowing Pennsylvania to attach strings to a woman's right to choose abortion, the *Roe* decision (which prevented virtually all restrictions imposed by a state during the pre-viability period) was partially overturned. But, as Justice O'Connor wrote, the "central holding" of *Roe*, allowing a woman's right to an elective abortion (albeit now with some strings attached) was upheld.

Justices forming the slim, five-person majority had different reasons for maintaining the "central holding" of *Roe*. This was a messy decision indeed. In fact, since the votes of eight of the nine justices had neatly stacked up to four in favor of retaining the right to an abortion with four in favor of completely undoing the *Roe* decision, everything had come down to how Justice Sandra Day O'Connor would vote. Whom would this swing voter side with this time? As noted above, she sided with the four who favored retaining the central decision to allow a right to an elective abortion. She wrote that, "While we appreciate the weight of arguments made on behalf of the State ... the reservations any of us may have in reaffirming the central holding of *Roe* are outweighed by the explication of individual liberty we have given combined with the force of stare decisis. We now turn to that doctrine ..."

Turning to "that doctrine" (stare decisis) O'Connor wrote that, "An entire generation has come of age free to assume *Roe*'s concept of liberty in defining the capacity of women to act in society, and to make reproductive decisions ... Within the bounds of normal *stare decisis* analysis, then, and subject to the considerations on which it customarily turns, the stronger argument is for affirming *Roe's* central holding, with whatever degree of personal reluctance any of us may have, not for overruling it." Emphasizing that *Roe* was just not some ordinary case, O'Connor went on to explain in detail why *stare decisis* should be followed here even more faithfully than might be done in "a less significant case." She said that, " ... the Court cannot buy support for its decisions by spending money, and except to a minor degree, it cannot independently coerce obedience to its decrees. The Court's power lies, rather, in its legitimacy, a product of substance and perception that shows itself in the people's acceptance of the Judiciary as to determine what the Nation's law means and to declare what it demands." She continued, "The Court must take care to speak and act in ways that allow people to accept its decisions on the terms the Court claims for them, as grounded truly in principle, not as compromises with social and political pressures having, as such, no bearing on the principled choices that the Court is obliged to make." O'Connor went on to say that *stare decisis* does not mean that a Court can never overturn itself when it has strong reasons to do so, but in a case so historic and tremendous as *Roe*, the Court would risk a real crisis of legitimacy if it were perceived by the public to have merely changed its mind.

Justice Scalia, writing on behalf of the four dissenters, blasted O'Connor's reliance on *stare decisis* as a primary basis for upholding abortion rights. He emphatically expressed his view that *stare decisis*, if truly followed, would prohibit the Court from upholding any of Pennsylvania's tough, new restrictions which were burdensome-enough to have clearly violated *Roe*. Yet, the Supreme Court just now chose to uphold these modifications. This strict constructionist jurist concluded by vehemently claiming that, "The Imperial Judiciary lives. We should get out of this area, where we have no right to be, and where we do neither ourselves nor the country any good by remaining."

Mechanics of an Appeal

What are the mechanics of an appeal? What are the steps lawyers go through to get their appeal heard? This is an area with which very few lay people are familiar. Nevertheless, it is an area to which criminal justice professionals and others who wish to be truly knowledgeable of our justice system should be exposed. The Table that is found shortly below does a neat, little job of outlining both the steps of an appeal and the purpose behind each of these steps. It is taken from the author's book, *Inside the Criminal Courts.*[21]

21. Lynch, David R. (2004). *Inside the Criminal Courts*. Durham, N.C.: Carolina Academic Press, at 270.

Mechanics of an Appeal

Step	Purpose
1. Objecting during trial (or raising motions)	Allows for immediate resolution and preserves the issue for later appeal to a higher court.
2. Post-trial Motions	Gives trial judge chance to correct own bad rulings or jury's unconscionable verdict.
3. Notice of Appeal	Makes higher court aware of appeal/ signals clerk of court to send trial transcript and other trial records to the higher court.
4. Submitting Briefs	Provides appellate court with a detailed presentation of the issues and legal arguments. Appellant files brief first then other side files a responsive brief presenting the other side.
5. Oral Arguments	Attorneys appear in person before appellate judges and orally present their arguments. Judges have the opportunity to quiz the lawyers regarding points of concern to them.
6. Opinion Issued	Informs parties of the appellate court's decision and gives the court's reasoning.

Appeals of Right vs. Discretionary Appeals

States and the federal system provide (by way of statute or state constitution) that anybody convicted at trial of a crime who wants to appeal must be granted at least one appeal.[22] This one, certain appeal is known as an **appeal of right**. All convicted people are entitled to their one appeal, no matter how air-tight and error-free their trial seems at first blush to have been. Because defendants have an appeal of right, nearly every trial-conviction in the U.S. is appealed. There is much for a convict to gain and virtually nothing to lose by appealing, especially if a free lawyer is being used.

After the appeal of right, appeals in most states become **discretionary appeals**, meaning that high appellate courts (such as state supreme courts and the U.S. Supreme Court) do not have to bother with them unless they find the issues interesting or of great public importance. (Lawyers submit a tiny summary of what the interesting issues would be in an attempt to lure the court into inviting them to submit a full-blown brief.) If the high appellate court agrees to hear a discretionary appeal, it **grants certiorari** and the parties are invited to submit briefs. If a court refuses to hear a discretionary appeal, it very tersely **denies certiorari** and the case is over.

22. See author's book, *Inside the Criminal Courts*, supra note 21, at 264 on which this discussion is based.

Right to Counsel in Appeals of Right

Most criminal defendants who wish to appeal are poor and cannot afford appellate counsel. Everybody knows that poor criminal defendants have the right to a public defender or other free lawyer at their trial. But what about for their appeal(s)? Should they be given a free lawyer to try to overturn their convictions? Should it depend on whether their appeal is one of right vs. a discretionary appeal? The following case looks into this area.

Douglas v. California

372 U.S. 353 (1963)

William Douglas was convicted of robbery, assault with a deadly weapon, and assault with intent to commit murder in a California trial court. He wished to appeal his convictions and was allowed to do so since California statute guaranteed him an appeal of right to the California District Court of Appeal. However, Douglas, who was very poor, was not given a free lawyer to craft and argue his appeal. The California District Court of Appeal, after simply reviewing the cold, trial transcript on its own, confirmed his convictions. Douglas then tried to appeal to the California Supreme Court. But, it considered Douglas's appeal to it discretionary and refused to entertain it. Douglas then asked the U.S. Supreme Court to hear his appeal and it agreed to do so.

The sole issue the U.S. Supreme Court agreed to consider was whether California's denying Douglas a free lawyer to craft and argue his original appeal of right denied him his constitutional rights. It ruled that it did. It grounded its ruling on equal protection, the requirement in the 14th Amendment that the government treat similarly situated people the same. The Court ruled that where the merits of the "one and only appeal" a poor person is entitled to are decided without the help of a lawyer, an "unconstitutional line has been drawn between rich and poor." The Court said that although absolute equality is not required by the Constitution, in the case of denying a person an effective appeal of right there can be no equal justice. An appellate court simply looking on its own at the barren trial transcript for hidden, appealable issues does not count as a true appeal. Lawyers are needed to make appeals meaningful. They have the time to carefully examine the transcript, engage in legal research, and marshal arguments on their clients' behalf. What the appellate court did in the case of Douglas in perusing the cold transcript and declaring no basis to complain was merely a "meaningless ritual," not a true consideration of an appeal. Rich people, who can afford to hire attorneys do not get "meaningless rituals" but "meaningful appeals." Equality, as demanded by the 14th Amendment, requires nothing less for the poor person.

The *Douglas* case above only considered the question of the right to a free lawyer in appeals of right. What about discretionary appeals? Eleven years after *Douglas* was decided the U.S. Supreme Court tackled this question when it ruled, in the case of *Ross v. Moffit*,[23] that the right to a state-paid lawyer did not extend beyond the first appeal of right. It reasoned that the right to a free lawyer was one of degrees.

23. 417 U.S. 600 (1974).

Anders Briefs and the Frivolous Appeal

Suppose you are a public defender who is assigned to represent a criminal in his or her first appeal of right. You search the trial transcript diligently for trial-errors but can only find some very frivolous, "harmless errors" at best. What should you do? You cannot simply do nothing because your client has an appeal of right and has the right to a free lawyer to advance it. You could counsel your client not to pursue an appeal but what if the client insists that an appeal be filed. What then?

One option (questionably ethical) would be for the attorney to simply look for the least frivolous of the frivolous issues he or she can find and argue that, knowing full well that he or she will lose. But, there is another option: the so-called "Anders brief." An **Anders brief**, named after the case of *Anders v. California*,[24] is a brief in which the attorney being forced by a client to file a frivolous appeal informs the appellate court that in the lawyer's professional judgment, there are no legitimate issues to raise on appeal. The lawyer writing the Anders brief is required to raise all conceivable issues and demonstrate how each one is indeed frivolous. Anders briefs can be more trouble than they are worth. They can be harder to write than simply picking the least frivolous of the frivolous issues and just arguing that. Also, clients get very angry at their attorney for filing an Anders brief, much angrier than they probably would become if the attorney pretended to work for the client by simply arguing a frivolous, dead-bang loser issue. (Two popular issues lawyers like to raise in doing merely perfunctory appeals is that the verdict was against the weight of the evidence or that the sentence was too long. When appellate courts see one of these standard, generic, **boiler-plate issues** raised and no others, they usually assume that the lawyer is merely going through the motions to get a client off his or her back.)

This completes the chapter on "Appellate Law." We began our journey by looking at the two purposes for appeals and ended it by discussing Anders Briefs. Some criminal defense attorneys (especially in large public defender offices) and some prosecutors (especially in large district attorney offices) never do trials but only do appellate work. They are often looked upon as the office intellectuals. Would you prefer to do trials or write and argue appeals? Or, would you enjoy being a small-office generalist who does both?

---

24. 386 U.S. 738 (1967).

Index

abscond, 98
actus reus, 16–18
admission by a party-opponent, 155
admissions, 155
affidavit, 154, 232
affirmation, 37–38, 135–136
aggravating factors, 246
Alford plea, 107–108
Allam v. State, 15
Allen charge, 200–202
Allen v. United States, 201
Amish, 10–11
Anders v. California, 297
Anders Brief, 297
anonymous juries, 195–196
appeal, mechanics of, 294
appeal of right, 295–297
appeals, discretionary, 295
Apprendi v. New Jersey, 218
arbitrary death sentences, 246
Argersinger v. Hamlin, 82–83
Arizona v. Fulminante, 286
arrest warrants, 56
arrests, 26, 53, 55–56
articulable facts, 54–55
Ashe v. Swenson, 280
assigned counsel, 63–64
Atkins v. Virginia, 248–249, 276
attorney/client privilege, 139–142
automobile searches, 48
bail bondsman, 98–99
bail, excessive, 94–96
bail, extralegal factors, 95–96
bail, types, 98
Ballew v. Georgia, 72
banishment, 213–215
Barker v. Wingo, 65
basic elements of a crime, 16
Berger v. United States, 75
best evidence rule, 118–120
Bill of Rights, 11, 243
birth control, 12–13
Bishop v. State, 23
Blakely v. Washington, 207
blended sentencing, 263–265
blended disposition, 267
boiler-plate issues, 297
Booth v. Maryland, 131
Bordenkircher v. Hayes, 80–81
bounty hunters, 98–99
Bowden, 248–249
Bowers v. Hardwick, 13, 292
Boykin Forms, 104
Brady v. Maryland, 76
Breed v. Jones, 274
brevity, requirement, 55
Brown v. Board of Education, 292
brutalization effect, 241
Byerly v. Ashley, 117
Cage v. Louisiana, 180
California v. Carney, 48
California v. Greenwood, 44
capital punishment, 192–195, 235, 238–239, 242–243, 246–248, 253
capitalis, 242
cash bond, 98
categories of evidence, 112–118
certiorari, denies, 295
certiorari, grants, 295
chain of custody, 117–118
challenged for cause, 69
Chapman v. California, 285
charge bargain, 101
charging decision, 78
children, mental incapacity and, 136–137
Chimel v. California, 52
circumstantial evidence, 112–113, 115–116

classical goals of criminal sentencing, 203
clear and present danger, 7–8
clergy/communicant privilege, 142–144
Coker v. Georgia, 252
Commonwealth v. Means, 130
Commonwealth v. Clair, 283
Commonwealth v. Webster, 172
commuted, 250
compelling interest, 10–11, 231–232
competent evidence, 133
Compulsory Process Clause, 146
concurrent jurisdiction, 263–264, 266
conditions of confinement, 222–223, 226–229
confession, mere, 184
confinement, conditions of, 227–229
Confrontation Clause, 146, 160
consent searches, 46
constitution, living, 290–292
constitutional limits on criminalizing, 5
constitutionality of guidelines, 207
contract systems, 64
corpus delicti, 184
count bargain, 102
courtroom workgroup, 73
crafting a sentence, extra-legal factors, 218
crafting a sentence, 215–218
crime-fraud exception, 140
crimes against the person, 4
crimes against public order, 4
crimes against property, 4
cross-section of the community, 70, 72, 190
cruel and unusual sentences, 209
Cruz v. Beto, 230
custodial questioning, 58–59
Daubert v. Merrell Dow Pharmaceuticals, Inc., 148
Dawson v. State, 210
deadlocked juries, 200
deadly force, 22–24
death penalty, juvenile, 249–252, 275–276
death penalty, race and, 247–248
death penalty, errors and, 253
death qualified jury, 192–195
death penalty for rape, 252
death penalty qualified, 70
declarant, 153
defense of property, 22–23
defense of others, 22
deinstitutionalization era, 261
Delaware v. Prouse, 54
deliberate indifference, 223, 225–228
delinquencies, 265
delinquent acts, 265
denies certiorari, 295
deposition, 155
detention centers, 268–269
deterrence, 203–204
deterrence, specific, 204
deterrence, general, 204
direct file statutes, 264
direct evidence, 112–113
discretionary appeals, 295–296
discretionary waiver, 263
dispositional hearing, 269
disproportionality, gross, 205
disproportionate sentences, 204
diverted, 269–270
doctor/patient privilege, 146
documentary evidence, 112, 118–120
Doe v. Miller, 214
double jeopardy, 274–275, 278–281
Douglas v. California, 296
Duncan v. Louisiana, 187–188
duress, 27, 31–32
duty to object, 281
duty to seek justice, 74–76
dying declarations, 160–162
dynamite charge, 200–202
effective assistance, 83–85, 108
Eisenstein, 73
electric chair, 210–212, 238
entrapment, 27, 32–34
error correction, 277–288
errors and the death penalty, 253
Estelle v. Williams, 128
Estelle v. Gamble, 226
evidence, four main categories, 112
exceptions to hearsay, 155
exceptions to the search warrant requirement, 39, 45–52
excessive bail, 94–98
excited utterances, 157–159
exclusion, statutory, 264
exclusion, legislative, 264

exclusionary rule, 39–43, 60
exculpatory evidence, 76–78
excuse defense, 21, 27
execution of public duties, 22–23
exigent circumstances, 46, 50
exonerated, 253
expert witnesses, 147–151
extra-legal factors in crafting a sentence, 218
extralegal factors in setting bail, 95
facially neutral and uniformly applied, 11
fact finders, 163
factual basis, 105–106, 108
fair cross-section of the community, 190
Farmer v. Brennan, 222
Federal Speedy Trial Act, 68
Felony Justice, 73
first appearance, 93
flight, mere, 183–184
Florida v. Bostick, 46
folkway violations, 5
four classical goals of criminal sentencing, 203
four key speedy trial factors, 67
freedom of speech, 7–9
freedom of religion, 9–11, 230–233
frisk for weapons, 46, 50–52
fruit of the poisonous tree, 41
fungible, 117
Furman v. Georgia, 245
future dangerousness, 96–97
Gallup Poll, 237–238
general deterrence, 204
get tough era, 262
Gideon v. Wainwright, 62–63, 82
Gilmore, Gary, 247
goals of criminal sentencing, 203
golden age of trials, 99
good faith exception, 41–42
grants certiorari, 295
Gregg v. Georgia, 246
Griswold v. Connecticut, 11
gross disproportionality, 205
guidelines, constitutionality, 207–209
guidelines, sentencing, 206–207
guidelines, mandatory, 207
guidelines, non-mandatory, 207
guilty pleas, 103–109, 177
guilty plea, withdrawing, 108–109
guilty pleas, types, 106–108
hands-off approach, 221
Harmelin v. Michigan, 204–205
harmless error doctrine, 285–288
hate speech, 8
hearsay, definition of, 153–154
hearsay, exceptions to, 155–162
hearsay, testimonial, 158–160
homosexuality, 8, 12–13
hooligan, 13–14
houses of reform, 256
Hudson v. Palmer, 229
Hudson v. McMillian, 224
husband/wife, 144–145
Hussein, Saddam, 235–236
impartial jury, 69–71, 187, 190
impeach a witness, 137
in spite of innocence, 253
in plain feel, 52
in plain view, 49–50, 52, 54
In re Grand Jury Subpoena, 140–142
In re Winship, 169–170, 172, 273
In re Gault, 153, 259–261
In re Grand Jury Investigation, 142–143
incapacitation, 203–204
indigent defense, 63–64, 82–83
ineffective assistance, 83–85
inevitable discovery, 42–43, 60
innocence, presumption of, 176
insanity, 27–30, 151
intake, 270
intoxication, 27, 35–36
investigative stops, 53–55
involuntary intoxication, 27, 35–36
Iowa v. Rutledge, 284
Jacob, 73
Jacobson v. United States, 33–34
jail clothes, 128
jeopardy attaches, 280
judicial participation in deal-making, 102
judicial review, 289–292
judicial waiver, 263–264
jurisdiction, concurrent, 266
jury nullification, 197–200
jury of one's peers, 190
jury, limitations of the right to trial by, 188–189
just deserts, 204
justification defense, 21–22

juvenile death penalty, 249–252, 275–276
juvenile murderers, 249
Katz v. United States, 43–44
Kaupp v. Texas, 55
Kent v. United States, 258–259
knowingly entered, 104, 108
Kumho Tire Company, Ltd., et al., v. Patrick Carmichael, et al., 149
Kyles v. Whitley, 77
law violation, 5
lawful arrest, search, 52
Lawrence v. Texas, 12–13, 291–292
lawyer's duty to object, 281
lay witness, 147–148
least restrictive means, 231–232
leg irons, 128–130
legal factors in crafting a sentence, 215–218
legislative exclusion, 264
lesser of two evils, 25–26, 32
Libby, 164
Libretti v. United States, 105
Lightner v. State, 25
living constitution, 290–291
Lockhart v. McCree, 70
Lockyer v. Andrade, 205
logical connection, 231
M'Naghten Rule, 28–29
mandatory sentencing guidelines, 207–208
mandatory waiver, 263
Mapp v. Ohio, 39–40
Marbury v. Madison, 289–290
material, 121
McKeiver v. Pennsylvania, 274
McVeigh, 236–237
mechanics of an appeal, 294–295
medical care, 226–227
mens rea, 16–19, 34
mental incapacity, 136
mentally retarded, 238, 248–250, 276
mentally disabled, 248
mere confession, 184
mere flight, 183
mere presence, 182–183
Michael Nowell v. City of Cincinnati, et al., 156
Michigan v. McMahan, 184
Miller v. Pate, 75–76
Minnesota v. Reha, 14–15
miranda rights, 58–61, 278
Miranda v. Arizona, 58–60
mirandized, 58, 60
mistake of fact, 31
mistake of law, 30–31
mitigating factors, 246
model penal code test, 29–30
moral certainty, 172–174, 180
mores violation, 5
Morissette v. United States, 18
necessity, 22, 25–26, 32
negligence, 17
New York v. Quarles, 60
New York House of Refuge, 256
Nix v. Whiteside, 87
Nix v. Williams, 60
nolo contendere plea, 107–108
non-judicially close, 270
non-mandatory sentencing guidelines, 207
non-unanimous jury verdicts, 181
North Carolina v. Alford, 107
numerical quantification, 174
oath or affirmation, 135
offensive speech, 7
offers to plea bargain, 125
opinion testimony, 147
ordeals, 178–179
pain, wanton infliction, 226–227
parens patriae, 257
parent/child privilege, 146
party-opponent, 155, 157
Payne v. Tennessee, 131
peers, jury of one's, 190–192
Penry v. Lynaugh, 248, 276
People v. Rokicki, 8
People v. Basciano, 116
per se unconstitutional, 246–247
per curiam, 245
peremptory challenges, 69
personal knowledge, 134–135
petition, 269
petty offenses, 188
plain feel, 52
plain view, 49–50, 52, 54
plain error, 281–285
Planned Parenthood of Southeastern Pennsylvania v. Casey, 293

plea bargaining, constitutionality, 100–101
plea bargaining, 73, 99–103, 125–127
plea bargains, types, 101–102
plea bargain, offers to, 125–127
Plessy v. Ferguson, 292
policy review, 277–278, 288–294
pre-sentence report, 100, 216
predisposed, 33–34
prejudicial evidence, 123–124
preponderance of the evidence, 169, 171–172, 174, 185
preserve an issue for appeal, 281
presumption of innocence, 165, 176–177
presumptive waiver, 263
pretrial detention, 272–273
preventive detention, 96–98, 272–273
priest/penitent privilege, 142–144
prior statements, 155
prior records, 124
private wrongs, 3–4
privileged communications, 137–146
probable cause to search, 38, 41, 48
probable cause to arrest, 38, 55
product test, 28–29
proof beyond a reasonable doubt, 163–186, 273
property bail, 98
proportionality, 205, 245
prosecution, selective, 80
prosecution, vindictive, 80–81
prosecutorial discretion, 78–81, 264
prosecutorial waiver, 264
protect the record, 281
psychotherapist/patient privilege, 146
public duties, 22–23
public safety exception, 60–61
public defender, 62–64, 296
Public wrongs, 3
R.O.R. bail, 98
race and the death penalty, 247
rape shield laws, 127
rape, death penalty, 252
rational basis, 15–16
real evidence, 116–118
reasonable suspicion, 52
reasonable doubt, proof beyond, 163–185
reasonable expectation of privacy, 43–46, 229–230
reasonable mistake of fact, 31
reasonable and proportional, 22
receiving, 268–269
recklessness, 17
recusal, 90, 92
referral, 268–269
regulatory searches, 52
rehabilitation, 203, 256–257
release on recognizance, 98
religion, freedom of, 9–11
religious belief, 9
religious practices, 9
Religious Freedom of Restoration Act, 11
requirement of brevity, 55
resisting unlawful arrest, 26
retarded, 15, 238, 248–250, 276
retribution, 203–204
reverse waivers, 264
Reynolds v. United States, 9
right to counsel, 61–64, 82–83, 85–86, 258–261, 296
Right to Privacy, 229–230
RLUIPA, 231–233
Robinson v. California, 6
Roe v. Wade, 12, 278, 292–293
Rommel v. Estelle, 204
Roper v. Simmons, 249–251, 276
Ross v. Moffit, 296
Saddam Hussein, 236
safe environment, 222–223
Santobello v. New York, 100
Scarlet Letter, 212–213
Schall v. Martin, 272
search incident to a lawful arrest, 52
search warrants, 37–39, 46
selective prosecution, 79–80
self-defense, 22
self-incrimination, 57–61, 259–260
sentence, legal factors in crafting, 215
sentence bargain, 101
sentencing, traditional powers, 207
sentencing, classical goals, 203–204
sentencing factors, 218–220
sentencing guidelines, 206–209
serious offenses, 188
shaming, 212–213
Sheppard v. Maxwell, 89
Simpson, 166–167, 172
size of juries, 71

slaves of the state, 221
Smith case, 11
Solem v. Helm, 205
South Carolina v. Gathers, 131
speciality courts, 271
specific deterrence, 204
speedy trial factors, 67
speedy trial statutes, 68
speedy jury trial, 57, 64
spousal privilege, 144–146
Spratt v. Rhode Island Department of Corrections, 231
Stack v. Boyle, 94–96, 97
stale warrant, 38
Stanford v. Kentucky, 250, 275–276
stare decisis, 292–294
State of Missouri v. Kobel, 183
State v. Vaillancourt, 182
State of California v. Simpson, 166
State v. Campbell, 285
State v. Long, 113
State v. Dalton, 17
State v. Davis, 102
status offenses, 6–7, 267–268
statutory exclusion, 264
stops, 52, 53–55
straight plea of guilty, 107
Strickland v. Washington, 83–85, 88
strict construction, 290
strict liability offenses, 19
Strunk v. United States, 65
subpoena duces tecum, 147
substantial capacity test, 29–30
Sumner, 4–5
targeting, 79
Taylor v. Louisiana, 190
Taylor v. Taintor, 98
Tennessee v. Garner, 24
Terry search, 52
Terry v. Ohio, 50–52
Terry stop, 52
testimonial hearsay, 158–160
testimonial evidence, 113, 146
Thompson v. Oklahoma, 275
Thompson v. Utah, 72
torture, 179, 210–212
totality of the circumstances, 38
traditional sentencing powers, 207
transfer or waiver statutes, 262
Trop v. Dulles, 221
ultimate issue, 151–152
United States v. Cronic, 85
United States v. Sewell, 35
United States v. Gementera, 212
United States v. Ball, 279
United States v. Brown, 121–122
United States v. Young, 282
United States v. Arney, 200
United States of America v. Allen J., 136
United States of America v. Jean Brito, 158
United States v. Thomas, 198
United States v. Stewart, 128
United States v. Leon, 41
United States v. Booker, 207–208
United States v. Withorn, 127
United States v. Mezzanatto, 125
United States v. Perez, 279
United States v. Salerno, 96
United States v. Sharpe, 55
United States v. Grayson, 216
United States v. Shinault, 190
United States v. Layton, 123
United States v. Gonzalez-Lopez, 85
United States of America v. Melvin Troy Two Shields, 161
unnecessary and wanton, 225–226
use of force, 224–225
utmost certainty, 174
vague statutes, 14
verdicts, non-unanimous, 181–182
viability, 12
victim impact evidence, 130
Victor v. Nebraska, 173–174
vindictive prosecution, 79–80
void for vagueness, 13–14
voir dire, 69
voluntarily and knowingly entered, 104, 108
voluntarily entered, 104, 106, 108
voluntary intoxication, 35–36
voluntary consent, 46–47
Wainwright v. Witt, 193–194
waiver, discretionary, 263
waiver, mandatory, 263
waiver, 263–265
waiver statutes, 262–264
waiver, judicial, 263

waiver, presumptive, 263
waiver, prosecutorial, 264
waivers, reverse, 264
wanton, unnecessary and, 225–226
wanton infliction of pain, 222, 225
warrantless searches, 45
Wayte v. United States, 79
Webster charge, 172–173
Weems v. United States, 245
Wilkerson v. Utah, 244
Williams v. Florida, 71
Wilson v. Seiter, 228
Winship, In re, 169–170, 172, 273
Wisconsin v. Yoder, 10
withdrawing one's guilty plea, 108
Witherspoon v. Illinois, 192–193
workgroup, courtroom, 73
writs of assistance, 37–38
youth courts, 271
youthful age, 34–35

Amendments

1 - Freedom of Religion, Press, Expression
2 - Rights to Bear arms
3 - Quartering of Soldiers
5 - Trial & Punishment, Compensation for takings
4 - Search & Seizure
6 - Right to Speedy trial, Confrontion of Witnesses
7 - Trial by Jury in Civil Cases
8 - Cruel & unusual Punishment
9 - Construction of Constitution
10 - Powers of the States & people